From Research to Practice in the Design of Cooperative Systems: Results and Open Challenges

Julie Dugdale • Cédric Masclet
Maria Antonietta Grasso • Jean-François Boujut
Parina Hassanaly
Editors

From Research to Practice in the Design of Cooperative Systems: Results and Open Challenges

Proceedings of the 10th International Conference on the Design of Cooperative Systems, May 30–1 June, 2012

 Springer

Editors
Julie Dugdale
LIG
University of Grenoble
Grenoble
France

Cédric Masclet
G-SCOP
University of Grenoble
Grenoble
France

Maria Antonietta Grasso
Xerox Research Group Europe
Meylan
France

Jean-François Boujut
G-SCOP
University of Grenoble
Grenoble
France

Parina Hassanaly
Institute of Political Study
Aix en Provence
France

ISBN 978-1-4471-6157-8   ISBN 978-1-4471-4093-1 (eBook)
DOI 10.1007/978-1-4471-4093-1
Springer London Dordrecht Heidelberg New York

Springer is part of Springer Science+Business Media (www.springer.com)

Preface

COOP 2012 is the 10th edition of the International Conference on the design of Cooperative Systems. It has now been 20 years since the first COOP event was organised by a small group of French researchers who identified an urgent need to investigate the complex issues involved in designing cooperative systems.

To mark this special anniversary we asked researchers and practitioners not only to report on recent advances, but also to reflect on successes and failures in our field. We have witnessed huge technological advances in the last twenty years in the ways that people communicate, cooperate and work. This has posed many challenges to systems design and development. With our current work in areas such as smart applications, tangible interfaces, the Internet of Things, web services, the integration of applications and devices, social media and our ever-growing virtual communities, new challenges will undoubtedly arise.

The underlying tenet of all the COOP conferences has been that such challenges can only be tackled through a multi-disciplinary approach. This has always been reflected in the contributions presented at previous COOP conferences. COOP 2012 continues this tradition, bringing together an exciting selection of state-of-the-art works that span the breadth of our domain. We hope that these works will engender a lively discussion throughout the conference and inspire new and valuable lines of work. The chapters of this book covers various themes: working in healthcare (Chaps. 1–3); social environments in support of work (Chaps. 4–6); understanding communities and global teams (Chaps. 7–9); working with tangible user interfaces (Chaps. 10–11); working with devices (Chaps. 12–14); working at distance (Chaps. 15–17); and understanding work and social settings (Chaps. 18–20).

The activity of COOP 2012 is not just confined to the conference but is supported by five workshops organised by leading researchers in their fields: Workshop 1 "Do we really need to share to cooperate" delves into the heart of what it means to cooperate and explores the underlying assumptions that we hold about sharing knowledge. Workshop 2 "Large scale idea management and deliberation systems" addresses the new challenge of how we can design and develop social and collaborative tools that will be used by crowds and extremely large groups. Workshop 3 "Fostering social interactions in the aging society" focuses on the social side of health and examines the challenges in developing community-oriented tools for elderly adults. Workshop 4 "Gamification of Production Environments" extends our knowledge of gaming elements and examines how the approach may be used in a variety of work contexts. Finally, Workshop 5 "Mobile CSCW" explores the nature of cooperation through mobile access and examines how we can work towards mobile, flexible and ubiquitous cooperation processes.

The work presented at this year's conference incorporates theoretical contributions, reports on empirical studies, software development experiences and methodological approaches spanning multiple disciplines, including CSCW, HCI, IS, knowledge engineering, multi-agent systems, organizational and management sciences, sociology, psychology, anthropology, ergonomics, and linguistics; incorporating a range of methodological approaches and specific domains of application. Submissions were subject to at least 3 double-blind reviews using the following criteria: relevance to COOP 2012, technical soundness, technical importance, originality, and presentation quality. 37 papers were submitted, of which 20 were finally accepted. Regarding the format of the conference we have chosen to have a sequential presentation of papers, rather than have parallel presentations in tracks. We believe that this supports our multi-disciplinary approach and fosters our community, and helps to prevent fragmenting our works into separate research fields in disconnected streams.

COOP 2012 would not have been possible without the help from a large number of people. Parina Hassanaly (as Conference Chair), Jean-Francois Boujut and Antonietta Grasso (as Scientific Chairs) have dedicated an enormous of their time and effort to COOP 2012. Thanks go to the reviewers and the Program Committee for their insightful comments, help and recommendations. Also, we are indebted to the Steering Committee that has helped to guide and hone the focus of COOP over these last years. Thanks are also due to David Martin who coordinated the 5 workshops. As with previous conferences Athissingh Ramrajsingh has provided invaluable help with the local organization, arranging sponsorship and managing the website. Julie Dugdale and Cédric Masclet as Proceedings Chairs coordinated the publication of this book. Lastly, thanks are due to all the contributors and participants, including Keynote speakers, without whom COOP 2012 could not take place. COOP 2012 provides the ideal setting for us to share knowledge and ideas, build our networks, and of course get to know one another a little better—thank you everyone for your hard work.

Julie Dugdale
Cédric Masclet
Maria Antonietta Grasso
Jean-François Boujut
Parina Hassanaly

Contents

Contributors

Malek Alaoui Troyes University of Technology (UTT), ICD/Tech-CICO—UMR CNRS 6279, 12 Rue Marie Curie—BP2060, 10010 Troyes Cedex, France
e-mail: malek.alaoui@utt.fr

Antonella de Angeli Department of Information Engineering and Computer Science (DISI), University of Trento, Via Sommarive, 5, 38123 POVO–Trento, Italy
e-mail: deangeli@disi.unitn.it

Fabien Badeig LIG, Université de Grenoble, UFR IM2AG—BP 53, 38041 Grenoble Cedex 9, France
e-mail: Fabien.Badeig@imag.fr

Pernille Bjørn IT University of Copenhagen, Technologies in Practice, Rued Langgaards Vej 7, 2300 Copenhagen S, Denmark
e-mail: pbra@itu.dk

Federico Cabitza Università degli Studi di Milano-Bicocca, Viale Sarca 336, 20126 Milano, Italy
e-mail: cabitza@disco.unimib.it

Jean Caelen LIG, Université de Grenoble, UFR IM2AG—BP 53, 38041 Grenoble Cedex 9, France
e-mail: Jean.Caelen@imag.fr

Stefania Castellani Xerox Research Centre Europe, 6, chemin de Maupertuis, 38240 Meylan, France
e-mail: Stefania.Castellani@xrce.xerox.com

Lars Rune Christensen IT-University of Copenhagen, Rued Langgaards vej 7, 2300 Copenhagen S, Denmark
e-mail: Lrc@itu.dk

Luigina Ciolfi Interaction Design Centre, Department of CSIS, University of Limerick, Limerick, Ireland
e-mail: luigina.ciolfi@ul.ie

Tommaso Colombino   Xerox Research Centre Europe, 6, chemin de Maupertuis, 38240 Meylan, France
e-mail: Tommaso.Colombino@xrce.xerox.com

Anthony D'Andrea   ISSP & Department of Sociology, University of Limerick, Limerick, Ireland
e-mail: a-dandrea@uchicago.edu

Paloma Díaz   DEI Laboratory, Computer Science Department, Universidad Carlos III, Madrid, Spain
e-mail: pdp@inf.uc3m.es

David Díez   DEI Laboratory, Computer Science Department, Universidad Carlos III, Madrid, Spain
e-mail: ddiez@inf.uc3m.es

Gunnar Ellingsen   Tromsø Telemedicine Laboratory, Telemedicine and e-health research group, University of Tromsø, 9038 Tromsø, Norway
e-mail: gunnar.ellingsen@hn-ikt.no

Catherine Garbay   LIG, Université de Grenoble, UFR IM2AG—BP 53, 38041 Grenoble Cedex 9, France
e-mail: Catherine.Garbay@imag.fr

Antonietta Grasso   Xerox Research Centre Europe, 6, chemin de Maupertuis, 38240 Meylan, France
e-mail: Antonietta.Grasso@xrce.xerox.com

Breda Gray   Department of Sociology, University of Limerick, Limerick, Ireland
e-mail: breda.gray@ul.ie

Sergio Herranz   DEI Laboratory, Computer Science Department, Universidad Carlos III, Madrid, Spain
e-mail: sherranz@inf.uc3m.es

Starr Roxanne Hiltz   DEI Laboratory, Computer Science Department, Universidad Carlos III, Madrid, Spain
e-mail: hiltz@njit.edu

Erik C. Hofer   School of Information, University of Michigan, 1075 Beal Avenue, Ann Arbor, USA

Petr Holub   Masaryk University, Botanická 68a, Brno, Czech Republic

Rasmus Eskild Jensen   IT University of Copenhagen, Technologies in Practice, Rued Langgaards Vej 7, 2300 Copenhagen S, Denmark
e-mail: raej@itu.dk

Roland Juchmes   LUCID-ULg—Lab for User Cognition and Innovative Design, University of Liège, 1 chemin des chevreuils B52, 4000 Liège, Belgium
e-mail: r.juchmes@ulg.ac.be

Eli Larsen   Tromsø Telemedicine Laboratory, Telemedicine and e-health research group, Norwegian Centre for Integrated Care and Telemedicine, 9038 Tromsø, Norway
e-mail: eli.larsen@telemed.no

Pierre Leclercq   LUCID-ULg—Lab for User Cognition and Innovative Design, University of Liège, 1 chemin des chevreuils B52, 4000 Liège, Belgium
e-mail: pierre.leclercq@ulg.ac.be

Myriam Lewkowicz   Troyes University of Technology (UTT), ICD/Tech-CICO—UMR CNRS 6279, 12 Rue Marie Curie—BP2060, 10010 Troyes Cedex, France
e-mail: myriam.lewkowicz@utt.fr

Marco P. Locatelli   University of Milano-Bicocca, viale Sarca 336, Milan, Italy
e-mail: locatelli@disco.unimib.it

Sanna Malinen   Tampere University of Technology (TUT), Human-centered Technology, P.O.Box 589, 33101 Tampere, Finland
e-mail: sanna.malinen@tut.fi

Osama Mansour   Linnaeus University, Pg Vejdes Väg, 35195 Växjö, Sweden
e-mail: osama.mansour@lnu.se

Valérie Maquil   Public Research Centre Henri Tudor, 29, avenue John F. Kennedy, 1855 Luxembourg, Luxembourg
e-mail: valerie.maquil@tudor.lu

Maria Menendez   Department of Information Engineering and Computer Science (DISI), University of Trento, Via Sommarive, 5, 38123 POVO–Trento, Italy
e-mail: menendez@disi.unitn.it

Zeno Menestrina   Department of Information Engineering and Computer Science (DISI), University of Trento, Via Sommarive, 5, 38123 POVO–Trento, Italy
e-mail: zeno.menestrina@studenti.unitn.it

Naja L. Holten Møller   The IT University of Copenhagen, Rued Langgaards Vej 7, 2300 Copenhagen, Denmark
e-mail: nhmo@itu.dk

Peter Novák   Masaryk University, Botanická 68a, Brno, Czech Republic

Jarno Ojala   Tampere University of Technology (TUT), Human-centered Technology, P.O.Box 589, 33101 Tampere, Finland
e-mail: jarno.ojala@tut.fi

Rune Pedersen   Department of Clinical Medicine, Telemedicine and e-health research group, University of Tromsø, 9038 Tromsø, Norway
e-mail: Rune.pedersen@uit.no

Eric Ras   Public Research Centre Henri Tudor, 29, avenue John F. Kennedy, 1855 Luxembourg, Luxembourg
e-mail: eric.ras@tudor.lu

Vít Rusňák Masaryk University, Botanická 68a, Brno, Czech Republic

Stéphane Safin LUCID-ULg—Lab for User Cognition and Innovative Design, University of Liège, 1 chemin des chevreuils B52, 4000 Liège, Belgium
e-mail: stephane.safin@ulg.ac.be

Carla Simone University of Milano-Bicocca, viale Sarca 336, Milan, Italy
e-mail: simone@disco.unimib.it

Petr Slovák Masaryk University, Botanická 68a, Brno, Czech Republic
e-mail: slovak@ics.muni.cz

Karine Lan Hing Ting LASMIC, Université de Nice-Sophia Antipolis, Nice, France
e-mail: karine.lan@gmail.com

Pavel Troubil Masaryk University, Botanická 68a, Brno, Czech Republic

Signe Vikkelsø Copenhagen Business School, Kilevej 14A, 2000 Frederiksberg, Denmark
e-mail: ssv.ioa@cbs.dk

Jutta Willamowski Xerox Research Centre Europe, 6, chemin de Maupertuis, 38240 Meylan, France
e-mail: Jutta.Willamowski@xrce.xerox.com

Olivier Zephir Public Research Centre Henri Tudor, 29, avenue John F. Kennedy, 1855 Luxembourg, Luxembourg
e-mail: olivier.zephir@tudor.lu

Chapter 1
Establishing a Core Health Record; A Case Study from Norwegian Healthcare

Eli Larsen and Gunnar Ellingsen

Abstract Information and communication technology (ICT) has become important for many public services as they seek to become more efficient and effective. Authorities in Norway have since 1997 formulated strategic plans for ICT in
healthcare, striving to obtain seamless care and funding in varying degree have been
allocated in order to achieve results. In this chapter we present several initiatives
concerning the establishment of a core health record in order to reveal the effects of
running ICT projects at a governmental level.

The study adheres to an interpretive research approach. Empirical data was collected through project participation, document studies, interviews and observations.

We found that the consequences of the authorities' influence in the information
system domain in the Norwegian healthcare seem to separate the users from the
system developers to an ever-increasing extent. We also found that reforms in the
hospital sector have created a powerful ICT organization in the hospital sector; this
organization seems to set the agenda within ICT in Norwegian healthcare, which
also includes the GPs and the municipality sector.

1.1 Introduction

Many stakeholders in healthcare seem to be very willing to work to control the
development of information systems within healthcare [1–4], and due to the substantial funding available for doing so, the authorities keep tabs on the development
process. These processes will encounter challenges that are different from those that
exist in free and consumer markets, and the actors have to maneuver in a landscape
of political signals, regulations, money flow, resources, power balance and alli-

E. Larsen (✉)
Tromsø Telemedicine Laboratory, Telemedicine and e-health research group,
Norwegian Centre for Integrated Care and Telemedicine, 9038 Tromsø, Norway
e-mail: eli.larsen@telemed.no

G. Ellingsen
Tromsø Telemedicine Laboratory, Telemedicine and e-health research group,
University of Tromsø, 9038 Tromsø, Norway
e-mail: gunnar.ellingsen@hn-ikt.no

J. Dugdale et al. (eds.), *From Research to Practice in the Design of Cooperative Systems:*
Results and Open Challenges, DOI 10.1007/978-1-4471-4093-1_1,
© Springer-Verlag London 2012

ances in order to establish new information systems. According to Greenhalgh, it is urgently necessary to carry out an interdisciplinary debate on priorities for research and policy within healthcare ICT with input from academics, service users, clinicians, policymakers, technical designers, research sponsors and the commercial IT sector [5]. This chapter contributes with empirical insight to a prolonged 8-year effort to establish an inter-organizational service, the Core Health Record, in Norwegian healthcare. We elaborate on how a municipal initiative has failed and how two public initiatives seem to compete with each other. By doing so, we address the following research question: How do the authorities exercise control and management in the information system domain and what are the consequences?

Our analysis proceeds along the following two dimensions: First, we elaborate how the authorities project management via the Directorate of Health [Directorate], have moved far from user-driven development philosophy and have led to a huge gap between the designers and the user groups. Secondly, we explore how the hospital sector has become an influential actor that makes it capable of setting set the agenda within ICT in the complete healthcare sector.

In this chapter we will show how the authorities influence the design of a Core Health Record/Patient summary in Norway. The work has gone on for about 8 years, and during the years, several powerful actors have influenced the work. However, the service is still on the drawing board.

The framing of the chapter is as follows: In the theory section we spell out characteristics with the healthcare information system. We review issues concerning planning and managing development of inter-organizational system. Our theoretical approach also includes design issues in the information infrastructure. We then outline our research method, and present the case, introduced by the overall description of the Norwegian healthcare sector and the level of ICT adoption. The case then describes three related initiatives in order to create a Core Health Record Service. In the analysis we discuss how the new top-down management strategy has affected the development of new services. A conclusion rounds off the chapter.

1.2 Theory

Modern professional and scientific practices, including healthcare, practices always include artifacts, architectures, paper, machines, systems etc. This requires attention to the fundamentally composite nature of these practices. Information systems in, for instance, a hospital, must therefore be adapted to the remaining structure. In healthcare the patient record is the key tool for many activities, both medical and mercantile. From the medical perspective, the healthcare provider needed relevant information about the patients and is also obliged to document findings, interventions and planned procedures. Similarly, the patient record also contains information that is fundamental for logistics, billing and statistics—which in turn plays a critical role in planning, financial management and control. The potential for ICT to integrate all this information into a single record has proven highly attractive to

policy makers, promising to improve quality and cut costs, providing a technological fix to the structural crisis—exponentially rising demand and the need to control
public expenditure—facing most public sector health systems [6]. The merged information system, called the electronic patient record, has taken a unique place in
the healthcare system as a gatekeeper for most of the information flowing within or
between the institutions. Private companies develop and sell these systems; design
issues are therefore a vendor-to-customer issue (ibid). The vendors each pattern
their electronic patient records differently, and replacing these systems is resource-
intensive for the users because they contain an enormous amount of data and are
intertwined with the working methods. In a healthcare institution, the electronic
patient record represents a substantial part of the information infrastructure which
Hanseth and Lyytinen define as a shared, evolving, heterogeneous installed base of
IT capabilities among a set of user communities based on open and/or standardized
interfaces. Such an information infrastructure, when appropriated by a community
of users offers a shared resource for delivering and using information services in a
(set of) community [7].

Designing and implementing effective information systems meant for inter-organizational co-operation is a difficult task to handle [8–10]. It relies on a joint venture
among the affected organizations and is dependent on several issues. Often, there is
no single obvious management in inter-organizational structures in charge of making the decisions necessary to trigger and impel the process. The actor who has the
most substantial interest in creating the inter-organizational system will try to enroll
and control the other actors in a way that caters to these actor's explicit interests.
These interests, as Latour [11] explains it, are:

> What lie between actors and their goals, thus creating a tension that will make actors select
> only what, in their own eyes, helps them reach these goals amongst many possibilities.

Through co-operation and stating some common goals, inter-organizational actors
can align their movements in the same direction and create a new system. However,
each of the actors will also have a subset of goals that do not necessarily overlap
with the other actor's goals. The subset of goals will control the behaviour in further
co-operation. Latour [11] argues that the mere 'possession' of power by an actor
does not automatically confer the ability to cause changes unless other actors can
be persuaded to perform the appropriate actions for this to occur. A "weak" actor
will break out of the co-operation if its interests are not taken care of, but this will
weaken the remaining group. In order to keep the actors enrolled, different negotiations take place. One powerful strategy is to convince the actors to take a detour in
the design process. The detour will appear as a faster way to the goal and will in
fact be a shortcut [12].

Co-operation is a key topic in the CSCW community and a number of scientists
have studied systems that is used by colleagues in several locations around the
world, such as the classic studies by Orlikowski [13] and Ciborra [9]. However,
while these studies analyze systems that are worldwide, they represent at the same
time co-operation systems that are within an organization. Co-operation systems in
healthcare represent challenges that also represent challenges in another dimension

because the co-operation must be performed between different organizations. Such inter-organizational information systems are even more challenging than systems within the same organization [14–16]. An actor that tries to manage the design of an inter-organizational system will face comprehensive challenges because objectives are multiple and often contested, and outcomes are not stable and may also be contested [17]. Creating inter-organizational systems increases the complexity of the picture by an extra dimension, because the co-operation is created between different institutions without a single over-arching management and who try to establish a common business culture.

The heterogeneous element of the information infrastructures means that creating a service that works between two structures will also demand relatively detailed knowledge about work practices. Agreement on the pure technological aspects of the system will not be sufficient.

1.3   Method

An interpretative approach [18] is used to gain a better understanding of the mechanisms influencing the development of electronic co-operation tools in the healthcare sector. The empirical material is gathered through a longitudinal process that began in 2004 and is still running today in Norway. In this period, the first author collected empirical data from the following information sources:

- Project participation in the Core Health Record (municipal initiative)
- Project reports from Core Health Record (owned by the Directorate), Central Medication Service (owned by the National ICT) and Core Health Record (municipal initiative)
- 42 semi-structured interviews with vendors, policy makers, healthcare personnel and public authorities. The interviews were conducted by the first author and lasted between approximately 60 and 160 min
- Strategic documents and evaluation reports for ICT in Norwegian health care for the period 1997 onwards.
- Minutes from the parliament
- Management document from the Ministry of Health.
- Minutes from meeting between Ministry of Health and the Regional Health Authorities.

The information from all data, except interview data, has been entered into a timetable in order to understand the background for the different events and how these have interfered with each other. The information from the interviews are transcribed and sorted into themes. By combining all information elements, it will be possible to understand the viewpoint from the different actors and how this has affected the progress in the field.

The first author was formerly a project member in the Core Health Record project (municipal sector) and has therefore been an insider to this process [18]. This has given her valuable insight into the discipline that has been studied and has enabled easier access to key actors who would otherwise be difficult to make appointments with. Nonetheless, throughout the data collection and analyses process, she had to re-examine her own perceptions of what was going on in these projects. After initially ascribing the problems and delays primarily to the vendors, she increasingly came to see the challenges as much more complex, involving interests, relationships and interdependencies between many actors.

The second author has been involved in several research projects on ICT in healthcare over a period of 12 years and has played the role of discussion partner and co-author in this chapter.

1.4   Case

The following case description will explain three initiatives that have taken place concerning creating a new service called the Core Health Record, a CSCW tool aimed at facilitating the patient's need for coordinated services among healthcare providers. The cooperation facility and content of the record has not yet been determined, but the involved actors have agreed that contact information and medication information is essential. However, *how* the information is put into the service and *by whom* is critical; these features are critical to the overall function. This service development illustrates the different perspectives and design solutions of the municipal sector, the hospital sector and the Directorate. The initiatives partly overlap one another chronologically and will be explained separately. First, we will explain how the healthcare sector in Norway is organized and the level of ICT adoption.

1.4.1   The State of Affairs in the Norwegian Healthcare Sector

The main actors in clinical healthcare in Norway consist of hospitals, general practitioners [GPs], municipal sector (home care service and nursing homes) and hospital sector. This structure has been stable for several decades. The sector is mainly public, but with various owner structures and funding.

GPs run private offices with strict regulations concerning refund rules from the authorities. Since the end of the 1990s, the majority of GPs have used electronic patient records.

Home care services and nursing homes are run by the municipalities, which receive frame funding from the local authorities. In general, the municipalities do not hire their own physicians, but use the GPs for medical services outside the hospitals. The municipal sector had, since the 1990s, slowly started to use electronic patient record for their patients—first of all for administrative and statistical concerns.

In 2002 a hospital reform transferred the responsibility for Norwegian hospitals from the counties to four regional health authorities and ownership was thereby centralized to the Ministry of Health. Based on the hospital reform, the Ministry of Health sent a management document in 2003 to the four regional health authorities and ordered them to establish a joint strategy group for ICT between the Ministry of Health and the regional health authorities. The purpose was to achieve benefits in terms of co-operational aspects. The basic idea was to achieve a hospital sector with systems that could operate together as an integrated community because this was considered to increase efficiency. The strategy group within the hospital sector became an established unit called National ICT with regular management group meetings, a separate budget and a project office running ongoing projects.

ICT in the healthcare sector became a priority area for several countries around the year 2000. Several countries, including Norway, started planning for new services that should cope with the challenges concerning fetching patient information that was stored in other institutions. The European Union put interoperability on the agenda in their eHealth conference in 2006, and the patient summary was one of the top prioritized issues.

After 2000, electronic referrals, discharge letters, x-ray photos, and other information were sent between actors in the Norwegian healthcare sector, but the scale of this electronic communication was limited compared to the expectations. The authorities supported some development activities but did not act as a superior coordinator. The lack of comprehensive progress in the field was stressed during several debates in the parliament in 2007. In recent years, the Directorate has taken charge of more and more national ICT projects. Three big projects have already been drawn into the organization map and two others are pending.

Another action that influenced the climate within ICT development to a large extent was the co-operation reform within healthcare that was approved by the government in 2009. It stated that: *All documentation and information exchange shall be carried out electronically*, and a new service—the Core Health Record—was given particular funding.

1.4.2   Core Health Record

In the remaining part of the case chapter we will describe three different activities related to the Core Health Record and explain how the main actors have approached the design issues. The three actors are: (I) a municipality, (II) the Directorate and (III) the hospital sector.

1.4.3   Core Health Record I—A Municipality Initiative (2004–2009)

The first attempt to create a Core Health Record was carried out by the Trondheim municipality. They experienced difficulties concerning user specifications and enrolling the electronic patient record vendors [EPR-vendors].

The municipality run the home care service, and they experienced that their professionals struggled to gain updated information about the medicine that their nurses administered to their clients, and the city council applied for funding to run a project creating a Core Health Record with the purpose of reducing adverse medicine events and contribute to better resource use in healthcare sector. They got 650,000 € in founding funds from the Directorate.

> The GPs are those who are responsible for our clients' medication as long as they are not hospitalized, and our Core Health Record will show the medication that the GPs have in their system, together with new prescriptions that other physicians, in the hospital or at the emergency service, have prescribed. [Project manager]

The project group considered it peremptory to integrate the Core Health Record with the electronic patient records in order to make a user-friendly service and they meant that the GPs' EPR system should be the most significant information source for the information in the Core Health Record.

From a technical point of view, the Core Health Record service should consist of two major elements; (1) a database containing the Core Health Records and (2) read/write functionalities in the electronic patient records. Trondheim City put out a limited tender and bought the database based on pre-specified requirements. Basically, the project team wanted to include as few EPR vendors as possible, but felt forced to include all the nine vendors, and to produce a national solution, because funding from Innovation Norway (a public business funding organization) was not available otherwise. Also the EPR-vendors wanted to have national specifications on such a service because otherwise would be too risky for them. After applying for more than 1 year, the project managed to receive funding—to cover some of the expenses in connection with integration work that the vendors had to carry out.

User workshops and technical workshops were arranged and specifications were further developed. The project was administered by well trained managers, but due to the complexity in the specification work, experts from Norwegian Centre for Informatics in Health and Social Care were hired to run the process. The specification work concerning integration with the electronic patent record was a difficult task and the EPR-vendors did not find the specifications suitable:

> It is not possible to start some kind of development based on the specifications—we must rewrite the whole damn thing. It is on such a theoretical level that all of it needs to be explained in a practical frame. [EPR-vendor]

None of the EPR-vendors started to make integrations in their systems for the Core Health Record. The vendor that developed the database delivered it and installed it in the local area network at the municipality and claimed that it was according to specifications. The City council, on their side, claimed that they had not received sufficient documentation together with the database. The following comment from the EPR-vendor illustrates the gridlocked situation:

> If they don't understand it, then it is because they don't understand their own project—and that is a bit curious! [EPR-vendor]

The project made no progress and was terminated in 2009 without achieving any kind of testing. A process concerning a national Core Health Record initiated by the Ministry of Health contributed to a lack of driving force.

1.4.4   Core Health Record II—A Task for the Directorate (2009–Ongoing)

The second initiative concerning the Core Health Record came from the politicians, and the Directorate was put in charge of a challenging compromise "race". The Core Health Record was established as an earmarked activity by the Ministry of Health and the Directory was put in charge of the preliminary work that took place in 2009 and 2010. The project group consisted of 10 persons, eight from the Directorate—lawyers, technicians, social scientists, economists, etc, and two hired employees on an hourly basis—as well as one general practitioner and one nurse from the home care sector. The Directorate arranged several workshops and established expert groups—all in order to gather information about the needs and ideas about how to carry on with the work. The Directorate delivered the pre-project report in January 2011, which outlined in the first version of the service that the dispatching information from pharmacies should be used as the information source for the medication. By using a web service, the healthcare providers could access their patient's prescription information. The Directorate thought that this approach would be the most effective way to realize the service within a couple of years.

> The politicians do not care about the contents in the Core Health Record, but they applied a lot of pressure in order to have a running service within a short time. We know that the first version of the Core Health Record will not be helpful for the Home Care sector and the general practitioners, but the emergency ward will be able to look up the medication that the patient has bought at the pharmacies the last 3 years. [Head of the Core Health Record Department, The Directorate]

The report was sent out for consultation by the Ministry of Health. Much of the input from the responders said that the Core Health Record should work seamlessly with the existing ICT-tools—which mean that it should be integrated with the electronic patient records.

> The service will not be integrated with the electronic patient record in the first version. That will cause us too much of a delay. [Member of the Directorate]

An important argument for not integrating with the electronic patient records was that the first version of the core health record should not be dependent on a commitment from the EPR-vendors. It was a well known de facto that the EPR-vendors represented a bottleneck in the healthcare ICT development, and the Directorate wisely put the integration with the electronic patient records on a 10 years schedule plan. The health care sector responded with mixed enthusiasm and a variety of different views. The home care sector was not at all happy with the suggested solution.

> It is not interesting for us to know what kind of medication the patient have purchased at the pharmacy, because we are in fact the ones that retrieve the medicine for our patients in the pharmacy. We need to know about prescribed medication as soon as a doctor has prescribed new medication, stopped or changed the medication dose. The solution that the Directorate has come up with is not valuable for us. It will take years and years before our needs will be taken care of in the Core Health Record Project! [Member of the Home Care Sector reference group]

The home care service that the municipalities run offers administration of the medication to their resident clients/patients who find it difficult to get the medicine at the pharmacy and/or struggle to take the medication at the right time of the day—often handicapped and old people. Thus, the home care sector needs to know the medication regime of their clients/patients as soon as a physician changes the medication regime. In the case of a new prescription, information would be available in the Core Health Record *after* the medicine was retrieved by the home care themselves at the pharmacy and termination and dose changes would not be available in the Directorate's Core Health Record. The co-operation function the home care hoped to get was not included:

> We were quite surprised when we saw the pre-project report—we have stressed that the Core Health Record is not suitable for the municipal sector as it is planned in the first versions. [Member of the reference group—municipal sector]

The general practitioners did not hail the Core Health Record.

> We have carried out an opinion poll that put the Core Health Record far down on the priority list. We have so many other ICT-related functionalities that are much more important. For instance, 60 % of general practitioners wanted to have a controlled electronic updating of the medication list when a patient is discharged from the hospital. The quality of patient care would increase significantly with this kind of functionality! Today we do so by means of a very challenging cut and paste exercise. [General Practitioner]

This opinion poll was also presented by a high profile department physician at one of Norway's biggest hospitals in a meeting with the Minister of Health. The physician claimed in his presentation that the Core Health Record was an ICT-moon landing compared to the controlled electronic updating of the medication list. The Minister was clearly provoked, and said: "I'm glad there's a table between us!" She also refused to believe the facts that the physician presented. However, the Norwegian Medical Association, which consists of 96.4 of all physicians in Norway, also pointed to this priority issue in their consultation letter to the Ministry of Health:

> The Norwegian Medical Association however, points out that there are a number of unresolved ICT tasks in the Norwegian health care system that must be resolved before the core health record can be developed as outlined in the final target image.

A general practitioner explained some of the issues:

> To build a Care Health Record is like building the attic before the foundation wall. We have several basic things that don't function well enough, for instance, electronic referrals and discharge letters. Several thousands of these electronic letters are sent to the wrong place or "disappear" in the system and cause bad headlines in the newspaper. The authorities should have spent money on fixing these issues instead of building a giant organization in the Directorate in order to build something fancy that some politicians want. [General Practitioner]

However, the response from the hospital sector was most positive:

> The dispatched medicine within the last 3 years can give us a good idea about a patient's
> medication status in case of an acute hospitalization. [Hospital Doctor]

The medication of patients within the Norwegian hospital is a process that has been documented on paper until recent years. However, some hospitals have introduced electronic services integrated with the electronic patient record—an integration that has cost a lot of effort and has been difficult to achieve. The medication is characterized by several intertwined processes, carried out by several professions: for instance, the physician prescribes the medication; nurses and nursing assistants are involved in the administration and distribution of the medicine. The process also has considerable logistical demands. From a medical point of view, several issues are important in the medication process, such as; (a) allergy to specific medicine, (b) the maximum level of medicine during a specific time slot cannot be surpassed, and (c) interaction between medicines that can cause adverse drug events. The way that the patient responds to the medication is also a matter of concern in the electronic patient record. Due to this intertwined situation between medication information and processes inside the hospital, the hospital sector underlined that their requirements had to be considered at an early stage in the Core Health Record process.

> We cannot use the Core Health Record inside the hospital, and this means that we have to
> build up a service parallel with the one that the Directorate builds. It will be quite similar. A
> waste of money if you ask me! [ICT procurement, Hospital Sector]

The mixed enthusiasm in both the municipal and hospital sector indicated difficult conditions for future work within the Core Health Record, but good funding might make it possible to overcome some of the obstacles. The project received 600 K € in 2011 and 10,3 million € in 2012. This is substantial on the Norwegian scale.

1.4.5   Core Health Record III—A Hospital Sector Initiative Called Central Medication Service (2009–Ongoing)

The third initiative came from the hospital sector because they needed electronic medication information when patients were hospitalized. The Central Medication Service (the hospital name of the Core Health Record) was the result of a subproject growing out of the ePrescription project—a project managed by the Directorate, aiming to send all prescriptions electronically from the physicians and to the pharmacies. The ePrescription project struggled to involve voluntary contributions from the hospital sector and had to push the sector via the Ministry. It was obvious that work concerning the electronic prescription had to be closely coordinated with the work concerning internal prescribing in the hospitals.

> We underlined as clearly as early as 2006 that we could not introduce electronic prescriptions without examining the context and internal prescribing and medicine administration.
> There has been quite a hefty letter exchange between the hospital sector and the Directorate. We have spent quite some time trying to understand each other. The Directorate is
> chasing goals such as, for example: x number of electronic prescriptions within x number

of years. The most interesting part is that the authorities are eager to get the electronic prescriptions because they need a copy of the prescriptions that they cover the cost of—an order from The Public Account Committee. The needs were not clinically embedded! [Project Manager Regional Health Authorities]

The National ICT put on hold the electronic prescriptions and instead focused their work on a Central Medication Service and in 2009 they drew up a plan to create a service that contained detailed information about the medication that was prescribed to a person/patient. Funding of the project was planned to be a cost-sharing between the four health authorities and National ICT. From a hospital point of view, this service had to be adapted in order to distribute and manage medicine for the hospitalized patients, including information about number of pills, time of day, maximum number of pills per day, patient has/has not swallowed medicine, etc. The Central Medication Service should also be able to send electronic prescriptions in order to meet requests from the authorities, 24/7, contain updated data and be able to access by healthcare personnel—also including GPs, homecare service and others outside the hospital after dispatching. Even though the service was intended to contain medication information exclusively, this was the most important information element in the Core Health Record as planned by the Directorate. However, the Central Medication Service was planned to be integrated into the "inner life" of the hospital, unlike the Core Health Record.

The Central Medication Service will be 90 % identical to the Core Health Record. The Directorate should reconsider this—but unfortunately—they have extreme political pressure on their back. We are much better equipped to run a project like this because we are in direct contact with the users. I think that it is strange that the Directorate has become such a strong independent operator and that they're supposed to build their own programming. [Project Manager Regional Health Authorities]

1.5 Discussion

In the following we will elaborate on how the authorities' control and management in the core health record case has affected the design of information systems in the health domain. With this top down strategy, it seems as if the hospital reform and the authorities' project management strategy have led to a huge gap between the developers and the user groups in the healthcare sector, and the hospital sector has become an influential actor capable of setting the agenda within ICT for the complete healthcare sector.

1.5.1 Designing ICT Within Healthcare—Not a Political Topic

The healthcare sector and the authorities have a common goal that focuses on improved quality of patient care, and this prepares the background for enrolling the actors [11]. However, in this section we will show how the authorities' time schedule hampers the collaborative climate.

The Core Health Record in the municipal initiative and the Central Medication Service in the hospital sector share a common interest, namely, to create a service that is built as an additional unit to their existing information system, or the installed base according to information infrastructure theory [7]. They also share a clinical interest in determining the basic function of the Core Health Record/Central Medication Service, namely, as a service that is updated as soon as a new medication regimen is introduced by a physician, either inside or outside of the hospital.

Neither the municipality nor the hospital sector expressed that the first version of the Directorate's Core Health Record would be a natural piece in their existing information system. The general practitioners are, first of all, concerned with the priorities of the authorities, i.e., the collaborative tools concerning medicine information transfer between the hospital and themselves, because they are in charge of the medication for discharged patients. Dispatched prescriptions during the last 3 years will hardly give them any added value. This illustrates the dilemma that the Directorate also faces, namely divergent interests and political pressure to deliver results within a short period.

> The process of the Core Health Record has been like the Night of the Long Knives the whole way! It has been like the Walk to Canossa for the Directorate to discuss with all types of health organizations and vendors and all other kind of actors to balance and come up with a compromise solution. Additionally, they need to change the law in order to establish the service within legislations. [Member of the Core Health Record reference group]

The strategy of moving management to a top level was put into place because the former initiatives of trying to establish sustainable electronic services had failed. The authorities have put themselves in a leading position and hope that by doing so they will be able to manage the problems. The ePrescription system that started in 2006 became the first project directly managed by the Directorate. They were put in charge of the project because such a service, with many independent actors, would be difficult to create without a single overarching management. By stating some common goals, the inter-organization actors, together with the Directorate, were able to create a new system. Despite the role of the Directorate, the project suffered from delays and over-delivery. The Core Health Record project was the second major inter-organizational project that the Directorate overtook, but it was the first that was clearly a result of political interference. By using reference groups as consultants and managing the project via the Directorate, the project has moved far from a user-driven development philosophy and has led to a huge gap between the designers and the user groups. According to research, this will result in information system development in poorly adapted services and seems to be a serious disadvantage to the strategy.

In the Core Health Record project, the actors seem to share a common goal, namely improving the quality of healthcare. Politicians, however, are so concerned with rapid results, that they suggested a detour, whereby they omit the EPR vendors. The lukewarm reception that this detour has been met with can be regarded as an outright diversion [12]. Political control of the development of ICT in healthcare does not seem to be a sensible choice.

1.5.2 The Hospital Sector or the Directorate—Who Is in Charge?

In this section we will show how the hospital sector has become an influential actor capable of setting the agenda within ICT in the complete healthcare sector.

The driving force within the Core Health Record in 2011 in Norway is the initiative managed by the Directorate. However, the other initiative run by the National ICT simultaneously seems to play a competitive role in the progress. Both parties seem to have a reasonable argument for their positions. The Directorate is aware of the tight coupling between the electronic patient record and the daily work occurring in healthcare. They have experienced the problems that occur when involving the electronic patient record vendors. The ePrescription project, the pilot program carried out in 2008, ended in total failure. The Directorate claimed that this failure was primarily due to the vendor's inadequacy. By avoiding these vendors in the first version of the Core Health Record service, many barriers could have been avoided. The information source that the Directorate has suggested is a spinoff of a service that they already use, namely the electronic prescriptions. However, this service has just been tested in a pilot involving GPs and pharmacies and does not yet include the hospital sector, even though they issue 20 % of the prescriptions. The decision by the Directorate is understandable when we consider a basic assumption in organizational theory that states that people are influenced by the organization to which they belong as well as by their individual socioeconomic status or career features. The Directorate is responsible for the electronic prescriptions, and thereby wants to include that functionality in the Core Health Record.

The Central Medication Service initiative by the hospital sector is managed by one of the regional health authorities that serve more than 50 % of the population, and is the biggest workplace, employing 56,000 staff members. By virtue of its size, it plays a role as the most significant healthcare entity in Norway. The Central Medication Service is supported by the National ICT, the uppermost strategic group within the hospital sector. None of the other sectors in healthcare have an ICT organization comparable to the hospital sector. It started as a strategy group, but has turned its focus from strict strategy work to more project-characterized work. National ICT represents a huge group of users in the healthcare sector—a huge group starting to speak with one voice and thus play a powerful role in development with ICT. In fact, the National ICT seems to have a more powerful position than the Directorate, not only because of the amount of users they represent, but also because of their close relationship with the EPR vendors, which represent an obligatory passage point [12]. This means that the hospital sector may set the agenda within ICT in Norwegian healthcare. However, this might not be preferable, because it puts, for instance, the GPs in the background, even though the GPs serve as a hub when it comes to the electronic patient information flow in Norway. The mere possession of power by the hospital sector does not automatically confer the ability to cause changes unless the other healthcare actors can be persuaded to perform the appropriate actions for this to occur. A service like the Core Health Record is dependent of participation from all actors; otherwise, the service would not be the collaborative tool that it is supposed to be. Being able to set the agenda is an advantage for the hospital sector.

1.6   Conclusion

We have presented the activities that been undergone in Norway for 8 years in order to establish a Core Health Record Service. We have found that during these years, the authorities have changed their approach to innovation within ICT in healthcare by establishing a growing project organization in the Directorate. We have also identified that the politicians seem to be concerned with quantitative outcomes and that this might not correlate with the aims of the healthcare personnel. The authorities have changed their role from that of a supporter (by allocating funds to projects on a low level in the health organization) to a designer (by being in charge of the design process and implementing a new service).

The consequences of the authorities' influence in the information system domain in Norwegian healthcare seem to separate the users from the system developers to an ever-increasing extent. In the future process, this separation has to be reconsidered and action must be taken in order to develop a more user-friendly and efficient systems. The authorities have to find methods for closing the gap by bringing users and developers together in innovative processes. A lot of the resources that are spent on consultants that create paper could be better spent on system developers and test-users.

References

1. Salmivalli, L.: Governing the Implementation of a Complex Information Systems Network: The Case of Finnish Electronic Prescription. ACIS 2006 Proceedings. 55, (2006)
2. Mundy, D., Chadwick, D.: Electronic transmission of prescriptions: towards realising the dream. International 2004; Conference: Citeseer (2004)
3. Nictiz.: https://www.nictiz.nl/ (2010)
4. NEHTA. Strategic Plan, Australia: http://www.nehta.gov.au/about-us/strategy (2009)
5. Greenhalgh, T., Potts, H.W.W., Wong, G., Bark, P., Swinglehurst, D.: Tensions and paradoxes in electronic patient record research: a systematic literature review using the meta-narrative method. Milbank Q. 87(4), 729–788 (2009)
6. Halford, S., Lotherington, A.T., Obstfelder, A., Dyb, K.: Getting the whole picture? Inf. Commun. Soc. 13(3), 442–465 (2010)
7. Hanseth, O., Lyytinen, K.: Theorizing about the design of Information Infrastructures: Design kernel theories and principles. Case Western Reserve University, USA. Sprouts: Working Papers on Information Systems, 4(12), (2004)

8. Dekker, H.: Control of inter-organizational relationships: evidence on appropriation concerns and coordination requirements. Account. Organ. Soc. **29**(1), 27–49 (2004)
9. Ciborra, C.: Mission Critical: Challenges for Groupware in a Pharmaceutical Company. In: Ciborra, C. (ed.) Groupware and Teamwork (pp. 91–119). Chichester: John Wiley & Sons Ltd. (1996)
10. Oliver, A., Ebers, M.: Networking network studies: an analysis of conceptual configurations in the study of inter-organizational relationships. Organ. Stud. **19**(4), 549 (1998)
11. Latour, B.: The powers of association. Power, action and belief. A new sociology of knowledge. Sociol. Rev. Monogr. **32**, 264–280 (1986)
12. Latour, B.: Science in Action. Harvard University Press, Cambridge (1987)
13. Orlikowski, W.J.: Learning from notes: organizational issues in groupware implementation. In: CSCW Proceedings, Conference, pp. 362–369 (1992)
14. Bossen, C.: Implications of shared interactive displays for work at a surgery ward: coordination, articulation work and context-awareness. Conference: IEEE, pp. 464–469 (2008)
15. Aarts, J., Ash, J., Berg, M.: Extending the understanding of computerized physician order entry: implications for professional collaboration, workflow and quality of care. Int. J. Med. Inform. **76**(Suppl. 1), S4–S13 (2007)
16. Ellingsen, G., Monteiro, E.: Seamless integration: standardisation across multiple local settings. Comput. Support. Coop. Work. **15**(5–6), 443–446 (2006)
17. Kushner, S.: The object of one's passion: engagement and community in democratic evaluation. Eval. J. Australas. **2**(2), 16–22 (2002)
18. Walsham, G.: Interpretive case studies in IS research: nature and method. Eur. J. Inf. Syst. **4**, 74–81 (1995)

Chapter 2
Standardizing Work in Healthcare Through Architecture, Routines and Technologies

Rune Pedersen

Abstract This chapter presents an in-depth longitudinal study of hospital work. It discusses standardization after the introduction of a computer-mediated nurse–nurse/interdisciplinary handover in a cardiology ward and its effect on collaborative work activities. The standardization also plays out in the physical architecture adopted by the hospital, which impact on the "who" and "how" collaboration progress—the impact of standardized spaces. The chapter focuses on the constant strive in health care to make work practice more effective by employing an increasingly broader approach towards standardization. The number of involved standards is central. Typically for this have been the introduction of the electronic patient record (EPR) system and a following chain of standards made feasible through possibilities from using an EPR system. Sociomateriality is used to illuminate the fact that standardization efforts cannot be investigated as isolated efforts, rather as one of several social and material interconnected ones. Particular to the case was how the physician–nurse handover was made computer mediated, which involves or alter interdisciplinary collaboration in the handover process. Although increased efficiency has been successfully achieved, the chapter discusses how altering some work impacts other processes, especially interdisciplinary collaboration, social relations, and informal learning. Further, architecture has gained sparse attention in the standardization of work processes in health care. Architecture contributes to standardized work practice when striving for efficiency and also become a conflicting standard in interdisciplinary collaboration.

2.1 Introduction

Standardization of work processes in hospitals has developed from particularly focusing on a single standard of various material or social status, towards focusing on several interconnected ones growing from the outset of the EPR and organizational changes making the process of standardization even more cumbersome [1].

R. Pedersen (✉)
Department of Clinical Medicine, Telemedicine and e-health research group,
University of Tromsø, 9038 Tromsø, Norway
e-mail: Rune.pedersen@uit.no

J. Dugdale et al. (eds.), *From Research to Practice in the Design of Cooperative Systems:*   17
Results and Open Challenges, DOI 10.1007/978-1-4471-4093-1_2,
© Springer-Verlag London 2012

The standardization of work processes is typically carried out with the objectives of improving efficiency, safety, and quality. However, the effort to standardize the work of, for instance, physicians and nurses has proven difficult to achieve [2–4]. One central work process in hospitals is that of the handover, i.e. when information about patients and work responsibilities is transferred from one shift to the next. The handover is particularly interesting because it is typically time-consuming and also crucial for patients' safety and the quality of care [5, 6]. The standardized nurse-nurse, and nurse–physician computer-mediated handover (pre- rounds meeting) became the focus of attention, where individual readings of the electronic patient record (EPR) system have replaced the oral pre-rounds meeting. The pre- round meeting is the process where all interdisciplinary information is merged to get an overview of the patient trajectory (the way patients are communicated between departments and personnel) through the hospitals, followed by the rounds where the physician and the nurse consult the patient. Further, the physical architecture (standardized space) of the hospital is given considerable attention as this impact on the way nurses and physicians collaborate.

With this as a backbone, we need a broader view on standardization based on the increasing number of installed standards, where success on one area of standardization tends to bring about consequences in other areas. Therefore we have asked: How does the variety of standardization initiatives shape healthcare work and particularly the collaboration between the professionals?

Recently, and parallel to the change from written accounts to an EPR system, efforts has been made at Akershus University Hospital (AHUS) to improve the nurse–nurse handover and the interdisciplinary pre-rounds meeting in an effort to overcome these presupposed efficiency and quality problems. Regardless of claimed project success, measured from user satisfaction, reduced overtime, and improved quality of the written documentation, there are concerns on the subject of increased standardization. Although increased efficiency has been successfully achieved, the chapter discusses how altering some work-oriented processes impact others, especially interdisciplinary collaboration, social relations, and informal learning.

Theoretically, the chapter draws on standardization literature and literature from Computer Supported Cooperative Work (CSCW) on collaboration, and sociomateriality as a tool to understand organizational work. Further, standardized architecture is discussed which confines and/or substantiates work process-oriented standardization.

2.2   Theory

Standardizing the work of healthcare personnel, for instance physicians and nurses, has proven extraordinarily difficult to comprehend [2, 4]. A fundamental characteristic of this work is its pragmatic fluid character with complex work activities that requires ad hoc and pragmatic response [7]. Healthcare work is further characterized by its distributed decision making, by 'multiple viewpoints' and by its 'inconsistent and evolving knowledge base'. The need to curb large and seemingly ever-increasing healthcare expenditure is an explicit feature of managerial agendas for increased standardization of healthcare work. The core activity is to manage patient trajectories of collective and cooperative enterprises [7] where standardization of information systems and work process-oriented standards are of increasing importance.

Traditionally, standardization in information systems (IS) has a history with a focus on technical issues like communication protocols, exchange formats and programming language [8]. There is an even stronger historical tradition of de facto standards for applications, operating systems, and file formats [9]. The Science and Technology Studies (STS) and CSCW literature [10, 11] promotes an approach where standardization is seen as a negotiation process between heterogeneous actors in a socio-technical network, consequently not just a technological issue, but rather a negotiation between technical artefacts, humans, work practice and procedures [2]. In this sense, there are several activated standards in one specific setting. Further, collaboration and interactions are essential properties in hospital work practices where information needs to be shared across time and space. Standardization is embedded in an effort to improve efficiency and quality in healthcare [2]. Hence, and despite the obvious potential for improvements, standardization efforts seldom meet their objectives [12]. Schaper and Pervanen [13] claim that it is clear that much of the work healthcare professionals do cannot be captured in procedures (standardization), as much is being done ad hoc and tailored to the patients' needs. The background for this is that hospitals are regarded as highly specialized, and despite the fact that some work follows routinized paths the never fully predictable nature of patients' reactions increases the complexity of the organization [14].

In healthcare, we see a move towards an increased number of standards [1] where the EPR system is one distinguished 'triggering' effort. EPR systems have a central function in accumulating and coordinating the extensive flow of the various kinds of information that is needed for providing 24/7 patient care. Compared to the paper-based record, the EPR system functions as a hub for coordinating a wider range of professionals, specialties, and in assembling information from different sources within a single system [15]. From the outset of standardizing hospital work through to the implementation and use of an EPR system, other standards have emerged, or have been shaped by the EPR, and have become mutual dependants. One way is through making the shift handover standardized, moving from oral to written accounts making the handover computer mediated and individual.

Handover is important when considering the continuity of care, and a hospitalized patient's demands, which extends beyond the resources of a single nurse or nursing team. In such 24-h work contexts, a shift handover mechanism is required to allow personnel changes with minimum disruption of the functioning of the ward or unit [16]. The traditional oral handover has been criticized for being inefficient, especially because many people are given information that is not directly relevant for their assigned tasks [6, 17, 18]. Further, efforts related to the nurses' handover has a scattered history between success and failure (see for instance [18, 19] that describes standardized handover as successful), and Arora et al. [20] has on the contrary shown that standardized handover tools not always lead to better outcomes or improved results. Further, Munkvold et al. [21] suggest that, despite a proclaimed success formalizing nursing handover, like reduced overtime, improved quality of the written documentation, and eliminated redundancy, a continuous urge to standardize increases the possibility for a collapse somewhere else in the system.

This chapter seek to find out what actually takes place in face-to-face reports between healthcare workers, which is invariably more than a simple transmission of information, and further interlink this to the development of the new standards. Hartwood et al. [22] claim that these interactions have a constitutive role in arriving at some shared sense of what the meaning of information actually is. Further, and in the same direction, Hughes [23] has documented how experienced nurses often help inexperienced residents by suggesting the way towards the diagnosis, or by hinting towards the necessary treatment. This makes it important that nurses and physicians have arenas to meet, and time to share information. Traditionally there has been a close relationship between written and oral accounts while organizing medical work [24]. Consequently, it is difficult to find a straightforward solution on how much this practice can be formalized and how much should remain oral.

In the prolongation of focusing on the human factors it is important to view them up against material factors. Architecture has for instance not been inherently explored as important for the standardization of work processes in hospitals, or seen as important for the relation between the EPR—information sharing—architecture. Information technologies are often depicted as possessing the potential to correct social inequalities by democratizing information access and economic opportunities. This view overemphasizes virtual spaces against the material and social conditions of technological infrastructures [25]. Further, when researchers eschew a substantive interrogation of materiality, they effectively 'black box' technologies as neutral artefacts, ignoring that these technologies, for instance, establish social order [26]. Orlikowski [27] claims that researchers in Information Systems (IS) have overlooked the ways in which organizing is bound up with the material forms and spaces through which humans act and interact. Therefore, the social and material are considered to be inextricably related, there is no social that is not also material, and no material that is not also social. In this broadened perspective on standardization, also the physical layout where hospital work is a part of the socio-material ensemble. Orlikowski [27] has suggested a shift in the conventional framing of organizational practices as 'social practices'. Instead she sees it as 'sociomaterial' which allows us to explicitly signify the constitutive entanglement of the social and the material in everyday organizational life. Even the most influential studies of IS and organization focus primarily on social dynamics or how people interact with each other, rather than providing evidence of what specific features people use, why they use them, and how and why their pattern of use shift over time [28]. Accordingly, the physical layout of the hospital wards—the architecture–becomes a key element of the sociomaterial and thus essential in integrated standardization efforts.

As listed above sociomateriality denote that standardization effort cannot be listed as isolated efforts, rather as one of several social and material interconnected ones, that overlap with each other, and increasingly become mutually interdependent, which curbs progress and may ultimately cause failure. This kind of "system accidents" are unforeseen, hard to diagnose, and have an interactive complexity that causes two components to interact in an unexpected way [29].

2.3   Method

The importance of social issues related to computer-based information systems has been increasingly recognized in IS, which has led researchers to adopt empirical approaches that focus particularly on human interpretation and meaning [30]. In practice, the movement of healthcare work activities is frequently much less linear than it is in other arenas, as it has flexibly defined roles. Interpretive research can help the IS researcher to understand human thought and action in a social and organizational context [31]. Further, interpretive studies assume that people create and associate their own subjective and inter-subjective meanings as they interact with the world around them. The interpretive researcher thus attempts to understand through accessing the meanings participants assign to them [32]. Our study adheres to an interpretive research tradition of this nature. In general, qualitative research methods, such as interviews and observations, are optimally suited to understand a phenomenon from the participants' point of view, and in particular the social and institutional context. Qualitative research techniques can provide deep insight, identify problems and answer the "why" and the "how" questions that quantitative studies cannot answer [33].

2.3.1   Data Collection

The data set consist of four modes of data collected during a period from Sept. 2009–March 2011: observations, semi-structured interviews, document analysis of central logs with general numbers on the use of nursing care plans. In total, the author conducted 170 h of observations and 12 semi-structured interviews with an average of 80 min at the Cardiology Department at AHUS in the period. The length of the observations varied from 1 to 8 h, and included tracing patient trajectories through the hospital to understanding the adoption and use of IT-based information carried out by nurses and physicians in different circumstances. The observations were done during the day, evening, and night shifts.

2.3.2   Data Analysis

The overall process of collecting data has been open-ended and iterative, with a gradually evolving focus on specific situations from work practice. The interviews were conducted using a tape recorder, and only a few open-ended questions that were semi-structured and shaped according to how the interviews evolved were posed. Crucial to the evolving questioning was interviews with experienced nurses, novices, and physicians. The analytical categories emerged from internal discussions and reading of field notes. Primarily nurses with varying experience from the department were interviewed; in addition a few residents were asked questions about the interdisciplinary collaboration and the lapse of the pre-round meeting. The interview guide consisted of a few structured questions about the routines at the ward, including a few on the topic of nursing handover, interdisciplinary collaboration, and the rounds. Handwritten field notes were transcribed shortly after the data was gathered. All transcriptions of the interviews were done immediately subsequent to the interviews themselves, as, according to Malterud [34], early transcription is crucial in order to clarify uncertainties and the meaning of unclear sentences. The findings have been discussed among fellow students, as well as between the author of this chapter and my supervisor who have a thorough understanding of and experience in working with IS studies, and also more specific with nursing plans and handovers.

2.3.3   Context of Study

The research was conducted at AHUS, which has approximately 4,700 employees and a total of 820 beds. The hospital has embarked on an ambitious effort aimed at a level of standardization of healthcare work unprecedented in Norway, and is built over a model from Johns Hopkins Hospital in Baltimore US. The Johns Hopkins Hospital is globally acclaimed for its exceptional services and programmes. For 19 consecutive years, it has topped US News & World Report's "Honour Roll" in the magazine's annual ranking of America's Best Hospitals. AHUS is one of the first and biggest hospitals in Northern Europe to follow this model. In November 2008, AHUS moved to its new $ 1.5 billion premises with the explicit objective of utilizing new and familiar technology to improve work practices.

2.4   Case

Important to this case was the implementation of a new large-scale EPR system delivered in 2005, which generated and contributed to new standardization efforts in work practice, which included technologies as well as artefacts and work practice-oriented standards. Nursing plans were standardized at the same time, and a computer-mediated handover between nurses was implemented at the Cardiology Ward followed by a nurse–physician computer-mediated handover in the same period of time. The EPR system used at AHUS included a module for nursing, a module for physicians, laboratory, and radiology. Care plans for nurses was introduced to replace the use of free-text in the documentation to establish a more common formalized language based on good clinical practice and global accommodated classification systems, named Nursing Intervention Classification (NIC) and North American Nursing Diagnosis Association (NANDA). Basically, the nursing plan is an overview of nurse-related diagnoses for a particular patient group combined with relevant interventions (NIC interventions, following the NANDA diagnosis). The diagnoses are represented by the international classification system of the NANDA, consisting of 206 nursing diagnoses [35]. The interventions are represented by the classification system, NIC, consisting of 486 interventions [36]. The care plan has been organized such that each diagnosis, dimension and action is firmly attached to the plan with a start and a stop date. When standardizing these plans, the nurse can easily choose several actions from a pre-defined list for the applicable diagnosis. By doing this, the nurse saves time, and at the same time the standardized sentences work as a quality indicator.

2.4.1   The Standardization of Nurses' Routines: And the Computer-mediated Nurse–nurse Handover

The success of a computer-mediated handover implementation was dependent on an effective EPR system for documentation in nursing practice. With the introduction of a collaborative EPR system in 2005, information work changed from a chronological status annotation into a process-oriented, structured document. The introduction of the EPR gave possibility for a change in the nursing handover process from oral handover to written handover. Further, the implementation of the EPR system increasingly led to a systematic use of standardized care plans. Previously, too much time was used on documenting unessential information such as, for example, 'eaten two slices of bread with jam and cheese,' and 'been for a walk' etc. Certainly, this also was a way to categorize information, making it more transparent for others to read, which shaped the documentation towards the prospective computer-mediated handover.

Standardized plans and a computer-mediated handover were introduced as a "package" late in 2005 in the Cardiology Ward. *"We wished to pursue a computer-mediated report for several reasons, our goals were to use less time compared to the oral report, hence there would be more time with our patients and improve quality of the documentation" (Administrative nurse).*

The nurses interviewed in this study were generally positive to the computer-mediated handover between nurses, as one experienced nurse pointed out: *"We spend much less time on the reports now than before when we had the oral handover. We spent too much time on small talk. The socialization aspect is important, but we always find time to socialize during the shift or during the lunch break."*

The nurses at the Cardiology Ward worked in accordance with a group nursing system divided in three shifts where one of the nurses took the leader position, and was thereby responsible for the care of six to eight patients, including the dispensing of medication, blood specimen collection, and participating in the physician's round. The same nurse was also responsible for the written nursing documentation on the patients, drawing on oral and written input from the other nurses throughout the day. The nurses were divided in the four units on a weekly basis, and they had a function of overlap where one nurse on the day shift arrived 1 h later with an overlap with the afternoon shift. The overlap secured a smooth change-over and foremost a possibility for the nurses on shift to read from the EPR without interruption. The whole staff of nurses had a common briefing in the morning where common information was delivered by the head nurse. Secondly, the nurses attended their selected unit and started out by reading the EPR (the computer-mediated handover procedure), while the night nurse watched over the patients. In addition to the formalized handover the nurse that went off shift gave an oral summary of the most important plans for the day including anything that might have happened during the last 30 min between shifts (information that not was entered into the EPR system). In general, some information had to be delivered orally between shifts because of the heterogeneity of work practice. The day shift was further divided as follows; one nurse had the coordinating responsibility. In the morning handover the nurses have approximately 20 min to read from the EPR. Different artefacts such as the chapter-based work schedule, appointment folder and EPR system were used in the search for information. Further, the nurse responsible at the unit normally had several days during the same week being responsible to uphold continuity. This nurse was responsible for the rounds, and thereby the communication with the physicians. The second and the third nurses were responsible for taking care of the patients throughout the shift, and ensure that everything that was ordered was executed. Further, the nurses had several small oral handovers, both to inform the coordinating nurse that was responsible for the documentation, and other information that varied between discussions about the patient trajectories, and cooperation within the unit. The number of small oral messages was not seen as interruptions of practice, as one nurse said; *"We have a small transparent unit, and it is never difficult to reach the nurse that is working by your side."*

2.4.2   The Computer-mediated Nurse–physician Pre-rounds Handover in Practice

The disestablishment of the oral interdisciplinary handover and thereby the change to a computer-mediated handover came in the same period of 2005 as the computer-mediated handover for nurses. Traditionally, nurses and physicians have had an oral meeting ('pre-visit') before the physicians did the rounds, usually together with the nurses. The purpose of this meeting was for the nurses to update the physicians on the status of the patients, and to discuss some patients in more detail before the rounds. At the Cardiology Ward, the oral pre-visit meetings could last for 1 1/2 h.

The advantage with the pre-visit was that both the physician responsible for the rounds and one or several more experienced physicians were present. In addition, both the responsible nurse and the primary contact for each patient were attending. Although much time was used, the discussion around each patient trajectory had several advantages. The advantages were two folded, firstly this was an arena for learning, and secondly the oral presentation of the patient trajectory on an interdisciplinary level were often clarifying towards details, for instance concerning medication or postponing examinations due to patient needs.

The physicians were expected to update themselves by reading the necessary information in the EPR, presuming that the physicians also read the nursing documentation. The physicians that were interviewed pointed out that the computer-mediated nurse–physician handover was successful in some respects, i.e. much time was now saved, and the sharing of information had never been better. Further, the use of EPRs in the nurse–physician handover process had made oral interdisciplinary communication more sporadic. Although the physicians and the nurses communicated orally and discussed patients throughout the day, the regular meeting point of the pre-visit meeting was no longer in place, and the chain of interdisciplinary work had become vulnerable (nurses' interpretation). The problem with this model was that the meeting activity between collaborating groups became unscheduled or not mandatory which, on the other hand, made it possible to choose where or when to "ask that particular question with great importance to the patient trajectory". In addition, the physicians used the previous interdisciplinary meetings to get an oral update on the nurses' documentation. Most of the residents asked agreed that the time used on oral handovers earlier often fluctuated, but reciprocal to that, the educational effect was highly valued by young residents. The advantage with computer-mediated handover was the time aspect (efficiency), but several pointed at some kind of face-to-face oral contact with the nurse as crucial while using a computer-mediated handover to get the complete overview. In some cases the physician responsible had problems obtaining the right picture of the patient trajectory just by reading the EPR in these cases it was important to consult the nurse. In addition, the physicians still had their morning meetings where new and complicated patient trajectories were discussed in a plenary session. This was crucial because the physicians work much more singlehandedly during the shift. Hence, the physician responsible for the rounds, often residents, typically discussed their patients face to face with the more skilled physicians during the shift, and before the rounds.

The group of interviewed physicians were all young residents with sparse clinical practice, and they had no complaints about the social relation between nurses and other healthcare personnel. The system, the computer mediated handover, and the architecture could according to the nurses make it easy not to meet, be social, and communicate. In contrast, the experienced physicians that had worked in the department over time and through different layers of standardization had a different viewpoint. These physicians had, according to the experienced nurses "a better social relation" with nurses and other healthcare personnel because of their long term relation to the department. Still, these physicians could from time to time take a professional liberty to take the rounds without the assistance of a nurse.

2.4.3   Outlining the Physical Space

Physical architecture and artefacts is central to our case, since the nurses are bound to their work stations, and the physicians are foremost located outside the ward. A standardized architecture contributed to a small, intimate and transparent work environment for nurses and physicians (the ones responsible for the rounds). This is central for this case, describing the establishment of the new AHUS premises in 2008. According to the nurses, there are both positive and negative implications towards small, intimate work stations. It is beneficial to have all patients and equipment gathered within a small area. This keeps all attending personnel within sight which makes the working environment more transparent for the nurse in charge and for the physician responsible for the rounds. Hence, what has been pointed out as the most negative effect is the absence of privacy, especially in terms of maintaining ethical and privacy rules, and the way physicians are less visible in the environment. In general, this solution makes the nurse and physician (the one responsible for the rounds) highly visible which is calming for the patient and their relatives, but it is also challenging because of continuous interruptions this causes for the personnel.

The department was modelled as follows: the four units were symmetrically gathered in a long, broad corridor with units from A to D (see Fig. 2.1). In the middle, dividing two and two units, there was a dining room and common area for patients and personnel, a separate area for garbage and laundry, and a cargo area. The four units were symmetric, meaning that they had the same facilities, three single-bed rooms and two double rooms and one open-based area where all other "daily activity" for personnel took place. In addition to a modern and standardized architecture a set of modern technological artefacts was introduced as a means of fulfilling the targeted standardization. This was everything from an intelligent IP phone system, to a fully automated medication system, and multifunctional patient screen systems.

The architecture puts efficiency first, and the structure of each unit reflected this very well as the two or three nurses on duty seemed to have a complete overview of their patients and their surroundings. The nurses could easily stay and work at the unit throughout the whole shift without crossing outside its perimeter. As one of the nurses noted, *"We have no overview outside the unit we are working on, and our focus is centred there throughout the shift"*. The physicians were physically located outside the department, with a conference room and their offices, which was structured as an open environment. Each week, one physician was associated to each of the four units. In this period, they used different facilities at the department for preparing the patient rounds, undergoing work tasks with the nurses, performing clinical examinations, and for completing documentation. These environments were situated around the ward, and were in immediate proximity to the patients and the work station. The physicians were, in general, positive towards how the architecture has structured their environment, although there was some initial resistance towards the common office premises.

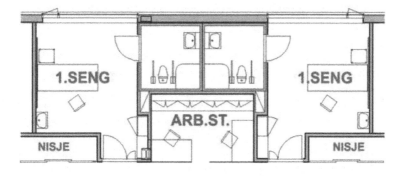

Fig. 2.1 The architecture, showing one of the units. The ward had four equal units divided with two on each side of a common area for both patients and personnel. SENG=bed, ARB.ST=work station, and NISJE=niche. There is further a common are in the middle, dividing two and two units

2.5   Discussion

2.5.1   The Broad Approach Towards Standardization, a Portfolio of Interconnected Standards

The purpose of using sociomateriality to frame the discussion is to illuminate the fact that standardization efforts cannot be investigated as isolated efforts, rather as one of several social and material interconnected ones [25, 27, 28]. The AHUS case includes an ambitious level of standardization with a portfolio of social and material standards that are interconnected. Orlikowski [27] sees organizational life as 'socio-material' which allows us to explicitly signify the constitutive entanglement of the social and the material in everyday organizational life. The effect of this is a physical layout where hospital work is a part of the socio-material ensemble, there is no social that is not also material, and no material that is not also social. The small, intimate units enable transparency, with three nurses restricted to the unit, and better knowledge about a limited number of patients, the EPR, the physical architecture, other artefacts, e.g. phone systems, and the computer-mediated handover. The effort has been ambitious: Increased focus on standardization of work processes in hospitals has developed from particularly focusing on a single standard of various material or social status, towards focusing on several interconnected standards of material and social character [1]. Winman and Rysted [15] claim that the nature of the gap between formal information and the demands of locally interpretive work depends on the nurses' oral presentation in handover meetings for putting information into practical use. This suggests that a computer-mediated handover has to be followed by a face-to-face oral meeting activity. In this chapter, work practice has changed from time-consuming handover conferences to a computer-mediated one. In addition to this, short oral handovers happen occasionally throughout the shift, something that should be considered as normal regardless of a standardized handover or not. The advantage here is that these "short conferences" are possible due to the physical architecture that provides a transparent working environment at this hospital. The nurses' work closely together, often three with one coordinating nurse, they are always within sight, and are also equipped with an IP phone system so that they are contactable for patients, their relatives, and other healthcare personnel. Further, the nurses share information about their patients by producing one document on each patient which is signed by the two or three nurses in the EPR system.

2.5.2 Suboptimal Effects of Standardization

The broad approach [25, 27, 28], and the increasing number of standards [1] increases the possibility of sudden or unpredicted events, which in terms (in this chapter) has been listed as 'suboptimal effects' of standardization. The suboptimal effects created become visible in the breakage point between gained success (efficiency) and unforeseen pitfalls as the interdisciplinary collaboration, and informal learning. The discussion is hinged in the fact that increased standardization is considered a success (on an in- house organizational level) measured in the primary goal, namely increased efficiency of the nurse–nurse handover. Also the standardization of the pre-round meeting is considered a success seen from a top-down organizational level. The nurses for instance value the computer mediated handover as a tool that has increased efficiency (time used on oral handover), and it has shaped and improved the written EPR based documentation. Based on this, and the case this chapter elaborate on the changes in social structure focusing on interdisciplinary collaboration caused by overly standardized routines, and a standardized physical architecture. The physicians are satisfied with the time spared on not having the oral pre- round meeting. Particularly, the case presents some unintended consequences, the loss of learning abilities and social relations on an interdisciplinary level. In turn this interdependency could, according to Perrow [29] turn in to unintended, unsuspected, and unsolvable accidents. In this segment we investigate how several standardization efforts tend to escalate, overlap with each other, and increasingly become mutually interdependent, which curbs progress and may ultimately cause failure. This kind of "system accidents" is unforeseen, hard to diagnose, and have an interactive complexity that causes two components to interact in an unexpected way [29]. Hughes [23] has for instance documented how experienced nurses often help inexperienced residents by suggesting the way towards the diagnosis, or by hinting towards the necessary treatment. Given the introduction of the computer-mediated nurse–physician handover, the most important arena for sharing documentation had vanished according to several nurses. Some examples from the case illustrates this: One aspect was the fact that the physicians in general were less visible in the work environment, therefore residents and inexperienced nurses could become uncertain about "how to accomplish interdisciplinary work" if they were executing it together: *"When the good clinical interdisciplinary relation disappears, so do the social and educational aspects. The relation created by interaction is crucial" (Experienced nurse).*

Architectural forms provides a particular register for social and professional discourses, within architectural theory social use is robustly connected to functionalism, and there is an on- going debate on the appropriateness of concepts such as function and utility among contemporary critics of architectural thinking [22]. In practice, this implies that the ones (in this case the residents) that were under education were under the impression that it was permitted to ignore social relations, and thereby the important formal learning that rests in this interdisciplinary collaboration. One experienced nurse had worked at the department for more than 10 years, and had been a vital part of the education of young physicians. She emphasized that young residents needed to be educated clinically and needed to obtain clinical experience, and that nurses contributed to this in particular.

Further, skilled physicians with years of experience in the ward have stated that the architecture was challenging in terms of upholding social relations.

2.5.3 Conflicting Standards

Recent research in IS are putting focus on an increasing number of interconnected standards in health care that in the next face could complicate the process of standardization to become even more cumbersome, see for instance [1]. This and the fact that all these standards don't stand substantially alone but are interconnected Orlikowski [27] is the basis for the arising of conflicting standards. The conflict of standards arises when nurses versus physicians as professional groups (different standardized work patterns and movement in the ward) fail to collaborate because of a 'restricting architecture'. The architecture separates nurses and physicians, and thereby the shaping of interdisciplinary learning and social relations. Some of the nurses were concerned about the possible effects of the physical and work-related separation of nurses and physicians: *"Some physicians are under the impression that it is suitable to work in this organization without having contact with nurses. The most experienced physicians value the interdisciplinary collaboration, but we have residents that pass through during their specialization..." (Experienced nurse).* What actually takes place in face-to-face reports between healthcare workers is invariable and more than a simple transmission of information [15]. Hartwood et al. [22] claim that these interactions have a constitutive role in arriving at some shared sense of what the meaning of information actually is. The social aspect was frequently mentioned by the nurses, and they agreed that the social relations between the nurses and the physicians had grown weaker over the years. There were several reasons for this, not only the computer-mediated report system, but also the standardized architecture which in some interest had decreased the possibility for social connections between the professions. The physicians had their offices outside the ward, and the nurses were very strongly attached to the small units, which were vulnerable (in terms of interdisciplinary collaboration) because of the small number of personnel attached to each unit. Another aspect to this was the simple fact that the possibility of having shared lunch and larger social gatherings had vanished since they no longer had a social meeting point.

2.6   Conclusion

Sociomateriality is used to illuminate the fact that standardization efforts cannot be investigated as isolated efforts, rather as one of several social and material interconnected standards. The number of standards is essential, and recent research in IS shows that standardization of hospital work includes increasingly more interconnected standards, which makes research in this area increasingly cumbersome [1]. The case has further pinpointed how physical architecture or "space" contributes to standardized work practices when striving for efficiency and how it further become a conflicting standard in interdisciplinary collaboration. Further, the physical architecture is a new interesting augmentation to the increasing number of standards involved. In the case of the computer-mediated nurse–physician handover, some aspects were described as successful in relation to efficiency. However, interdisciplinary collaboration has been reduced, and the social relations between nurses and physicians and informal learning may have been affected. We suggest that these practical implications should be taken into account in future implementations of interdisciplinary computer-mediated handovers.

References

1. Pedersen, R., Ellingsen, G., Monteiro, E.: The standardized nurse: mission impossible? IFIP. Adv. Inf. Commun. Technol. **356/2011**, 163–178 (2011). doi: 10.1007/978-3-642-21364-9_11
2. Timmermans, S., Berg, M.: Standardization in action: achieving universalism and localization through medical protocols. Soc. Stud. Sci. **27**, 111–134 (1997)
3. Ellingsen, G., Monteiro, E., Munkvold, G.: Standardization of work: co-constructed practice. Inf. Soc. **23**, 309–326 (2007)
4. Bowker, G.C., Star, S.L.: Sorting Things Out. Classification and Its Consequences. The MIT Press, Cambridge (1999)
5. British Medical Association.: Safe Handover: Safe Patients. Guidance on Clinical Handover for Clinicians and Managers. British Medical Association, London (2004)
6. Riesenberg, L.A., Leisch, J.J.M.: Cunningham, nursing handoffs: a systematic review of the literature. Am. J. Nurs. **110**, 24–34 (2010)
7. Berg, M.: Patient care information systems and health care work: a sociotechnical approach. Int. J. Med. Inform. **55**, 87–101 (1999)
8. Schmidt, S.K., Werle, R.: Coordinating Technology. Studies in the International Standardization of Telecommunication. The MIT Press, Cambridge (1998)
9. Hanseth, O., Monteiro, E., Hatling, M.: Developing information infrastructure standards: the tension between standardisation and flexibility. Sci. Technol. Hum. Values. **21**(4), 407–426 (1996)
10. Hanseth, O., Lundberg, N.: Designing work oriented infrastructures. Comput. Support. Coop. Work. **10**(3–4), 347–372 (2001)
11. Pollock, N., Williams, R., D'Adderio, L.: Global software and its provenance: generification work in the production of organizational software packages. Soc. Stud. Sci. **37**(2), 254–280 (2007)
12. IOM.: Institute of Medicine. Crossing the Quality Chasm: A New Health System for the 21st Century. IOM. National Academy Press, Washington, DC (2001)
13. Schaper, L.K., Pervan, G.P.: A model of information and communication technology acceptance and utilization by occupational therapists. Int. J. Med. Inform. **76**(Suppl 1), 212–221 (2007)
14. Berg, M.: Accumulating and coordinating: occasions for information technology in medical work. Comput. Support. Coop. Work. **8**, 373–401 (1999)
15. Winman, T., Rystedt, H.: Electronic patient records in action: transforming information into professionally relevant knowledge. Health Inform. J. **17**(1), 51–62 (2011)
16. Kerr, M.P.: A qualitative study of shift handover practice and function from a socio-technical perspective. J. Adv. Nurs. **37**(2), 125–134 (2002)
17. Nadzam, D.M.: Nurses' role in communication and patient safety. J. Nurs. Care Qual. **24**, 184–188 (2009)
18. Sexton, A., Chan, C., Elliot, M., Stuart, J., Jayasuriya, R., Crookes, P.: Nursing handovers: do we really need them? J. Nurs. Manag. **12**, 37–42 (2004)
19. Meum, T., Ellingsen, G.: "Sound of silence"—Changing from oral to a computermediated handover. Behav. Inform. Technol. **30**(4), (2011). (Special issue: Medical team meetings: Utilizing technology to enhance communication, collaboration and decision-making)
20. Arora, V.M., et al.: A theoretical framework and competency-based approach to improving handoffs. Qual. Saf. Health. Care. **17**, 11–14 (2008)
21. Munkvold, G., et al.: Formalizing work—reallocating redundancy. Comput. Support. Coop. Work. **6**, 59–68 (2006)
22. Hartwood, M., et al.: Making a case in medical work: implications for the electronic medical record. Comput. Support. Coop. Work. **12**(3), 241–266 (2003)
23. Hughes, D.: When nurse knows best: some aspects of nurse/doctor interaction in a casualty department. Soc. Health. Illn. **10**, 1–22 (1988)
24. Atkinson, P.: Medical Talk and Medical Work. Sage Publication Ltd., London (1995)

25. Monahan, T.: Picturing technological change: the materiality of information infrastructures in public education. Technol. Pedagog. Educ. **17**(2), 89–101 (2008)
26. Winner, L.: The Wale and the Reactor: A Search for Limits in an Age of High Technology. University of Chicago Press, Chicago (1986)
27. Orlikowski, W.: Sociomaterial practices: exploring technology at work. Organ. Stud. **28**(9), 1435–1448 (2007)
28. Leonardi, P.M., Barley, S.R.: Materiality and change: challenges to building better theory about technology and organizing. Inform. Organ. **18**, 159–176 (2008)
29. Perrow, C.: Complexity, coupling and catastrophe. In: Normal Accidents, pp. 62–100. Princeton University Press (ed.), Princeton (1984)
30. Walsham, G.: Interpretive case studies in IS research: nature and method. Eur. J. Inform. Syst. **4**, 74–81 (1995)
31. Klein, H., Myers, M.: A set of principles for conducting and evaluating interpretive field studies in information systems. MIS Q. **23**, 67–94 (1999)
32. Orlikowski, W., Baroudi, J.: Studying information technology in organizations: Research approaches and assumptions. Inform. Syst. Res. **2**(1), 143–169 (1991)
33. Ash, J.S., Berg, M., Coiera, E.: Some unintended consequences of information technology in health care: the nature of patient care information system-related errors. J. Am. Med. Inform. Assoc. **11**, 104–112 (2004)
34. Malterud, K.: Kvalitativ metode I medisinsk forskning: 2. utgave. Universitetsforlaget. (2003)
35. NANDA-1.: Nursing diagnosis: Definitions and classification 2007–2008. In: Heather Herdman, T. (ed.) NANDA international, p. 6. Weley (2007)
36. Bulechek, G.M., Butcher, H.K., Dochterman, J.M.: NIC. Nursing Interventions Classification, 5th edn. Mosby/Elsevier, St. Louis (2008)

Chapter 3
The Clinical Work of Secretaries: Exploring the Intersection of Administrative and Clinical Work in the Diagnosing Process

Naja L. Holten Møller and Signe Vikkelsø

Abstract Diagnostic work is often defined by the skill of clinicians whereas the contributions of non-clinicians, for example secretaries, tend to fade into the background. The secretaries are deeply involved in diagnostic work through the eligible administration of patients in the collaborative electronic information systems. This study explores the *secretaries' role* in diagnostic work, focusing specifically on the context of diagnosing cancer. It identifies four key activities of secretaries that are essential for diagnosing patients: We argue that the secretaries' role is positioned at the intersection of clinical and administrative practices and not limited to support of articulation work of clinicians and administrative work. Secretaries also carry out activities that fall under the core definition of clinical work. This clinical dimension of the secretaries' work, we argue, should be embedded in the design of collaborative systems to support the diagnosing process.

3.1 Introduction

Diagnostic work is often understood as a particular type of collaborative work that is "clinical" or "medical" at its core [1–4]. So it is the work of clinicians, ranging from physicians assessing patients, to technicians running tests, and nurses tending to patients while taking note of their condition. Secretaries, from this perspective, are the "right hand" of clinicians, ensuring that physicians, test results, and patients are brought together at the right time and place [5–9]. Despite the fact that secretaries are central to the core of clinical work (defined by Bardram [5] as examining the patient's illness and condition, requesting and interpreting clinical information, decision-making concerning the patient's illness and condition, further medical treat-

N. L. H. Møller (✉)
The IT University of Copenhagen, Rued Langgaards Vej 7, 2300 Copenhagen, Denmark
e-mail: nhmo@itu.dk

S. Vikkelsø
Copenhagen Business School, Kilevej 14A, 2000 Frederiksberg, Denmark
e-mail: ssv.ioa@cbs.dk

J. Dugdale et al. (eds.), *From Research to Practice in the Design of Cooperative Systems: Results and Open Challenges*, DOI 10.1007/978-1-4471-4093-1_3, © Springer-Verlag London 2012

ment of the patient's illness and condition, and monitoring the effect of it), and that diagnostic work is defined in relation to this core clinical work, surprisingly little attention has been paid to the role of secretaries in diagnosis. This study empirically investigates the role of secretaries in both a radiology department and a medical department. We find that secretaries are central to diagnostic work and identify four particular activities where this is evident when secretaries: (a) examine the patient's condition, (b) interpret the clinical information, (c) monitor the follow-up, and (d) further inform the patient's trajectory. These activities constitute an intersection of clinical and administrative work where secretaries become involved in the handling of patients through the collaborative electronic information systems. The formal distribution of power when secretaries become involved in diagnosis is not the focus; the analysis focuses strictly on how to further specify the secretaries' role.

In the following we start by introducing the collaborative electronic information systems, RIS-PACS and OPUS-OCW, that were the subject of the secretaries' work in the study reported here. Then, we explore four specific examples of how secretaries contribute to the diagnosis of patients in a radiology department and a medical department. Third, we discuss the combined clinical and administrative content of these examples and point to the way in which it specifies the secretaries' work. Finally, we conclude that a detailed understanding of secretaries' work as intersecting is crucial to the support of collaborative systems.

3.2 Background

In Denmark, collaborative electronic information systems such as RIS-PACS (Radiological Information System—Picture Archiving and Communication System) and OPUS-OCW (Open Clinical Workspace) were implemented in recent years as part of a national strategy for the digitalization of the health service [10]. In terms of diagnostic work, the national strategy is focusing in particular on support of radiology to ensure better and faster diagnosis. Secretaries' work is an implicit part of the national strategy that has as its purpose the connection of the entire health service in Denmark. RIS-PACS and OPUS-OCW are both multi-module access portals. RIS-PACS is primarily oriented toward radiology (administration and picture archiving). The medical department uses OPUS-OCW, which supports a broader spectrum of clinical practices (administration, medication, monitoring, etc.). These systems are intended to support continuous and smooth coordination of the clinical and administrative work. While systems such as RIS-PACS and OPUS-OCW are increasingly prevalent in diagnostic work, there are several reasons why it is crucial to place secretaries at the center of analysis. First, the development of, and experimentation with, collaborative electronic information systems has been occasion for reappraising rather than dismantling the role secretaries play. Second, the implementation of these systems has not simply supported existing practices but rather entailed reorganization of activities and responsibilities [9, 11]. This reorganization confirms the classic argument of Hughes and others: that new kinds of technology may interfere with existing roles and the organization of work [1, 12]. Given that roles are in flux, the very understanding of what kinds of work practices comprise diagnostic work needs to be re-examined.

3.3   Theoretical Framework

In order to understand the organizational positioning of the secretary, we will argue that this role cannot be understood simply within administrative or "supportive" terms or by the concept of "articulation work." The secretary is deeply involved in the core "clinical work", but this aspect has remained under-theorized. In the following we will briefly review the way secretaries work has been conceptualized in the literature.

3.3.1   Secretarial Work

Secretarial work is by no means a new subject. Research within CSCW and related fields has expanded our understanding of the secretary's role in various fields of collaboration. Secretarial work has been addressed broadly in relation to directing assistants [13, 14], secretaries [15–17], medical secretaries [5, 7, 18–21], clerical workers [1, 22], office workers [23, 24], and coders [25]. A shared departure for this research is the argument that secretarial work is something that cannot be performed by everyone. Pointing to the knowledge work, CSCW research has demonstrated that understanding the role of secretaries is important for the design of collaborative electronic information systems in various fields of collaboration.

Secretarial work, as has been demonstrated in CSCW, is rarely recognized as knowledge work. Instead, a secretary is often thought of as someone who simply connects clients with software or answers phones and types. In contrast to this simplified picture, it has been shown, for example, that the software relies on secretaries' work in different ways [14, 25]. Müller demonstrated how the work of a particular type of secretaries—telephone operators—is about collaborative refinement of clients' requests and not just connecting the software (database of telephone numbers) and the clients. Hence, knowledge work is defined by the domain-specific memory and use of domain-specific patterns of meaning, and Müller demonstrates that this is also a characteristic for telephone operators [14].

Somewhat related, the key activities of the medical secretary have been characterized as: printing clinical information [20], transcribing and filing physicians' dictations [26], locating files [19], and being a receptionist [7, 37] Often, however, the secretary's role is described as "collaborating" with nurses and physicians or "providing clerical support" [5, 7, 19, 20, 26, 37]. It remains somewhat unclear how the work of the medical secretary is "knowledge work" and how it relates to what is seen as the core clinical work, which diagnosis is a part of.

3.3.2   Clinical Work

"Clinician" is a rather broad term that covers professions doing work in a clinic or work that is related to the observation and diagnosis of patients [27]. The performance of clinical work typically relies on different types of specialties and is thus essentially collaborative. This is particularly true in relation to complex diseases, such as cancer [7]. Bardram characterizes the performance of clinical work as a circular process roughly consisting of five activities [5]: (a) examining the patient's illness and condition, (b) requesting and interpreting clinical information, (c) decision-making concerning the patient's illness and condition, (d) further medical treatment of the patient's illness and condition, and (e) monitoring the effect of it. These activities define clinical work, Bardram argues; but they are determined by the actual condition of the patient [5]. Clinical work varies across patients (for example, how fast symptoms develop and hence can be diagnosed). This variety very much affects the work environment of clinicians. Few settings are as rich in detail as clinical settings [5, 20, 27], which, in the words of Strauss et al., consist of places "where very different resources (space, skills, ratios of labor force, equipment, drugs, supplies, and the like) are required" to carry out the work ([27], p. 6). At the same time, clinical work is dispersed across time and space; and, the coordination or articulation of this work is pivotal.

3.3.3   "Articulation Work" in Clinical Settings

The support of articulation work—or the reduction of effort involved in articulation work of others—is a classic job of secretaries besides administrative work. The organization of clinical work relies on articulation work to bridge the various types of specialties involved in clinical work [5, 8, 27]. Articulation work, from this perspective, defines a type of "supra work process" that supports the accomplishment of distributed activities [28]. Articulation work is an ongoing and shared concern of clinicians to make the collective work add up to more than discrete bits of accomplished work [27]. Secretaries are reported as part of this process, for example, when they structure and send information in collaborative electronic information systems that support the clinical work [5–7, 20, 21]. Here, the articulation work of clinicians, for example, structuring information, is the core work of secretaries.

Emphasis has often been placed on the role of shared repositories and objects for this articulation work [26, 29]. The concept of "boundary objects" points to objects that are "weakly structured in common use and become strongly structured in individual-site use" ([30], p. 393). In a clinical setting boundary objects can serve *different* purposes for different communities of practice (such as clinicians and secretaries) and still maintain some common sense of purpose across them [26, 29–31]. Equally important, the central concept within CSCW of "common information space" [32], such as that provided by a collaborative electronic information system, also allows different communities of practice to pursue *different* purposes. Secretaries clearly play a role in the establishment and maintenance of such "boundary objects" or "common information spaces," and hence in the support of articulation work [33]. It is in relation to the pursuing of a *shared* purpose of different communities of practice that the secretary's role in diagnostic work is explored.

3.3.4 The Clinical Work of Secretaries?

While we find the above conceptualizations of secretaries' work important, we also note that the secretary tends to be seen as an administrative function or as part of the articulation of clinical work [5–9]. There is no explicit account of the way secretaries might also be partaking directly in the clinical work, which diagnosis is a part of. While this is no surprise in light of both common sense and formal distinctions between the job of physicians, nurses, and secretaries, we will show that secretaries also carry out tasks that fall under the core definition of clinical work.

3.4 Research Method

The study reported here was conducted in a mid-sized hospital that specializes in patients with general symptoms. These patients are particularly important when investigating the initial diagnosis because they often fail to meet the formal criteria for referring patients to hospital departments that specialize in cancer. The study focused on two departments: the radiology department and the medical department. *The radiology department* provides important examinations critical for the initial diagnosis of complex diseases such as cancer. The staff in the radiology department includes specialists of radiology, radiographers, and secretaries. *The medical department* has several sub-sections specializing in different areas of medicine (such as diabetes, gastroenterology, cardiology, etc.) as well as four outpatient clinics and an acute care section. The medical department diagnoses a number of patients with cancer every year in collaboration with other departments, although, this is not the specialty of the department. The staff of the medical department includes specialists of medicine, secretaries, and nurses.

The study was ethnographically informed [34, 35]. The initial diagnosis process—and the secretaries' role—was explored through detailed analysis of ethnographic notes from observations of practices related to diagnostic work, as well as *in situ* interviews and semi-structured interviews, artifacts (schedules, classification

Fig. 3.1 Distribution of
responsibilities during the
initial diagnosing process

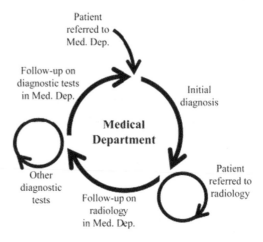

Fig. 3.1 Distribution of responsibilities during the initial diagnosing process

schemes, etc.), and images. Observations were conducted by the first author over a period of 13 months. In total, the first author spent 118 h observing practices and conducting *in situ* and semi-structured interviews. Prior to commencing these observations, preliminary observations were conducted, in total, 14 h. Data were analysed right from the beginning of the data-constructing process. In this way, data collection and data analysis together formed an iterative process of analyzing themes that emerged as being essential for the process of diagnosis, for example, variations of secretaries' work. Data were continuously contested by presenting it to the secretaries and clinicians when observations were resumed. Secretaries' as well as clinicians' insight provided useful interpretations for further collection and analysis of data. In this way the contesting of data in one stage became the preconception for the collection of data in the next stage and a way of reasoning in the analysis [36].

3.5 Analysis: The Clinical Work of Secretaries

In Denmark, secretaries are often the first hospital staff to handle requests of diagnostic examinations and incoming referrals, which positions secretaries as central to diagnostic work. In the following analysis, we explore the role of secretaries in four specific examples of activities involved in diagnostic work. First, we analyze how secretaries participate in the examination of a patient's condition in order to ensure that severe patient cases are given first priority. Second, secretaries' clinical interpretations are analyzed. Third, we analyze how secretaries evaluate patients to make sure they received appropriate follow-up. Finally, we analyze how secretaries further inform the patient trajectory. Figure 3.1 illustrates the relationship between the radiology and the medical department and the distribution of responsibilities during the initial diagnosing process.

3.5.1 Examining the Condition

To even begin the process of diagnosing a patient will have to be referred to a clinical department. In the medical department the referrals are received by the general secretaries' office (the medical secretariat) before patients are distributed to the "local" secretariats in the sub-sections. Most referrals are received electronically, but they may also be received as paper referrals. The referrals are printed (if received as paper referrals they are scanned so that they are also registered in the electronic information system) and then distributed to plastic trays that each sub-section has in the general secretariat. Although, it might seem to be a somewhat trivial task, while distributing the printed referrals to the sub-sections, this secretary, the following example shows, is simultaneously examining the patients' conditions. Reading through the free-text of one of the referrals the secretary quickly realizes that she has to take action. The free-text reads:

> 77 year old woman, known to have COLD [chronic obstructive lung disease] as well as afli [atrial fibriliation], recently started treatment with Maravan. Referred acute since the patient has macroscopic hematuria and development of various ecchymosis of OE. Had INR [international normalized ratio] taken in lab > 7.5. (Referral for the medical department, September 30th 2009)

The secretary's examination, in this example, is highly relevant for the diagnosing of the patient. The electronic referral template allows the referring physician to indicate the condition as either "acute" or "planned". The patient in this example is categorized in the referral template as "planned" indicating that this patient may wait. However, the free-text tells the secretary an entirely different story: Reading through the free-text, the secretary underlines the text "acute" with a yellow marker and then explains that an INR > 7.5 (a measure of the blood coagulation) is problematic, before she comes to the conclusion that this patient will have to be handled "acute" and not as a patient that can wait. The patient, the secretary explains, is not supposed to have an INR this high.

When she looks up the patient in the collaborative electronic information system her suspicion is confirmed. In the collaborative electronic information system it is registered that the patient (despite the fact that the referral was sent electronically to the general secretariat) has already been admitted physically through the hospital's acute care section. Knowing this, the secretary may cancel the referral in the collaborative electronic information system. To make sure that it is also clear to the clinicians why the referral is canceled, she notes this information in the comment field. When done, the secretary throws out the printed copy of the referral and continues to read through the rest of the referrals received in the general secretaries' office that morning.

The example illustrates exactly how the secretary gets involved in diagnostic work (examining the condition of the patient). While this work is not something that any of the clinical staff are aware of (unless they read the comment in the collaborative electronic information system), it influences the diagnostic work. If the patient had not been admitted, it would have been a potentially dangerous situation.

Even if the patient had been admitted (physically) but the secretary had not reacted adequately (electronically), this would have been disturbing to the diagnostic work. Eventually the clinical staff would have been the ones to make sure this patient was receiving proper diagnostic care. However, in terms of timing, this assurance would have occurred much later than when the secretary noticed the seriousness and took action.

3.5.2   Interpreting the Clinical Information

Another department equally important for the diagnostic work is the radiology department. Radiology often guides the next diagnostic step as clinicians are trying to understand the nature of patients' symptoms. The secretary is the first person to receive referrals for radiology. The rule is, the secretary in the radiology department explains, that all referrals should be scheduled the day they are received, as a way to ensure that patients are not waiting because of the administration of the referrals. In this way, the radiology department tries to avoid patients waiting for reasons other than clinical ones. The incoming referrals are lined up in a list in the radiology information system, RIS-PACS.

Also the radiologist on call, located downstairs in the protected space of the CT-scanner and MR-scanner, takes notice of the referrals as the electronic list of referrals fills up. The radiologists have a work space next to the CT-scanner and the MR-scanner so that they can pay attention to the scanners and access the collaborative electronic information system at the same time. RIS-PACS is used by the radiologist for describing the scans, and in between the description of scans the radiologist interprets the information in the referrals so that the secretary can continue to schedule them.

Back in the secretaries office the next electronic referral for a CT-scan is waiting to be scheduled. The referral is received like any other electronic referral (automatically listed one after the other in RIS-PACS). The radiologist has added a priority and specified the program and sequence of the particular scan. Reading through the electronic referral template, the secretary interprets the wording of the referring physician and the radiologist, which both says something about the way the scan is to be carried out, she explains. Scheduling a CT-scan is not the same as scheduling an MR-scan or any of the other scans, it is revealed when the secretary glances at a protocol hanging above the secretary's desk entitled "CT—The short version".

The presence of the protocol in the secretaries office is surprising at first due to the clinical nature of it. The exact same A3-sized (11.7×16.5 inch) protocol is hanging downstairs next to the radiographers as well as in the radiologists' work space. The CT-protocol is a clinical tool used by the radiologists; the CT-scans each require specification of the appropriate sequence and program before the radiographer can perform the CT-scan. The CT-protocol, for example, specifies that "tumour detection" corresponds to sub-protocol number 6A in RIS-PACS and also specifies the situations where, for example, contrast is needed. The secretary confirms that the various clinical information corresponds.

The example illustrates how the secretaries' work (specifying the protocol and sequence while scheduling the CT-scan) involves an artefact (the CT-protocol) that is strictly clinical while checking the clinical history for other conditions that may influence the way the CT-scan is carried out (contrast or not). Although the clinical information on the choice of program and sequence is not filled in by the secretary, she does become involved in the diagnostic work when she once again interprets it. In the convey of information the secretary makes sure that the patient is supposed to have contrast when this is specified.

3.5.3   Monitoring the Clinical Follow-up

When the scan has been performed it appears in a list in RIS-PACS. The medical department can then retrieve the scan for their department and sub-sections. The responsibility for retrieving scan results in the medical department is placed with the "local" secretaries in the sub-sections. In the sub-section for medical acute care patients, the secretaries share the office space with the physicians and nurses. There are always two secretaries on duty; one takes care of the many *ad hoc* tasks and the other types the physicians' dictations. The secretary who is responsible for *ad hoc* tasks retrieves the results of patients' scans in RIS-PACS and makes sure that a physician takes responsibility for the particular scans so that they are followed-up.

This routine was established, the secretary explains, to avoid adverse events. Before this, the sub-section sometimes experienced that it was unclear who was responsible for the follow-up, which presented a risk to the patients if the result was, for example, cancer related. The secretary explains this while sorting printed copies of scan results into three piles: (1) scan results that have to be signed by the physician responsible for the patient; (2) scan results that the physician on-duty may sign before it is sent to the patient's GP; and (3) scan results that must be signed by another department because the patient has been transferred there. The secretary carefully reads the result of the scan and then reads the newest part of the continuation (clinical notes). In this way, she tries to make sense of the results and how they should be sorted (as 1, 2 or 3). When the secretary is uncertain, she consults the physician on-duty.

The physicians also monitor RIS-PACS, but only when they have requested the scan themselves. It is possible that a physician will call their colleague in the radiology department prior to the release of a scan, the secretary explains, to have a first indication of whether the result points in one direction or the other (cancer or not). The secretary gets up to consult the physician on-duty working at a computer in the background. The scan results are not printed simply to be distributed; the secretary's responsibility is quite literal, she says, when the secretary returns with the signature of the physician. The secretary's name is printed at the bottom of the paper copy that is later saved in the patient record. If no physician has signed for the printed result it is her responsibility, the secretary explains and points to her name at the bottom of the paper.

The example illustrates that while printing scan results might seem as extra work or doing the same work twice, in the sense that a physician already has the scan in mind, the secretary is not just printing scan results to remind the physician. The real task is the sorting and the overall monitoring involved in this activity where physicians share the responsibility for the patient. The secretary does not monitor the single patient like the physicians do; instead the secretary monitors all the patients. Physicians schedule changes, and since the physician may be at the ward 1 day and in the clinic or at a conference the next, patients are sometimes left in a vulnerable situation. The secretary makes sure scan results are followed-up and therefore gets involved in the diagnosing process in a crucial way.

3.5.4   Further Informing the Clinical Trajectory

The "local" secretary in the medical sub-sections is the person responsible for registering that the diagnosing process has come to an end in the collaborative electronic information system, OPUS-OCW. The act of registering this clinical milestone (a) indicates the change of responsibility for the patient (if responsibility is to be turned over to another clinical department or the GP) and (b) signals to the medical department itself that no further action is taken. In this way, diagnosing is accomplished by the secretary who registers the final diagnosis—at least in a formal sense.

The secretary, sitting with the paper record in front of her, looks up the patient in the system (OPUS-OCW). The physicians in the medical department decided that they could not come any closer to a final diagnosis for the patient. The secretary now has to find out how to close the patient's case, she explains. This happens every now and then, that no diagnosis is set, but the patient's case still has to be closed. Flipping through the paper record, the secretary notices that there are several pages in the continuation (the clinical notes) that are obsolete. The secretary prints a new, complete edition of the electronic continuation and replaces the previous one.

The electronic registering is part of a larger setup where the patient's status is reported to The National Patient Register (LPR). Although the purpose of the registering is somewhat clear to the secretary, who is also aware of and tries to register the patient according to the registering guide (spending time reading through it several times), it does not help her. To get her work done, the secretary instead interprets the patient's "unknown" diagnosis in a way that to some extend informs the further diagnosis process. The secretary's interpretation is that she can "close" the patient's trajectory to one of two patient categories in the electronic information system:

"HA" [The patient is already diagnosed]
"HF" [The patient is being diagnosed]

After some time of going back and forth between the registration guide the secretary finally decides to register the patient as "HF," although, she notes, this does not fit the registration guidelines if taken literally. The code "HF," the secretary explains, is used to register that the patient is still being diagnosed. Therefore, to register the patient as "HF" (being diagnosed) is somewhat contradictory to the fact that "HF" in this case is "closing" the diagnosis of the patient. But, a decision has to be made, and that is what she chose to do. In this way the secretary becomes involved in diagnostic work by deciding how to close the diagnosis of the patient that further informs the diagnosis process in other departments—or, the process if the patient returns.

3.6   The Intersection of Clinical and Administrative Work

Articulation work, according to Strauss et al., is the ongoing and shared concern of clinicians to make the collective work add up to more than discrete and conflicting parts [27]. Strauss et al. do not explicitly mention secretaries' work (the underlying point being that articulation work is carried out not only by administrators but also by clinicians), which is perhaps why the opposite point is not made: that clinical work is carried out not only by clinicians but also by "administrators" such as the secretaries explored in this study. While "articulation work" and "work" are analytical concepts difficult to separate in practice, this is not only an omission of Strauss and colleagues. Secretaries' work is well described within CSCW and related fields. However, it tends to be conceptualized using the limited terminology of secretaries as administrators, or support of clinicians' articulation work to manage the intersection of administrative and clinical work [5–9]. In general, a considerable part of secretaries' common work is to support the articulation work and administrative work necessary for the diagnosis of patients, but not all of it can be understood as such.

In addition to these supportive and administrative functions, we have shown that secretaries also play an important role in the diagnosis of patients: examining the condition; interpreting the clinical information; monitoring the follow-up; and further informing the trajectory. At the intersection of administrative and clinical work, the secretary carries out activities that fall under the core definition of clinical work, for example, when the secretary distributes referrals. To distribute the referral is formally the secretary's task; however, while doing this task she simultaneously becomes aware that the patient is at risk of not receiving the sufficient treatment and therefore takes action. Bardram describes how a core clinical activity of a physician is the change of a request if the physician, for example, finds it insufficient to address the stated problem of the patient [5]. The example illustrates how the secretary also carries out clinical work in the same way as the physician. However, the direct partaking of the secretary in clinical work should not be understood as coincidental practice. Rather, we argue, this partaking follows from the positioning of the secretary at the "intersection" of, formally separate but practically enmeshed practices, namely administrative and clinical work.

We emphasize the concept of "intersection" in order to draw attention to the fact that formal and common sense definitions of tasks and job responsibilities do not always, and in fact seldom, mirror exactly the reality of work. This is by no means a new observation [21, 27]. But, as we have illustrated, the understanding of the work of medical secretaries in previous research has stayed relatively true to such common sense and formal distinctions, even though organizational reality can be empirically shown to be different. The concept of "intersection" entails that clinical work does not come in clearly demarcated chunks and that practitioners often seesaw between tasks in a fashion that makes it hard to distinguish where one type of work ends and another begins. This is particularly relevant to CSCW because the design and use of collaborative electronic information systems often suffers from poor understandings of the actual collaborative work and of the specific ways in which this work is divided and coordinated. The concepts of "common information spaces" and "boundary objects" seek to address the same type of intersecting or "crossing" activities that we argue also characterize diagnostic work. However, the use and discussion of these concepts tends to be concerned with how to support articulation work for practitioners to be able to collaborate across their *different* practices [26, 29–32].

While Bannon and Bødker point to a need for more attention to the issues of managing boundaries [32], their focus is predominantly on the handling of articulation work and not so much the crossing or intersecting activities. We address the intersecting work of secretaries and clinicians. Based on the empirical examples of secretaries' work, we argue that, in relation to the work itself, it is necessary to be open about the division of work when designing collaborative electronic information systems. This is, for example, evident when the secretary takes care of the follow-up of the scan results: to formalize her responsibility the secretary has to print a copy of the scan result and sign it. The system reveals the name of the physician who requested the scan and therefore formally is responsible for the follow-up. Hence, this example shows that it is not enough to assume the reality of formal boundaries or job descriptions. The secretary also plays a central role in the follow-up. Therefore, these collaborative electronic information systems should be designed to support the practices at the intersections of conventional boundaries as well.

3.7 Conclusion

Secretaries' work is of central interest to CSCW. Despite this interest, the secretary's role has been given surprisingly little attention in relation to diagnostic work. We have emphasized the need to explore the secretary's role as part of diagnostic work just as is done in other fields of collaboration. Diagnostic work is often defined by the skills of clinicians while secretaries' work tends to slide into the background. Some of the most significant CSCW research emphasizes how articulation work is carried out by physicians, which is perhaps why the opposite point is not often made: that clinical work is also carried out by secretaries.

Secretaries handle patients in collaborative electronic information systems. As collaborative electronic information systems that integrate administrative and clinical tasks are becoming increasingly prevalent in diagnostic work, there is good reason to place secretaries at the center of attention. We aim to further specify the "intersection" of clinical work and administrative work in relation to the process of diagnosing patients. The research question we explored is: what role do secretaries play in diagnostic work, and how is it related to the use of collaborative electronic information systems?

We explored this question in our analysis of various activities of secretaries in a radiology department and a medical department. The two departments are often involved in the initial diagnosing of potential cancer. Diagnosing potential cancer is a complex, collaborative activity that involves various specialties, particularly in the initial part of the process where symptoms can point to a range of conditions. The secretaries reduce the effort involved in clinicians' articulation work during this process. However, as the analysis illustrated, the secretaries' contribution is also achieved through work that fall under the core definition of clinical activities—this may be an advantage from a timely perspective.

Subsequently, the contribution of this study lies in empirically showing how secretaries, in addition to their administrative tasks and their support of clinicians articulation work, also carry out clinical tasks. Thus, we specify how exactly the secretaries work is located in between, or at the "intersection" of, formally separate but practically enmeshed practices, namely administrative and clinical work. This suggests, we argue, that the clinical dimension of secretaries' work should be embedded in the design of collaborative systems supporting diagnostic work.

Acknowledgments   Our thanks to all staff—in particular, the secretaries—at the medical department and the radiology department, Køge Sygehus. Also, thanks to colleagues for providing comments and, in particular, Pernille Bjørn, Marisa Cohn and Laura Watts.

References

1. Aydin, C.E., Rice, R.E.: Bringing social worlds together: computers as catalysts for new interactions in health care organizations. J. Health Soc. Behav. **33**(2), 168–185 (1992)
2. Büscher, M., O'Neil, J., Rooksby, J.: Designing for diagnosing: introduction to the special issue on diagnostic work. Comput. Support. Coop. Work. **18**, 109–128 (2009)
3. Berg, M.: Accumulating and coordinating: occasions for information technologies in medical work. Comput. Support. Coop. Work. **8**(4), 373–401 (1999)
4. Saunders, B.F.: CT Suite. The Work of Diagnosis in the Age of Noninvasive Cutting. Duke University Press, Durham (2008)
5. Bardram, J.E.: I love the system—I just don't use it! In: Proceedings of the 1997 International ACM Conference on Supporting Group Work, pp. 251–260 (1997)
6. Paul, S.A., Reddy, M.C.: Understanding together: sensemaking in collaborative Information seeking. In: Proceedings of the 2010 ACM Conference on Computer Supported Cooperative Work, pp. 321–330 (2010)
7. Schmidt, K., Wagner, I., Tolar, M.: Permutations of cooperative work practices: a study of two oncology clinics. In: Proceedings of the 2007 International ACM Conference on Supporting Group Work, pp. 1–10 (2007)

8. Bardram, J.E., Bossen, C.: Mobility work: the spatial dimension of collaboration at a hospital. Comput. Support. Coop. Work. **14**, 131–160 (2005)
9. Vikkelsø, S.: Subtle reorganization of work, attention and risks: electronic patient records and organizational consequences. Scand. J. Inf. Syst. **17**(1), 3–30 (2005)
10. Digital Sundhed.: National strategi for digitalisering af sundhedsvæsenet 2008–2012—til fremme af befolkningens sundhed samt forebyggelse og behandling. Digital Sundhed, 1–53 https://www.sundhed.dk/content/cms/6/3406_national-strategi-2008-2012.pdf (2008)
11. Berg, M.: Practices of reading and writing: the constitutive role of the patient record in medical work. Sociol. Health Illn. **18**(4), 499–524 (1996)
12. Hughes, E.C.: The Sociological Eye. Selected papers. Transaction, New Brunswick (1984)
13. Lawrence, D.E., Atwood, M.E., Dews, S.: Surrogate Users: mediating between social and technical interaction. In: Proceedings of the 1994 SIGCHI Conference on Human Factors in Computing Systems, pp. 399–404 (1994)
14. Müller, M.J.: Invisible work of telephone operators: an ethnocritical analysis. Comput. Support. Coop. Work. **8**, 31–61 (1999)
15. Ehrlich, S.F.: Social and psychological factors influencing the design of office communications systems. ACM SIGCHI Bull. **18**(4), 323–329 (1987)
16. Grudin, J.: Why CSCW applications fail: problems in the design and evaluation of organizational interfaces. In: Proceedings of the 1988 ACM Conference on Computer Supported Cooperative Work, pp. 85–93 (1988)
17. Pipek, V., Wulf, V.: A groupware's life. In: Proceedings of the Sixth European Conference on Computer Supported Cooperative Work, pp. 199–218 (1999)
18. Møller, N.H., Bjørn, P.: Layers in sorting practices: sorting out patients with potential cancer. Comput. Support. Coop. Work. **20**, 123–153 (2011)
19. Reddy, M.C., Jansen, B.J.: A model for understanding collaborative information behavior in context: a study of two healthcare teams. Inf. Process. Manag. **44**, 256–273 (2008)
20. Reddy, M.C., Spence, P.R.: Collaborative information seeking: a field study of a multidisciplinary patient care team. Inf. Process. Manag. **44**(1), 242–255 (2008)
21. Svenningsen, S.: Den Elektroniske Patientjournal og Medicinsk Arbejde—Reorganisering af Roller, Ansvar og Risici på Sygehus. Handelshøjskolens Forlag http://www.adlibris.com/dk/product.aspx?isbn=8762902326 (2004)
22. Glenn, E.N., Feldberg, R.L.: Degraded and deskilled: the proletarianization of clerical work. Soc. Study Soc. Probl. **25**(1), 52–64 (1977)
23. Markussen, R.: Politics of intervention in design: feminist reflections on the Scandinavian tradition. AI Soc. **10**, 127–141 (1996)
24. Rouncefield, M., Viller, S., Hughes, J.A., Rodden, T.: Working with "constant interruption": CSCW and the small office. Inf. Soc. **11**(3), 173–188 (1995)
25. Blomberg, J., Suchman, L., Trigg, R.H.: Reflections on a work-oriented design project. Hum. Comput. Interact. **11**, 237–265 (1996)
26. Bossen, C., Markussen, R.: Infrastructuring and ordering devices in health care: medication plans and practices on a hospital ward. Comput. Support. Cooper. Work. **19**, 615–637 (2010)
27. Strauss, A.L., Fagerhaugh, S., Suczek, B., Wiener, C.: Social Organization of Medical Work. The University of Chicago Press, Chicago (1985)
28. Clement, A., Wagner, I.: Fragmented exchange: disarticulation and the need for regionalized communication spaces. In: Proceedings of the Fourth European Conference on Computer Supported Cooperative Work, pp. 33–49 (1995)
29. Bossen, C.: The parameters of common information spaces: the heterogenity of cooperative work at a hospital ward. In: Proceedings of the 2002 ACM Conference on Computer Supported Cooperative Work, pp. 176–185 (2002)
30. Star, S.L., Griesemer, J.R.: Institutional ecology. 'Translations' and boundary objects: amateurs and professionals in Berkeley's 'Museum of Vertebrate Zoology'. Soc. Stud. Sci. **19**(3), 387–420 (1989)
31. Lee, C.P.: Boundary negotiating artifacts: unbinding the routine of boundary objects and embracing chaos in collaborative work. Comput. Support. Coop. Work. **16**, 307–339 (2007)

32. Bannon, L., Bødker, S.: Constructing common information spaces. In: Proceedings of the Fifth European Conference on Computer Supported Cooperative Work, pp. 81–96 (1997)
33. Schmidt, K., Simone, C.: Coordination mechanisms: towards a conceptual foundation of CSCW system design. Comput. Support. Coop. Work. **5**, 155–200 (1996)
34. Forsythe, D.: "It's just a matter of common sense": ethnography as invisible work. Comput. Support. Coop. Work. **8**, 127–145 (1999)
35. Luff, P., Jon, H., Heath, C.: Workplace Studies: Recovering Work Practice and Informing System Design. Cambridge University Press, Cambridge (2000)
36. Klein, H., Myers, M.A.: A set of principles for conducting and evaluating interpretive field studies in information systems. MIS Q. **23**(1), 67–93 (1999)
37. Tellioglu, H., Wagner, I.: Work practices surrounding PACS: the politics of space in hospitals. Comput. Support. Coop. Work. **10**, 163–188 (2001)

Chapter 4
Exploring the Virtual Space of Academia

Maria Menendez, Antonella de Angeli, and Zeno Menestrina

Abstract The aim of this chapter is to provide a view on how researchers present themselves in a social network specifically developed for supporting academic practices, how they share information and engage in dialogues with colleagues worldwide. We analysed data from 30,428 users who have registered on a publicly available website to study the effect of academic position, university ranking and country on people's behaviour. Results suggest that the virtual network closely mirrors physical reality, reproducing the same hierarchical structure imposed by position, ranking, and country on user behaviour. Despite the potential for bridging and bonding social capital the networks have not achieved substantial changes in structures and practices of the academic context. Furthermore, our analysis highlights the need of finding new strategies to motivate the users to contribute to the community and support equal participation, as so far the community is mainly exploited as a static website.

4.1 Introduction

A consistent corpus of research in social networks has linked this technology to social capital, the value derived from being member of a community [2, 7, 16]. Social networks can increase the establishment and maintenance of weak-ties by bridging social capital and have some positive effect also on strong ties by bonding social capital [16]. Social capital is an important personal and organisational asset. It tends to improve processes of knowledge management and information sharing [7], a desirable outcome in many professional contexts, and in particular in research work. In this chapter, we provide some insights on how researchers have structured

M. Menendez (✉) · A. de Angeli · Z. Menestrina
Department of Information Engineering and Computer Science (DISI),
University of Trento, Via Sommarive, 5, 38123 POVO–Trento, Italy
e-mail: menendez@disi.unitn.it

A. de Angeli
e-mail: deangeli@disi.unitn.it

Z. Menestrina
e-mail: zeno.menestrina@studenti.unitn.it

J. Dugdale et al. (eds.), *From Research to Practice in the Design of Cooperative Systems:*   49
Results and Open Challenges, DOI 10.1007/978-1-4471-4093-1_4,
© Springer-Verlag London 2012

themselves into an on-line community specifically developed to support academic practices. In particular, we look at self-presentation strategies, information sharing, and on-going dialogues supported by the community. This knowledge can facilitate our understanding of how technology shapes organizational practices and how to design technology for supporting positive changes in existing structures [13].

The chapter is structured as follows. First, we review related work on the use of social networks in professional contexts with an emphasis on barriers and drivers in the adoption. Then, we present the main social networking websites for academics available on the web and present methods and results of our study. Finally, we discuss the findings and propose directions for future work.

4.2 From Personal to Professional Networks

In the last decade, many different types of social networks have appeared on the Internet with some astonishing success stories. Facebook is the winner in terms of users and number of academic studies [4, 6, 8, 9, 15, 17]. As for 2011, it entered the life of 800 millions people worldwide. Facebook was initially established as a tool for university students, but nowadays it pervades many other population segments. The move into the workplace has not been easy due to several tensions between personal and professional life. For instance, social networks challenge the organisational requirement to maintain confidentiality within the firewall, and the individual requirement to keep personal and professional life separated [15]. Enterprises usually have strict policies on data protection and security. A recent study commissioned by the Internet Security Company Webroot revealed that over 50 % of American and British business with up to 500 employees has restricted access to any public social network. Yet, social networks may play an important and productive role in organisations. They can contribute to building social capital [16] and facilitate knowledge management and information sharing processes [7].

To lessen security threats and the difficult overlapping between professional and personal life, a number of ad-hoc social networks have been developed to be used within the company intranet [3, 5, 14, 16]. Research, however, suggests that adoption and contribution rates are far from satisfactory. For instance Beehive, the internal IBM social network, collected registration from some 15 % of the total employees over 2 years, and only some 30 % of registered users visited the networks in a month [16]. Several studies have investigated motivational factors related to participation in social networking. Results highlight five basic dimensions addressing different needs related to functional, organizational, social, personal and technological factors.

Sharing and obtaining information are reported as main *functional* drivers for joining and contributing to professional social networks [19]. This source of motivation can be enhanced by *individual* predispositions and *organisational* culture which foster a perception of knowledge as a public good, belonging not to individuals, but to the whole organization [1]. Another important *functional* driver is the creation of new contacts, maintenance of old connections, and finding domain experts [1, 5, 14]. Surveillance of people's activity in the network has also been mentioned as a *functional* driver, especially at the managerial level of the organization [1]. However, some people perceive social networks as a waste of time [3].

Social factors facilitating adoption are linked to attraction by similarity. Users join groups and networks with whom they share some interests and passions [12, 16], and avoid places with content that they consider unsuitable [1, 17]. *Personal* exposure has been identified both as a driver and a hindrance. For some users, it increases visibility [1], opening opportunities for obtaining quality feedback on personal work [1] and self-expression [1, 18]. However, personal exposure can also be perceived as a privacy thread, preventing users from joining and contributing to social networks [1, 14]. *Technological* factors also play an important role in adoption. Suitability of functionalities [18] drives users to join and use social networks, while accessibility issues, such as registration requirements, network security, and usability issues, [1, 15] are listed within the technology related barriers.

4.3   Social Networks for Researchers

In the last years there has been an increasing number of public social networks targeted to professionals, in particular to academics and researchers. Most of these sites aim to create communities of professionals, where users can build their social networks by connecting to colleagues, finding old connections, and creating new links with professionals relevant to their work. Most of these social networks also aim at increasing personal visibility by creating online profiles and sharing work-related content [12, 15]. Figure 4.1 illustrates the establishment of academics social network in time, and provides (where available) information on the number of users as for October 2011. Lalisio was one of the first public social network target to researchers, but it was not until Linkedin was launched that public social networks for professional became popular. Linkedin was not specifically targeted to researchers, but the community quickly adopted it. The period between 2007 and 2008 was especially active in the creation of social networks for researchers. Many of them (e.g., labspaces, pronetos, colaboratree, bioexperts, biocrowd, and labroots) focus on Life Sciences, such as Biology and Medicine. These fields of research were the ideal targets for social networks, as they require exchange of complex experimental protocols and expensive datasets. Furthermore, in these fields it is important that not only the significant findings, which are usually published in traditional academics journals, but also the failures reach the community in order to save funding and time.

Despite the growing number of social networks for researchers little is known yet on the specific characteristics of these communities. This chapter attempts to fill this gap by presenting a detailed analysis of use of Academia. In particular, we aim to answer the following research questions: Who are the users of social networks for

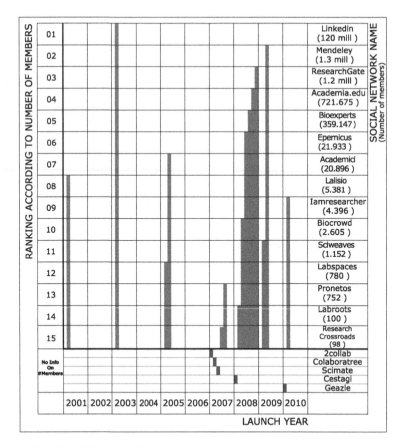

Fig. 4.1 List of Social Networks for researchers with ranking and launch year

academics and researchers? How do they use these social networks? Do individual, organizational, and cultural characteristics affect how they use them?

4.4 Method

As a case study for our investigation we selected Academia.edu as it as it allows tracking individual contributions to the community in a 'wall' available on the participants home page, following the typical Facebook metaphor. Academia.edu is advertised as a "platform for academics to share and follow research" and it was launched in October 2008. Every user has a personal webpage with information such as name, university, department or thesis title, and an open text field where they can write personal content. Name and surname are compulsory fields. University, department, and position are compulsory fields, unless the user registers as "independent researcher".

The webpage also contains research interests: primary and secondary (at registration users have to state, at least, one primary interest). Users can upload documents such as books, papers, talks, teaching documents, blog posts, CV, and websites to their pages. Documents can be, although not necessarily, tagged with research interests. Recent updates (up to 25 actions) are automatically shown in every webpage. Examples of updates are: ("*x followed the research interest: Web design*", "*x answered "What do you use Academia.edu for?"*", and "*X started following the work of eight people*"). Explicit connections among users are represented by department networks, followers, and followees. Department networks are automatically created by the system clustering all the users working at the same department, and can be manually adjusted by the users. Users can also connect to external people by following them, without needing permission from the followed person. Users can interact with other community members by posting questions and answers. For a question to be posted, it needs to be tagged with at least one research interest. Questions and other content related items, such as paper and books, can also be followed.

4.4.1 Procedures

Data were automatically collected between the 1st and the 16th of May 2011 using an algorithm developed within the group, and stored in off-line databases. Data were anonymized and no information which allowed retrieving users' identity was stored. Data collection was divided in three stages. During the first stage, user's webpages were manually analyzed to identify important information elements to be used in the analysis. In total, 33 variables were selected to describe information contained in webpages. These variables include information on user profile (e.g., position and affiliation), absence/presence of specific fields (e.g., picture, email address, and CV), number of elements per field (e.g., number of research interests, followers, and papers), and activity information (e.g., date of the first and last update). In the second stage, the identified variables were collected from users affiliated to a medium-size European University and to a large North American University. Data from 147 and 1295 users respectively were collected. This first data collection evaluated the potential of the variables to generate relevant user information. The variables showed interesting information on user's profile, activity, and content. However, the method used for data collection limited the potential of the dataset by bounding the affiliations to a predefined list.

During the last stage, a larger data set was collected. In order to overcome the limitations of the previous method, data were collected by research interest. Eight interests from different academic disciplines were selected to cover a broad range of fields (i.e., Anthropology, Biology, Biomedicine, Chemistry, Computer Science, Medical Sciences, Medicine, and Philosophy). Data from 30,428 users following, at least, one of the eight research interests were collected.

Table 4.1 Variables categorized by dependent and independent

Category	Factors	Collected/computed variables
Independent variables	*Position*	User's *Position*
	Ranking	Absence/presence of *affiliation* in the best 400 Universities
	Country development	*Affiliation* country clustered by Human Development Index (HDI)
Dependent variables	Indices	Collected/computed Variables
	Personal information	*Picture, Status, About, CV, Homepage*
	Content contribution	*NPaper, NBooks, NTalks, NTeaching Documents, NBlogs, NWebsites*
	Research interests	*NPrimary Research Interests, NSecondary Research Interests*
	Openness to contact	*Homepage, Address, Phone, Skype ID, email*
	Popularity	*NFollowed by—NFollows*
	Interaction among users	*NAsked Questions, NAnswered Questions, NFollowing Questions*
	Level of engagement	*Day's interval, NUpdates*

4.4.2   Variables

The independent variables used in this study are information contained in, or computed from, compulsory registration fields. In particular we took into consideration the researcher *position*, the *human development index* of the country where the researcher was affiliated and the affiliation *ranking* according to the Times Higher Education. These factors were used to analyse variations on a set of indices created by combining conceptually related variables. All these variables were retrieved by facultative fields contained in the user's webpage, as we wanted to analyze variations in the quantity of information voluntarily provided. A summary description of independent and dependent variables is reported in Table 4.1. Independent variables are detailed in the remaining of this paragraph, whereas a description of each dependent variable is reported in the result section.

4.4.2.1   Position

At sign up users could select their position from a list containing "faculty member", "post-doc", "graduate student", "emeritus/emerita", "undergraduate", "alumnus/ alumna" or "independent researcher". Alternatively, they could enter a label in a blank field. Some 97 % of the users selected their position from the list. For the sake of simplicity, the remaining 3 % were not included in the analysis. Furthermore, users whose position suggests not direct professional use of the system were not included in the analysis (i.e., "Emeritus/emerita", "undergraduate", and "alumnus/ alumna"). This led to the deletion of some 15 % of the users. The sample was finally composed of graduated students (49 %), faculty members (36 %), independent researchers (9 %), and post-docs (6 %).

Table 4.2 Academia.edu affiliations distributed by *university ranking* (excl. Affiliations with no ranking and independent researchers)

Ranking in the list of the best 400 Universities	Frequency	Percentage
1–50	3877	35
51–100	1550	14
101–150	1464	13
151–200	1144	10
201–250	904	8
251–300	822	8
301–350	776	7
351–400	477	4

4.4.2.2 Country Development

As no information on the country of the affiliation was collected at sign up, we evinced this information from the content manually entered by the user in the field *affiliation*. These data were very noisy, due to the open question style. Thus, the text was standardized by a string search tool, which correctly identified 94 % of the affiliations. The standardized affiliations were matched to a country by an external web service[1], which automatically covered some 70 % of the sample, with a very high reliability as evinced by a human rater performing double coding on some 10 % of the sample. The remaining entries were checked manually, allowing disambiguation of some 94 % of the standardized affiliations (99 % of the users). Most of the uncovered entries were international companies or Universities based in more than one country.

The dataset included 142 countries. The majority of the users worked for research institutions in the USA (29 %), UK (12 %), India (8 %), Canada (5 %), and Brazil (3 %). Overall North America accounted for some 34 % of the people, Europe 25 % and Asia 19 %. The remaining 10 % was evenly spread between Central and South America, Oceania, and Africa. A *country development* index was computed by using the country's Human Development Index (HDI)[2]. A large part of the users were affiliated in very-high developed countries (72 %), followed by users in high developed countries (13 %), medium (13 %) and low developed countries (2 %). Given the very skewed distribution of the country development index, medium and low developed countries were clustered together, to be used as independent variables in the analysis.

4.4.2.3 Ranking

A University *ranking* index was calculated by matching the standardized affiliation name to the list of the best 400 Universities published by the Times Higher Education[3]. Some 9 % of the users' affiliations appeared in the list. Frequency and percentage of users affiliated to ranked Universities are reported in Table 4.2, grouped

---

[1] http://univ.cc.

[2] http://hdr.undp.org.

[3] http://www.timeshighereducation.co.uk.

by eight intervals. A dichotomous (presence vs. absence) variable was finally computed, to be used in the analysis.

4.5   Results

The dependent variables were analysed by a set of one-way analysis of variance with Position (4), Country development (3) and Ranking (2) as between subjects variables. Due to the fact that the factors subsume different sample size (e.g., independent researchers did not report a country) and that ranking and country development are strongly correlated, a full factorial design was not possible. Post-hoc comparisons were based on the Least-Significance Difference method. Partial eta-squared (η_p^2) was used as an estimate of effect size. As a general guideline, $\eta_p^2=0.01$ are considered small, $\eta_p^2=0.06$ medium, $\eta_p^2=0.14$ large.

4.5.1   Personal Information

A personal information index was computed by adding a value of 1 for each piece of information provided by the user to the fields: picture, homepage, about, status, and CV. The index ranged from 5 (all information provided) to 0 (no information provided). The mean was 1.02 (SD=1.19), but some 44 % of the users did not provide any *personal information*. Overall, *Pictures* were the most frequently uploaded items (47 %), followed by *Homepage* (18 %), *About* (16 %), *Status* (13 %), and *CV* (9 %).

The one-way analysis of variance returned a significant effect of *position* ($F_{(3,30424)}=162.25$, $p<0.001$, $\eta_p^2=0.02$), *country development* ($F_{(2,26534)}=280.56$, $p<0.001$, $\eta_p^2=0.02$), and *ranking* ($F_{(1,27570)}=107.01$, $p<0.001$, $\eta_p^2=0.04$) on *personal information*. On the average, people affiliated to ranked universities disclosed more information than people affiliated with non-ranked universities. As regards the effect of position, post-hoc tests indicated a scale with significant intervals between faculty members, who submitted more information, post-doc, graduate students, and independent researchers. The effect of country development was due to users affiliated in very high developed countries which shared more information than users in high and medium-low developed countries, and users in high developed countries who shared more information than users affiliated in low-medium developed countries. Among the very high developed countries, we compared researchers in the US and Europe. A significant effect of location ($F_{(2,19032)}=47.61$, $p<0.001$, $\eta_p^2=0.005$) emerged as Europeans disclosed more personal information than North Americans.

4.5.2 Content Contribution

A *content contribution* index was computed by adding all items uploaded relatives Papers, Books, Talks, Teaching Documents, Blogs, and Websites. On the average, users uploaded some 4.55 files (SD=10.05). Some 10 % of the users did not upload any file. Users most often contributed papers (23 %), non-personal websites (10 %), books (6 %), talks (4 %), teaching documents (2 %), blogs (1 %). There was a positive correlation between *personal information* and *content contribution* indices r=0.38; p<0.01, highlighting a general predisposition to contribution in both variables.

The quantity of content contributed to the community varied as a function of *position* ($F_{(3,30424)}=435.01$, $p<0.001$, $\eta_p^2=0.04$), *country development* ($F_{(2,26534)}=128.28$, $p<0.01$, $\eta_p^2=0.01$), and university *ranking* ($F_{(1,27570)}=55.4$, $p<0.001$, $\eta_p^2=0.002$). The post-hoc test on position indicated that faculty members contributed significantly more than post-docs, who contributed more than graduate students and independent researchers. The post-hoc test on development indicated a scale with significant intervals between pairs, starting from user affiliated in very-high developed countries, who contributed more content, to users in high developed countries and medium-low developed countries. Among the very-high developed countries, there was an effect of location on the amount of contributed content ($F_{(2,19032)}=33.95$, $p<0.001$, $\eta_p^2=0.004$). Europeans contributed more than North Americans. People affiliated to ranked universities contributed more material than people affiliated to non-ranked universities.

4.5.3 Research Interest

The research interest index was computed by adding all items indicated as primary or secondary. *Primary research interest* was a compulsory field at sign up. Some 43 % of the users reported only one *primary research interest* (mean 8.94, SD=30.83). Some 80 % of the users did not report any *secondary research interests* (mean 0.44, SD=3.67). The minimum value for the global *index* was 1 and the maximum was 3,869 (mean 9.4, SD=31.49)

There was a significant effect of *position* ($F_{(3,30424)}=9.06$, $p<0.001$, $\eta_p^2=0.001$) and *country development* ($F_{(2,26534)}=64.67$, $p<0.001$, $\eta_p^2=0.005$) on *research interest*, but no effect of *ranking*. Post-hoc analysis indicated that the independent researchers reported more interests than users from any other position, and faculty members followed more research interests than post-docs and graduate students. The effect of country development followed the same scale with significant intervals between very-high developed countries, who reported more research interests, to high, and finally medium-low developed countries. Among the very-high developed countries, there was an effect of location on the number of research interests ($F_{(2,19032)}=8.8$, $p<0.001$, $\eta_p^2=0.001$). Users working in Europe reported more research interests than users in North America.

4.5.4 Openness to Contact

Openness to contact was computed by adding 1 mark for the presence of homepage, address, phone and Skype ID and subtracting 2 marks for the absence of e-mail. This choice was due to the fact that *e-mail* was a compulsory field at sign up and it was a public field by default. Users must intentionally change their default settings for their email address to be private. Hence, the absence of this information was considered a negative indicator of openness to contact. Some 14 % of the users changed their email to private. Users most often disclosed their homepage address (18 %), address (9 %), phone (6 %), and Skype ID (4 %).

There was a significant effect of *position* ($F_{(3,30424)}=572.4, p<0.001, \eta_p^2=0.05$), *country development* ($F_{(2,26534)}=73.08, p<0.001, \eta_p^2=0.005$), and *ranking* ($F_{(1,27570)}=46.54, p<0.001, \eta_p^2=0.002$) on *openness to contact*. People affiliated to ranked universities shared more contact information than people affiliated to non-ranked universities. Post-hoc tests indicated that the effect of position was due to the same scale, previously reported, with significant intervals between faculty members, who shared more contact information, post-docs, graduate students and independent researchers. The effect of country development was due to users affiliated in very high and high developed countries, who were more open to contact than users in medium-low developed countries. Considering just very high developed countries, an effect of location was found ($F_{(2,19032)}=58.3, p<0.001, \eta_p^2=0.006$). Post-hoc tests indicated that users affiliated to universities in very high developed countries in Europe were more open to contact than users in very high developed countries in North America and the rest of the world.

4.5.5 Popularity

The average number of contacts followed by a user was 9.67 (SD=30.15) and the average number of contacts following a user was 10.89 (SD=22.62). There was a significant correlation between the number of contacts followed by and following a user (r=0.61 p<0.01). The average number of colleagues was 12.59 (SD=19.62). A *popularity* index was computed by subtracting the number of people followed by a user from the number of followers of that user. The average *popularity index* was 1.21 (SD=25.21).

The Anovas indicated a significant effect of *position* ($F_{(3,30424)}=96.56, p<0.001, \eta_p^2=0.01$), *country development* ($F_{(5,26534)}=35.7, p<0.001, \eta_p^2=0.003$), and *ranking* ($F_{(1,27570)}=61.88, p<0.001, \eta_p^2=0.002$). The effect of position reflected the scale dividing faculty members by post-docs, graduate students and independent researchers. As regards location, users affiliated with very-high developed countries were more popular than users affiliated with high and medium-low developed countries. No significant effect between researchers in the US and Europe was found. Users affiliated to ranked universities were more popular than users affiliated to universities with no ranking.

4.5.6   Interaction Among Users

A very small number of people followed, asked, and answered questions. The maximum number of questions asked by a user was 13; the maximum number of questions answered by a user was 11; and the maximum number of questions followed by a user was 41[4]. There was a positive correlation but weak between the number of asked and answered questions, $r=0.23$; $p<0.001$.

The Anovas returned a significant effect of *ranking* on *number of asked* $(F_{(1,27570)}=12.29,\ p<0.001,\ \eta_p^2=0.000)$, *answered* $(F_{(1,27570)}=16.93,\ p<0.001,\ \eta_p^2=0.001)$, and *followed questions* $(F_{(1,27570)}=20.81,\ p<0.001,\ \eta_p^2=0.001)$. Users affiliated with ranked universities interacted more than those in non-ranked universities. No significant effect of *position* was found on *number of asked questions* or *of followed questions*. A significant effect of *position* was found on *number of answered questions* $(F_{(3,30424)}=6,\ p<0.001,\ \eta_p^2=0.001)$. Faculty members answered more questions than graduate students and independent researchers, but not of post-docs.

There was a significant effect of *country development* on the *number of asked* $(F_{(2,26534)}=19.8,\ p<0.001,\ \eta_p^2=0.001)$, *answered* $(F_{(2,26534)}=27.82,\ p<0.001,\ \eta_p^2=0.002)$, *and followed questions* $(F_{(2,26534)}=30.07,\ p<0.001,\ \eta_p^2=0.002)$. Post-hoc tests indicated that all effects were due to users affiliated in very-high developed countries who asked, answered, and followed more questions than users affiliated in high and medium-low development countries. No significant effect between Europe and North America emerged.

4.5.7   Level of Engagement

To measure the level of engagement with the network we computed the *Day's interval* between the first and the last update. This value was equal to zero for 45 % of the sample, showing that almost half of the sample did never modified their initial profile. Among the users who did some changes, the average *day's interval* was 3, 23.3 (SD=245.17) with a maximum of 1,072 days between the first and the last update. The average number of updates per user was 5.6 (SD=6.2) with a minimum of 0 and a maximum of 25 updates. There was a positive correlation between the *number of updates* and *interval* between the date of the first and the last update, $r=0.49$; $p<0.01$.

This level of engagement varied as a function of *position* $(F_{(3,30424)}=264.61,\ p<0.001,\ \eta_p^2=0.03)$, *country development* $(F_{(2,26534)}=30.07,\ p<0.001,\ \eta_p^2=0.002)$, and *ranking* $(F_{(1,27570)}=258.56,\ p<0.001,\ \eta_p^2=0.01)$. Post-hoc tests indicated that post-docs and faculty members had higher engagement level than graduate students, who are significantly more engaged than independent researchers. Users affiliated with very-high developed countries had higher level of engagement than

---

[4] In Academia.edu, users who asked or answered a question, also follow that question by default.

Table 4.3 Summary of results by variable and factor

	Position	Ranking	Country Development
Personal information	Faculty member (FM)- Post-doc (PD)- Graduate student (GS)- Independent researcher (IR)*	Ranked (R)- Non ranked (NR)*	Very high-developed (VH)- High develop. (H)/ Medium-Low develop. (ML)*
Content contribution	FM-PD-GS/IR*	R-NR*	VH-H-ML*
Research interests	IR-FM-PD/GS*	No effect	VH-H-ML*
Openness to contact	FM-PD-GS-IR*	R-NR*	VH/H-ML*
Popularity	FM- PD- GS- IR*	R-NR*	VH-H/ML*
Asked questions	No effect	R-NR*	VH-H/ML*
Answered questions	FM/PD-GS/IR*	No effect	VH-H/ML*
Followed questions	No effect	R-NR*	VH-H/ML*
Level of engagement	PD/FM-GS-IR*	R-NR*	VH-H/ML*

Small(*), medium(**), large(***) effect

users in high and medium-low developed countries (all difference significant). Considering just very-high developed countries, an effect of location was found ($F_{(2,19032)} = 34.44$, $p < 0.001$, $\eta_p^2 = 0.004$). Users affiliated with universities in Europe were more engaged than users in North America and the rest of the world. The effect of university ranking was due to users affiliated to ranked universities, who had higher level of engagement than users affiliated to non-ranked universities.

4.6   Discussion

A summary of results is reported in Table 4.3. A number of significant results were found and despite being small effect size they all reflect the same trend, namely the hierarchical structure of real-life academia, where position, reputation, and availability of funding (a factor strongly associated to country development) play a major role on people's visibility, contribution to the community, and integration within the network. For instance, faculty members (the highest hierarchical position in the University system) shared more personal and contact information than users in any other position. They also contributed with more content, and interacted with users by answering questions. In some cases, the difference between faculty members and post-docs was not significant (i.e., number of answered questions, level of engagement), but the gap was always significant between them and people at the beginning of their career (e.g., PhD students) and people who were likely to have less institutional support (e.g., independent researchers).

Independent researchers were the least popular users, since they were the group with the largest difference between the number of followed contacts and the number of contacts following them, possibly reflecting the lack of an institutional network provided by the academic environment. Initially, we expected that independent researchers could try to compensate for the lack of workplace connections by exposing themselves more than other users on the virtual network to bridge and bond social capital [16]. However, they were found to be the least open to share personal and contact information. Independent researchers just scored high in number of research interests, being the group following the most of them, probably reflecting the higher variability of professional life as compared to an academics one. However, these results might suggest an interesting self-presentation strategy: research interests may not be used only as a source of information but also as a way to disclose information about themselves. The definition of research interest may be used as a means to establish common ground, a fundamental element in fostering cooperation between participants, especially when little is known about them [9].

Following real life trends, users affiliated to ranked universities scored higher in all variables than users in non-ranked universities. Similarly, users in very high developed countries scored higher than users in high and low-medium developed countries, reflecting a difference in economical possibilities between them. An interesting difference was found between North American and European researchers. Users affiliated in Europe were more open to share personal and contact information. Europeans contributed more content than users from any North American affiliation, possibly indicating a need for self-affirmation in an academic world where the old continent is still substantially less represented than North America. European users followed more research interests, which might reflect the higher specialization of North American professionals.

4.7 Conclusion

This study presents a number of limitations. First, the results are only based on a quantitative approach, which is currently work in progress. Second, the available data on users' social network did not contain information on individual connections. This information would have contributed to the analysis of social dynamics related issues, such as the effect of using a non-hierarchical online social network to target a stratified professional community. Finally, cultural and language factors linked to the use of a professional social network in English by native and non-native users, were not researched.

Organisational structures and practices are dynamic elements of any technological ecosystem. They play an influential role in the definition of requirements, and are expected to be modified by technology appropriation [13]. Although the Internet has been presented as a democratic virtual space where physical boundaries are blurred, this chapter provides evidence that professional real-life characteristics such as position, university ranking and country level of development affect the way users build and interact in their professional virtual life. In spite of the potential of public social networks for researchers to provide equal opportunities and the interest triggered within the research community, no full advantage of these technologies has been taken yet.

Our studies suggest that these systems are mainly used to host online resumes, as a virtual business card, very similar to traditional personal web pages. The problem of motivating users to participate in and contribute to is an old major theoretical and practical challenge in the design of any type of groupware [10], and social academia does not seem to escape from it.

This exploratory study provides the foundations for understanding the dynamics in social technologies for academics and researchers. Future work will focus in better understanding users' behaviour and attitude towards public social technologies in order to develop new strategies to motivate users to contribute to the community and support equal participation.

Acknowledgments Our thanks to Academia.edu for allowing this research and, in particular, to Richard Price for kindly answering all our questions.

References

1. Ardichvili, A., Page, V., Wentling, T.: Motivations and barriers to participation in virtual knowledge-sharing communities of practice. J. Knowl. Manag. 7(1), 64–77 (2003)
2. Boyd, D.M., Ellison, N.B.: Social network sites: definition, history, and scholarship. J. Comput. Mediat. Commun. 13(1), article 11. http://jcmc.indiana.edu/vol13/issue1/boyd.ellison.html (2007)
3. Brzozowski, M.J., Sandholm, T., Hogg, T.: Effects of feedback and peer pressure on contributions to enterprise social media. In: Proceedings of the ACM 2009 International Conference on Supporting Group Work (GROUP '09), pp. 61–70, ACM Press, New York (2009)
4. DiMicco, J.M., Millen, D.R.: People Sensemaking with Social Networking Sites. CHI 2008 (2008)
5. Farrell, S., Lau, T., Nusser, S., Wilcox, E., Muller, M.: Socially augmenting employee profiles with people-tagging. In: Proceedings of the 20th Annual ACM Symposium on User Interface Software and Technology (UIST '07), pp. 91–100, ACM Press, New York, NY, USA (2007)
6. Gangadharbatla, H.: Facebook me: collective self-esteem, need to belong, and internet self-efficacy as predictors of the iGeneration's attitudes toward social networking sites. J. Interact. Advert. 8(2), 1–28 (2008)
7. Huysman, M., Wulf, V.: IT to support knowledge sharing in communities, towards a social capital analysis. J. Inf. Technol. 21(1), 40–51 (2006)
8. Joinson, A.N.: 'Looking at', 'Looking up' or 'Keeping up with' People? Motives and Uses of Facebook. CHI 2008 (2008)
9. Lampe, C., Ellison, N., Steinfield, C.: A Familiar Face(book): Profile Elements as Signals in an Online Social Network. CHI 2007 (2006). doi:10.1145/1240624.1240695
10. Lampe, C., Wash, R., Velasquez, A., Ozkaya, E.: Motivations to Participate in Online Communities. CHI 2010 (2010)
11. Papacharissi, Z.: The virtual geographies of social networks: a comparative analysis of facebook, linkedIn and ASmallWorld. N. Media. Soc. 11(1–2), 199–220 (2009)
12. Ploderer, B., Howard, S., Thomas, P.: Being online, living offline: the influence of social ties over the appropriation of social network sites. In: Proceedings of the 2008 ACM conference on computer supported cooperative work (CSCW 1908), pp. 333–342. ACM, New York, NY, USA (2008). (doi:10.1145/1460563.1460618)
13. Rhode, M.: Building social capital in an Iranian NGO community system. In: Huysman, M., Wulf, V. (eds.) Social Capital and Information Technology. The MIT Press, Cambridge (2004)

14. Richter, A., Riemer, K.: Corporate social networking sites—modes of use and appropriation through co-evolution. In: 20th Australasian Conference on Information Systems (2009)
15. Skeels, M.M., Grudin, J.: When social networks cross boundaries: a case study of workplace use of facebook and linkedIn. In: Proceedings of the ACM 2009 International Conference on Supporting Group Work (GROUP '09), pp. 95–104. ACM Press, New York, NY, USA (2009)
16. Steinfield, C., DiMicco, J.M., Ellison, N.B., Lampe, C.: Bowling online: social networking and social capital within the organization. In: Proceedings of the Fourth Communities and Technologies Conference (2009)
17. Toma, C.L.: Affirming the Self through Online Profiles: Beneficial Effects of Social Networking Sites. CHI 2010 (2010). doi:10.1145/1753326.1753588
18. Väänänen-Vainio-Mattila, K., Wäljas, M., Ojala, J., Segerståhl, K.: Identifying Drivers and Hindrances of Social User Experience in Web Services. CHI 2010 (2010)
19. Wu, A., DiMicco, J.M., Millen, D.R.: Detecting Professional versus Personal Closeness Using an Enterprise Social Network Site. CHI 2010 (2010). doi:10.1145/1753326.1753622

Chapter 5
The Not-So-Open Wikis: Structures of Collaboration At Work

Osama Mansour

Abstract The current chapter discusses issues related to the use of the wiki technology at the workplace for social knowledge collaboration and sharing. This kind of technology is principally flexible and free in the sense of allowing people to create, edit, and shape content collaboratively. However, this chapter argues that the application and use of a wiki within an organizational setting might be influenced by social and structural properties that govern collaboration and sharing. It is based on empirical data obtained through 11 semi-structured interviews with employees working for a large multinational organization. The theory of structuration was used as a theoretical framework to guide the empirical inquiry. Eventually, the chapter concludes with discussing a number of structures associated with evolving norms, interpretations, and resources that govern and shape the use of a wiki as a tool for social and open collaboration.

5.1 Background

The evolution of the web has enabled novel forms of collaboration, interaction, and knowledge sharing. Social media represent this evolution that is associated with fundamental changes in the way people work and interact with each other on the web [13]. They refer to Internet-based applications that build on the ideological and technological foundations of web 2.0 [12]. Web 2.0 is the platform for the evolution of social media. It represents an assortment of social and open technologies such as wikis, blogs, and social networks, tools as well as new norms of self-governance and freedom of information ownership [24]. These kinds of technologies allow for dynamic and flexible social interactivity through the co-creation of content, engagement and participation in online communities, and openness and free expression on the web [5, 12, 17]. For instance, a wiki is described as a tool for open and social knowledge collaboration that allows anyone to create

O. Mansour (✉)
Linnaeus University, Pg Vejdes Väg, 35195 Växjö, Sweden
e-mail: osama.mansour@lnu.se

J. Dugdale et al. (eds.), *From Research to Practice in the Design of Cooperative Systems:*   65
Results and Open Challenges, DOI 10.1007/978-1-4471-4093-1_5,
© Springer-Verlag London 2012

and edit content collaboratively. It consists of a set of dynamic web pages that are continuously updated by communities of people [6, 26]. Ward Cunningham, the inventor of wiki, provided a number of principles that characterize the nature of a wiki such as open, simple, incremental, organic, etc. [2]. Openness is one of the most intriguing aspects of wikis. In principle, a wiki is open and allows its users to jointly create, edit, change, and delete content [21]. It also allows for knowledge shaping which is a purposeful activity to transform existing knowledge on the wiki into more useful knowledge through reorganizing, rewriting, and integrating content [26].

In this respect, given their potential, organizations continue to apply and use wikis at the workplace [6, 15, 24, 26]. As such, wikis are often used by professional communities for knowledge collaboration and sharing [4, 26]. For instance, wikis can be used as conversational knowledge management tools where by which individuals and groups create and share knowledge through collaborative dialogues and conversations [5]. Kosonen and Kianto [14] maintained that due to their easiness and flexibility, wikis enable fluid patterns of collaboration that support the free exchange of knowledge. Accordingly, many scholars argued (e.g. [7, 8, 14]) that the use of wikis is driving more flatter, democratic and horizontal structures in organizations as users become more free and engaged. For instance, Faraj et al. [4] argued that knowledge collaboration, that involves creating, sharing, transferring, and accumulating knowledge, in online communities can occur without the traditional structures often associated with this kind of collaboration such as stable membership, interdependence among group members, etc. They further claimed that the lack of such structures might partly free the collaboration from social conventions, ownership, and hierarchy. We take a dubious stance on such arguments and claims aiming at addressing issues related to the potential development of social structures (cf. [16]) in the course of using social and open technologies for knowledge collaboration and sharing.

In addition, research addressing the use of wikis in organizational settings is increasing (e.g. [3, 7, 8, 15, 25, 26]). However, this research lacks the focus on understanding socio-structural dynamics of using wikis at work and how these dynamics shape social collaboration and sharing. To this end, the current chapter, drawing upon the theory of structuration, focuses on examining social structures that might evolve when using a wiki for open knowledge collaboration and sharing at the workplace. Hence, it seeks to answer the questions of: what kind of structures might evolve in the course of using a wiki for open knowledge collaboration sharing? And how these structures shape the process of social collaboration and sharing? The rest of the chapter is divided as follows: the next section presents the theoretical framework. Then the third section describes our empirical inquiry. The fourth section shows the findings of the research. The fifth section provides a general discussion of the findings and finally the sixth section includes the conclusions of this chapter.

5.2   Theoretical Framework

5.2.1   Structuration Theory

Structuration theory was developed by the English sociologist Antony Giddens. Giddens described his theory as an "ontology of social life" which can be used as a sensitising device in any social study [25]. In this respect, Jones and Karsten [10] maintained that the theory of structuration deals with social phenomena at a high level of abstraction rather than their particular instantiation in a specific context. Further, Jones et al. [11] explained that Giddens aimed at developing a theory that serves as a middle way between two competing traditions in sociology: naturalistic sociology and the interpretive tradition of phenomenology. Giddens sought to transcend the limitations of these two traditions by rejecting traditional dualistic views that see social phenomena as determined either by objective social structures or by autonomous human agents [10]. Eventually, Giddens proposed the theory of structuration which emphasizes that structure and human agency should be understood as a mutually constitutive duality [10, 11].

Structuration theory is heavily used in many academic disciplines [11, 25]. Wanda Orlikowski has published several works on structuration theory in which she developed new extensions and understandings of the theory (e.g. [18, 19]). One example is her structuration model of technology (see [18]). In this model, Orlikowski draws upon the structuration theory in the sense of maintaining that human actions are enabled and constrained by structures and that these structures are still the result of previous actions. As such, she argued that technology is created and modified by human actions while at the same time technology is used by humans to accomplish specific goals. She referred to this understanding as the duality of technology. In the next section we describe the main components of structuration theory that have been used to frame our theoretical and empirical efforts in this chapter.

5.2.2   Modalities of Structuration Theory

Three central modalities or components of structuration theory have been used to help in framing our empirical inquiry. These components include interpretive schemes, norms, and resources [10, 18–19, 22]. But before we discuss these components it is important to clarify some concepts. Structuration is defined as a social process that involves the reciprocal interaction of human actors and structural features of organizations [11, 18]. Structure, as defined by Giddens, refers to rules and resources organized as properties of systems and exists as structural or institutionalized properties [11, 18, 19, 22]. Given this definition, Gidden's understanding of structure emphasizes the dynamic process of social interaction rather than static properties or patterns [10]. All three modalities provide the linkage between human action (agency) and institutionalized properties (structure) [9, 20]. Each modality can be understood differently from either an agency or structural perspective.

From an agency perspective, human interaction involves the communication of meaning which is achieved via interpretive schemes. Interpretive schemes from a structural perspective represent structures of signification which are organizational rules that inform and define interaction (e.g. a person wearing a white coat suggests he is a doctor) [18, 20]. Resources from an agency perspective are related to power relations. Power plays an important role in human interaction as it provides organizational capabilities for human to accomplish certain outcomes. The impact of power from this perspective is understood as transformative capacity that is the power of humans to transform the social and material world [18, 20]. This transformative power is mediated in organizations through two kinds of resources: authoritative that is extending power over people and allocative that is extending power over objects or material phenomenon. From a structural perspective, these resources reflect structures of domination [18]. In respect to norms, from an agency perspective, they refer to organizational conventions and rules governing legitimate or appropriate conduct. From a structural perspective, norms constitute organizational structures of legitimation which are used to maintain organizational order through rituals and tradition.

In addition, Orlikowski and Robey [20] explained that these three modalities determine how the institutional properties of social systems mediate deliberate human action and how human action constitutes social structure. For instance, people in their everyday lives draw upon their knowledge of their prior action or situation in hand, the facilities available to them (e.g. technology), and the norms that inform their ongoing practices. As such, the application and use of these elements in social interaction lead to structuring their current actions [19]. In this view, human agency, that is humans in their ongoing interactions, and structure, that is institutionalized properties of social systems, are treated as mutually interacting duality [9]. Eventually, structure is always seen as enabling as well as constraining.

5.3   The Case and the Method

The case in this study was conducted at IBM which is a large multinational technology corporation. IBM is specialized in developing computer software and hardware and also offering consulting, hosting, and infrastructure services in areas ranging from mainframe computers to nanotechnology. IBM was founded in 1911 and is considered the largest technology company in the world and often ranked among the largest 30 companies worldwide. The company has more than 425,000 employees in more than 200 countries.

One major part of IBM technology services is IBM Social Business and IBM Collaboration Solutions where the current case took place. This section of IBM was initially called IBM Lotus Notes that mainly focuses on providing enterprise collaboration solutions. Nowadays, this section is called IBM Social Business &

Table 5.1 Characteristics of research participants

Role	Wiki experience	Gender	Nationality	Interview
Learning intelligence leader	3–4 years	Male	UK	Skype
Engagement manager	1 year	Female	Denmark	f2f
Software developer	5–6 years	Male	Denmark	f2f
Client technical professional	3–4 years	Female	Denmark	f2f
Marketing production manager	5–6 years	Male	USA	Phone
Information developer	3 years	Female	USA	Phone
Technical sales professional	3 years	Male	Denmark	f2f
Social business evangelist	3–4 years	Male	USA	f2f
Information architecture lead	4 years	Male	USA	Phone
Social computing evangelist	9 years	Male	Spain	Skype
Project manager	3–4 years	Male	UK	Skype

Collaboration Solutions that is specialized in providing various social collaboration services for businesses with emphasis on integrating social software capabilities. One main social collaboration technology that is developed by IBM Collaboration Solutions is IBM Connections. This software combines multiple social collaboration tools including file sharing, status updates, blogs, micro blogs, tagging, wikis, communities, and many other social collaboration tools.

The IBM Connections software was the tool studied in this case with a particular focus on the wiki technology. The aim was to understand the structures surrounding the use of the wiki by employees at the IBM Collaboration Solutions. As such, participants in this study were mostly working at the IBM Collaboration Solutions and using wikis for different collaboration purposes such as documentation, activity management, scheduling, content and file sharing, a point of reference, etc. It is important to mention that people using IBM Connections are free to use any tools available in the system the way they like. So the participants in this research have either been users of wikis created by others or creators of wikis related to their work. The system also allows them to set up a wiki to be either open for anyone or accessible only to specific members.

The semi-structured interview method was the vehicle for collecting data in this study. The choice of the interview method was motivated by the need to understand people's experiences and interpretations of using the Wiki technology. The total number of the interviews was 11 of which three were conducted via Skype online video conferencing, three conducted over the phone, and five were face-to-face (f2f) interviews at different IBM locations in Copenhagen, Denmark. Table 5.1 describes the characteristics of these participants.

The contact details of these interested people were then shared with the authors by the main contact at the department and an official interview invitation had been sent to all of them by the first author. The email contained information about the focus of the interview and practical issues such as time and date and the communication method. The interviews were planned, conducted, and completed during the months of September and October 2011. The average interviewing was not less than 45 and no more than 60 min. An interview protocol was developed to guide the conversation with the participants. This protocol included several questions developed based on the theory of structuration and drawing upon three central modalities of human agency: interpretive schemes, norms, and resources. The discussion of these modalities is presented in the theoretical framework above.

These modalities were used as "sensitising devices to generate some searching questions on the nature, purpose and value of computer-based representations within and between communities of practice in organizations" ([25], p. 12). While the interview protocol contained a structured list of questions, the conversation was rather fluid and flexible to allow for active engagement with the participants. At the beginning of the interview, each interviewee was informed about the research and the purpose of the interview as well as confidentiality and privacy issues. In this respect, a number of the interviewees requested their names to be hidden. Others preferred that only their first names are to be used or a nick name to replace their real names when quoted. Also, some of them asked to be informed about any quotes before using them in the chapter. As such, these participants were contacted at the time of writing the chapter in order to get their consent for including and publishing their quotes. In the same vein, the validation of empirical data was achieved mainly through member checks. The transcript of each interview was sent to individual participants for verifying their answers.

In addition, the analysis of qualitative data obtained from the interviews was based on a hermeneutical approach [1, 2]. Each interview was fully transcribed into text. It is important to mention that the analysis of the data was started during the transcription phase. This has been done through associating themes to important parts of the text and making highlights for later deeper analysis. The actual analysis of the text was purely hermeneutical in the sense of emphasising the participants' interpretations and beliefs about their use of the wiki technology. The application of hermeneutics during the analysis was characterized by the iterative processes of reading and rereading the text to see how different parts of the text make sense in respect to the overall textual or qualitative data. Open and axial coding techniques were used to support the development and the association of themes to specific textual data segments [23]. More clearly, open coding was used to create themes and categories that represent central meanings in specific data segments and axial coding was used to connect and associate these themes based on their relevancy and significance to the main purpose of the research. It is important to mention that these themes were developed in light of the research purpose, that is identifying and understanding the evolution of social structures that might govern knowledge collaboration and sharing with wikis, and the theoretical components used to frame our empirical data collection.

The hermeneutical analysis of the data aimed at understanding the essence of the text in order to identify specific structural categories and then connect them with each other. For example, the statement "...*the second factor is potentially people might not be willing to submit questions in a more public arena... I think certainly which myself has experience you know not wanting to put my name out there because I look stupid...*" was interpreted to imply an open or network structure. Also, influenced by structuration theory, we've been able to account for the "belief" or the perception associated in this statement that is the idea that open sharing might possibly cause embarrassment for the contributor in front of a large audience. This process of hermeneutical interpretation and analysis was applied into each data segment iteratively allowing us to identify a number of dominant categories and link them with each other, which are described in the next section.

5.4   Findings

The findings from our interviews are presented in this section. During our empirical data collection we have been able to identify and examine a number of structures that evolve in the context of using a wiki for open knowledge collaboration and sharing at the workplace. These kinds of structures are either emergent or reflection of existing structures in the organization. Existing structures refer to established rules and resources at the organization. So during the interviews we asked the participants about, for instance, their roles at the workplace, the tools they use to accomplish certain tasks, etc. in order to understand the influence on the use of the wiki. In contrast, emergent structures, drawing on structuration theory, refer to rules, resources, and interpretive schemes that evolve in the course of knowledge collaboration and sharing using a wiki. Accordingly, the analysis of the empirical data resulted in a number of evolving and emergent structures that describe, for instance, new rules that govern the way people use the wiki at work. This section aims to present and discuss the empirical evidence for these structures that span technological, organizational, social, behavioral and cultural properties. These structures are presented below together with empirical evidence addressing the structural variations in the wiki environment.

5.4.1   Open or Network Structure

The open or network structure is primarily determined by the open nature of wikis. The fact that wikis are editable, open and visible to a large audience creates several implications for the users of wikis. For instance, a learning intelligent leader explained the influence of openness on his perception of using a wiki:

> people might not be willing to submit questions in a more public arena... Because I don't know maybe they are worried about looking stupid, I think certainly which myself has experience you know not wanting to put my name out there because I look stupid.

In the same vein, a software developer described how sharing information in the open space affects the way he engages with others to collaborate for the improvement of content:

> putting the information out in the open i feel responsible for it and if someone makes me aware that it could be improved and changed then i would engage that person and find out

what they mean about it. And of course if openness and accessibility mean someone could go and change it and maybe make it less correct or remove important parts of it i would feel bad about it because then i would have to go in and redo it.

This implies that sharing with others openly entails some responsibilities to maintain what has been contributed and shared with a public audience. As such, some people might however perceive this kind of open exposure on the wiki to be a demanding behavior. A client technical professional said:

One of the comments I hear when I talk to colleagues about this is that they say well I don't want to be a subject matter expert, I don't want everyone to point to me, I don't want all this fame and glory because typically it adds to my workload…The other comment is also well is it not included in my job description.

In the same vein, a technical sales professional explained his view about contributing and sharing knowledge in open wikis:

if you put it on something that is open for editing then you actually invited me to see if i can improve on it…and when i do something it is only to improve the quality, it is not to be seen or anything on a personal level.

In a similar sense, the fact that any contributions made on the wiki are open and publicly accessible by others makes contributors more careful about what they contribute. An information architecture lead explained this:

…this is gonna be in the public record that says Keith added this information and deleted this information on the wiki page and I know that's going to be within IBM for as long as I am here. So i spent extra time to make sure that these are really good changes.

Further, a social computing evangelist explained the network effect of openness and how it helps people to trust each other as they share what they know openly:

by being open about what you know, who do you know, and what do you contribute … you're giving people an opportunity to figure out for themselves whether they can trust you or not.

Accordingly, this suggests that exposing and sharing what people know in the open space would create a comfortable atmosphere at the workplace which may lead to fostering trust amongst them. An example was given by a technical sales professional and how the openness of the wiki helped him to connect with people:

I look at who contribute. Who has got a sale that makes sense that i am interested in … I mean I go in here to get educated.

5.4.2 Relationships Structure

Members of groups or project teams tend to determine their contributions into the wiki based on their relationships to each other or affiliation to a group. A learning intelligence leader, explained how his relationship with the team would make him eager to contribute to the wiki:

> Within the environment of my own team I know that I am informed, I know that I have certain subject matter expertise. I think of it more as a matter of talking to a colleague over the phone.

This statement shows the importance of the relationship with the team which gives people the ability to realize and use their expertise, thus make them more capable to contribute and share with others. Another interesting dimension of the relationships structure is the creation of new relationships among people. A technical sales professional reflected upon this experience:

> if one goes in and changes something, I invite them to my network. Because they are most likely made a valuable contribution so I would like to be closer to them. So as you can see (showing his profile on the wiki) I currently have 90 friends and we have commonalities in topics of interests.

The wiki in this case serves as a networking tool that helps people connect and get introduced to each other. In addition, something that we also found relevant to these networking opportunities is related to the credibility of content on the wiki. More clearly, the ability to know the background of the contributors not only helps in creating new relationships with them but also in ensuring that their content is credible. A social business evangelist maintained that:

> it is important for us to remember in any of our information discourses even wikis to be able to know the person doing the editing gives you a perspective on credibility.

5.4.3   Hierarchical or Experience Structure

One of the most important structures that evolve in the wiki environment is related to the hierarchical and experience variations. Hierarchy in this sense refers to divisions among employees and their levels of expertise. We found that hierarchical divisions among employees are well manifested in the wiki environment and shape the perception and behavior of wiki users. For instance, a learning intelligence leader and a software developer said respectively:

> I am a quite senior resource within our team I would be very surprised first of all to see other team members editing my manager's post or even editing my post.

> the knowledge can be difficult for less experienced person to go in and edit something that i would say a subject matter expert has rendered.

Sometimes, however, people do not give much weight for the hierarchical levels of contributors. Instead, they emphasize the importance of the contributor's knowledgeability in the subject. A client technical professional explained this:

> I don't check whether or not the guy who has written the wiki is higher in the hierarchy than I am. I would rather check I mean if he has the right level of knowledge. Because we can see what contributions you have done, what information you already have provided....its more the value, or the picture of their knowledge that is more important than the role they have.

Further, we asked our participants about the influence of hierarchical and experience levels on editing others' contributions on the wiki. A marketing production manager said:

> I am 48 years old and I've been at the company for 20 something years. You know I am confident in what i know and i am confident in what my colleagues know so people wouldn't get insulted if someone posted something and I had a better answer or more accurate information to contribute. They wouldn't get offended just like i would be… i think that's a maturity thing.

In the same vein, a technical sales professional said:

> If I, let me formulate, am absolutely sure I know better, then I correct it directly. If i am unsure, will I understand it correctly or will they know more than I do then I would not edit directly. I will comment on it. I will say could you please explain this further.

This implies that people tend to be cautious about the expert levels of contributors and that would have a determining impact on the way they actually collaborate with others. In other words, the variations of contributors' expertise limits the free editablity of the wiki. An additional dimension of hierarchy that exists in the wiki environment is related to the perceptions of people of whether a wiki is a tool they should use or not. An example provided by the marketing production manager explaining how the use of the wiki by their executive has legitimized the wiki as a tool for collaboration and knowledge sharing:

> we have our vice president do that in wiki so that people will take it seriously because when our audience simply see our leaders and executives using these new forms of communication, that legitimizes it for them all, this is a real thing.

5.4.4   Social or Behavioral Structure

This kind of structure is related to the social dynamics or social conduct among groups of individuals. These social norms can either be agreed upon by the group or emergent because members are accustomed to do or perceive certain things in certain ways. For instance, one of the software developers explained the routine or norm within his team when it comes to editing something on the wiki:

> Typically in a group … when there is a subject matter expert, other members would look for this person and expect the changes coming from him.

He further commented on editing his contributions on the wiki by others as follows:

> I would find that this person is breaking a social habit. Without contacting me first and putting a comment or anything that would be a bit weird.

As such, the social norms that exist within the group get reflected into the wiki, thus shape the editing behavior of group members. In a similar sense, an information developer described how she perceives editing content made by others:

> I hesitate to just go in and edit people's content without asking them first. I just don't, maybe I feel like it is being a little rude.

In respect to social norms which are agreed upon by a group using a wiki, an information architecture lead explained an example describing a master-writer collaboration model in which they agree that one person writes content and anyone else can only be a commentator:

> the whole wiki is open to everybody but we just have an agreement okay here is the master writer for this one document and Sally is the master for this one and Bob is the master for this one and everybody else just comment.

Further, a social business evangelist explained the social or behavioral norms when it comes to editing content on the wiki that is not yet agreed upon by the group:

> It is almost a socially accepted practice that if I asked you your opinion and you give it to me I should respect you. And if your opinion is valid, great. If not, let me tell you why.

As such, editing or changing content on the wiki is subject to prior discussions about the reasons for making an edit as well as agreeing upon any potential changes. The social computing evangelist argued that this behavior is a barrier for harnessing the essence of wiki openness:

> Someone would typically bump into a wiki, which will be open to everyone not only read but also edit access and he will go and see a paragraph in a wiki page that is not entirely correct and that needs fixing and they know the fix. So instead of them going ahead and privately click on edit and make the update, they are actually calling the person who created that wiki to make the update for them.

5.4.5   Technology Structure

The technology structure refers to the way the wiki is setup either as a private or public platform. For instance, there are wikis set up for public accessibility, thus people are allowed to add, edit, and change content. In contrast, there are other wikis which are setup for private communities to serve specific people for specific purposes. An engagement manager described this:

> I think the way they are working is a lot of pushing knowledge out. And projects use them for their own business. Like I use them for my RFP, then other people use it for their webinars. So it is more like their knowledge sharing more than it is actually people sharing knowledge.

A marketing production manager explained to us how the setup of the wiki determines his content-editing behavior:

> if i see that a wiki is setup in a way that anyone can edit, that tells me that the culture and the way that this application is setup, they allow that, they expect it and then I can help them, no one will be offended, no one is going to mind if i did it. But the only thing if I went to a wiki that didn't allow that and required me to submit a comment or ask, that tells there is some sort of a cultural component in this particular wiki that they expect me to work in another way.

Further, the technical sales professional discussed the nature of the tools they use at the workplace. He emphasized that the flexibility of the technology enables sharing as follows:

> ...because many of our internal tools are built like that. So many of the tools we use encourage us to do this kind of exchanges...I mean from that aspect we take our product suit and create them to be open and encourage people to share.

In addition, the technology structure is also related to technical skills needed to use the wiki. The marketing production manager explained that sometimes the lack of such skills would be a barrier for people to use the wiki:

> Interestingly that for some of our users it has become a barrier because wikis are so flexible and because they are so easy to edit... There is a certain part of people who know a little bit of HTML; people who know a little bit about HTML, they know how to edit it and make it look exactly the way they want. But the majority of people get scared of that.

5.4.6   Task Structure

Task structure describes wikis that are designed for certain purposes (e.g., creating and editing articles in specific subjects) and there are people assigned to achieve these purposes. As such, contributing to the wiki whether through creating and editing articles or structuring and rearranging content becomes the responsibility of particular people. Also, task structure is related to the way wiki users perceive their roles as well as the roles of others in the wiki environment. A client technical professional provided an example of how she experiences this:

> when I look at this wiki (a product documentation wiki) I can see that it is very few people working on it, and it is the developers more or less who are trying to put marketing terms into things and try to explain for ordinary users. And if you see almost only the same authors then I have this feeling why should I jump in and write, it is not my job really, kind of let them do it. So I could come with a comment and say this is an area where it is lacking information please go and do.

Another example that describes the task structure is when someone is assigned to work with the wiki. In other words, some person has the job to create and edit content on the wiki. The marketing production manager has such responsibility as he described it:

> you know i would meet with the executive, we discus what it is (subject to be shared on the wiki), and then I would write for her the article and would go out under her name even though it was written by me.

In addition, the information architecture leader has further provided an example that describes another form of assigning people to work with the wiki:

> Sometimes... we sort of have a person whose a writer, our main writer, so she tends to be the master writer for everything and everybody comments on it...This is our documentation focus project so the documentation is the most important we deliver so we have somebody whose job is to do that.

5.5   General Discussion

The structural variations that exist in the wiki environment suggest that collaboration and sharing with open and social technologies is not a straightforward process. Our quest to understand the development of social structures in the context of using a wiki for open collaboration and knowledge sharing is based on the premise that social structure is continuously created and recreated through the flow of everyday social practice [10].

As such, based on the three modalities of structuration theory (see [10, 19]) we looked at the perceptions of using a wiki among coworkers, dominant protocols and social conduct, facilities and resources available to them, and power relations among individuals and groups. In this respect, the use of social and open technologies, like a wiki at the workplace, represents a dynamic social production of new structures and reproduction or reflection of existing structures. For instance, the perception that a person is in a subject matter expert position within the team was reflected into the wiki in the sense that people tend to avoid editing his or her contributions on the wiki, thus creating a sense of hierarchy that constrains collaboration and sharing. Also, even when people decide to make comments or changes on the content made by a person higher in rank they tend to consult with him or her in order to avoid any implications caused by hierarchical divisions. As such, the hierarchical structure in this case was transformed into the wiki creating barriers for people to collaborate and share with each other freely.

In other cases, structures are emergent resulting from the dynamic social interactions on the wiki. An interesting example was observed when discussing openness and editing content made by others publicly. A number of participants explained that sharing content on a wiki suggests that this content is subject to changes since their understanding of the concept of a wiki implies that content is open and thus anyone can make edits and changes (cf. [2, 21, 26]). This kind of what we call open or network structure is driven by the open interactions that take place when people share content with each on the wiki. These interactions are visible and anyone can see what others have contributed especially in public wikis that are accessible by a large audience.

In this respect, Jones and Karsten [10] argued that human agents draw on social structures in their actions, and at the same time these actions serve to produce and reproduce social structures. The interpretation of people that content shared on the wiki is open and subject to changes represents a manifestation of this argument. On the one hand, people collaborate and share knowledge with each other at the workplace because either it is part of their job or because they are eager to share their experience and knowledge with others. For both reasons, the drivers are determined by social structures such as a jobs requirement or eagerness to share. In this view, the action to collaborate and share is driven by existing structures which can be seen as an outcome of a social structure reproduction process. On the other, social collaboration and sharing on the wiki involves a production of new social structures. The example about open or network structure shows how people's interpretation of sharing content on the wiki has created new rules or resources that govern their collaborative and sharing behavior in the open space. Accordingly, the production or emergence of new social structures either enable or constrain action [10, 18]. An example from the empirical data that shows how new structures might enable collaboration and sharing is related to hierarchical or experience structure. The fact that people can see their executives using the wiki has motivated and even legitimized its use at the workplace. This can be understood as one form of structures of legitimation [20] that can help in maintaining collaboration on the wiki.

In addition, contrary to arguments for the flat, horizontal, and democratic structures suggested by the literature (e.g. [4, 7, 14]), our findings suggest that knowledge collaboration and sharing using open and social technologies such as a wiki is not free of structures. The use of a wiki in an organizational setting is governed by both emergent and reflected social structures. The interplay between existing and emergent structures is central in understanding the dynamic of social and open collaboration in organizations. These kinds of structures shape the social dynamics of collaboration using a wiki through diverse interpretations, norms, and resources associated with each structure. For instance realizing the importance of affiliation to particular teams and groups makes people more motivated to share openly (relationships structure). Also, the influence of hierarchy in social collaboration (hierarchical or experience structure) becomes a resource of power that influences the way people perceive and use the wiki. Further, the development of a sense of responsibility to maintain contributions on the wiki that is open and public tends to become a norm or a routine task among the contributors (open or network structure). In this respect, while wikis allow for social interactions to be free and more flexible, these interactions are implicated by the norms, resources, and interpretations associated with social and open collaboration using a wiki. In this view, the interplay between norms, resources, and beliefs available at the workplace and the open space of a wiki drives the development of new rules, norms, and resources that people draw upon in their interactions, thus shape and govern the wiki. In other words, wikis are not so open.

5.6   Conclusions

The chapter aimed at examining the development of social structures that might evolve in the course of using a wiki for social collaboration and sharing at the workplace. It concludes with providing a number of social structural including open or network, social or behavioral, relationships, technological, task, and hierarchical or experience structures. This chapter showed that these kinds of structures manifest evolving interpretations, norms, and resources that govern collaboration and sharing using a wiki. Noteworthy, these structures should not only be treated as either enablers or inhibitors of collaboration and sharing using a wiki but also as mediums for the production and reproduction of social structures. Such kinds of structural properties might be volatile in the sense that the open and dynamic nature of wiki collaboration among people may continually drive their evolution. In other words new structural properties may arise or evolving properties might get institutionalized. Hence a promising direction for further research is to examine and understand both the evolution and the institutionalization of these structures and their influence on the design and use of social and open collaborative technologies. Longitudinal studies would be effective tools to achieve such an understanding.

References

1. Cole, M., Avison, D.: The potential of hermeneutics in information systems research. Eur. J. Inf. Syst. **16**, 820–833 (2007)
2. Cunningham, W.: Wiki design principles. http://c2.com/cgi/wiki?WikiDesignPrinciples (2004). Accessed Oct 2011
3. Danis, C., Singer, D.: A wiki instance in the enterprise: opportunities, concerns, and reality. In: Proceedings of the Computer Supported Cooperative Work, San Diego, USA (2008)
4. Faraj, S., Jarvenpaa, S., Majchrzak, A.: Knowledge collaboration in online communities. Organ. Sci. **22**(5), 1224–1239 (2011)
5. Gruber, T.: Collective knowledge systems: where the social web meets the semantic web. Web Semant. **6**, 4–13 (2007)
6. Happel, H., Treitz, M.: Proliferation in enterprise wikis. In: Proceedings of the 8th International Conference on the Design of Cooperative Systems, Carry le Rouet, France (2008)
7. Hasan, H., Pfaff, C.: Emergent conversational technologies that are democratizing Information Systems in organizations: the case of the corporate Wiki. In: Proceedings of the Information Systems Foundations (ISF): Theory, Representation and Reality Conference, Australian National University, Canberra, Australia (2006)
8. Holtzblatt, L., Damianos, L., Weiss, D.: Factors Impeding Wiki Use in the Enterprise: a case study. In: Proceedings of the 28th ACM Conference on Human Computer Interaction, Atlanta, USA (2010)
9. Jones, M., Karsten, H.: Review: Structuration Theory and Information Systems Research. Research papers in management studies, Judge Institute of Management, University of Cambridge, England (2003)
10. Jones, M., Karsten, H.: Gidden's structuration theory and information systems research. Manag. Inf. Syst. Q. **32**(1), 127–157 (2008)
11. Jones, M., Orlikowski, W., Munir, K.: Structuration Theory and Information Systems: a critical reappraisal. In: Mingers, J., Willcocks, L. (eds.) Social Theory and Philosophy for IS. Wiley, West Sussex (2004)
12. Kaplan, A., Haenlein, M.: Users of the world unite! The challenges and opportunities of social media. Bus. Horizons. **53**, 59–68 (2010)
13. Klein, H., Myers, M.: A set of principles for conducting and evaluating interpretive field studies in information systems. Manag. Inf. Syst. Q. **1**(23), 67–94 (1999)
14. Kosonen, M., Kianto, A.: Applying wikis to managing knowledge—a socio-technical approach. Knowl. Process. Manag. **16**(1), 23–29
15. Majchrzak, A., Wagner, C., Yates, D.: Corporate wiki users: results of a survey. In: Proceedings of WikiSym'06, Odense, Denmark (2006)
16. McAfee, A.: Enterprise 2.0: new collaborative tools for your organization's toughest challenges. McGraw-Hill Professional, Boston (2009)
17. O'Reilly, T.: What is Web 2.0: design patterns and business models for the next generation of software. Commun. Strategy. **65**, 17–37 (2007)

18. Orlikowski, W.: The duality of technology: rethinking the concept of technology in organization. Organ. Sci. **3**(3), 398–427 (1992)
19. Orlikowski, W.: Using technology and constituting structures: a practice lens for studying technology in organizations. Organ. Sci. **11**(4), 404–428 (2000)
20. Orlikowski, W., Robey, D.: Information technology and the structuring of organizations. Inf. Syst. Res. **2**(2), 143–169 (1991)
21. Rafaeli, S., Ariel, Y.: Online motivational factors: incentives for participation and contribution in Wikipedia. In: Barak, A. (ed.). Psychological Aspects of Cyberspace: Theory, Research, Applications. Cambridge University Press, Cambridge (2008)
22. Rose, J.: Evaluating the contribution of structuration theory to the IS discipline. In: Baets, W. (ed.) Proceedings of the 6th European Conference on Information Systems, pp. 910–924, Euro-Arab Management School, Aix-en-Provence, France (1998)
23. Rowlands, B.: Employing interpretive research to build theory of information systems practice. Australas. J. Inf. Syst. **10**(2), 3–22 (2003)
24. Stenmark, D.: Web 2.0 in the business environment: the new Intranet of a passing hype?. In: Proceedings of the 16th European Conference on Information Systems, Galway, Ireland (2008)
25. Walsham, G.: Knowledge management systems: representation and communication in context. J. Commun. Inf. Technol. Work. **1**(1), 6–18 (2005)
26. Yates, D., Wagner, C., Majchrzak, A.: Factors affecting shapers of organizational wikis. J. Am. Soc. Inf. Sci. Technol. **61**(3), 543–554 (2010)

Chapter 6
Harvesting Collective Agreement in Community Oriented Surveys: The Medical Case

Federico Cabitza

Abstract The chapter discusses the role of simple and lightweight Web-based systems in promoting a different approach to the externalization of practice-related knowledge within communities of professionals. This approach exploits common online questionnaire systems to collect the preferences of large numbers of domain experts to interesting paradigmatic work cases and proposes a statistically sound evaluation of these responses to evaluate the agreement reached within the community. We tested this approach in a case study that involved a large international medical association, that we chose as an example of a large and highly distributed community of expert professionals; in this study we challenged more than 1,000 surgeons about some border-line clinical cases where tacit notions based on life-long practice and situated experiences coexist (and sometimes clash) with scientific evidences drawn from the specialistic literature. We make the point that a sound evaluation of the collective agreement is a necessary precondition to use such lean Web-based tools in bottom-up knowledge elicitation initiatives. To this aim, existing measures of agreement and survey-related heuristics can be exploited to get a more precise picture of the "opinion of the many" in collective settings like communities of practice.

6.1 Background and Motivations

Surveys and polls are important means to collect information since the beginning of the nineteenth century [19] and the rationalization of both the instruments and methods to process, analyze and interpret the collected data can be said coeval to the development of the machines that were to evolve in the modern programmable computers [20]. Surveys have been used extensively in different disciplines, like sociology, psychology, economics, education and also in medicine. In this domain, they have been frequently used for a range of different objectives, from the collection of data on the beliefs, attitudes and behaviors of both patients and doctors [27],

F. Cabitza (✉)
Università degli Studi di Milano-Bicocca, Viale Sarca 336, 20126 Milano, Italy
e-mail: cabitza@disco.unimib.it

J. Dugdale et al. (eds.), *From Research to Practice in the Design of Cooperative Systems: Results and Open Challenges*, DOI 10.1007/978-1-4471-4093-1_6,
© Springer-Verlag London 2012

to the collection and analysis of quantitative data that are essential in clinical epidemiology and health services research [32]. In the last 10 years, due to the crescent diffusion of personal ICTs, either computer-assisted or online questionnaires have been increasingly employed to leverage the clear advantages that Web-based surveys provide in terms of both total costs, recruitment effort and analysis efficiency. A simple research on Pubmed on the expressions "Web-based surveys" and "online surveys" in either the title or abstract of indexed publications reveals less than five papers written before year 2000 against more than 1,700 contributions written since 2000 to date.

Yet, despite their number, their cost and the level of interest in their findings, surveys conducted among physicians usually get inadequate response rates, thus raising concerns that non-response bias could affect the validity and generalizability of the findings [27]. Quite surprisingly (if considering, e.g., the very high level of digitization of general practice in Europe [9]) the phenomenon of low response rates is observed to be significantly *worse* for Web-based surveys in comparison to surveys that are based on traditional mail and telephone [5, 28, 31, 42, 46]. Many researchers have focused on various and complementary strategies for achieving higher rates of response [44] where assurance of confidentiality, monetary incentives and keeping questionnaires short are the most frequent recommendations within more general and complex framework for sound surveying (e.g. [8]). Since no magic formula probably exists, even recently researchers advocate further studies in this vein [13]. Our point is that one of the reasons why surveys do not attract a vast interest from doctors lies in the actual use that researchers make of the results coming from such initiatives. For instance, when a survey is employed to probe respondents on their preferences about clinical procedures and indications, the related analyses are usually kept at the simple level of comparing response percentages and the agreement among respondents is characterized in very qualitative ways, e.g., by merely confronting percentages of responses (e.g., [33]). This a problem that begins to emerge even in the specialist literature [10] and that, together with the correlated problem of low response rates, undermines the reliability of these initiatives, and therefore their potential to become reliable but lightweight methods to extract tacit knowledge from the grassroot level of medical communities.

This will be the main point of the chapter, as it will be articulated in some detail in Sect. 6.2 and in particular in Sect. 6.5, where we will briefly discuss how to possibly improve reliability in medical surveys. Section 6.3 will review some of the methods by which the agreement among the respondents of a survey can be measured with some objectivity, as a necessary precondition to ground on these estimates the externalization/production of new knowledge on the practices carried out within the surveyed community; Sect. 6.4 reports a case study where these ideas were first applied all together to extract consensus-based "best practices" from a medical association counting more than 1,000 members all around the world. Section 6.6 will conclude the chapter by providing some indications of how this work could be extended in next similar initiatives.

6.2 Surveys as Tools for Knowledge Externalization

Our initial point is that the real impact that surveys may have on the process of knowledge externalization and sharing within a community does not lie on the instrument in itself, but rather on the method and rigour with which questionnaires are designed and applied, responses are collected and analysed and results are interpreted and returned to the respondents and policy makers: this is especially true in those ambits where the existence of reliable and socially valued knowledge has an important impact on professional practice and this, in turn, has an impact on themes that rightly catch the attention of the commonalty, like healthcare quality, treatment appropriateness and patient safety [6, 34]. Our more specific point is that online questionnaire systems have a potential to contribute to medical knowledge (and hence medical practice) that has not fully been explored so far, especially in light of the increasing pervasiveness that characterizes Web-based technologies and, in particular, of the recent interaction modalities that are enabled by the so called "Web 2.0" platforms [45].

The key point here is "scalability". It has always been impractical for investigators to administer a questionnaire to all potential respondents in a target population, e.g. the members of a community of practice; for this reason, it has been a common (yet delicate) practice to address a so called "sampling frame" instead of the whole population, i.e., the target population from which to extract a sample by means of different sampling techniques according to the research objectives and resources (e.g., random sampling, cluster sampling). Nowadays in the healthcare sector, like many other sectors where public registries of professionals exist and are constantly maintained, it is much easier and cheaper to identify large populations of possible respondents and contact them at very low cost; indeed, almost every member of a speciality association and employee of an healthcare facility has (at least) an email address and most of the addresses of health professionals can be found in either private or public registries (e.g., MMS[1], NHSnet[2]). The large numbers that ICT can help achieve account for nothing less than *increased* precision and descriptive power, as it is known that the margin of error in survey-based researches does not depend on the size of the population of interest but rather on the sample size (at a desired confidence level). But the larger the numbers involved, not only the higher the statistical precision; we may wonder if reaching the grassroot levels of an arbitrarily large community of professionals could allow the investigators to end up by probing phenomena that are more traceable back to the concept of "collective intelligence" [21, 26] than to those of either census of practices or survey of attitudes/preferences. In what follows, we will concentrate on these themes in the specific domain of medicine, but we are confident that many of the results gained in such a delicate and knowledge-intensive domain can be also applied or better yet, can inform, research that is oriented to other professional domains.

---

[1] http://www.mmslists.com/.

[2] http://www.nhs.net.

In the healthcare domain, relatively small-sample surveys have been recently employed to assess knowledge of and compliance with evidence-based recommendations (e.g. [35, 47]) of practitioners in their actual practice. In this same vein, our current research question is whether community-wide online surveys can contribute in shedding light on those "treatments of choice" and rationales for decision (e.g., particular indications that make a specific treatment or procedure advisable) that the majority of practitioners prefer over possible alternatives in the context of border-line and exemplificatory cases; and whether such indications, which attract the interest and earn the preference of a multitude of (usually silent) experts, can rise to the status of *collective consensus-based recommendations*. As ICT researchers, we focus on the tools that could enable the explicitation and formalization of these recommendations and leave to the debate of the medical communities whether the preferences that emerge from the "rank and files" of hospitals and private practices could flank and, maybe, complement, what are now considered the "scientific evidences" of lowest level in medicine, the so called evidences of level III or D [3], which are built on the basis of the opinions of (a limited number of) respected authorities or of (allegedly) respected and influential expert committees.

To address this research question, our approach focuses on a rigorous approach towards two aspects of (online) surveys: *generalizability* of findings (tackled from the perspective of the interrater reliability); and "consensus quality" (or agreement assessment). Agreement assessment regards how much it is true that the practitioners agree on a specific treatment. To this respect, our contribution will be presented in Sect. 6.3 and regards the experimentation and consolidation of heuristics proposed elsewhere in the literature, as well as the introduction of a novel measure, that is simple to calculate and is more sensitive to large numbers of respondents. Generalizability regards how much the collected respondents are representative of a whole category of practitioners; to this respect, in Sect. 6.5 we will discuss a novel heuristics to determine the optimal timing for sending a reminder and therefore to help assess and minimize non-response bias.

6.2.1 The Quest for Objectivity in (Online) Surveys

For the success of initiatives of online surveying, scholars have underlined the importance of proper design and of compliance to recommendations that gave some evidence of efficacy (e.g., [1, 6, 13, 46]). In addition to good design (e.g., survey length) and effective strategies (e.g., incentives, reminders), it is also important to make the best use of the responses collected. To this aim, proper analytical procedures and techniques must be applied in a proper manner. It is the employment of these techniques (eventually embedded in the response processor of the computer-based system) that makes a research survey essentially different from the most trivial online survey systems like, for instance, the almost ubiquitous Web-based *polls*; these are usually very lean tools, more and more frequently made available in mashups form, that are becoming increasingly common in several web sites, ranging between institutional newspaper websites, corporate portals and social network platforms (e.g., blogs) to probe the readers' opinion on almost any subject.

The differences between knowledge-oriented surveys and discussion-oriented polls lie, as simple as it can be, on how questions are asked and how responses are analyzed; or, in more technical terms, on the "study design" and on the "hypothesis formulation". In fact, assuming that the right questions (i.e., which are able to raise the interest of a competent community) are formulated in the right manner (i.e., without revealing a specific preference or discriminating and biasing the respondents), the point is not in the underlying technology per se, but on the result analysis and how this can affect discussion and consensus-building practices that are triggered and supported by incremental uses of the system. In particular, to detect consensus and concordance patterns in a heterogeneous and distributed community of practitioners, such a system must be designed so that statistical processing of responses can be carried out as objectively as possible. Only in this way, the system can be seen as a technology at least potentially capable to contribute—in ways that were simply not possible before—in building wide-consensus-based evidences that take the real attitudes, habits and practices of the "rank and file" of practitioners into account.

The simplest output that a system collecting responses to closed questions can provide is the frequency with which each possible alternative has been selected by the respondents. Yet, knowing how these frequencies distribute over the full range of responses is not sufficient to draw the knowledge that can enable further informed discussion and comparison of alternatives, as it is expressed in the following two questions: "what is the degree of agreement that we observe among respondents (in our case, doctors)?"; and "to what extent these agreements can be generalized and reproduced?". While the first question seems to refer only to what scholars call *interrater reliability*, the latters seems to refer to generalizability and replicability; as a matter of fact, both aspects are tightly intertwined.

In the domain of treatment evaluation, generalizability (and therefore the external validity of the user study) refers to the extent to which the assessment of appropriateness for a specific treatment is influenced by the specific doctors involved; or, alternatively, to the extent a different group of doctors would have yield the same responses within a tolerable margin of error. This is a thorny matter since much of what pertains to doctors' evaluation (e.g., diagnosis, prognosis) is bound to their specific experience, sensitivity and interpretative capabilities; to this respect, subjectivity and interpretive differences are unavoidable factors of medical profession and could be considered a source of bias only from the merely statistical point of view. Yet, provided that researchers have selected respondents randomly from a population of potential practitioners, if they detect that the respondents' answers are affected by an excessive degree of subjectivity this could indicate the need for further refinement for either the case descriptions, the expression of the alternatives or the choice of the evaluation categories. For this reason, reproducibility can be seen as a kind of reliability, arguably the strongest to achieve and demonstrate. Reliability accounts for the degree of agreement that is observed among independent observers; therefore, the more observers agree on the responses they provide, the more comfortable we can be that their responses are exchangeable with those provided by other observers [17], reproducible, and trustworthy.

6.3   How to "Gauge" Collective Agreement?

In this section we focus on interrater reliability. In Sect. 6.5 we will see a contribution to make a reliable survey more soundly generalizable. Interrater reliability is defined as the extent to which different evaluating doctors (more than two and independent from each other), each assessing the same treatment for the same case, come to the same decision, i.e., either select the same treatment/option or assign the same appropriateness category for the option in hand.

The simplest and most common method of reporting interrater reliability is the percent agreement statistic, also called 'proportion of agreement' (Po). Po is an estimation of the probability that two (randomly selected) raters assign the same appropriateness grade to a given treatment. Unfortunately, this measure tends to overestimate the degree of clinically important agreement since it does not take into account the agreement that would have been expected due solely to chance[3]. To overcome this shortcoming, scholars often employ the Fleiss's (multirater) Kappa score[4]. This score is interpretable as a measure of agreement beyond that due solely to chance, where values between 1 and 0 indicate agreement better than chance, a value of 0 indicates a level of agreement that could have been expected by chance, values between 0 and −1 indicate levels of agreement that are worse than chance.

Although Kappa is a measure of interrater reliability that is often found in literature, some authors have argued that it is not suitable for the majority of agreement analysis. In fact, the Fleiss' Kappa is overly conservative [38] especially when evaluation includes several categories. In these cases the possibility of chance agreement appears negligible, thus leading to several cases in which the Kappa score is very low even when proportions of agreement are very high [10]. Moreover, others argue that the Fleiss Kappa should be applied only when the number of ratings on each subject (treatment) is constant [40] and when assessments are limited to nominal data with no clear order between categories [18].

Since ordinal variables are a convenient way to assess both the appropriateness of treatments and the level of personal accordance with some option, in our analyses we opted for two complementary measures that can be used with any number of observers, namely the free-marginal multirater Kappa [40], which is not influenced by prevalence bias and do not require an a priori knowledge of marginal distributions; and the Krippendorff's Alpha [18], which generalizes across different scales of measurement and can be computed with or without missing data. Both are scores that define a reliability scale from 1 for perfect agreement and 0 for absence of

---

[3] Obviously a doctor does not choose a treatment by chance; but it is the doctors that are (should be) recruited by chance.

[4] Not to be confused with the Cohen Kappa, suitable for multi-case two-rater assessments.

agreement. Yet, a test of the null hypothesis that all agreement is due to chance and agreements are not reliable ($K=0$, $A=0$) often relates to a statistically significant but mediocre level of real agreement. For this reason, to assess the strength of agreement conventional benchmarks are proposed in the literature: in regard to the Kappa score, Landis and Koch [30] characterized values of Kappa less than 0 as indicating no agreement, values between 0 and 0.20 as slight, 0.21 and 0.40 as fair, 0.41 and 0.60 as moderate, 0.61 and 0.80 as substantial, and between 0.81 and 1 as almost perfect agreement; Fleiss proposed a two threshold benchmark where values less than 0.4 are associated with poor agreement, values between 0.4 and 0.75 with intermediate to good agreement and values above 0.75 with excellent agreement [14]. In regard to the Krippendorff's Alpha, social scientists commonly consider generalizable agreements with reliability greater than 0.8, while they draw only tentative conclusions for data whose agreement measures are less than that threshold [29].

In addition to Alpha and Kappa scores, we also propose a heuristic-based measure of agreement that is simply based on a Chi Square test (performed on the difference in distributions between alternative categories), from the obvious observation that the higher the Chi square score, the more polarized responses are (that is, the farer the respondents from perfect balance between the options). This latter score is highly sensitive to large samples of respondents, assuming that the fact that several people agree on a specific option is more significant than the mere proportions between options (i.e., 8 vs. 2 is associated to a smaller agreement than 800 vs. 200). Our simulations carried out on samples of more than 30 respondents for both nominal and ordinal data[5] led to proposing the following indicative thresholds: no agreement below 10, poor agreement up to 20, good agreement from 30 up (obviously the higher the score, the better the agreement).

All that said, although interrater reliability is a generally accepted indicator of how much consensus lies in the ratings/opinions given by a group of people/experts, there is no general...consensus on how this indicator should be precisely measured and related scores interpreted. This uncertainty calls for further research and for validation of formal approaches through tests run at the field of work. In those cases, we should also address the fact that an excellent agreement on a specific treatment choice (e.g., like that reported in Sect. 6.4 for the case no. 8) should not induce researchers to discarding the opinion of small minorities, but rather bring them to considering why, say, one (out of ten) expert doctor expresses an opinion that contrasts that of the other nine. In fact the point of initiatives where agreement is assessed should not in erasing differences or in making opinions more extreme [2]; but, on the contrary, these systems should be seen as tools to let hidden common preferences emerge, share rationales for such preferences, make practitioners aware of differences and help them understand the reasons for divergence, as well as probe them whether a candidate solution can be the best compromise.

---

[5] In this latter case we compared the values of Chi with the Kendall's coefficient of concordance, which is a normalized score between 0 and 1 as the above mentioned Alpha and Kappa.

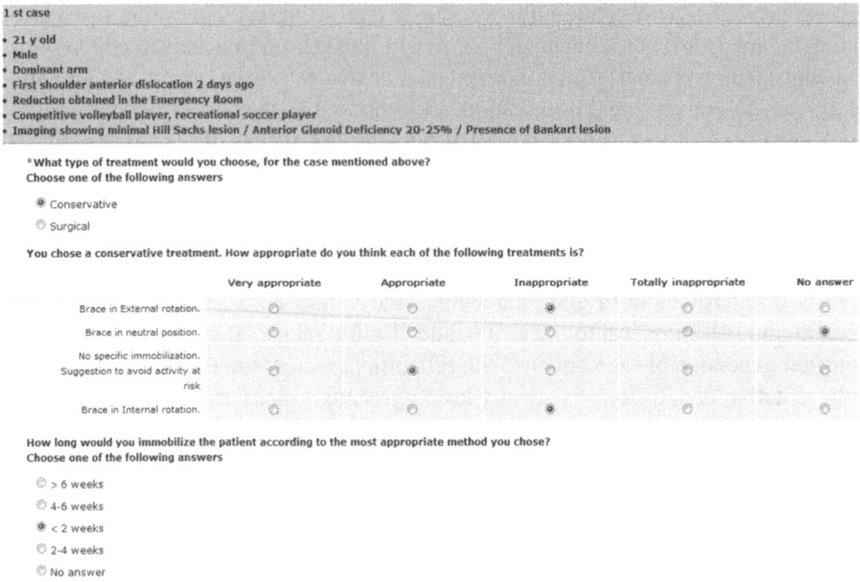

Fig. 6.1 A screenshot from a page of the ESSKA survey

6.4 The ESSKA Case Study

In order to validate our approach, we conceived a multi-page survey in which the members of a large community of specialists were invited to either choose their treatment of choice or rank alternative treatments in the context of eight fictitious clinical cases. These cases were conceived to be somehow "borderline" with respect to which treatment would be the best one (i.e., the most appropriate) to apply and they were described in terms of short summaries at the top of each survey page (see Fig. 6.1 to see how a typical case was shown in each page of the online question-naire). The initiative was co-designed and then patronaged by the scientific board of an international association of surgeons specialized in sports traumatology and knee surgery, ESSKA and this made it noteworthy for two main reasons. First, this association counts more than 1,000 members from 66 countries from all five conti-nents; in that, it represents a heterogeneous gathering of professionals that, on one hand, share all the same interests and competencies in a specific medical specialty (i.e., sport traumatology) but that, on the other hand, have been trained and practice in quite different settings and environments. Second, surgery specialities are gener-ally known to be the most conservative ones with respect to the adoption and inclu-sion in daily practice of evidences drawn from the academic literature [11]; for this reason, the scientific board of the association shared with us the research objective to see if lightweight Web-based tools, like online surveys are, could be leveraged to find potential agreement and achieve consensus on best practices in their specialty, even in those cases where no scientific evidence exist or is effectively applied by the grassroot level of their members.

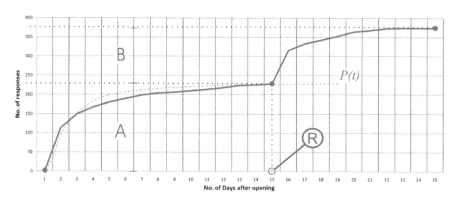

Fig. 6.2 The response rate of the survey

At the end of the survey, we collected 374 completed questionnaires (36 % of the target population), 38 partial questionnaires and 25 contacts, i.e., respondents that opened the first page of the survey but did not proceed. Almost three fourth of the respondents were from a European country. All together, we gathered 412 questionnaires where at least one case had been considered (i.e., a question addressed), accounting for a final response rate of 40 % of the target population. This was in line with, or even beyond, the initial expectations, not only considering the really tight schedule of orthopaedic surgeons (57 % of respondents declared to perform more than 200 operations yearly) and the nature of their work (that does not imply long stays at a computer), but also with respect to other survey initiatives involving orthopaedic surgeons [31] and populations of similarly great size (i.e., > 1000 respondents) that are characterized by loose social control, high distributedness and lack of incentive structures [15]. Figure 6.2 depicts the particular response rate that we obtained: the dispatch of a reminder message after approximately 2 weeks since the opening of the collection session caused the increase of the 63 % of responses as we will see in more details in Sect. 6.5.

The design of the study and the statistical results gathered through the online questionnaire have been described in another contribution [39]. In what follows, we will focus on the responses collected about two specific clinical cases that were considered of particular interest for the community due to their potential overlapping (or clash) with existing medical evidences of level I and II (i.e., the highest available for the community at hand). We present these cases in a row by presenting the concise description that was conveyed to the respondents and then discussing how these expressed their opinions and how their preferences can be matched with the existing literature in their field.

case 1   **21 years old Male; Dominant arm; First shoulder anterior dislocation 2 days ago; Reduction obtained in the Emergency Room; Competitive volleyball player; recreational soccer player; Imaging showing minimal Hill Sachs lesion/Anterior Glenoid Deficiency 20–25 %/Presence of Bankart lesion**

	conservative	surgical	Po	Kappa	Alpha	Chi Square	Agreement
case 1	27.6%	72.4%	0.6	0.2	0.2	80	slight/poor
case 8	4.3%	95.7%	0.9	0.8	0.8	313	excellent/perfect

Fig. 6.3 Response proportions and agreements for the selected cases

In regard to whether a patient presenting a case like that should be operated or not (conservative vs. surgical treatment), the proportions of responses indicated a clear majority in favor of the surgical approach (72 vs. 28 %, in Fig. 6.3); that notwithstanding, the measures of agreement proposed in Sect. 6.2.1, gave results that are heuristically interpreted in terms of either slight or poor agreement (see the assessments of agreement in the right-most column in Fig. 6.3). This is an interesting point in favor of a more objective approach to the assessment of response proportions, as these can bring to intuitive results that highly overstate the actual agreement existing in communities (thus polarizing opinions and indications towards an unfounded consensus). If we focus on conservative options (the choice of the large majority of the respondents), we observe results by which we can assert that 'Brace in Internal rotation' and 'Brace in neutral position' are appropriate management techniques of similar cases with statistical significance. These two treatments are preferred with respect to the others ($p=0.003$, 63 vs. 37 %) but between these two, we cannot say which one is the preferred one ($p=0.118$); yet, "Brace in Internal rotation" was considered the most appropriate treatment on the 37 % of cases (vs. 26 %). This finding clashes with the lack of evidence from randomised controlled trials that a conservative management is more appropriate than others [16]. Moreover, differently from what asserted in a randomized controlled trial performed on 2007 [22], which asserts that external rotation is better (in terms of risk of recurrence) than the conventional method of immobilization in internal rotation, the community considers this treatment not appropriate ($p<0.001$). To this regard, yet, respondents did not exhibit a significant agreement (P0, percentage of overall agreement 50 %, Kappa score$=0.004$). In regard to the optimal length of immobilization period for those who chose external rotation, we detected that the community expresses a clear preference ($p=0.025$, 50 vs. 30, associated with the second treatment) toward a length between 2 and 4 weeks. This finding complements the lack of evidence coming from a study of level II [41]

case 8   **69 years old Diffuse knee arthritis (all the compartments); Relative improvement from conservative treatments done elsewhere (VAS 8 to 5); Shows up again complaining for increase of daily pain. 75 kg, 181 cm**

This is one of the cases in which the respondents reached the most clear consensus; obviously, they were unaware of each other's opinion and this marks the most notable difference between traditional ways to reach consensus on medical treatment, i.e., through focus groups where experts discuss cases and evidences at length till some agreement is reached. The survey indicated that most of the surgeons would go for a surgical treatment (96 vs. 4 %) and this high polarization of preference is reflected by scores of almost perfect agreement. Also in regard to the kind of implant, respondents exhibited a clear preference ($p=<0.001$) for the Cemented Total Knee implant. This confirms the inclusion in practice of corresponding evidences from literature [12]. Likewise, where there is a lack of evidence between Posterior Cruciate Retaining Implant and Posterior Stabilized Total Knee Prosthesis [23], respondents split quite evenly for either techniques (163 vs. 171, $p=0.662$).

From the cases outlined above, we make the point that where statistical significance is achieved, and agreement assessed, the system can provide practitioners with "evidences" that either confirm or oppose those drawn by scientific methods. On the basis of how much sound the findings are, the system could then pass these results to the discussion of the experts. These, in turn, could try to understand the status of the findings and address whether it is reasonable to rank their level of evidence somehow in between evidences drawn from case-series studies and those based on the opinions of few experts of clear and respected authority[6]. We leave it to the reader's opinion whether to deem the agreed opinions on very specific matters of a wide majority of skilled professionals more authoritative than the opinion of "the chosen few", where the agreement level is backed by an analytical survey system that is properly tailored to specific research questions.

6.5 A Proposal to Improve Generalizability of Findings

Threats to the (external) validity of a study like the reported one regard those elements that can negatively affect the confidence that the findings can be generalized from the sampling frame to the entire population of interest, and from the context of the study to other contexts, i.e., other people, communities, places and times. At the end of the survey, when we presented the preliminary results to the ESSKA board during their biannual congress (that was hold just 1 week after the conclusion of the study), we have been asked whether the opinions gathered from the respondents could be representative of the whole community of the ESSKA members. As we said in Sect. 6.2.1, generalizability is a major point to address for any study and consensus-oriented studies enabled by online surveys should make no exceptions.

In our case, a little less than half of the target population (i.e., all the ESSKA members) returned their questionnaire, thus making participation a partial success.

---

[6] These are, respectively, evidences of level II-3 and III or level C and D according to the evidence ranking developed by either the U.S. Preventive Services Task Force or the Oxford Centre for Evidence-based Medicine.

We could not pick every actual respondent in a purely random manner, and this irreversibly thwarted the fact that the size of the sample would be sufficient for reliable results at a standard confidence level. Therefore, we had to consider the probability that non-response bias could affect the generalizability of the findings. In the present study, non-response bias refers to the condition in which the surgeons who did not fill in their questionnaires have opinions on the treatments of choice that are systematically different from the opinions of those who completed their surveys.

In order to test for non-response bias, then, we decided to consider who responded after the reminder had been sent as *proxies* for non-respondents; this is a technique that has been proved adequate in regard to homogeneous groups of potential respondents, such as physicians in one specialty [43], in the assumption that the variations that do exist within such groups may not be as associated with willingness to respond. To this aim, we compared the responses of those who completed the questionnaire *before* the reminder (group A in Fig. 6.2), to those who completed *after* it (group B in Fig. 6.2), as the latter ones can be considered a sample of non-respondents (to the first mailing). Now, this comparison can be considered arbitrary in the general case, but it is not if one considers the cumulate response rate curve, we reported in Fig. 6.2. As Barclay et al. noted almost incidentally, looking at when the curve seems to "flatten out" enables to decide on the right timing when to deploy a reminder to the completion of the questionnaire [4]. Our point is that the study of the best interpolating curve can not only be used to determine when it is a good time to send an effective reminder but, more significantly, to begin sampling the "catchment area" of the population of non-respondents. An assessment of the slope of the cumulative response rate curve allows to estimate whether the questionnaire will be completed by many other respondents or, on the contrary, very few others will remember to complete the questionnaire (and hence consider an invitation they received weeks or even months earlier). In our case, the pattern that we detected by minimizing the summation of the squared deviations between our data and a generic S-shaped logistic curve [36][7] suggests that very few respondents of the "second" turn would be just late comers of the first turn. The corresponding logistic function P(t) saturates after a certain value of x (i.e., number of hours/days) over a value that is not noticeably incremented not even for very high values of x, thus backing our approach to non-response bias[8]. Also in this case, we propose a heuristic to determine whether the response rate has reached a value of y (i.e., number of responses) that is very close to the hypothetical maximum; this value, indicated with R in Fig. 6.2 corresponds when the first derivative of the logistic function[9] becomes less than 0.01. Once that point has been detected, investigators can send a reminder and begin considering responses col-

---

[7] The logistic regression model we obtained is represented by the function $y(x) = a/b + ce^{-ax}$ with $a \approx 1.04$, $b \approx 0.004$, $c \approx 0.06$ and it is indicated with P(t) in Fig. 6.2.

[8] This holds in the assumption that responses from the second turn are representative of the nonresponses, and that people that can get convinced by a single reminder end up by exhibiting similar opinions to those that, conversely, are refractory to any reminder at all.

[9] $y' = abce^{cx}/(b + e^{cx})^2$.

lected from then on as representative of the rest of the population and consequently partition responses in two groups, namely early-respondents and late-respondents, respectively A and B in Fig. 6.2, with group B taken as proxies of potential non respondents. Coming back to our case study, we performed a Pearson Chi test and a Wilcoxon-Mann-Whitney test on the variables of interest in these two groups, and detected no significant difference (Asymp. Sig. > 0.4); the reweighting of the results according to the response/non-response proportions produced a negligible impact on the observed values.

6.6 Conclusions and Future Work

Porter pointed out that the basis for authority in science must be *quantitative objectivity* as "reliance on nothing more than seasoned judgment seems undemocratic" ([37], p. 7). We agree with this stance but we also came to wonder whether a fully "democratic judgment" can also be taken as reliable. To this aim, in this chapter we have addressed the general problem of how to reach "quantitative objectivity" in the analysis of survey-related responses and, at the same time, how lightweight Web-based technologies can support the "democratic" creation of (medical) knowledge on the basis of this objectivity. The methods we proposed and tested in our case study can be taken as a first contribution toward the consolidation of enabling technologies and methods to "give voice" to the usually silent multitude of experts, the so called "grassroot level" of a community of practice. To validate our approach, we proposed and discussed the use of an online survey system as a flexible and convenient means to collect the preferences and attitudes of doctors towards appropriate treatments in medical practice.

The doctors involved in the initiative responded favourably to the survey and to the specific tool we designed: some of them even contributed with suggestions on how to improve the tool, recognizing its potential especially for the younger and less expert surgeons. For this reason, we plan to further develop this idea by deploying an online survey that could adapt even more flexibly to the respondents' specialization, experience and demands for the apt interpretation of the clinical cases proposed. The challenge posed by such a system is to find a way to offer to the users (i.e., to the doctors in the considered domain) pieces of information that are meaningful and "structured" enough to convey and evoke the experiential knowledge they need to make sense of a given context [7].

As a last remark, we believe that the potential for systems that are designed with the precise aim to collect collective preferences and soundly assess the agreement over these preferences is overly underestimated. We believe that further research should be undertaken to fully take advantages of their use in community-based domains. In fact, applications may range from the generic domains of distributed consensus conferences and distributed expert panels, to more specific ambits like, in medicine, the support of Delphi processes [24] and diagnosis team meetings [25]; in the academic domain, the support of the review process of novel research contributions for conference program committees and journal editorial boards; in the software engineering domain, the support of the phases of requirement elicitation, prioritization and validation. In particular to this latter domain, such systems would help analysts and designers probe the preferences and attitudes of a large number of potential users and stakeholders of a prospective system, thus contributing in the improvement of one of the most delicate phases in software development within the usually pressing time and cost constraints of ICT projects in cooperative settings.

References

1. Aday, L.: Designing and Conducting Health Surveys. Jossey-Bass, San Francisco (1996)
2. Alstyne, M.V., Brynjolfsson, E.: Global village or cyber-balkans? Modeling and measuring the integration of electronic communities. Manag. Sci. 51(6), 851–868 (2005)
3. Atkins, D., Eccles, M., et al.: Systems for grading the quality of evidence and the strength of recommendations: critical appraisal of existing approaches. BMC Health. Serv. Res. 4(1), 38 (2004)
4. Barclay, S., Todda, C., Finlayb, I., Grande, G., Wyattc, P.: Not another questionnaire! Maximizing the response rate, predicting non-response and assessing non-response bias in postal questionnaire studies of gps. Fam. Pract. 19(1), 105–111 (2002)
5. Braithwaite, D., Emery, J., de Lusignana, S., Sutton, S.: Using the internet to conduct surveys of health professionals: a valid alternative? Fam. Pract. 20(5), 545–551 (2003)
6. Burns, K., Duffett, M., Kho, M., Meade, M.: A guide for the design and conduct of self-administered surveys of clinicians. Can. Med. Assoc. J. 179(3), 245–252 (2008)
7. Cabitza, F., Simone, C., Sarini, M.: Knowledge artifacts as bridges between theory and practice: the clinical pathway case. In: KMIA'08: Proceedings of the International Conference on Knowledge Management in Action. Held in Conjunction with the 20th IFIP World Computer Congress, 7 Jan 2008, Milan, Italy (2008)
8. Dillman, D.: Mail and Internet Surveys: The Tailored Design Method, 2nd ed. Wiley, New York (2000)
9. Dobrev, A., Haesner, M., Hüsing, T., Korte, W., Meyer, I.: Benchmarking ict use among general practitioners in Europe. Tech. rep., European Commission—Information Society and Media Directorate General (2008)
10. Feinstein, A.R., Cicchetti, D.V.: High agreement but low kappa: I. the problems of two paradoxes. J. Clin. Epidemiol. 43(6), 543–549 (1990)
11. Ferlie, E., Wood, M., Fitzgerald, L.: Some limits to evidence-based medicine: a case study from elective orthopaedics. Qual. Health. Care. 8, 99–107 (1999)
12. Gandhi, R., Tsvetkov, D., Davey, J., Mahomed, N.: Survival and clinical function of cemented and uncemented prostheses in total knee replacement. J. Bone. Joint. Surg. 91-B(7), 889–895 (2009)
13. Grava-Gubins, I., Scott, S.: Effects of various methodologic strategies. Can. Fam. Physician. 54(10), 1424–1430 (2008)
14. Gwet, K.: Handbook of Inter-rater Reliability. STATAXIS Publishing Company, Gaithersburg (2001)
15. Hamilton, M.B.: Online survey response rates and times. background and guidance for industry. Technical report, Ipathia, Inc./SuperSurvey (2009)
16. Handoll H.H.G., Hanchard N.C.A., Goodchild L.M., Feary J.: Conservative management following closed reduction of traumatic anterior dislocation of the shoulder. Cochrane. Database. Syst. Rev. 25(1) (2006). (Art. No.: CD004962, doi:10.1002/14651858.CD004962.pub2)

17. Hayes, A.: Statistical Methods for Communication Science. Lawrence Erlbaum Associates, Inc., Mahwah (2005)
18. Hayes, A.F., Krippendorff, K.: Answering the call for a standard reliability measure for coding data. Commun. Methods Meas. 1(1), 77–89 (2007)
19. Headrick, D.R.: When Information Came of Age: Technologies of Knowledge in the Age of Reason and Revolution, pp. 1700–1850. Oxford University Press, New York (2000)
20. Heide, L.: Punched-card Systems and the Early Information Explosion, pp. 1880–1945. Johns Hopkins University Press, Baltimore (2009)
21. Hiltz, S., Turoff, M.: Network Nation: Human Communication via Computer (Revised Edition). The MIT Press, Cambridge (1993)
22. Itoi, E., Hatakeyama, Y., et al.: Immobilization in external rotation after shoulder dislocation reduces the risk of recurrence. a randomized controlled trial. J. Bone. Joint. Surg. Am. 89(10), 2124–2131 (2007)
23. Jacobs W, Clement D.J., Wymenga A.A.B.: Retention versus sacrifice of the posterior cruciate ligament in total knee replacement for treatment of osteoarthritis and rheumatoid arthritis. Cochrane. Database. Syst. Rev. 19(4) (2005). (Art. No.: CD004803, doi:10.1002/14651858. CD004803.pub2)
24. Jones, J., Hunter, D.: Consensus methods for medical and health services research. BMJ. 311, 376–380 (1995)
25. Kane, B., Luz, S.: Achieving diagnosis by consensus. Comput. Support. Coop. Work 18(4), 357–392 (2009)
26. Kapetanios, E.: Quo vadis computer science: from turing to personal computer, personal content and collective intelligence. Data. Knowl. Eng. 67(2), 286–292 (2008)
27. Kellerman, S., Herold, J.: Physician response to surveys. A review of the literature. Am. J. Prev. Med. 20(1), 61–67 (2001)
28. Kongsved, S., Basnov, M., Holm-Christensen, K., Hjollund, N.: Response rate and completeness of questionnaires: a randomized study of internet versus paper-and-pencil versions. J. Med. Internet. Res. 9(3), e25 (2007)
29. Krippendorff, K.: Content Analysis: An Introduction to Its Methodology. Sage, Thousand Oaks (2004)
30. Landis, J., Koch, G.: The measurement of observer agreement for categorical data. Biometrics. 33, 159–174 (1977)
31. Leece, P., Bhandari, M., Sprague, S., Swiontkowski, M.: Internet versus mailed questionnaires: a controlled comparison. J. Med. Internet. Res. 6(4), e39 (2004)
32. Lipton, R., Liberman, J., Cutrer, F., Goadsby, P.: Treatment preferences and the selection of acute migraine medications: results from a population-based survey. J. Headache. Pain. 5(2), 123–130 (2004)
33. Marx, R.G., et al.: Beliefs and attitudes of members of the American academy of orthopaedic surgeons regarding the treatment of anterior cruciate ligament injury. Arthroscopy. 19(7), 762–770 (2003)
34. McColl, E., Jacoby, A., Thomas, L., Soutter, J.: Design and use of questionnaires: a review of best practice applicable to surveys of health service staff and patients. Health. Technol. Assess. 5(31), 1–256 (2001)
35. Mosca, L., et al.: National study of physician awareness and adherence to cardiovascular disease prevention guidelines. Circulation. 111, 499–510 (2005)
36. Parasuraman, A.: More on the prediction of mail survey response rates. J. Mark. Res. 19(2), 261–268 (1982)
37. Porter, T.M.: Trust in Numbers: The Pursuit of Objectivity in Science and Public Life. Princeton University Press, Princeton (1996)
38. Potter, W.J., Levine-Donnerstein, D.: Rethinking validity and reliability in content analysis. J. Appl. Commun. Res. 27, 258–284 (1999)
39. Randelli, P., Cabitza, F., Arrigoni, P., Cabitza, P., Ragone, V.: Current practice in shoulder pathology: results of a web-based survey among a community of 1,084 orthopedic surgeons. Knee. Surg. Sports. Traumatol. Arthrosc. 20(5), 803–815 (2012). (doi:10.1007/s00167-011-1673-z)

40. Randolph, J.J.: Free-marginal multirater kappa: An alternative to fleiss' fixed-marginal multi-rater kappa. In: Proceedings of the Joensuu University Learning and Instruction Symposium 2005, Joensuu, Finland, 14–15 Oct (2005)

41. Scheibel, M., Kuke, A., Nikulka, C., et al.: How long should acute anterior dislocations of the shoulder be immobilized in external rotation? Am. J. Sports. Med. **37**(7), 1309–1316 (2009)

42. Seguin, R., Godwin, M., MacDonald, S., McCall, M.: E-mail or snail mail? Randomized controlled trial on which works better for surveys. Can. Fam. Physician. **50**(5), 414–419 (2004)

43. Sobal, J., Ferentz, K.: Assessing sample representativeness in surveys of physicians. Eval. Health. Prof. **13**, 367–372 (1990)

44. Thorpe, C., Ryan, B., Burt, A., Stewart, M., Brown, J.: How to obtain excellent response rates when surveying physicians. Fam. Pract. **26**(1), 65–68 (2009)

45. Van De Belt, T.H., Engelen, L.J., Berben, S.A., Schoonhoven, L.: Definition of health 2.0 and medicine 2.0: a systematic review. J. Med. Internet. Res. **12**(2), e18 (2010)

46. VanGeest, J., Johnson, T., Welch, V.: Methodologies for improving response rates in surveys of physicians: a systematic review. Eval. Health. Prof. **30**(4), 303–321 (2007)

47. Webster, B.S., Courtney, T.K., et al.: Physicians' initial management of acute low back pain versus evidence-based guidelines. Influence of sciatica. J. Gen. Intern. Med. **20**, 1132–1135 (2005)

Chapter 7
Classifying Communities for Design

A Review of the Continuum from CoIs to CoPs

Sergio Herranz, David Díez, Paloma Díaz, and Starr Roxanne Hiltz

Abstract Cooperative design is a complex process that usually involves participants from different cultural and social domains, with different backgrounds and experiences. In this context, the need for social structures that support sharing and common understanding is an essential requirement. The response to such a need can be found in the creation of 'Communities of Practices' and 'Communities of Interest'. Both types of structures have successfully and extensively been applied in different domains; however, a detailed analysis of these concepts points up the need for additional research that leads to their application to cooperative design. This chapter presents a review of the 'Communities of Practices' and 'Communities of Interest' concepts in order to propose a systematic process for classifying communities. This process might allow practitioners to identify which kind of structure is more suitable to support specific cooperative design processes.

7.1 Introduction

Sharing and common understanding are common activities in open source development. In such a domain, a community of software developers cooperatively construct systems to help solve problems of shared interest. Using open source development as a successful model for cooperative design, it is possible to highlight the creation of both 'Communities of Practice' (CoPs) and 'Communities of Interest' (CoIs) as significant organizations to support cooperative design [1].

S. Herranz (✉) · D. Díez · P. Díaz · S. R. Hiltz
DEI Laboratory, Computer Science Department, Universidad Carlos III, Madrid, Spain
e-mail: sherranz@inf.uc3m.es

D. Díez
e-mail: ddiez@inf.uc3m.es

P. Díaz
e-mail: pdp@inf.uc3m.es

S. R. Hiltz
e-mail: hiltz@njit.edu

J. Dugdale et al. (eds.), *From Research to Practice in the Design of Cooperative Systems:*   97
Results and Open Challenges, DOI 10.1007/978-1-4471-4093-1_7,
© Springer-Verlag London 2012

One of the most accepted definitions for CoP is "a group of people who share a concern, a set of problems, or a passion about a topic, and who deepen their knowledge and expertise in this area by interacting on an ongoing basis" [2]. Nevertheless, other authors, such as Hildreth and Kimble [3], understand this structure in a very different way, pointing out the professional experience of community members as the essential aspect to conform a CoP. Similarly it is possible to collect several different CoI definitions [1, 2]. As a consequence, there is not a universally accepted criterion about what CoPs and CoIs mean, when they must be applied, or how they should be supported; on the opposite, distinction between these structures exists in varying degrees, "they are not black and white" [2] entities, and the space from CoPs to CoIs should therefore be understood as a continuum.

Different kinds of communities have different needs and they also have to be managed in different ways. For that reason, it is essential to understand what kind of particular community should be defined as a way of effectively supporting the cooperative design process. With the goal of achieving this purpose, this chapter aims to deepen knowledge about these structures, firstly reviewing the CoP and CoI concepts, and secondly analysing their characteristics and aspects to provide a community model. The resulting systematic process for classifying structures within the continuum from CoPs to CoIs is discussed. The final section compiles conclusions and further work.

7.2 Reviewing Concepts of Community

There is not a unique or uniform classification of the different kinds of communities. McDermott [4] classifies communities based on the degree of connection and shared identity among members. He distinguishes among user groups, communities of interest, and communities of practice. There are also classifications based on the purpose. For instance, Carotenuto et al. [5] see a landscape of communities formed by communities of practice, communities of interest, communities of purpose, and communities of passion. Allen [6] classifies communities into two types, 'internal and extended communities of practice' and 'knowledge and business networks'. Fischer [7] simplifies the space and just identifies two kinds of design community: communities of practice and communities of interest. Wenger et al. [2] distinguish between CoPs and other complementary structures: formal departments, operational teams, project teams, communities of interest, and informal networks. Thus, there is no single uniform criterion to distinguish different types of communities. However, communities of practice and communities of interest can be found as different structures in most classifications. In this section, a review of these two structures is presented.

7.2.1 Reviewing the CoP Concept

CoPs are a well-studied topic with a large number of publications. Nevertheless, each one of these publications has a particular point of view and a different way to understand the definition space of a community of practice. In addition, the use of term 'community of practice' has not been uniform [8]. Sometimes it is a conceptual way to express the social construction of meaning in a group. At other times it is used to refer to a community or informal group sponsored by an organization to facilitate learning or knowledge exchange. The usage of the term has been very diverse. In this section, the CoP concept and its evolution will be reviewed.

Wenger [9] understands a CoP as a special type of community where practice is a source of the coherence to pursue a joint enterprise. In this work, CoPs are defined by the following three features: (i) mutual engagement, (ii) joint enterprises, and (iii) shared repository. Later, he redefines the concept of community of practice, explaining that it is not just a collection of best practices, "it is a group of people who interact, learn together, build relationships, and in the process develop a sense of belonging and mutual commitment. Having others who share your overall view of the domain and yet bring their individual perspectives on any given problem creates a social learning system that goes beyond the sum of its parts." [2]. In this definition we can notice that Wenger's community of practice concept has evolved. In 1998 Wenger explains a community of practice as the collaborative space for workers to pursue a joint enterprise creating a shared repository of practices. He explains it describing the daily work routine in a claim processor office. However, in 2002 Wenger's definition is different. It is a group of people interested in the same thing, not just to pursue a common enterprise. Interest is focused on learning together and sharing ideas, not just on doing some particular job. According to Cox [8] this change is "a popularisation and a simplification but also a commodification of the idea of community of practice".

A community of practice is redefined by Wenger along three dimensions that combine the three fundamental elements: "(i) a domain of knowledge; (ii) a community of people who care about this domain; and (iii) the shared practice that they are developing to be effective in their domain" [2]. Based on all these ideas, Wenger et al. [2] propose a brief definition of a CoP that is one of the most accepted one: "groups of people who share a concern, a set of problems, or a passion about a topic, and who deepen their knowledge and expertise in this area by interacting on an ongoing basis". Keywords of this definition are "passion" which denotes voluntary participation, "deepen their knowledge and expertise" which can be translated to learning, and "interacting" which is the process that the "group of people" performs in order to learn. In this definition the bidirectionality of the learning process is missed. They want to "deepen their knowledge and expertise" (learn), but also they want to share their knowledge to develop practice.

In addition, other important definitions are proposed by Hildreth and Kimble [3], and Fischer [7]. Based on Wenger's definition [9], Fischer understands a CoP as a "group of practitioners who work as a community in a certain domain undertaking similar work" [7]. On the other hand, Hildreth and Kimble define a CoP as a "a group of professionals informally bound to one another through exposure to a common class of problems, common pursuit of solutions, and thereby themselves embodying a store of knowledge" [3].

Table 7.1, summarizes the differences among the Fischer [7], Wenger et al. [2], and Hildreth and Kimble [3] conceptions. Firstly, while Wenger et al. understand a CoP

Table 7.1 Comparative CoP concepts

	Fischer [7]	Wenger et al. [2]	Hildreth and Kimble [3]
Definition	A group of practitioners who work as a community in a certain domain undertaking similar work	A group of people who share a concern, a set of problems, or a passion about a topic, and who deepen their knowledge and expertise in this area by interacting on an ongoing basis	A group of professionals informally bound to one another through exposure to a common class of problems, common pursuit of solutions, and thereby themselves embodying a store of knowledge
Members	A group of practitioners	A group of people	A group of professionals
What holds them together?	A common expertise about a certain domain	Share a concern, a set of problems, or a passion about a topic	Exposure to a common class of problems, common pursuit of solutions
Purpose	Undertaking similar work	Members deepen their knowledge in this area	Embodying a store of knowledge

as a group of people, Hildreth and Kimble understand it as a group of professionals. More close to this idea is Fischer's definition, encompassing a group of practitioners with expertise in a particular domain. According to Fischer, and Hildreth and Kimble, membership depends just on expertise and includes only people who have a high degree of expertise could belong to the community. Wenger et al. see CoP membership as depending also on members' passion about the community domain. For that reason, in their opinion passion about the community domain is essential to hold members together. In contrast, solving common problems is the main reason to hold members together for Hildreth and Kimble. In terms of purpose, according to Wenger et al., the purpose of a CoP is to deepen members' knowledge and expertise in the area, which means they belong to the community because they want to learn. Nevertheless, Hildreth and Kimble's CoP purpose is more complex because it consists of "embodying a store of knowledge", including contributing knowledge. Fischer points out a more practical purpose related to undertaking similar work within the community.

7.2.2 Reviewing the CoI Concept

Not all communities are communities of practice [2]. An interesting kind of community used for cooperative design is communities of interest (CoI). A community of interest is a group of people who share a common interest and who want access to community information [2]. This common interest is usually a shared goal in the framing and resolution of a problem [7] or just to be informed [2]. CoI membership is usually open, everybody who is interested in the information that is managed by the community can access it [2]. Individuals are involved in the community in an adhoc manner [10], when they want to exchange questions and solutions about the

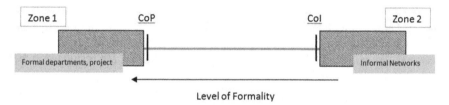

Fig. 7.1 First approach of the problem

common interest [4]. This exchange among community members produces mutual needs that are the motivation to hold them together [11].

For Fischer [1] CoIs are heterogeneous design communities that can be composed of different CoPs that share a common interest. However, a CoI has a lesser level of formality than a CoP. Relaxing this formality level, CoIs have a great potential to be more innovative and creative [1]. CoI members do not have a strong identity because relationships are always shifting and changing [12].

In conclusion, a community of interest is a different structure than a community of practice. A CoI is characterized by a shared common interest and its purpose is that everybody interested can access and exchange information. CoI members hold together because they want to be informed.

7.3   Community Model: A Continuum from CoP to CoI

The analysis of the CoP and CoI concept has shown that there is not a uniform criterion about when these structures should be used, and how they should be supported. Nevertheless, it seems quite clear that it is possible to define a set of characteristics that determines whether a social structure conforms to a community type. The analysis of these characteristics allows systematizing the classification process. This section defines a model for the continuum from CoPs to CoIs, establishing the scope of the model and a set of characteristics to distinguish among different types of communities.

7.3.1   Scope

There is a large variety of communities. For that reason, it is necessary to determine the scope, limiting the model to the continuum space from the CoPs to CoIs. Level of formality is one of the most promising features to distinguish between CoPs and CoIs. Based on level of formality we could design a first approach to the problem. This approach can be defined by a scale where we would locate CoP and CoI concepts (Fig. 7.1). At the left of the CoP concept, we would find structures whose skeleton is rigid and determined by the organization that supports them, such as business units, formal departments or project teams. We will refer to this zone as zone 1. On the other hand, at the right of the CoI concept, we would find flexible and informal structures that are out of our established range, for instance informal networks. We will refer to this as zone 2. Then, our problem space is situated in the scale between these two end points.

In zone 1 we find structures more formal than CoPs. We are able to distinguish any of these structures from a CoP. The following features are indicators of structures more formal than CoPs that would be located in zone 1:

- Domain and enterprise are clear, closed and it is imposed by the organization that supports it. There is not a joint enterprise that it is negotiated by community members. (An example might be the organization of volunteers in the Red Cross). In a CoP the enterprise "is never fully determined by an outside mandate, by a prescription or by any individual participant" [9].
- The primary purpose is to deliver a product or accomplish a task. A CoP is focused on developing practice, expanding and exchanging knowledge about a specific domain. A domain is different from a task. It is an area of shared common interest that the community explores while it is developing its practice. This does not mean that a CoP cannot have a specific goal but its primary scope is to encourage knowledge and learning.
- Roles and relationships are established by the organization. In a CoP leadership can be emergent or assigned. However, a CoP leader "brings people together and enables the community to find its direction" [2]. It is not possible that the organization or the particular leader decides the member's power and relationships of a community member. In a CoP members' power depends on participation, passion for the domain and expertise. An expert usually has more power than a novice but this power comes from the ability to contribute to the community, not from formal authority. Relationships are based on mutual engagement and they grow through mutual interest. For that reason roles and relationships cannot be closely defined nor depend on institutional affiliation.
- Boundaries are extremely clear. In a CoP boundaries are fuzzy [2].

Summarizing all these ideas, CoPs will differ from any structure of zone 1 because they are more connected, informal and self-managed than these structures, even when they are institutionalized. They have joint enterprises and their membership is based on participation, passion and expertise more than institutional affiliation [2].

On the opposite point we observe zone 2, where we can find structures more informal that can be determined based on the following guidelines:

- There is not a shared common interest. People access these structures just for communicating with friends or business acquaintances.
- The main purpose is just to pass and receive specific information. Besides this information does not correspond to a particular common interest. It is business information or information just to know who is who in the community. However, the purpose of a CoI is to be informed about the common interest of the community.

- There are no boundaries. Although they are fuzzy, a CoI has boundaries [2]. An example might be an unmoderated listserver to which anyone may belong, or the followers of an entity on Twitter.

In conclusion while a CoI is a structure whose purpose is to be informed about a shared common interest or concern, more informal structures located in zone 2 are just a set of relationships whose purpose is to disseminate specific information.

7.3.2 Characteristics

The proposed model is based on a set of features useful to identify differences within the continuum from CoP to CoI concepts. However, not all of these have the same degree of importance. There are a set of features that are identified as fundamental elements to distinguish between a CoP and a CoI [2, 9]:

- **Purpose of the community**. This refers to the general main scope of the community. It is established by Wenger as a key factor in the comparison between CoPs and other structures [2, 11].

  - CoP: the purpose of a CoP is to create, extend and exchange knowledge in order to learn and develop individual capabilities. It is also related to learning through sharing best practices. Finally, a CoP's purpose is focused on developing practice by expanding and exchanging knowledge about a specific domain.
  - CoI: the purpose of a CoI is less specific. It consists of being informed, discussing and sharing understanding about a particular topic, problem or concern that interests community members.

- **What is the community about?** The community is interested in something. In this feature we analyze what is 'this something'.

  - CoP: according to Wenger, a CoP is about a specific domain of knowledge [2]. The enterprise of the community is negotiated by community members based on this domain of knowledge and community members develop their practices about this specific and shared domain. Wenger identifies this process as joint enterprise [9].
  - CoI: do not have an enterprise nor a domain of knowledge. CoIs are about a shared common interest formed by multiples domain [1].

- **How does the community function?** This means how the community regulates the activity and members' interactions.

  - CoP: a CoP has to encourage participation and interaction, building a collaborative relationship based on negotiated rules. It is determined by Wenger as including mutual engagement [9] and the community concept [2]. This mutual engagement generates an atmosphere of openness to facilitate learning.

Table 7.2 Summary of fundamental elements to compare CoPs & CoIs

Characteristic	CoP	CoI
Purpose	To create, extend and exchange knowledge to learn and develop individual capabilities. Learning and sharing best practices	To be informed, discuss and share understanding about a specific topic or concern that interests the community members
What is it about?	Joint enterprise about a specific domain of knowledge	No enterprise. There is a shared common interest formed by multiples domains
How does it function?	Mutual engagement builds a collaborative relationship based on negotiated rules	It is not regulated. Suitable to encourage creativity and innovation
Produce any capability	Shared repository of common resources that serve as future practice. Store of knowledge	Not necessarily

- CoI: a CoI does not have any regulated function. There is no specific way to build either a collaborative relationship or negotiated rules. As a result, it is a more suitable structure to encourage creativity and innovation.

- **If the community produces any capability**. Does the community produce or support a specific practice?

  - CoP: it is required that a CoP develop a specific shared practice about the domain of knowledge. Wenger identifies this feature as the shared repository [9] and the shared practice [2, 6]. Hildreth and Kimble speak about the store of knowledge [3]. Practice should capture tacit and explicit interactions and it has to be useful for practitioners.
  - CoI: it is not necessary that CoIs develop a practice (Table 7.2).

On the other hand, there exist other features that, although they are not fundamental to identify the kind of community, are very useful to adjust the classification:

- **Who belongs to the community**. This means what kind of people belong to the community and upon what this process depends.

  - CoP: membership can be self-selected or partially assigned but always based on expertise and passion for the topic [2]. People cannot belong to the community just because it is mandatory. They have to feel a personal passion or expertise about the topic developed by the community.
  - CoI: whoever is interested in the common shared topic or concern of the community can join. This structure could bring together stakeholders from different domains and even CoPs [1], collecting different perspectives and enhancing diversity.

- **What holds community members together**. This means what is the reason that community members hold together and collaborate.

  - CoP: CoP members start to belong to the community because of personal passion or expertise about the topic developed by the community. Then they hold together because they continue having this passion and also they develop a commitment and identification with the group of people who form the community and their expertise [2, 9].

- CoI: CoI members hold together just because they want access to information and participation about a collective interest or concern with the resolution of a particular problem.

- **On what is the community membership based?** This means on what features or characteristics the community members level of engagement is based.

  - CoP: in a CoP, newcomers and old-timers have different degrees of membership [13]. This level of engagement is based on participation, expertise and passion for the topic.
  - CoI: it is dynamic and based just on participation. Because CoIs are structures formed by stakeholders from multiples domains, they are considered both experts and novices at the same time: they are experts when they communicate their knowledge to others, and they are novices when they learn from others who are experts in domains outside of their own knowledge [14].

- **Composition of the community**. Is the community more or less heterogeneous or homogeneous?

  - CoP: a CoP is usually a more homogeneous community than a CoI. Although in a CoP it is not unusual to find diversity, this diversity will always be less than in a CoI. CoP members share a common expertise or passion about a specific topic. They work as a community in a certain domain undertaking similar work [9].
  - CoI: CoIs are usually heterogeneous communities [7]. In fact, a CoI can be composed of different CoPs that share just a common interest or concern.

- **Lifespan of the community**. It means how the community evolves over time and how long its estimated duration is.

  - CoP: evolve and end organically [2]. Although, there is not a specific default lifespan, CoPs usually have a longer lifespan than CoIs.
  - CoI: as with CoPs, CoIs evolve and end organically [2]. However, CoIs are usually more temporary than CoPs [7] because they come together in the context of a specific common interest and when this interest becomes less important, the community tend to dissolve itself (Table 7.3).

7.4 Classification Process

Based on the previously determined characteristics, a systematic process has been defined for classifying communities within the continuum space from CoPs to CoIs. This process, apart from the discarded areas established above, contains three main zones: structures that resemble CoPs, structures that resemble CoIs, and fuzzy structures somewhere in between (Fig. 7.2).

Table 7.3 Summary of "not fundamental" elements to compare CoPs & CoIs

Characteristic	CoP	CoI
Who belongs?	It is based on expertise and passion for the topic	Whoever is interested in the common shared topic or concern. Stakeholders from different domains
What holds them together?	Commitment, identification with the group, expertise	Access to information and participation about a collective interest, or concern with the resolution of a particular problem
Membership	Depends on expertise, passion for the topic and participation	Dynamic and depends only on participation
Heterogeneous or homogeneous?	More homogeneous because there is a common expertise or passion for a specific topic	Heterogeneous
Lifespan	Evolve and end organically. They are usually longer-lived than CoIs	Evolve and end organically. More temporary

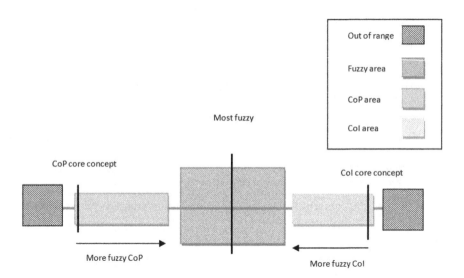

Fig. 7.2 Scale: a continuum space from CoP to CoI

The first area corresponds to structures that resemble CoPs. This means that in this area we will find structures which satisfy fundamental principles already identified for CoPs. The opposite area corresponds to structures that resemble CoIs. These structures must satisfy fundamental principles already identified for CoIs. Finally, between these two areas, we find a fuzzy area composed of structures which do not satisfy all fundamental principles for either CoPs or CoIs. After we have situated the structure in one of the three areas defined in the scale, the "not- fundamental" principles will serve to adjust the accuracy of the classification by situating the structures more or less right or left inside this area.

Fig. 7.3 Stage 3 for CoP area

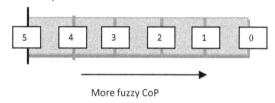

Based on this idea we propose a process to situate a specific structure in the continuum space from CoPs to CoIs. The model is defined by three stages. The first stage is to check that the structure we want to situate is not out of the limits of our scale. The second stage consists of situating the structure in the suitable scale area and the third stage adjusts the accuracy inside this area.

Once we have checked that the structure is inside the limits of our scale, we will move to stage 2. This second stage is the most important one. In this stage, we will assess the specific structure we want to situate based on the fundamental principles described above. Afterwards we will be in one of these three scenarios:

- Satisfy all fundamental principles for CoPs. In that case, we would have a structure that resembles a CoP (left blue area in Fig. 7.2).
- Satisfy all fundamental principles for CoIs. In that case, we would have a structure that resembles a CoI (right green area in Fig. 7.2).
- The structure does not satisfy all fundamental principles for either CoPs or CoIs; for instance, a structure that satisfies three principles for a CoP and one for a CoI. In that case the structure would be in the fuzzy area (middle area in Fig. 7.2).

Finally, in stage 3 we will adjust the position in the scale within the stage 2 selected area. For accomplishing that, we will use the "not fundamental" principles defined above. Firstly, we will divide the stage 2 selected area into a specific number of parts. This number is determined by the number of principles that apply. It is possible that all of the "not fundamental" principles cannot be applied. For instance, if you are situating a structure that has been recently created, maybe you will not be able to identify its lifespan (it is one of the "not fundamental" principles). When you have divided the area you will take into account the number of not fundamental principles that the particular structure satisfies. Based on this number we will situate the structure this number of positions more left (satisfies more CoP "not fundamental" principles) or right (satisfies more CoI "not fundamental" principles). In order to explain better this stage we are going to divide the problem into three categories, depending on the area selected in the stage before:

- **Case 1, CoP area**. Imagine you can apply all "not fundamental" principles. Before performing stage 2, a structure would be situated at the highest point to the right (point 0, Fig. 7.3). We will check how many "not fundamental" principles for CoPs satisfy the particular structure. If none, the structure would be at the starting point (point 0, Fig. 7.3), if it satisfies one it would be a bit more left

Fig. 7.4 Stage 3 for CoI area

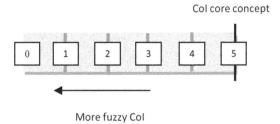

CoI core concept

More fuzzy CoI

(point 1, Fig. 7.3). Then it would be the same process until one checks if it satisfies all principles. If the structure satisfies all the "not fundamental" principles it would be in the CoP core concept (point 4, Fig. 7.3).

- **Case 2, CoI area**. Imagining we could apply all not fundamental principles, the process would then be the same as case 1 but in the opposite direction and taking into account if the structure satisfies CoI not fundamental principles (Fig. 7.4).
- **Case 3, fuzzy area**. Imagine you can apply all not fundamental principles; you will divide the fuzzy area into double the number of "not fundamental" principles (10 parts). Before performing stage 2, a structure would be situated at the middle (point 5, Fig. 7.5). We will check how many not fundamental principles for CoPs and CoIs satisfy the particular structure. For each principle that the particular structure satisfies for CoPs we will add one to the actual point (remember that the initial point is 5). On the other hand, for each principle that it satisfies for CoIs we will subtract one point.

Based on theoretical points, the scale proposed provides an effective way to situate a community in one of the proposed areas (CoP area, CoI area or fuzzy area). However, we must highlight that this scale provides an approximate position inside the selected area. Further work could be related to improving the accuracy inside the selected area by providing different weights to each not fundamental principle according to its importance.

7.5 Conclusions

Complexity of cooperative design problems requires communities to address them [14]. In this sense this work has reviewed and analyzed two effective forms of organization to cooperate and share knowledge, namely Communities of Practice (CoP) and Communities of Interest (CoI). The review of both concepts has shown the lack of a uniform and universally accepted criteria about what these structures mean. Furthermore, the defining characteristics of these structures establish a continuum model from CoP to CoI. Based on these characteristics, this work presents a systematic process aimed at classifying a particular community.

This systematic process allows practitioners to identify which kind of community is more suitable to support a specific cooperative design process. In terms of

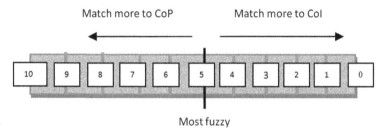

Fig. 7.5 Stage 3 for fuzzy area

collaborative or cooperative design, the CoP could be a better candidate than the CoI. CoPs have a definite goal and set of tasks to be supported, and tend to be longer lived, so that investment in custom software is worthwhile. They have a body of knowledge that needs to be organized into a framework that will allow it to be added to, modified, and rated by members. But, since they have a definite social structure and roles, it is important to identify leaders within the CoP and to include them in the design and evaluation process.

Nevertheless, in some particular cases, the CoI could also be a good structure for cooperative design. CoIs have a great potential for creativity and innovation, gathering different perspectives and backgrounds to explore a new solution [14].

In conclusion, each of these structures could be suitable, depending on the particular features of the specific design process. For instance, a cooperative design to create a new and innovative artefact will need a structure to encourage creativity, diversity and exploration of alternatives in breadth. In this case, it could seem more suitable to rely on the idea of CoIs as a structure to support cooperative design. However, a cooperative design to refine an existing artefact will need an initial well-established knowledge of the existing artefact and examination of the problem in depth. This is more related to the idea of CoPs.

Future work could include studying the different ways that practitioners perform cooperative design, providing a taxonomy for communities of design.

Acknowledgments This work has been partly supported by the urTHEY project (TIN2009-09687) funded by the Ministry of Science and Innovation (MICINN) of *the Government of Spain.* Dr Hiltz's work on this project was supported by a Cátedra de Excelencia appointment at U. Carlos III of Madrid for 2010–2011.

References

1. Fischer, G.: From reflective practitioners to reflective communities. In: Proceedings of the HCI international conference (HCII) (2005)
2. Wenger, E., McDermontt, R., Snyder, W.M.: Cultivating Communities of Practice. Harvard Business Press, Boston (2002)
3. Hildreth, P., Kimble, C.: Knowledge Networks: Innovation Through Communities of Practice. Idea Group Publishing, London (2004)

4. McDermott, R.: Nurturing three dimensional communities of practice: how to make the most out of human networks. Knowl. Manag. Rev. 2(5) 26–29 (1999)
5. Carotenuto, L., Etienne, W., Fontaine, M., Friedman, J., Muller, M., Newberg, H., Simpson, M., Slusher, J., Stevenson, K.: Community Space: Toward Flexible Support for Voluntary Knowledge Communities. Changing Places workshop, London (1999)
6. Allee, V.: Knowledge Networks and Communities of Practice. OD Practitioner. http://www.odnetwork.org/odponline/vol32n4/knowledgenets.html (2000). Accessed 2 Sept 2011
7. Fischer, G.: Communities of interest: learning through the interaction of multiple knowledge systems. In: Proceedings of the 24th Annual Information Systems Research Seminar in Scandinavia, Norway (2001)
8. Cox, A.: What are communities of practice? A comparative review of four seminal works. J. Inf. Sci. 31(6) 527–540 (2005)
9. Wenger, E.: Communities of Practice: Learning, Meaning and Identity. Cambridge University Press, Cambridge (1998)
10. Nousala, S., William, P.H.: Emerging Autopoietic Communities—Scalability of Knowledge Transfer in Complex Systems. 2008 IFIP International Conference on Network and Parallel Computing (2008)
11. Wenger, E., Snyder, W.M.: Communities of practice: The organizational frontier. Harv. Bus. Rev. (2000)
12. Andriessen, J.H.E.: Knowledge Communities in Fives. Delft Innovation System Papers (2006)
13. Lave, J., Wenger, E.: Situated Learning: Legitimate Peripheral Participation. Cambridge University Press, Cambridge (1991)
14. Fischer, G., Ostwald, J.: Knowledge communication in design communities. In: Bromme, R., Hesse, F., Spada, H. (eds.) Barriers and Biases in Computer-mediated Knowledge Communication and How They May Be Overcome. Kluwer Academic, Dordrecht (2005)

Chapter 8
The Trouble with 'Knowledge Transfer': On Conduit Metaphors and Semantic Pathologies in Our Understanding of Didactic Practice

Lars Rune Christensen

Abstract It is a feature central to cooperative work that practitioners develop and maintain their collective competences and skills, and one will in many settings find elaborate didactic practices that reflect this state of affairs. The concept of 'knowledge transfer' that plays a key role in the knowledge management research area offers an obvious framework to the study of mutual learning. However, the notion of 'knowledge transfer' is a semantic pathology despite its widespread use in academia and everyday language, or more precisely, it is a conduit metaphor that mystify the very concept of didactic practice. The argument is that we need to abandon the conduit metaphor all together and present a viable alternative. In this paper we suggest that talking about 'didactic practice' is one such alternative and substantiate this assertion by presenting an ethnographic study of didactic practice in the building process.

8.1 Introduction

It is a feature central to cooperative work that practitioners develop and maintain their collective competences and skills, and one will in many settings find elaborate didactic practices that reflect this state of affairs. These aspects of cooperative work are pertinent to CSCW and the concept of 'knowledge transfer' that plays a key role in the knowledge management research area offers an obvious framework. However, the notion of 'knowledge transfer' is a semantic pathology, or more precisely, a conduit metaphor that mystify the very concept of didactic practice. The notion of 'knowledge transfer' may be deemed a conduit metaphor as it alludes to the (false) idea that knowledge is somehow a thing that may be transferred by the conduit of words and information technology from actor A to actor B. Contrary to what is often assumed, then, the notion of 'knowledge transfer' tends to impair and obscure the CSCW essential focus on actual didactic practices.

L. R. Christensen (✉)
IT-University of Copenhagen, Rued Langgaards vej 7, 2300 Copenhagen S, Denmark
e-mail: Lrc@itu.dk

J. Dugdale et al. (eds.), *From Research to Practice in the Design of Cooperative Systems:*   111
Results and Open Challenges, DOI 10.1007/978-1-4471-4093-1_8,
© Springer-Verlag London 2012

The ironic thing is that although a large number of studies within CSCW and related research fields (e.g. [2–5]) are very critical of the notion of 'knowledge transfer' i.e. that knowledge is a thing that can be stored, retrieved, and distributed in a thing-like manner through the conduit of information technology, the term or metaphor remains in heavy use.[1] Szulanski ([10], p. 12), for example, state in a well cited article that "even though transfers of knowledge are often laborious, time consuming, and difficult, current conceptions treat them as essentially costless and instantaneous." It appears that the notion of 'knowledge transfer' is hardly mentioned without being criticized in the same breath (at least in academia) for in one way or the other making allusions to unproblematic conduit of knowledge from one person to the next and yet its use as an analytical category seem to flourish unhindered. Perhaps, and this is the assertion here, this is because of a lack of a better alternative.

In this paper it is pointed out that talking about 'didactic practices' is a viable alternative to using the misleading metaphor 'knowledge transfer' in the study of mutual learning in cooperative work. This assertion is substantiated by presenting an ethnographic study of didactic practice in the building process. In this manner this article attempt to contribute to the critical agenda and share the critical spirit of the work of for example Huysman and de Wit's [4], Fitzpatrick [3], Bansler and Havn [2], and Huysman and Wulf [5]. The critical literature on 'knowledge management' relocates the problem of knowledge and mutual learning in a number of ways, stressing issues such as the social distribution of expertise, and the importance of 'who knows', as well as the contextual nature of much knowledge articulation, use, and mutual learning. Not least, it reminds us that not all solutions are technical solutions. Broadly speaking, this study shares this outlook. More specifically, the contribution of this paper is to point out that talking about 'didactic practices', rather than 'knowledge transfer' will make our lives as CSCW researchers and practitioners much simpler as it presents us with a way out of the conceptual muddle than is the notion of 'knowledge transfer'.

We will proceed in the following manner. First we will discuss 'knowledge transfer' as a conduit metaphor. Secondly, we will consider the methods of our ethnographic study. Third, we will present and investigate a case of didactic practice in the building process. Fourth, we will discuss our findings. Finally, a conclusion and some perspectives will be provided.

8.2 Knowledge Transfer as a Conduit Metaphor

As mentioned above, although opposition to the notion of unproblematic 'knowledge transfer' is present in CSCW and related research fields (see e.g. [2–5]), the very expression or metaphor 'knowledge transfer' is far from being stamped out in

---

[1] A search on 'knowledge transfer' in the ACM Digital Library (http://dl.acm.org/) returns no fewer than 18,307 results (on December 8, 2011).

everyday language and academic discourse.[2] What is it about the term 'knowledge transfer' that makes it so pervasive still? The short answer is that 'knowledge transfer' is a conduit metaphor, a semantic pathology, pervasive to the English language in general and this is why it is so resilient even in the face of relentless critique from CSCW and elsewhere. Let us elaborate.

The eminent linguist Michael J. Reddy [9] coined the term *the conduit metaphor* in an effort to describe what he regarded as a semantic pathology pervasive to the English language. According to Reddy, the English language alone hosts more than a hundred expressions based on what he calls 'the conduit metaphor' [9]. Reddy calls it 'the conduit metaphor', because it implies that thoughts or ideas are transferred from actor A to actor B through some conduit or other. Reddy argues that it is almost impossible for an English speaker to discuss communication without committing to some form or other of that metaphor. A Conduit metaphor is a linguistic term, then, referring to a dominant class of figurative expressions used when discussing communication itself.

In his seminal article Reddy [9] discussed the conduit metaphor's distorting potential in culture and society. For example, he points out that the expression 'You'll *find* better *ideas* than that *in the library*' is a conduit metaphor asserting that ideas are in words, which are on pages, which are in books, which are in libraries—with the result that "ideas are in libraries." One implication is that libraries full of books, tapes, photographs, videos and electronic media contain 'culture'.

Importantly, according to Reddy there are no ideas in the words; therefore, none in libraries. Instead, there are patterns of marks, bumps or magnetized particles capable of creating patterns of noise and light. Using these patterns people can (re) construct content such as for example a cultural heritage.

Because culture does not exist in books or libraries, people must continually reconstruct it. Libraries preserve the opportunity to perform this reconstruction, but if language skills and the competences of reconstruction are not preserved, there will be no culture. Thus, Reddy asserts that the only way to preserve culture is to train people to 'regrow' it in others.

He stresses that the difference of viewpoint between the conduit metaphor and his view is profound. Humanists—those traditionally charged with reconstructing culture and teaching others to reconstruct it—are increasingly rare. Reddy proposes that, despite a sophisticated system for mass communication, there is actually less communication; and moreover, that people are following a flawed manual. The conduit-metaphor influenced view is that the more marks and signals moved and preserved, the more ideas "transferred" and "stored." Society is thus often neglecting the human ability to reconstruct meaning such as cultural heritage based on e.g. marks on the pages of books. This ability atrophies when what is deemed 'extraction' is seen as a trivial process not requiring instruction past a rudimentary level [9].

---

[2] A search on "knowledge transfer" in Google Scholar (http://scholar.google.com/) returns no fewer than 102,000 results (on December 8, 2011).

Reddy concludes that the conduit metaphor may continue to have negative technological and social consequences: mass communications systems that largely ignore the achievement of (re)construction of meaning and the skills that go into it. Because the logical framework of the conduit metaphor indicates that people "capture ideas in words"—despite there being no ideas "within" the ever-increasing stream of words—a burgeoning public may be less culturally informed than expected [9]. In this manner Reddy convincingly describes the distorting potential that conduit metaphors may have on culture and society at large.

Moving form society at large to concerns more specific to CSCW we may, following Reddy [9], ask this: What are the distorting potential of the metaphor 'knowledge transfer' on knowledge management and the design of knowledge management systems?

Turning to a widely cited review article in MIS Quarterly by Alavi and Leidner [1] may give us part of the answer. Without referring to the work of Reddy or the linguistic term 'conduit metaphor', Alavi and Leidner [1] describe how the 'knowledge management' literature has been plagued by the entire repertoire of conceptual pathologies associated with the conduit metaphor: 'Knowledge' as an 'object', something that can be 'encoded, stored, and transmitted' [1].

Furthermore, the experience with 'knowledge management systems' has often been one of disappointment. Considerable effort and resources have been invested in the development and deployment of such systems but with very few results in terms of productivity and profitability to show for it (see e.g. [2, 7, 8]). To take but one example from the literature:

> A good example of how information technology alone cannot increase the leverage of professional knowledge comes from a large consumer products company. As part of reorganization, the company decided to improve professional work. Professional staff was instructed to document their key work processes in an electronic database. It was a hated task. Most staff felt their work was too varied to capture in a set of procedures. But after much berating by senior managers about being "disciplined," they completed the task. Within a year the database was populated, but little used. Most people found it too general and generic to be useful. The help they needed to improve their work processes and *share learning* was not contained in it. The result was an expensive and useless information junkyard. Creating an information system without understanding what knowledge professionals needed, or the form and level of detail they needed, did little to leverage knowledge. ([6], p. 104)

In this manner McDermott [6] describe a common experience of failed 'knowledge management systems' and give us a window into the consequences of the use of conduit metaphors when performing knowledge management and designing knowledge management systems. McDermott [6] does not himself attribute these troubles with pervasive use of conduit metaphors in the English language—this is the argument that we are trying to make.

It turns out, then, that just as there were consequences for the use of conduit metaphors in relation to culture and society at large (recall the Reddy's case above), there are grave consequences using conduit metaphors when performing and studying knowledge management and designing knowledge management systems. As indicated above, it may for example lead to the (uncritical) assumption that knowledge is a thing that can be managed in the sense of being stored, retrieved, and distributed in a thing-like manner through the conduit of information technology.

How do we move forward? An analytical concepts or category such as 'knowledge transfer' does not loose its misleading allusions merely by being criticised again and again in the literature. It is too deeply entranced in our discourse and everyday language to be altered or tempered by criticism alone—no matter how sophisticated and well argued this critique may be. That is, critique of the notion of 'knowledge transfer' is not enough we need to abandon this conduit metaphor all together.

Abandoning the use of a well-entranced conduit metaphor such as 'knowledge transfer' involves presenting an alternative; it involves supplanting it, not with another conduit metaphor, but with something different. What are the alternatives then? There are perhaps many. We will in all modestly present one, namely, to speak of 'didactic practice' instead of 'knowledge transfer'. The notion of 'didactic practice' takes as its starting point those activities of the actors that are centred on developing and maintaining the collective competences and skills of the cooperative ensemble, rather than alluding to the effortless and instantaneous. The rendering of the case below will serve as a substantiation of this argument. Before moving on to our case we will consider the methods of the study.

8.3 Methods

The case presented below springs from (part of) an ethnographic fieldwork carried out in the course of 14 months on a building sites and architectural offices. In this period, work within the domains of architecture, engineering and construction was studied. The building project, the development of the new domicile for a publishing house, is a multi-storey building in glass, steel and concrete constructed at the city of Copenhagen's waterfront. It is a relatively large building of 18,000 m² distributed across eight floors. A combination of observation and interviews was used. The fieldwork also included collecting (scanning, taking screenshots or photographs of) artifacts used and produced by the actors engaged in the building project.

8.4 A Case of Didactic Practice in Construction Engineering

We will now turn to an investigation of didactic practice in the building process where an apprentice and an accomplished actor engage in didactic activities as part of their cooperative work practice. We will do so in an attempt to show that talking about didactic practice represents a viable alternative to engaging in studies of 'knowledge transfer'. Let us commence and start by providing some context.

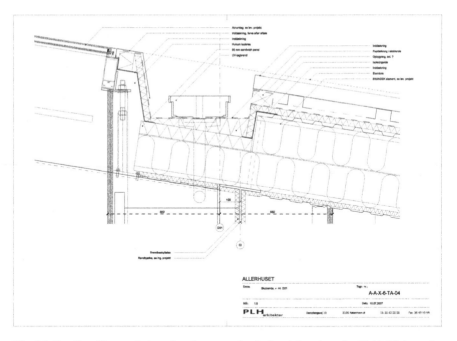

Fig. 8.1 Detail architectural plan of roof construction before it is coloured with highlighters for coordinative purposes

An accomplished practitioner and an apprentice are engaged in coordinating building construction work on a large project advanced to the latter stages of construction work, more precisely, the construction of the roof. The physical location for the case studied is the site manager's trailer on a construction site. Complex roof construction work requires the coordination of a diverse ensemble of actors (i.e. various contractors such as carpenters, plumbers, electricians, roofers etc.) each performing a range of specialised construction task.

The particular representation, shown in Fig. 8.1, is of a *section view*, a view from the side virtually cut through the building. It shows the roof construction around a drainage. To demarcate what the team believes to be different areas of responsibility, the architectural plan is marked with highlighter pens in different colours. For example, blue marks the area that one particular subcontractor is responsible for, and yellow is the colour for another. This is a task that involves two people. One assesses the areas of responsibility, he reports the area out loud, e.g. "the roofing felt is going to cover the sandwich panels—KBK should do this." A second engineer marks the area in question. After finding the right area on the architectural plan he highlights it with the chosen colour. What we find here is a practice that encompasses talk, architectural plans and writing tools as the two actors collaborate on inscribing areas of responsibility onto the architectural plans (subsequently these plans are scanned and sent as PDF files to the various subcontractors involved in order to inform them of their responsibilities as seen by the manager). It is in this context that the didactic activities that we are going to investigate plays out.

The action that we will now consider begins with a request from Peter, the caller, to Steen, the colourer (lines 1–2).

1. Peter: The roofing felt is going to cover the sandwich panel
2. KBK[3] should do this.
3. (Pause)
4. No, No. Not there.

However, before Steen, who is an apprentice, has coloured anything, indeed before he has said a word, Peter, who is his manager, challenges him, telling him what he is doing is wrong. How does he know that there is something wrong with what Steen hasn't even done yet? Here no talk has yet been produced by Steen, but talk is not the point. Providing an answer in this practice encompasses something other than talk. Steen must locate and colour the relevant part of the architectural plan in order to respond according to Peter's expectations. His movement of the highlighter to what Peter regards as the wrong place on the architectural plan is the visible event that prompts Peter's intervention (line 4). However, Steen's response to the correction calls this presupposition into question. Steen does not immediately colour the architectural plan but instead hesitates (line 5), before replying with an "hmm".

5. Steen: (Pause) Hmm.
6. Peter: Wherever the roofing felt goes.
7. Steen: Ahh.

In line 6 Peter moves from request to coaching by talking to Steen and telling him what to look for in the architectural plan, i.e., "Wherever the roofing felt goes".[4] In the present case, in order to use what Peter has just said in their collaborative effort, Steen must be able to find the course of the roofing felt in the plan—knowing what 'roofing felt' means in the abstract is not enough. Wittgenstein notes: "If language is to be a means of communication there must be agreement not only in definitions but also (queer as it may sound) in judgments" ([12], p. 75, § 242). As the manager setting the task, Peter is in a position to evaluate Steen's practical judgment.

8. (Pause)
9. Peter: See, like right here, and down here.
10. (Tracks it with a pen across the architectural plan)
11. Steen: All right, yeah ok.

In line 10, instead of relying on talk alone to reveal the course of the material in question that Peter wants Steen to colour, Peter moves his pen onto the architectural plan and tracks the course of the roofing material. He shows it to him in the plan. What Steen is taught is not simply 'definitions' (he already knows what 'roofing felt' means in the abstract), but rather a practice, i.e. how to code the relevant perceptual field in terms of categories that are relevant for his work. The activity in

---

[3] KBK is the acronym for a subcontractor that was responsible for some elements of the roof construction.

[4] Roofing felt' is also sometimes referred to as 'asphalt roofing'.

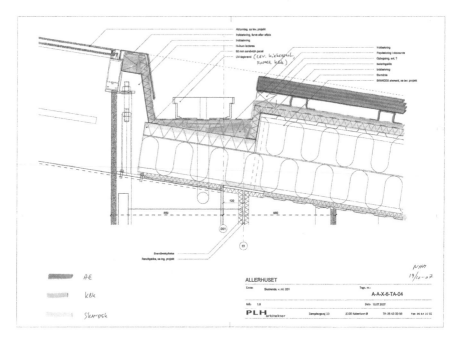

Fig. 8.2 Detail architectural plan of roof construction after it has been sketch with highlighters for coordinative purposes

progress, including the sequence of talk, provides a language game in which these judgments are taught, a language game about precisely which features of the complex perceptual field in question to attend to. Peter is instructing Steen how to 'see' the architectural plan.

As master and novice carry on planning the construction of the roof, further tasks are delimited, pointed out and assigned to particular contractors.

12. Peter: Right (Pause)
13. Scandek is supposed to mount their elements.
14. Steen: The roof slab?
15. (Points to the architectural plan)
16. Peter: Yes.

In this manner the task continues until the result shown in Fig. 8.2 is reached. In line 12–16 yet another part of the roof construction is assigned to a particular contractor. That is, the responsibility for mounting the central reinforced concrete roof slab is assigned to a subcontractor named 'Scandek'.

As indicated above, we could suggest that what happens within this sequence of didactic activities internal to the cooperative work practice of the actors is a not least a progressive expansion of Steen's ability to comprehend what he must do in order to carry out the task assigned to him as Peter explicates it. We could suggest that 'patches of ignorance' on the part of Steen are revealed and transformed into practical ability sufficient to get the job done. Steen is gradually able to grasp what it is Peter wants him to do and how to see the architectural plan in order to do it (note how casting these activities in terms of 'knowledge transfer' could easily gloss over the work involved here).

Furthermore, according to Wittgenstein [12, e.g. § 143–155, § 179–181], the situation for the novice or apprentice is in stark contrast to that of the accomplished actor. Wittgenstein differentiates the role of the two participants in didactic practice ([11], p. 204), and it is this that we may highlight with reference to our case. The accomplished actor momentarily acting in the capacity of teacher is the one whose judgment is unchallenged precisely because he has mastered the practice himself, and now he sets the standards for what is correct as far as the apprentice is concerned. The apprentice does not have and is not required to have all the skills or techniques that are necessary for the successful participation in practice. As indicated above, this differentiation enables the accomplished actor to extend a courtesy or show consideration for the shortcomings of the apprentice's performance. The stage setting, the background necessary for judgment, is within the domain of the accomplished practitioner. That is, the behaviour of the apprentice is shaped and made intelligible by the competences of the accomplished actor. In this manner, the background for judgment of the apprentice's actions is the competence of the accomplished actor who masters the practice, and in this process of 'judgement' or guidance the practice is explicated (albeit to a limited degree).

In addition, it would be quite wrong to delimit the unit within which this is lodged as comprised of solely the two actors Steen and Peter. Instead the unit (with very soft boundaries) is the building process understood as a community of practice or set of related communities of practice within which the skills of building engineering and the task in question are lodged. The skill to handle the task, including the complex perceptual field of the architectural plans, and to see for instance 'where the roofing felt goes', is central to what it means to see the world through the eyes of a building engineer. Being able to highlight certain aspects of a representation of a building according to a specific task is part of what it means to be an accomplished building engineer, and it is these standards that Steen is being held accountable to—standards that also include mastery of techniques such as scale and projection discussed above. The relevant unit of analysis, then, is not these two individuals as an isolated entity, rather it is the wider building process where a community of competent practitioners are engaged, most of whom have never meet each other, but who nonetheless expect each other to categorise and act in this domain in ways that are relevant and predictable and pertain to the work, tools and artifacts that constitute the community of practice, including the didactic activities within it.

8.5 Discussion

In contrast to the conduit metaphor, the view of didactic practice, as we have attempted to cast it in the case above, does not rely on the notion of knowledge as a thing that may be propelled back and forth between actors like a tennis ball in a game of tennis. In didactic practice there is no fixed form of meaning that may be transferred from actor A to Actor B through the conduit of words, artifacts and computer systems. Hence, the fallacy of expressions such as 'knowledge transfer'. In contrast, actors in cooperative work continually have to reconstruct and maintain their collective competences and skills in elaborate didactic practices that may be part of their cooperative efforts as in the case above. This is based on the fact that there are no ideas or fixed forms of meaning in the words, drawing or artifacts. Instead, there are patterns of marks, bumps or magnetized particles capable of creating patterns of signs. Using these patterns actors can (re)construct content appropriate to the norms and rules internal to their community of practice given that they have the competences and skills. Whether constructing meaning based on e.g. the artifacts of a given practice is easy, hard or even possible dependents on the skills and experience of the individual actor. Maintaining and developing such skills is crucial to cooperative work practice. In the case presented above we saw how the apprentice, mentored by the experienced engineer, had a steady expansion of his practical ability to construct meaning and get the job done based on the marks and signs on the architectural plans before him. Talking about 'knowledge transfer' in this context will only mystify and obscure what is actually going on. The conduit metaphor mystifies, and even as it is being critiqued heavily, its semantic pathology persists buried deep in our everyday language as exposed by Reddy [9]. It must be abandoned. As stated in the introduction, we must shift our focus to the actual didactic practices that are part of cooperative work and see how they are integrated with cooperative work practice. We must do so in order to move forward. This is in line with the impressive efforts conducted elsewhere in the CSCW community (see e.g. [2–5]).

8.6   Conclusion and Perspectives

In this article is has been argued that investigations of mutual learning in cooperative work may take as their starting point the analytical category of didactic practice, rather than frame the such activities in terms of 'knowledge transfer'. This position spring from the observation that the term or metaphor 'knowledge transfer', despite its continued widespread use in academia and everyday language, is a conduit metaphor that obscures the actual didactic practices pertinent to CSCW. Relying on a conduit metaphor such as 'knowledge transfer' may for example lead to the (uncritical) assumption that knowledge is a thing that can be managed, i.e. stored, retrieved, and distributed, in a thing-like manner through the conduit of information technology.

The situation is acerbated by the fact that the notion of 'knowledge transfer' and associated allusions does not loose their misleading qualities merely by being criticized again and again in the CSCW community and elsewhere. The conduit metaphor in general is too deeply entranced in our discourse and everyday language to be altered or tempered by criticism alone—no matter how sophisticated and well argued this critique may be. We need to abandon the conduit metaphor, in all its variations, all together and present a viable alternative. In this paper we have suggested that talking about 'didactic practice' is one such alternative and have substantiated this assertion by presenting an analysis of didactic practice in the building process. This is in line with important CSCW research on the subject.

The challenge for CSCW emerging from this is to focus on the actual didactic practices that are part of cooperative work and see how they are an integrated part of cooperative activities. We must look and see in order to move forward.

Acknowledgments A warm thanks goes to the employees of PLH Arkitekter A/S as well as E. Pihl & Søn A/S for allowing me to take up so much of their time. In addition, the contributions of the anonymous reviewers are greatly appreciated.

References

1. Alavi, M., Leidner, D.: Knowledge management and knowledge management systems: conceptual foundations and research issues. MIS Q. **25**(1), 107–136 (2001)
2. Bansler, J., Havn, E.: Building community knowledge systems: an empirical study of IT-support for sharing best practices among managers. Knowl. Process. Manag. **10**(3), 156–163 (2003)
3. Fitzpatrick, G.: Emergent expertise sharing in a new community. In: Ackerman, M., Pipek, V., Wulf, V. (eds.) Sharing Expertise: Beyond Knowledge Management, pp. 77–106. The MIT Press, Cambridge (2003)
4. Huysman, M., de Wit, D: A critical evaluation of knowledge management practices. In: Ackerman, M., Pipek, V., Wulf, V. (eds.) Sharing Expertise, pp. 27–57. The MIT Press, Cambridge (2003)
5. Huysman, M., Wulf, V.: IT to support knowledge sharing in communities: towards a social capital analysis. J. Inform. Technol. **21**, 40–51 (2006)
6. McDermott, R.: Why information technology inspired but cannot deliver knowledge management. Calif. Manag. Rev. **41**, 103–117 (1999)
7. Newell, S., Scarbrough, H., Swan, J.: From global knowledge management to internal electronic fences: contradictory outcomes of intranet development. Br. J. Manag. Learn. **12**, 91–111 (2001)
8. Orlikowski, W.J.: Learning from NOTES: organizational issues in groupware implementation. In: Mantei, M.M., Baecker, R.M., Krau, R.E. (eds.) Proceedings of the Conference on Computer-supported Cooperative Work, 31 October–4 November 1992, Toronto, Canada, pp. 362–369. ACM Press, New York (1992)
9. Reddy, M.J.: The conduit metaphor: a case of frame conflict in our language about language. In: Ortony, A. (ed.) Metaphor and Thought. Cambridge University Press, Cambridge (1979)
10. Szulanski, G.: The process of knowledge transfer: a diachronic analysis of stickiness. Organ. Behav. Hum. Decis. Process. **82**(1), 9–27 (2000)
11. Williams, M.: Wittgenstein, Mind and Meaning: Towards a Social Conception of Mind. Routledge, London (1999)
12. Wittgenstein, L.: Philosophical Investigations. Blackwell, Oxford (2001)

Chapter 9
Divergence and Convergence in Global Software Development: Cultural Complexities as Social Worlds

Rasmus Eskild Jensen and Pernille Bjørn

Abstract This study reports the results of a workplace study of globally distributed software development projects in a global software company. We investigated cultural complexities as social worlds and sought to understand how differences in social worlds between geographically distributed developers become salient in their everyday interactions. By analysing both interviews and observations we identified two types of situations where social worlds become salient in the everyday interactions between developers working at different geographical locations: (1) the divergence of concept and meaning and (2) the convergence of concept but divergence of meaning. We argue that these situations are grounded in social worlds and pose a challenge to work practices in the form of miscommunication and misinterpretation of shared tasks.

9.1 Introduction

Working in globally distributed teams is increasingly becoming the norm for many large international organizations. Globally distributed work settings are malleable and allow work to be transferred across organizational, national, and cultural boundaries [1], which is attractive for organizations involved with flexible and transferable work like software development. Despite the numerous benefits of globally distributed work settings, there are challenges to coordinating work across sites, including establishing common ground [2], creating suitable work practices [3], and overcoming cultural differences [4]. One key challenge for global software development (GSD) concerns communicating and interpreting implicit knowledge, which is not easily shared out of context [5]. Implicit knowledge is socially embedded within work practices and it is not easily shared across contexts. Communication

R. E. Jensen (✉) · P. Bjørn
IT University of Copenhagen, Technologies in Practice, Rued Langgaards Vej 7,
2300 Copenhagen S, Denmark
e-mail: raej@itu.dk

P. Bjørn
e-mail: pbra@itu.dk

J. Dugdale et al. (eds.), *From Research to Practice in the Design of Cooperative Systems:*   123
Results and Open Challenges, DOI 10.1007/978-1-4471-4093-1_9,
© Springer-Verlag London 2012

requires the development of common ground, and common ground is established through grounded processes [6]. When people collaborate and communicate across social and geographical boundaries, such as languages, organizations, and national borders, the risk of misunderstanding and misinterpretation is high.

Investigating communication complexities in geographically distributed situations, CSCW researchers have examined how people with different national cultures interact with each other and apply different types of media [7–9]. Such studies refer to intercultural communication in terms of national culture, with many referring to Hofstede's [11] different dimensions of understanding the disparities between, for example, Western and Asian countries [10]. However, this perspective on culture as a stable entity has recently come under fire, and it has been suggested that culture should instead be investigated as a social construction between people [11]. We join other CSCW researchers [5] in taking a practice-based approach to examining the cultural complexities in GSD by dealing with the issue of culture as part of practice rather than a stable construct based on nationality. GSD is an interesting area to investigate geographically dispersed collaboration because this type of work comprises closely coupled collaborative tasks and, as such, requires a lot of communication.

While we agree that culture beneficially can be understood as a social construct, we discovered particularly complex and pertinent aspects of communication in our empirical case. These aspects can be linked to the society in which the participants are situated and, as such, are related to culture. This observation made us wonder whether we could think about culture as part of practice without submitting to a national culture framework and yet still take the incidents related to society into account. In this study, we suggest that one way to capture the national perspective on culture without submitting to the categories of Hofstede is to think in terms of social worlds. Investigating the communication within GSD, we therefore asked: How can we identify situations where the differences in social worlds between geographically distributed developers become salient in their everyday interactions?

We report on an ethnographic study of GSD practices within an organization that develops IT systems for Danish customers, with developers dispersed across the Philippines and Denmark. The way people work together in GSD is not always apparent. Too often assumptions are made about the task without examining the underlying implicit knowledge embedded within the task. By making visible situations where differences between developers' social worlds are pertinent to the task at hand, we can better understand how social worlds affect collaboration within GSD.

In the following we start by presenting related work on GSD and communication in virtual teams. Then we present the methodology, our empirical case, and the study results. Finally we discuss our empirical observations and offer conclusions.

9.2   Theoretical Framework

Aside from cost-savings and despite increased collaborative challenges, the key motivators for developing software across geographical locations are interest in leveraging knowledge diversity, exploiting knowledge capabilities, and scaling activities [3].

Some of the collaborative challenges in GSD identified through ethnographic studies include awareness of distributed collaborators [12], coordination [13], and organizational learning [14]. While these are all important, several researchers have pointed to communicating and interpreting the requirement specifications of the IT system under development as a key challenge [e.g. 15, 16].

One of the visions for GSD in any given project is to achieve a shared understanding of the system requirements across the various local sites that are part of the project. System requirements are a key artefact of collaborative practices in all types of software development, and they are used to guide, negotiate, coordinate, and communicate about the tasks shared between developers. However, communication is also considerably more difficult across geographical distances because many details need to be made explicit, yet knowledge is often taken for granted. Empirical workplace studies of GSD have shown that the interpretation of system requirements often causes problems and, in some cases, delays projects or even reduces the quality of the final product [16, 17].

One strategy for solving this problem is process standardization, stipulating explicit and detailed requirements. Many large global IT companies (e.g., Infosys and TCS) have chosen this strategy. However, recent studies of GSD question the standardization approach because it restricts a company's flexibility and agility, which may be its core competencies [e.g. 3]. If standardization alone is not the solution, we need to find alternative strategies for dealing with the interpretation of inexplicit system requirements created using taken-for-granted knowledge and background assumptions.

9.2.1 From Culture to Social Worlds

To investigate how taken-for-granted knowledge and background assumptions affect communication concerning system requirement specifications in GSD, we need a theoretical perspective from which we can examine collaborative practices across cultural boundaries. We define culture as a "reference framework, which stipulates roles and interpretations, and which is dynamically negotiated by the actors in the course of their daily work" ([5], p. 20). This view of culture comprises multi-layered assemblages of intertwined practices, values, beliefs, and attitudes that cannot be isolated or directly examined. It includes lived experiences that guide people's behaviour and attitudes, which consist of unarticulated and taken-for-granted knowledge and beliefs ([18], p. 229). In this way, culture serves as implicit directions shaping the interpretation of events. In a collaborative situation culture operates as a filter through which collaborators can observe and interpret the actions of others ([19], p. 133). While it is impossible to study culture as an isolated factor in collaborative practice, we can study culture by examining the manifestations of culture in practice. This approach to studying culture entails investigating practices, artefacts, and activities as they emerge within GSD with the focus of identifying situations where particular cultural aspects are pertinent for interpreting the situation. However, the question remains how to address cultural aspects when investigating the practical circumstances in GSD.

In collaborative practices, cultural differences are most often invisible until a communication breakdown occurs. Communication breakdowns in geographically distributed teams appear to take place within a shared meaning context comprising three levels: work practice, organization practice, and life world practice ([18], p. 231). Importantly, although a communication breakdown may appear at the work practice level, it might be grounded in either the organizational or the life world level. Thus, we are focused on identifying situations in which communication challenges experienced as part of the work practice level are grounded in the life world level. We speculate that essential miscommunications derived from the life world level are grounded in the social worlds that the participants have grown up and lived their lives in. We propose that the meaning participants assign to particular situations or their understanding of a common task is dependent on the background knowledge they have internalized as part of living in particular social worlds [20]. Social worlds can be described as the institutions and notions about society that is shared among a larger population of people. The social worlds influence our perception and understanding of particular incidents we encounter, including communicating with colleagues who are globally dispersed from us.

By investigating situations where social worlds become salient in the everyday work practice we hope to conceptualize and understand how cultural differences affect communication between geographically dispersed participants involved in GSD.

9.3   Methods

To answer the research question, we chose workplace studies as our methodological approach [21]. Workplace studies seek to investigate and observe the world as it is and try to understand how people act in the world, making it a suitable approach for investigating communication between practitioners during their everyday interactions. The focus of our case study was GlobalSoft, a GSD company of Danish origin with 1,500 employees. Typically clients contact GlobalSoft with particular needs for a new IT system; GlobalSoft also answers public calls for tender specifying the requirements for proposed IT systems. Regardless of how the connection between GlobalSoft and the client is created, all projects begin with key negotiations about the scope of the project. In most cases GlobalSoft negotiates directly with the client, with little or no involvement from offshore partners. Once the project scope is defined, it is divided into tasks, some or all of which are sent to the Philippines, depending on the project. The Filipino department's only input on the project prior to this is when they are asked to do a task proposal estimating the number of hours required for at given task. One of the key documents in this process is the requirement specification, which is meant to define the scope of the entire software project.

As part of a large research project on GSD, we initiated a workplace study with GlobalSoft in November 2010 (study ongoing). In total, three researchers conducted 22 audio-recorded interviews (14 in Denmark, 8 in Philippines) lasting 30–60 min (average 50 min). Practices were observed in Manila, Philippines, for approximately 180 h over three periods (December 2010, July 2011, November 2011). In Copenhagen, Denmark, observations of a particular project were conducted for approximately 80 h. Four workshops (two in Denmark, two in Philippines) were conducted, and various documents and presentations were collected. Employees at many different organizational levels were interviewed, allowing us to compare perceptions of the corporate vice president of GSD with those of the developers.

9.4 Results

We documented several incidents where the challenges developers experienced could not be explained by normal communication issues like trust [2] or social context [22]. Instead, these incidents were related to the local social worlds of the different participants. Here we present four examples of situations where the differences in social worlds between geographically distributed developers become salient in their everyday interactions: Prescriptions and pharmacy, CVR and CPR, food and health inspections, and retirement plans. We also present two examples of social worlds at work: Inventory facility management system and children with special needs.

9.4.1 Diversities in Social Worlds

9.4.1.1 Prescription and Pharmacy

Our data suggest that the Danish employees often experienced their Filipino colleagues misinterpreting or misunderstanding the intended meaning of the requirement specification. The requirement specification contains overall descriptions of all the tasks for a given project. But the descriptions of the tasks are often part of a predefined context, which is the result of assumptions that are embedded in the requirement specification and which can cause misinterpretations and misunderstandings. A Danish manager from GlobalSoft explained the situation:

> [The Danes] should also understand that they [the Filipinos] may not recognize everything. That they spend time talking about what a prescription is. And what a pharmacist is. (Manager)

The manager quoted above spoke about how different understandings of a concept can influence the project. In this example he mentioned prescriptions and pharmacists as concepts that were perceived differently by the Filipinos. In Denmark, all pharmacists have undergone 5 years of university training and are strictly governed by official authorities. All prescriptions are sorted in IT systems and are efficiently monitored by the authorities. Doctors authorize prescriptions after patient consultations and submit them to a general database that all pharmacists can access. Patients can then go to the nearest pharmacy and collect the medicine. The Danish manager recognized that the Filipino employees might not fully comprehend the complexities of how prescriptions and pharmacies are integrated and administrated by the officials in the Danish system. It therefore became essential to talk about what a prescription or a pharmacist was to develop a common understanding of these concepts. The manager was describing the challenge of understanding the local context of Danish pharmacies and prescriptions—a challenge grounded in the social worlds between the Danish and Filipino employees.

9.4.1.2   CVR and CPR

A Danish IT architect described the challenge of communicating possible differences in social worlds:

> But there are also some things we take for granted. I do not need to tell a Danish programmer what a CPR number is, or a CVR number, or many other things, because we take it for granted…. But when we are speaking with the Filipinos…then it is not certain that they have the same knowledge. Such cultural issues, which are something we [the Danes] all know about, are not known outside the borders of the country. And that can easily cause misunderstandings. (IT-architect)

The IT architect described the Danish Central Personal Registry number (CPR), which is unique to Denmark. Every Danish citizen is given a CPR number at birth used as identification for every Danish citizen. In some ways it is equivalent to a social security number, except that it is not optional; everyone must have one. All interactions between the public and the municipalities or the government such as healthcare, taxes, day care, and education, are managed through a CPR number. Thus, the CPR number in an integral part of the social world in Denmark. However, the extensive use of the CPR registration is viewed as controversial in other countries, such as United States, where it is often perceived as unnecessary governmental control of citizens in a democratic country. This example illustrates that outside of Denmark, the concept of the CPR is not fully comprehended, yet the development of IT systems for Danish institutions will require a comprehensive understanding of the concept and the criteria surrounding it. The Central Company Registry number (CVR) is used for registered companies of a certain size. Companies with revenue of 50,000 Danish kroner or more have to register for a CVR number in a centralized database called Virk.dk and cannot function legally without one. According to the IT architect, there is considerable taken-for-granted knowledge about Danish society that is not easily communicated. This became evident when the Danes were trying to communicate the meaning of the CPR number to their Filipino colleagues, because they lack a shared context.

9.4.1.3 Food and Health Inspections

Another challenge we documented involved communicating the use context for a particular IT system. In 2001, the Danish government initiated a public food inspection program in an attempt to secure the health of Danish citizens. Inspectors travel the country regularly visiting restaurants and giving them a general hygiene rating. These ratings correspond to various smiley faces, where the cleanest restaurants get a full smiley face and the less clean get a sad face. A Danish project manager had the following experience when working with his Filipino colleagues on a scheduling system for governmental food and health inspectors:

> Yes it [the project] is about route schedules. In this case, an inspector who should visit two restaurants in the course of 1 day, and each visit should take approximately 1 h. To a Dane, this is clearly a mistake, because what was the inspector going to do for the rest of the day? But for the Filipinos, (...) well, they did not relate it [the product] to the application. (Project manager)

The project manager quoted above presented an example of how different perceptions of a concept caused a misunderstanding. The developers in the Philippines were coding a scheduling system where data (i.e., number of inspectors and number of restaurants to be checked) were entered and the system generated route schedules. However, at some point an error occurred in the system, resulting in inspectors being assigned to only two visits a day. The Filipino developers tested the IT system using various use-case scenarios and did not find this error. They did not realize that two inspections a day translates into a 2-h workday, which, by Danish standards, is not a sufficient use of resources. To the Danes, this was clearly a mistake. But, according to the Danish project manager, the mistake was grounded not in the Filipino developers' lack of ability but rather in a fundamental lack of understanding of the IT system and how it would be used in Danish society. We suggest that the Danish developers identified the error not based on a superior understanding of the requirement specification but due to a fundamental understanding of the Danish society. As the manager stated, the Filipinos did not understand the use context and therefore could not relate the IT system to the use situation. Not being able to relate the task to a given context is a challenge that both the Filipinos and the Danes are aware of. Yet it still remains a source of miscommunication.

9.4.1.4 Retirement Plans

The following example illustrates the challenge of interpreting system requirements with unknown terminology, in this case, while developing an IT system for retirement plans. A Danish manager explained:

> We had a couple of discussions regarding the retirement concept (efterløn) and your public pension age (folkepensionsalder), which was misunderstood. They [the Filipinos] had understood it in one way and we had another idea of the concept. And this meant that our testing did not match, and at some point the client got involved, because the correction of one error resulted in new errors, basically because they had corrected more than they

were supposed to. And it was all caused by this confusion of concepts. (Advanced Project Manager)

In Denmark, everyone gets a public pension at the age of 65, but many also have a privately funded pension. On top of that, many Danes are part of a public retirement fund called "efterlønsordningen," which is a supplement to the national pension plan aimed specifically at blue collar workers. This voluntary plan is intended to retire the older generation and create demand for younger workers by allowing workers with physically demanding jobs to retire at 60 instead of 65. In the Philippines they have a social security system where the employer and employee each make monthly contributions based on the employee's monthly wage. The contributions depend on the salary, and the employer matches the amount contributed by the employee. This is a mandatory minimum that legally obliges Filipino workers and companies to create retirement funds. Workers become eligible for their pension around the age of 55–60, and there is no public pension plan. Furthermore, Filipino law requires companies to pay 1 month of salary for every year of service to employees who have been with the company for at least 10 years when they turn 55.

These very different retirement plans are built on the particular social worlds of their respective countries. Thus, constructing an IT system to manage retirement plans requires significant knowledge of the social systems in the given country. This knowledge is not easily transferred between developers; it requires considerable communication not only about the system requirements but also about the society in which the IT system will be implemented.

According to the Danish manager, the differing pension systems led to different interpretations of the concept, which led to errors in the IT system that were eventually detected by the Danish testers. This example illustrates the invisibility of different background assumptions and taken-for-granted knowledge. The manager saw a strong relationship between the problems they experienced in the project and the lack of a common vocabulary for the project because the developers shared the concept, but not the meaning behind the concept.

9.4.2   Social Worlds at Work

9.4.2.1   Inventory Facility Management System

When the Filipino employees are given a task, it is often in the form of a paper-based requirement specification. We observed two Filipino project managers discussing a task proposal sent from Denmark. They discussed how to determine the scope of the task and how to estimate the number of hours required to complete the task. During the discussion, the developers turned to us and reflected on how difficult and prone to misinterpretation this activity is:

Project Manager: Then there are these requirements like: There should be a…
Interviewer: Bruttoliste?

> Project Manager: Yeah, see, we can't understand that. What is that? So what kind of list is
> that? My assumption is, like, gross list. I am not sure, but based on our assumptions, brut-
> toliste is like a contract list. So, I am not sure how we can use that term.

The Filipino project manager did not understand the term "bruttoliste", a Danish word related to calculating inventory. If the word is directly translated, it means a gross list, but, according to the Filipino manager, it could be interpreted as a contract list. The project manager tried to relate the concept to its meaning, which is key to understanding the IT system they are going to create. The challenge was further complicated in this case because the Danish developers did not translate the word bruttoliste. Forgetting to translate is a common mistake in GlobalSoft, despite assumptions about the concept being used to create a sense of meaning for the proposed IT system. To overcome this challenge, the Filipino project managers created a list of assumptions showing how they have interpreted the task description.

> There are a lot of assumptions in this project. There are, like, 16 assumptions. Yes, it is quite
> a lot. Because of the requirements. Did you see the requirements? How would we work on
> that? (Project manager)

The Filipino project manager was clearly frustrated with the difficulty making sense of the requirements. Creating assumptions was their way of trying to overcome the uncertainties in the task proposal. In this case, they had to create a list of 16 assumptions to estimate the number of work hours for the project. If any of these assumptions are wrong, then a new estimation of time and resources is required. A Filipino project manager continued discussing the gross list IT system:

> (...) this facility asset thing...we are not used to those kinds of systems. So, as mentioned
> before, it basically comes down to the domain knowledge frustration. So, we don't have any
> domain knowledge about this system. (Project manager)

The manager explained they do not always fully understand the requirement specification. She referred to this problem as "domain knowledge frustration."

9.4.2.2 Children with Special Needs

It is not only the lack of a common vocabulary that creates challenges for communication. In GlobalSoft, we also saw examples where differences in social worlds became pertinent for the collaboration. While working to create an IT system for children and youth with special needs, a Danish team leader experienced both a lack of understanding and scepticism as a result of different social worlds:

> We had a project about a system for handling children and youth with special needs. And
> we had negotiated the scope, but they [the Filipinos] never realized that this was a big
> project of great importance because, in their eyes, they believed that, frankly, you cannot
> allocate that much money for these activities. They [the children] should be able to look
> after themselves. Because this is how they do it in their [Filipino] society. (Team Leader)

In Denmark, the social welfare system is investing heavily in children and youth with special needs ranging from learning difficulties to severe physical disabilities.

It is a high-priority issue that has general support from most political parties. However, the Danish team leader indicated that the Filipino developers could not grasp the importance of the project. In this example, social worlds became salient. Even after the scope of the project was the negotiated, the project leader found it difficult to convince the Filipino developers why the project was important. They showed disbelief that so much money could be allocated to children with special needs. In Filipino society, such children have to look after themselves and would not be supported by the government. The team leader described further:

> So it was linked as a central solution to an important project and we had money prioritized for these things, right? But they [the Filipinos] never really took it seriously. Because, in their context, this seems like a completely ridiculous way to spend money. (Team Leader)

This quote illustrates how social worlds become salient in global work. The Danes felt they had a solid project with a straightforward solution and that overall the project was important and highly prioritized by the client—the Danish government. But the Filipino developers were sceptical about the project. They struggled to understand the willingness to spend so much money on children with special needs. Because the Filipino employees had trouble relating this project to a meaningful situation, they were, according to the manager, not able to collaborate in a serious manner.

> No, this can be a real challenge because sometimes they [the Filipinos] find it very hard to understand…to understand what really concerns people in Danish society, and why many things can be important in Denmark when they do not understand them at all. (Team Leader)

According to the team leader, the real challenge is a basic lack of insight into the different social worlds embedded in the geographically distributed teams. The Filipino developers have trouble understanding the social contexts in which the IT systems will be applied. This lack of contextual knowledge is an obstacle for the collaboration and may increase the risk of communication breakdowns.

9.5 Discussion

We have been investigating situations in practice where differences in social worlds between Danish and Filipino developers became salient. Our empirical observations demonstrated how social worlds became a pertinent part of collaborative work in relation to concept and meaning. We set out to identify the types of situations in which the differences between the developers' social worlds were visible and affecting the collaboration. We propose two general situations where social worlds become salient: (1) divergence in concept and meaning and (2) convergence in concept but divergence in meaning. We do acknowledge that the categories "meaning" and "concept" might be a simplistic model for illustrating complex situations of matches and mismatches, but we propose it as a way to unpack the concept of culture.

9.5.1 Divergence in Concept and Meaning

We saw several examples where concepts essential for the design of the IT system were not part of the social world of the remote site, including the CPR number, a key part of the structure of Danish society that is thus crucial for IT systems designed for the Danish government. Social security numbers are used in the Philippines, but there are clearly differences between Danish CPR numbers and Filipino social security numbers. The divergence between social worlds in Denmark and the Philippines is quite evident, so the parties are aware of the differences. They know they do not share knowledge and must therefore make extra efforts to explain the concept as well as the meaning behind the concept to the remote site. In situations where concepts relevant for the interpretation of the system requirements are localized in the social world of one location, and where the concept is not part of the shared meaning context of the other location, identifying the issue and resolving communication breakdowns is a process of explaining, negotiating, and creating a shared meaning context [18].

In the food and health inspector example, we observed the Filipino developers' failure to relate the IT system to the use context, leading to errors that were easily identified by the Danish testers. In such a situation it is crucial that the remote party identify and question the assumptions embedded within the system requirements, as others have argued [16, 17]. We suggest that situations of divergence in concept make it easier to identify the divergence in meaning of the concept because in the remote location, the concept does not exist. In these situations, reinterpretation of the meaning behind the concept is not needed.

9.5.2 Convergence in Concept but Divergence in Meaning

As we have shown, high diversity in domain vocabulary across sites creates extra work that is critical to creating a shared meaning context for the project. In high diversity situations, developers working across sites might be aware of the risk of misunderstandings, and thus will use considerable resources translating domain-specific knowledge in documents like the requirement specification and the product description. It is relatively easy to identify instances of divergence in concept because the lack of a shared vocabulary is obvious. However, our analysis revealed a different type of situation where the local social world was evident—situations where the concept is shared across locations but has different meanings for the different social worlds, such as the case of the retirement system. The retirement systems in Denmark and the Philippines appeared quite different and were dependent on the social world of each country. We label this a situation where there is convergence in concept but divergence in meaning across different social worlds. Differences in social worlds prove challenging for the design and development of IT systems in cases of a divergence in meaning of key concepts used in both local contexts. Both Denmark and the Philippines have an interpretation of the concept of a pension plan, and the concepts have similarities across locations, such as similar retirement age. There are, however, distinct differences in how the two societies have structured their pension systems, but these differences may not be immediately apparent to the development teams.

The lack of visibility of different parties' interpretations of a common concept makes it difficult to detect this source of misunderstanding. We saw this in the retirement system example, where crucial errors were not detected early by the Filipino testers and were only later discovered by the Danish testers. This suggests that communication breakdowns caused by diversity in meaning of shared concepts are more likely to happen at later stages because participants may perceive a "false" sense of common ground, making the lack of shared understanding harder to identify. Common ground occurs when parties share knowledge and know they share it [2]; however, developing common ground requires a grounding process where the parties rearrange their knowledge according to each other's utterances [6]. In cases of convergence in concept but divergence in meaning, detecting a lack of common ground is difficult and, in some situations, even impossible. In many cases, the lack of common ground will not appear until technical decisions based on false assumptions become manifested in the IT system. This kind of miscommunication is more costly for the company because the cost of fixing errors rises exponentially as the product reaches the delivery deadline. It is essential that the remote party not only identify and question the assumptions embedded within the system requirements, but also that they are aware of the divergence in meaning of what might seem to be a shared understanding of key concepts. We believe identifying situations of convergence in concept but divergence in meaning is difficult but critical to reducing the risk of miscommunication throughout the development process. We argue that re-interpreting the meaning behind the concept is required for developers to establish a shared understanding of the development of IT systems. Yet, because of the initial shared understanding of the concept, development teams tend not to allocate resources to communicating it's meaning and thus fail to address the challenge of divergence in meaning.

You may also wonder about situations of convergence in concept and meaning. We detected no such cases when examining our data for situations where differences in social worlds between sites became salient for communication. We might assume that in situations of convergence in both concept and meaning, no differences in social worlds exist, and thus they are not problematic. Perhaps our empirical material revealed no such situations because they do not result in communication breakdowns, and thus our respondents did not identify these instances as challenges for collaboration in GSD.

We have argued that social worlds can become salient as either divergent in concept and meaning or convergent in concept but divergent in meaning. We propose that that these social worlds pose a risk for miscommunication between developers, and we have observed examples of these miscommunications in practice. In the inventory facility management example, where the Filipino project leaders found it challenging to comprehend the IT system's use context, these challenges lead to frustration because a list of assumptions had to be created as a way to address these challenges. Workaround creation in GSD processes has also been noted by other researchers [3]. In such situations, social worlds become salient and project leaders create ways to work around them.

The development of an IT system for children with special needs was another example of social worlds at work. In this case, differences in social worlds led to scepticism among the developers across locations and created a challenge for the collaboration. Thus, the lack of implicit directions for shaping the interpretation of events hindered the developers' ability to enact shared meaning [18].

Based on our observations of social worlds and their impact on collaboration, we suggest the need for further research into understanding how divergence and convergence in concept and meaning affect collaborative work in GSD. We propose that divergence in concept and meaning is easier for participants to identify and comprehend and will therefore often be present early in the development process. In contrast, convergence in concept but divergence in meaning is harder to identify and more complicated to comprehend because it requires reinterpretation of familiar concepts and we suggest that these situations will occur later the development process.

9.6 Conclusion

In this study, we present an analysis of a work place study in a global software development company. We sat out to investigate how to identify situations where the differences in social worlds between geographically distributed developers become salient in their everyday interactions. In our analysis, we identified two types of situations where social worlds became pertinent: (1) situations of divergence in concept and meaning and (2) situations of convergence in concept but divergence in meaning. While we acknowledge that the conceptualization of concept and meaning might be somewhat simplistic, we believe this to be a first step into unpacking culture as part of collaboration. Based on our empirical findings we have argued that by identifying and describing these situations, we can better understand how and why communication breakdowns occur in intercultural collaborative work practices.

Acknowledgments This research has been funded by the Danish Agency for Science, Technology and Innovation under the project "Next Generation Technology for Global Software Development", #10-092313.

References

1. Majchrzak, A., Rice, RE., Malhotra, A., King, N., Ba, S.: Technology adaptation: the case of a computer-supported inter-organizational virtual team. MISQ. 24(4), 569–600 (2000)
2. Olson, G.M., Olson, J.S.: Distance matters. Hum. Comput. Interact. 15, 139–178 (2000)

3. Avram, G., Bannon, L., Bowers, J., Sheehan, A.: Bridging, patching and keeping the work flowing: defect resolution in distributed software development. Comput. Support. Coop. Work. **18**, 477–507 (2009)
4. Krishna, S., Sahay, S., Walsham, G.: Managing cross-cultural issues in global software outsourcing. CACM. **47**(4), 62–66 (2004)
5. Boden, A., Avram, G., Bannon, L., Wulf V.: Knowledge management in distributed software development teams: does culture matter? Paper presented at the international conference on Global Software Engineering (ICGSE), Limerick, Ireland, 13–16 July (2009)
6. Clark, H., Brennan, S.: Grounding in communication. In: Resnick, L., Levine, J., Teasley, S. (eds.) Perspectives on Social Shared Cognition, pp. 127–149. American Psychological Association, Washington, DC (1991)
7. Massey, A.P., Hung, Y.-T.C., Montoya-Weiss, M., Ramesh, V.: When culture and style aren't about clothes: perceptions of task-technology "fit" in global virtual teams. In: GROUP, pp. 207–213. ACM Press, Boulder (2001)
8. Nardi, B.A., Whittaker, S., Bradner, E.: Interaction and outeraction: instant messaging in action. Paper presented at the Proceedings of the 2000 ACM conference on computer supported cooperative work, Philadelphia, Pennsylvania, United States (2000)
9. Setlock, L., Fussell, S.: What's it worth to you? The costs and affordances of CMC tools to Asian and American users. Paper presented at the Computer Supported Cooperative Work (CSCW), Savannah, Georgia, US (2010)
10. Duarte, D., Snyder, N.: Mastering Virtual Teams: Strategies, Tools, and Technoques that Succeed. Wiley, San Francisco (2006)
11. Søderberg, A.-M., Holden, N.: Rethinking cross cultural management in a globalized business world. Int. J. Cross Cult. Manag. (CCM). **2**(1), 103–121 (2002)
12. Souza, C.D., Redmiles, D.: The awareness network: to whom should I display my action? And, whose actions should I monitor. Paper presented at the European Conference on Computer Supported Cooperative Work (ECSCW), Limerick, Ireland (2007)
13. Espinosa, A., Slaughter, S., Kraut, R., Herbsleb, J.: Team knowlegde and coordination in geographically distributed software development. J. Manag. Inf. Syst. **24**(1), 135–169 (2007)
14. Boden, A., Nett, B., Wulf, V.: Operational and strategic learning in global software development: implications from two offshoring case studies in small enterprises. IEEE Softw. **27**(6), 58–65 (2010)
15. Herbsleb, J.: Global software engineering: the future of socio-technical coordination. Paper presented at the Future of Software Engineering (FOSE), Washington, DC, USA (2007)
16. Boden, A., Nett, B., Wulf, V.: Trust and social capital: revisiting an offshoring failure story of a small German software company. Paper presented at the European Conference Computer Supported Cooperative Work (ECSCW'09), Vienna, Austria, 7–11 Sept (2009)
17. Herbsleb, J., Paulish, D., Bass, M.: Global software development at Siemens: experience from nine projects. In: International Conference on Software Development (ICSE), pp. 524–533, St. Louis, Missouri, USA, ACM, IEEE Xplore, (2005)
18. Bjørn, P., Ngwenyama, O.: Virtual team collaboration: building shared meaning, resolving breakdowns and creating translucence. Inf. Syst. J. **19**(3), 227–253 (2009)
19. Ngwenyama, O., Klein, H.: An exploration of the expertise of knowledge workers: towards a definition of the universe of discourse for knowledge acquisition. Inf. Syst. J. **4**, 129–140 (1994)
20. Star, SL., Griesemer, J.: Institutional ecology, translations and boundary objects: amateurs and professionals in Berkeleys museum of Vertebrate Zoology, 1907–39. Soc. Stud. Sci. **19**, 387–420 (1989)
21. Randall, D., Harper, R., Rouncefield, M.: Fieldwork for Design: Theory and Practice. Springer, London (2007)
22. Jarvenpaa, S.L., Leidner, D.E.: Communication and trust in global virtual teams. Organ. Sci. **10**(6), 791–815 (1999)

Chapter 10
Creating Metaphors for Tangible User Interfaces in Collaborative Urban Planning: Questions for Designers and Developers

Valérie Maquil, Olivier Zephir, and Eric Ras

Abstract Designing tangible user interfaces (TUIs) means to deal with a complex number of issues related to the particular mixture of the physical and digital space. While a number of existing guidelines and frameworks propose issues and themes that are relevant during design, we still miss a more specific guidance on how to address such issues. This chapter analyses the difficulty of designing and developing TUIs by considering the principle of metaphors. Based on an analysis of the different types of targets of metaphors in TUIs, we identify the complexities of TUI adoption by users across physical, digital, and application domains. We propose a series of questions that support designers and developers in dealing with these complexities in the context of a TUI for collaborative planning and discussion of urban concepts. Our work is based on and illustrated through various insights collected during the development of the "ColorTable", a complex TUI for collaborative urban planning.

10.1 Introduction

The concept of Tangible User Interfaces (TUIs) allows us to go beyond the limitations of desktop computing and to create new applications based on interactions with a physical environment. TUIs provide the same computational capabilities as desktop computers, but are able to offer the richness and familiarity of physical actions. We believe that the strength of TUIs lies within this particular mixture of physical and digital interactions and representations. Through the physical space, we can create social effects, such as an increased collaboration (e.g., [7]), whereas

V. Maquil (✉) · O. Zephir · E. Ras
Public Research Centre Henri Tudor, 29, avenue John F. Kennedy,
1855 Luxembourg, Luxembourg
e-mail: valerie.maquil@tudor.lu

O. Zephir
e-mail: olivier.zephir@tudor.lu

E. Ras
e-mail: eric.ras@tudor.lu

J. Dugdale et al. (eds.), *From Research to Practice in the Design of Cooperative Systems:*   137
Results and Open Challenges, DOI 10.1007/978-1-4471-4093-1_10,
© Springer-Verlag London 2012

the interactive representations mixing physical and digital elements offer new types of human experiences and understanding (e.g., [12]).

Due to this intense combination of physical and digital interactions and representations, we are faced with a new complexity related to the design of TUIs. To deal with this complexity, researchers from diverse directions identified the need for general approaches to the description, the design, the implementation, and the evaluation of TUIs. In literature, we find a number of frameworks, guidelines, models, or taxonomies that all provide a certain type of guidance during design, evaluation, and description of different types of TUI systems (e.g., [1, 7, 9, 22]).

As noted by Mazalek and Van den Hoven [18], each of the frameworks provides a different perspective on tangible interaction design and supports designers and developers in a different way. We agree with Hornecker [6] that the existing frameworks tend to be theoretic and abstract and are difficult to use as step-by-step guidance in practice. Current works provide interesting lists of issues or themes that should be considered during design, whereas a more specific guidance for solving or addressing these issues throughout a design process is still missing.

This chapter approaches the tangible interaction space by drawing on theories of external and distributed cognition, i.e., by considering that cognitive processes are distributed and coordinated between internal and external elements of our environment [5]. Hence, in our work, we refer to the information and knowledge that is available in both the people's mind and the world: We consider actions and behaviour to be caused by "a combination of internal knowledge and external information and constraints" [19]. Therefore, we take into account, at the same time what users intend to do, and what is represented through the physical and digital space of a TUI.

To be able to analyse these two types of knowledge, we focus on the different types of metaphors and metaphorical links that can be found in a tangible user interface. We believe that this approach allows us to get an understanding on the multiple dimensions of a TUI and to formulate a workflow that integrates them. Our aim is to provide practical guidance for those who need to design and develop a new TUI to support activities within a contextual and social environment. The structure and workflow presented in this chapter is a first step in identifying a sequence of the main questions to be addressed in the design activities. We invite everyone to contribute to this structure, namely to refine and complete the questions, and to provide methods and guidance for solving them.

The questions and sequence provided in this chapter are based on the multiple experiences made from the 4 years iterative development of the ColorTable [15, 16]. As this TUI was built to support collaborative planning and discussion of urban projects, the work primarily serves as guidance for this type of application context. In future work, we seek to generalize and adapt the workflow to a larger range of use cases.

We specifically address our work to designers *and* developers, since our approach requires skills from several disciplines. In our analysed context of the ColorTable, the main skills needed to advance in the design were found in design and computer science.

This chapter starts with the related concepts and works that provided us with the insights to define a series of questions: the principles of metaphors and affordances, and the complex TUI called ColorTable. We base our work on the idea that we are confronted with three types of domains (i.e., physical, digital, and application) when using or designing TUIs. Through analysing the types of targets the user needs to deal with when adopting a TUI, we define a set of issues related to user understanding of a TUI. We propose a series of questions that designers and developers need to answer when defining metaphors in TUIs. We finish the chapter with our conclusions and future work.

10.2   Background

10.2.1   Metaphors

The idea of metaphors has been a central and popular element in the design practice of graphical user interfaces. In our work, we use the most common and popular definition, which is based on a cognitive approach, considering a metaphor as a basic mental operation. It was formulated by Lakoff and Johnson: "*A metaphor is a rhetoric figure, whose essence is understanding and experiencing one kind of thing in terms of another* [14]". In 1987, Johnson provides an even more specific definition, stating that a metaphor is "*a pervasive mode of understanding by which we project patterns from one domain of experience in order to structure another domain of a different kind* [11]." Based on these definitions, the concept was intensively elaborated and discussed to become a key component in the design of graphical user interfaces. In TUI research, the idea was caught in several works, claiming that the physical properties of objects and space are particularly interesting for metaphorical links [4, 8, 20].

Our work is based on these previous works on TUI metaphors and interface metaphors in general [9, 13], which support us in understanding how the physical, digital, and application domains are connected. Based on this understanding, we identify the design activities for creating TUI metaphors and to structure a design workflow spanning multiple domains.

10.2.2   The ColorTable

To be able to study the design of metaphors in TUIs, we take the ColorTable [15] as example. The ColorTable is a TUI enabling the collaborative discussion and debate of different ideas and concepts around urban planning projects. It is a tabletop interface presenting a collaborative planning and discussion space—users are motivated to share their ideas and visions by moving colour tokens of different shapes and colours on the table. The tokens enable users to set urban elements such as buildings, streets, pedestrian flows, or ground textures. The table view uses a physical map, which is augmented with digital information to provide a top-down view onto

Fig. 10.1 Evaluating the ColorTable during participatory
workshops on real sites

the project site. A vertical projection renders the scene against a background, which is produced by either a video stream, a panorama image of a view onto the site, or a see-through installation and creates a perspective mixed reality view.

The ColorTable was developed in a participatory design process of 4 years, and passed eight iterations, each covering the identification of the needs, the design, the implementation of interactive prototypes, and the evaluation. The prototypes had been designed and developed in a multi-disciplinary team, collaborating with experienced urban planners, and integrating material from field works. Each of the iterations was connected to an on-going urban planning project, providing a range of urban issues to be of interest for participants. The prototypes were evaluated in close cooperation with users, using ethnographic and observational methods within the scope of participatory workshops (Fig. 10.1). During the different iterations, we improved the design of objects, table, and space around (a) to facilitate the use for multidisciplinary groups of participants and (b) to support a more and more enhanced range of application functions.

During the long-term development process of the ColorTable, we had the opportunity to experiment with different design solutions and to improve individual aspects several times. A multimodal analysis of the observational data in the multi-disciplinary team, allowed us to deeply understand the characteristics of a tool, supporting groups of stakeholders to discuss urban planning decisions in a truly collaborative and participatory manner. This approach allowed us to collect and analyse a large amount of insights on the individual design activities and their importance in the development of a TUI.

10.3   The Complexities in a TUI

To identify the types of complexities in a TUI, we refer to one of the most popular notion used in a metaphor definition: the *source* and *target* domain. The target is the original idea, a new or complex concept, to which the metaphor is referring to. The source is the borrowed idea, a familiar concept that helps us in understanding the target [14]. The mapping from source to target is called the metaphorical projection [13].

In the context of TUIs the source domain uses characteristics of physical objects and tangibility to refer to familiar concepts. As Fishkin [4] points out, this context is particularly appropriate for applying a metaphor-based design approach, because of the high number of physically afforded metaphors: "*A designer can use the shape, the size, the colour, the weight, the smell, and the texture of the object to invoke any number of metaphorical links.*"

The target domain is the unfamiliar structure in and around the TUI that needs to be understood by the user when appropriating a TUI. As described in [2], the interface can be seen as some representation that helps the user to understand the abstract operations and capabilities of the computer. This idea is in line with the work of Ullmer and Ishii [10, 21], comparing the TUI paradigm with the GUI paradigm. They discuss two levels, the physical and the digital level: tangible and intangible controls and representations allow users to interact with, and experience from an underlying digital information model. According to this perspective, *digital information and computation* is the target domain, which is presented as is it was something else that the user might already understand.

We agree with this view of seeing the interface as metaphorical representation of the operations and capabilities of the computer, but believe that in TUIs, and especially mixed reality (MR) based TUIs, we are faced with a whole series of different sources and targets that are mapped through metaphorical projections.

To better understand the different levels where complexities can be found, we analyse in more detail the way tangible interaction is structured in related literature. In his influential book "The design of everyday things" [19], Norman discusses the concept of affordances in everyday artefacts. He uses the notion of *conceptual model* to refer to the actions, operations, and effects of an artefact, as well as the relations in between. Affordances, constraints, and mappings allow the user to construct an own mental model of an artefact in order to understand how a system can be used. Since TUIs use everyday artefacts, the same reflexions on conceptual models can be done for TUIs: a user constructs a mental model of the TUI in order to understand how the different parts can be physically manipulated. In contrast to the digital information model of Ullmer and Ishii, the conceptual model concentrates on *physical actions, and their effects*, which can be considered as second type of target.

In the work of Dourish on embodied interaction [3], we can find an additional, broader view on tangible interaction. His idea behind this concept is to consider interaction as embedded in the real world. It illuminates "*not just how we act on technology, but how we act through it*". Artefacts of interaction can be used in many different ways and users can create different levels of meaning through their actions. He considers computation as a medium for communication; meaning is conveyed through a technology and through the practices that surround it. In other words, a transmitted meaning is something unknown and complex, which is explained through different kinds of patterns in our gestures, talk, and physical actions. This meaning created through the activities of the users can be considered as third type of target in a TUI. We name this domain as *application* domain.

Fig. 10.2 Exploring and understanding how the digital space reacts to physical manipulations

10.3.1   Case Study—The ColorTable

To further motivate and illustrate these three different types of targets, we make use of the ColorTable. In the *physical* domain, the user needs to understand the physical manipulations that can, or should be done with the TUI. This includes the area where objects should be placed (i.e., the tabletop), and that they can be moved or rotated. The patterns used for explanation are, for example, the flat bottom side of the objects, the flat tabletop, and the directional form of the rectangles.

The second type of target concerns the computational information model, i.e., the *digital* domain. The user needs to build a mental model of the kind of digital objects and scenes that can be created and how they react to the different physical manipulations (Fig. 10.2). Characteristics of the physical and digital representations support understanding how digital data is computationally represented and controlled.

Finally, a third type of target can be found in the *application* domain. Characteristics of the physical and the digital actions support users in conveying a meaning, i.e., expressing different kinds of properties of their urban vision. For example, they can communicate quantities, such as the position, or size of certain urban elements, but also more qualitative aspects such as the desired atmosphere, or the kind of people meeting there.

A more detailed description of these three types of targets is provided in [17].

10.4   Questions for Designers and Developers

The proposed three types of targets show the levels on which complexities in a TUI exist and need to be understood by the users. In the following, we address the three types of targets (a) from the perspective of the user and (b) from the perspective of the designer or developer. Based on our experiences with the ColorTable, we propose a series of questions which allow to better understand the targets of the TUI design space, and through which design activities they can be addressed. We illustrate our work through multiple observations and insights from the participatory workshops with the ColorTable.

10.4.1 Understanding the Targets of the ColorTable

Throughout the different evaluation workshops of the ColorTable, we refined our approach of explaining the ColorTable and its different features. During the last workshops we started the sessions with a specific tutorial and developed and refined a protocol for it. The final protocol was based on four main steps, which are explained in the following.

In the first step, the starting configuration of the TUI is made, through selecting a background panorama, a paper map and 11 contents cards. The criteria for this selection are that the content gives insight into what type of urban elements the system can illustrate. However, it needs to be sufficiently neutral and not address critical issues in order to prevent users of discussing urban decisions at this point.

In the second step, the users are explained the basic principle and components of the ColorTable. This includes the table and the different tokens. The users are explained that the positions, orientations, and colours of the objects are tracked through a camera above the table, and that feedback is projected onto the map.

In the third step, the users each are provided with some of the preselected content cards. This makes them to the active user and forces them to try out the different manipulations.

In a final step, each of the features is explained individually. The list of features is made based on the different urban interventions that can be expressed through them, rather than the technical possibilities of the system. Examples for such features are: setting roads, creating zones, navigating, placing urban objects, etc. The feature is explained through (a) explaining a potential use in an urban discussion, (b) showing the physical move, and (c) showing the digital reaction.

From this sequence, we can extract elements of how the three domains and the corresponding targets are addressed. At the beginning of the tutorial, the users are explained which physical objects are part of the system, and what physical manipulations can be done (i.e., are tracked).

When explaining the features, the users are informed on what digital objects can be created, and how they can be manipulated through which physical manipulation. The examples of digital objects are selected in a way that they reflect a typical urban planning content, i.e., a building, a bridge, or a road, in order to illustrate what types of meanings can be transmitted through the tool.

In the workshops we observed that when following this protocol, the users were able to understand the physical and the digital domain, and could proceed to selecting the objects and manipulations in order to express their own urban vision.

In contrast, on occasions where some of the tools had not been explained on the three layers, they have mostly not been used at all. A typical example of such an improper explanation is to explain the algorithm behind a digital intervention and using a "funny" example to illustrate it. Explaining that objects are visualized as pictures on invisible canvasses being placed in 3D space and illustrating this through placing a heroic figure in front of St Stevens Cathedral (the emblem of Vienna, Austria), is interesting for people which want to understand the algorithms in virtual and augmented reality. However, when users are interested in novel tools and methods for urban planning, they want to understand how the TUI can be used in this application area, and the above example is, in this case, of no help. Such an illustration does not show how to use the physical and digital space as metaphor for urban interventions, and requires a large mental effort of the users to imagine useful examples by themselves.

10.4.2   Questions Related to Use

The three types of targets that have been identified in the previous section imply that the design space can structured into three domains, each of them to be characterized through a type of target. When focusing on the way users approached the three targets, we can build a structure showing the unknown aspects the user faces when adopting a TUI (Fig. 10.3).

In the *physical domain*, those are about the physical objects and the respective manipulations that can be made with them. Since a TUI is always accessed in a physical space, the user first needs to find out what objects within that space are the objects of interaction (*Which physical objects are parts of the TUI?*). Further, s/he needs to learn how these objects can be manipulated, for example, whether they are moved, rotated, pressed, assembled, or twisted (*Which physical actions can be done with which physical objects?*). There may also be constraints for the manipulations, like movements that can only be done in a in a specific area, e.g., a tabletop, and other characteristics of the action, like the precision.

In the *digital domain*, the targets are the digital objects and the digital manipulations which can be done with them. A first unfamiliarity is what types of digital objects (i.e., shapes, lines, images, sound) can be produced with the TUI (*Which digital objects can be created?*). Second, the user needs to find out which actions can be done with those digital objects, i.e., whether they be moved, rotated, coloured, scaled, or distorted, and to what extend and how precisely (*Which digital actions can be done with which digital objects?*). Finally, s/he needs to learn which physical manipulation has which effect on which digital object (*How are the physical and the digital manipulations connected?*).

In the *application domain*, the unfamiliar aspect is the meaning which is communicated. It needs to be expressed by one user, and interpreted by the rest of the group. To be able to effectively use a TUI for communicating a meaning, the user needs to find out which of the hybrid interaction elements, i.e., the augmented phys-

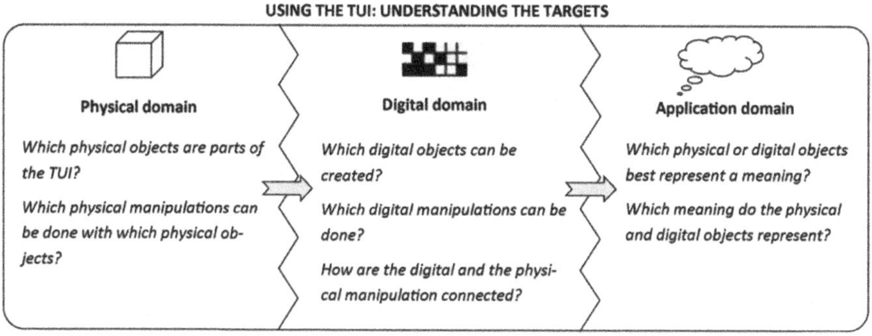

USING THE TUI: UNDERSTANDING THE TARGETS

Fig. 10.3 Three types of targets which the user is confronted with

ical objects and manipulations, show the important aspects that characterize the meaning a user wants to convey (*Which physical and/or digital objects best represent a meaning?*). The rest of the group needs to interpret this representation and understand which characteristics of the shapes, images, sounds, and tokens, as well as the related manipulations, provide which information about the meaning which is communicated (*Which meaning do the physical and digital objects represent?*).

Guided through the tutorial sessions in our participatory workshops, the users approached the targets in the aforementioned order. They first tried to understand the physical objects and the manipulations that can be done with them. Then they sought to understand how the digital objects and manipulations can be controlled, and finally they were ready to use the tool as support to communicate about concepts and their properties (i.e., meaning) in the application domain.

10.4.3   Questions Related to Design

Based on the above specification on the different levels of understanding of the user, we are able to define design questions which directly address these targets (Fig. 10.4).

To explain the *application domain*, we need to understand and specify the meanings users can convey and define metaphors for expressing them with the TUI. As a first step, we need to elaborate the topics the users want to address and discuss, as well as how precisely they want to discuss them (*Which meanings do the users want to convey?*). Further, a decision needs to be taken on how each of the topics and related qualities of discussion is represented through physical and digital objects and manipulations, i.e., what types of images, shapes, sound, physical objects refer to the important characteristics of the conveyed meaning (*Which characteristics of the physical and digital objects best explain the meanings?*).

To explain the *digital domain*, we need to elaborate the digital possibilities and the corresponding metaphorical links to the physical domain. In this step, we need to find solutions for creating digital objects showing the qualities elaborated in the previous domain. So we need to determine the digital actions, e.g., translations,

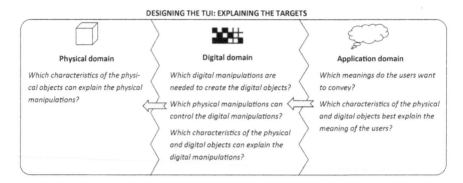

Fig. 10.4 Designing the TUI based on the tree types of targets the user is confronted with

rotations, scaling procedures, distortions that are required for creating the desired digital effect and appearance (*Which digital manipulations are needed to create the digital objects?*). Further, we need to investigate which physical manipulations can be technically sensed, through which type of physical object this manipulation can be realized, and under which circumstances the physical manipulation can be linked to the variables of the digital manipulation (*Which physical manipulations can control the digital manipulations?*). Lastly, we need to think about the properties of the physical and digital objects that show the users the possibilities for digital manipulations (*Which characteristics of the physical and digital objects can explain the digital manipulations?*).

Finally, in the *physical domain*, we have to design the physical properties to explain the physical actions. We need to elaborate which properties of the physical objects show the users the possibilities for physical manipulations (*Which characteristics of the physical objects can explain the physical manipulations?*).

When focusing on the levels of understanding of the user, it suggests itself to approach the design space starting from the application domain, then working towards the digital and the physical domain. However, in a user-centred design perspective, several iterations and simultaneous adaptations are needed. This means that the designer also needs to redefine the outcome of each step several times and adjust design decisions based on previous evaluations and user feedback. This will, for instance, allow him to adjust decisions of the application domain based on issues of the physical domain.

10.4.4 Case Study—The ColorTable

Although this structure was not used during the development of the ColorTable, we can show that the proposed questions have all been addressed at some moment during the different iterations. In the following, we describe the issues around each of the questions, as well as our approach for solving them.

Fig. 10.5 Representing the specific details of an ambiance through photos

Which meanings do the users want to convey? This question was mainly addressed by the urban specialists in the team. These selected an ongoing urban planning project and suggested a set of 'urban themes' they considered as particularly relevant. They illustrated these themes by providing a number of visual examples, such as scale, temporality, borders and layers, fuzziness, ambience and mobility. Using participatory design techniques (e.g., cultural probes, narrative interviews), these issues have been detailed with user's own vision of the future site. Different scenarios of statements have then been elaborated, such as 'work with issues of connectivity', 'discuss allocation of spaces for different uses', or 'activities and ambiances'.

Which characteristics of the physical and digital objects best explain the meanings conveyed by the users? Based on the elaborated scenarios, we created and selected ways to represent the statements with digital and physical objects. This was mainly done through intense collaboration with an artist and wide exploration of different visual and technical possibilities. Outcomes of this step were, for instance, that urban elements need to be represented through photos, as these better visualize the specific details of an ambiance compared to 3D models (Fig. 10.5). The photos need to be placed on any position in order to link the ambiance with a specific location. User feedback during the workshops allowed us to refine the characteristics of physical and digital objects. For instance, users were repeatedly mentioning that objects 'are not on the ground', or 'are floating' (Fig. 10.6). We therefore identified the necessity of positioning any type of objects in a way that they are perceived to be on the ground. Further, users were mentioning the need for smaller physical objects.

Which digital manipulations are needed to create the digital objects? In this step we defined the digital manipulations that can create the visual effects elaborated in the previous design step. This was mainly done through exploring technical possibilities, implementing them, and evaluating how they are perceived by the users. Outcome of this step was, for example, the requirement for 3D positioning and scaling of each object. To create the impression that a certain photo has been placed on a specific position on the ground in the panorama, the object needs to be lowered depending on the perspective in its own photo, correctly scaled, and be occluded through 'real' objects in the panorama.

Fig. 10.6 A playground
which is not perfectly
adjusted to the background is
perceived to be 'floating'

Which physical manipulations can control the digital manipulations? In this step
we analysed which physical manipulations can be sensed and connected to the digital manipulation. Possibilities for physical manipulations depend on the choice of
the sensing technology and are created through combining a technology with different types of physical objects. In the case of the ColorTable, this step was done in an
intense collaboration between designers and computer scientists, by exploring technical and physical possibilities and doing creative combinations. Outcome of this
step was, for instance, the manipulation of tokens of different colours and shapes
to control positions, and the placement of small cards on dedicated colour areas to
control other parameters (Fig. 10.7 right).

*Which characteristics of the physical and digital objects can explain the digital
manipulations?* Knowing the possibilities for physical manipulations and the requirements for digital manipulations, we can make links between the two. When
defining these links, we need to elaborate how the digital manipulations can be
explained to the user by well selecting physical and digital objects. This step heavily relied on the feedback and observation of users provided in the participatory
workshops. A design of metaphorical links was implemented and then iteratively
adapted based on the results of the workshops. In the example of placing photos,
the positioning on the XY plane (corresponding to the floor) was controlled through
positioning the colour tokens on the tabletop (Fig. 10.7 left). Since this imitates the
behaviour of objects in the real world, the link is easy to understand. The manipulation of size and offset to the ground was decided to be controlled via command
cards placed on RFID readers (Fig. 10.7 right). However, this is more difficult to
understand since the physical manipulation does not refer to any familiar metaphorical source. We therefore explained this manipulation digitally using textual
information popping up and indicating size and offset in meters. Better metaphors
for modifying the size of objects could, for instance, be based on stacking or rotat-
ing mechanisms on the objects themselves.

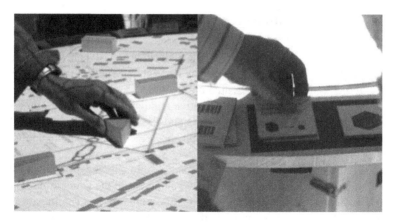

Fig. 10.7 Moving physical objects (*left*) to control positions and placing a small card on a color area (*right*) to increase the size

Which characteristics of the physical objects can explain the physical manipulations? In this step, we thought about the design of the objects themselves and how they can support the user in manipulating them correctly. This was mainly done through collaboration with an industrial designer and exploration of physical possibilities as well as their alignment to requirements developed in previous steps. Outcomes were, for example, a flat bottom side that motivates the user in placing the objects on the table. A certain height allows her/him to grasp them from the side and avoid occlusion on the camera image. A certain weight infers that they are comfortable to hold in the hand while thinking.

When considering the design and development of the ColorTable, we can see the importance of each of the proposed questions and how they affect design decisions for the related domains. Although a basic approach was to define digital and physical manipulations after having elaborated an understanding of the application domain, the case study showed that this sequence was not followed rigidly. For instance, as mentioned before, outcomes of the 'digital' and 'physical' step have influenced decisions taken related to the application domain. The physical objects needed to have a certain size in order to be detected by the colour vision framework. This means that on a large urban site, the objects physically held a place on the map that corresponds to a large building. Because of this issue we decided that it makes no sense for using 'small' urban elements, like a tree or a bench, when the urban site is rather large.

The common strategy of the design process of the ColorTable was to start with a loose definition of each of the domains, and then specify each of the domains of the design space in more and more detail. The first prototype built upon the idea of a tabletop using physical objects and a mixed reality view to represent urban planning elements. Based on this concept, the TUI has been more and more refined in order to respond to the requirements and outcomes related to the different questions of the three domains.

10.5   Conclusions and Future Work

This chapter proposes a range of questions which support designers and developers in designing TUIs while considering both the internal knowledge in the users' mind, and the external knowledge represented on the tabletop. Our work is based on the different insights collected during the iterative and participatory design process of the ColorTable. The principle of metaphors and the elaborated three types of targets allowed us to consider aspects of the physical, the digital, and the application domain in TUIs.

In our discussion we provided examples on how and why the different questions had been addressed during the design and development of the ColorTable. The approach shows that each of the related steps features an important complexity which can be managed using skills of multiple disciplines.

Structuring the design space in three domains allowed us to identify a range of questions to be integrated in the design process of a TUI, addressing issues of its usage as a tool within a broader context. In particular, the provided structure highlights which kinds of associations between components of the physical, digital, and application domain need to be made explicit to the user in order to ensure successful design.

Our work is a first step towards a more specific workflow of design activities in TUIs. It provides a range of issues that need to be considered during design, and points out how the different decisions are interconnected. However, there is still a lot to do. On one hand, the questions need to be completed and refined through a high number of case studies. Further, existing guidelines and methods, which support finding a solution to these questions, need to be aligned with the structure. There is also the need for new guidelines and methods to fill currently existing gaps. While we provide first hints on a kind of sequence for addressing the questions, this workflow needs to be elaborated further in order to create a more effective and efficient design process.

In our future work, we will test and refine the questions in two different case studies dealing with collaborative service design activities using tabletops. Our aim is to complete and refine the questions and to develop a design support for this particular domain. We believe that through our metaphor-based approach to TUIs, linking multiple domains, we will be able to define a design workflow, which allows us to more effectively and efficiently design new TUIs.

Acknowledgments The majority of the research underlying this chapter was conducted by the first author as Ph.D work within Vienna University of Technology. It was partially funded by the European Union Integrated Project IPCity under contract no. FP6-2004-IST-4-27571. We would like to thank all researchers who contributed to the work of this chapter, in particular the team of Vienna UT: Lisa Ehrenstrasser, Stephan Gamohn, Michal Idziorek, Ina Wagner, and Mira Wagner.

References

1. Antle, A. N.: The CTI framework: informing the design of tangible systems for children. Proceedings of the 1st International Conference on Tangible and Embedded Interaction. Baton Rouge, Louisiana, pp. 195–202, ACM Press (2007)
2. Blackwell, A.F.: The reification of metaphor as a design tool. ACM Trans. Comput. Hum. Interact. **13**(4), 490–530 (2006)
3. Dourish, P.: Where the Action Is: The Foundations of Embodied Interaction. The MIT Press, Cambridge (2004)
4. Fishkin, K.: A taxonomy for and analysis of tangible interfaces. Pers. Ubiquitous Comput. **8**(5), 347–358 (2004)
5. Hollan, J., Hutchins, E., Kirsh, D.: Distributed cognition: toward a new foundation for human-computer interaction research. ACM Trans. Comput. Hum. Interact. **7**(2), 174–196 (2000)
6. Hornecker, E.: Creative idea exploration within the structure of a guiding framework: the card brainstorming game. In: Proceedings of the Fourth International Conference on Tangible, Embedded, and Embodied Interaction, pp. 101–108, ACM Press (2010)
7. Hornecker, E., Buur, J.: Getting a grip on tangible interaction: a framework on physical space and social interaction. In: Proceedings of the SIGCHI Conference on Human Factors in Computing Systems, pp. 437–446, ACM Press (2006)
8. Hurtienne, J., Israel, J.H.: Image schemas and their metaphorical extensions: intuitive patterns for tangible interaction. In: Proceedings of the 1st International Conference on Tangible and Embedded Interaction, pp. 127–134, ACM Press (2007)
9. Hurtienne, J., Weber, K., Blessing, L.: Prior Experience and Intuitive Use: Image Schemas in User Centred Design. Designing Inclusive Futures. P. Langdon, J. Clarkson and P. Robinson, pp. 107–116, London, Springer (2008)
10. Ishii, H.: Tangible bits: beyond pixels. In: Proceedings of the 2nd International Conference on Tangible and Embedded Interaction, pp. xv-xxv, Bonn, Germany, ACM Press (2008)
11. Johnson, M.: The Body in the Mind. The University of Chicago Press, Chicago (1987)
12. Klemmer, S.R., Hartmann, B., Takayama, L.: How bodies matter: five themes for interaction design. In: Proceedings of the 6th Conference on Designing Interactive Systems, pp. 140–149, ACM Press (2006)
13. Kuhn, W., Frank, A.U.: A formalization of metaphors and image-schemas in user interfaces. Cogn. Linguist. Asp. Geogr. Space. **63**, 419–434 (1991)
14. Lakoff, G., Johnson, M.: Metaphors We Live By. University of Chicago Press, Chicago (1980)
15. Maquil, V.: The ColorTable: An Interdisciplinary Design Process. Vienna University of Technology, Wien (2010)
16. Maquil, V., Psik, T., Wagner, I.: The ColorTable: a design story. In: Proceedings of the 2nd International Conference on Tangible and Embedded Interaction, pp. 97–104, Bonn, Germany (2008)
17. Maquil, V., Ras, E., Zephir, O.: Understanding the characteristics of Metaphors in Tangible User Interfaces. Proceedings of the Workshop Be-GreifbareInteraktionat the Conference Mensch und Computer, Chemnitz, Germany, pp. 47–52, GI (2011)
18. Mazalek, A., van den Hoven, E.: Framing tangible interaction frameworks. Artif. Intell. Eng. Des. Anal. Manuf. **23**(3), 225 (2009)
19. Norman, D.A.: The Design of Everyday Things. Basic Books, New York (2002)
20. Svanaes, D., Verplank, W.: In search of metaphors for tangible user interfaces. In: Proceedings of DARE 2000 on Designing Augmented Reality Environments, pp. 121–129, ACM Press (2000)
21. Ullmer, B.: Emerging frameworks for tangible user interfaces. IBM Syst. J. **39**, 915–931 (2000)
22. Zuckerman, O., Arida, S.: Extending tangible interfaces for education: digital montessori-inspired manipulatives. In: Proceedings of the SIGCHI Conference on Human Factors in Computing Systems. (2005)

Chapter 11
Collaborative Problem Solving with Objects: Physical Aspects of a Tangible Tabletop in Technology-based Assessment

Valérie Maquil and Eric Ras

Abstract This chapter analyses how the physical objects and space of a tangible user interface supports groups of participants to collaboratively solve a problem. Our aim is to understand which characteristics of the physical space support the participants in thinking collaboratively. We describe a user study with a tangible tabletop for technology-based assessment. We identify a series of patterns extracted from a video analysis using the Collaborative Learning Mechanism framework. In our discussion, we elaborate the characteristics of the TUI that support interactions based on the observed patterns: the physical interaction objects, the shareability of the space, and the non-responsive spaces.

11.1 Introduction

Technology-based assessment (TBA) can facilitate learning and instruction in ways that paper and pencil cannot. Besides assessing that a learner has a certain level of competency (i.e., assessment *on* learning), it allows optimizing the learning process for both the student and the teacher, i.e., assessment *for* learning. During the last years, topics such as measuring solving strategies (i.e., measurement of dynamics in a test) and *collaborative problem solving* are getting more attention. Such approaches could allow assessing higher levels of comprehension and synthesis, e.g., the students' critical-thinking skills [1]. While current, web-based e-assessment frameworks (e.g., TAO [14]) exploit multimedia capabilities of graphical user interfaces to support a large range of different questions types, their possibilities for supporting and measuring aspects of collaborative problem solving are extremely limited. Hence, we need new technologies that support and allow collaborative activities in a setup, supporting more natural activities and interactions.

V. Maquil (✉) · E. Ras
Public Research Centre Henri Tudor, 29, avenue John F. Kennedy,
1855 Luxembourg, Luxembourg
e-mail: valerie.maquil@tudor.lu

E. Ras
e-mail: eric.ras@tudor.lu

J. Dugdale et al. (eds.), *From Research to Practice in the Design of Cooperative Systems:*
Results and Open Challenges, DOI 10.1007/978-1-4471-4093-1_11,
© Springer-Verlag London 2012

A potential solution are tangible user interfaces (TUIs), which create new types of interaction combining physical and digital elements as part of a physical space. Exploratory, design-focused studies have suggested that TUIs provide some learning benefits, due to the additional haptic dimension, the better accessibility for example for children, and the shared space that supports group interactions [9, 22]. According to Klemmer et al. [8] our human bodies and our interactions with physical objects have an essential impact on our understanding of the world. Bodily actions, physical manipulations, and tangible representations are an active component of our cognition; they act as cues for our memory [21] and allow us to think in a tangible way [17].

While a number of projects have provided different insights on how tangible interfaces are suitable for collaborative learning [2, 5, 11, 19, 22], we lack of a more detailed understanding of how collaborative problem solving is done on a TUI. A better characterization of the different interactions on a tabletop TUI could allow us to understand which aspects of TUIs support and describe our thinking processes in a collaborative problem solving activity.

In this chapter we explored a tangible version of a matching test item that recalls knowledge (i.e., facts) about our planets. The test item provides a task to the test takers (i.e., assign names to the planets), which we consider as simple problem that can be solved in a group on the tabletop. Our aim is to investigate the characteristics of the physical space that support different kinds of actions in a collaborative problem solving activity. Our approach is to analyse an effective collaboration situation around a tangible tabletop and to extract those patterns of external, physical actions that are used as a support for cognition.

On our prototype, physical cards labelled with names of planets could be matched to their visual representations on the tabletop. The test item was solved by eight groups of three subjects in August 2011. Based on a video analysis we extracted a number of patterns related to actions in the physical space and classified them according to a set of mechanisms, provided through the Collaborative Learning Mechanisms (CLM) framework [4]. In our discussion we describe three properties of the physical space that were considered being particularly relevant for external actions of collaborative thinking: the physical interaction objects, the shareability of the space, and the non-responsive spaces.

11.2   Related Work

A number of researchers are working on the development of learning environments using tangible user interfaces, without emphasizing onto assessment. For example, the Chromatorium [16] is an environment where children may discover and experiment with mixing of colours. A similar type of setup allows students to learn about the behaviour of light [12]. Through manipulating a torch and blocks on a table surface, the students could explore concepts of reflection, absorption, transmission, and refraction.

Another type of learning system implements the concept of digital manipulatives [15], computationally enhanced building blocks, which allow the exploration of abstract concepts. This principle is followed by SystemBlocks and FlowBlocks, two physical, modular interactive systems, which children can use to model and simulate dynamic behaviour [22]. The approach of concept mapping for self-regulated learning is followed in [10]: A tangible tabletop allows users to reflect and evaluate their learning tasks through externalizing and representing their knowledge on concept maps. They can, for instance, place physical tokens, assign names, make connections, and use tokens as containers.

Only a few systems go beyond the learning aspects, and implement possibilities for assessment. The Learning Cube [20] acts as a tangible learning platform where multiple choice tests can be done. One side shows a question while up to five answers are shown on each of the other sides. The user turns the cube to the side with the right answer and then shakes it to select it. Another example provides new possibilities for assessing spatial and constructional ability. The Cognitive Cubes [18] are a set of cubes that are used for reconstructing a target 3D shape. The change of each shape is recorded and scored for assessment.

The learning benefit of TUIs has been reflected in a number of design-focused and empirical studies. The use of large artefacts and physical props encourages collaboration as it slows down interaction, makes them more visible to others, and gives everyone "a vote" [19]. A comparative study [5] revealed that TUIs, in contrast to GUIs, are more inviting to use and provide a better support for active collaboration. A tangible programming space showed that physical cards support thinking and negotiating about design decisions of the programed game [2]. The multiple senses engaged in interactions with tangible objects correspond to the natural way that children learn [22]. Further, the shared space of TUIs enables social interactions, such as shifting the focus of a conversation or organizing themselves into subgroups [2], and encourages interference which often leads to argumentation and collective knowledge building [11].

Although a number of publications can be found that describe different kinds of strengths of TUIs for learning applications, there is still a lack of knowledge for using TUIs to assess different kinds of skills and competencies in technology-based assessment. We are missing a detailed understanding of how to design the physical objects and space in a TUI in order to support and measure the individual skills in a collaborative problem solving activity. In this chapter we contribute to this problem through providing the results of a user study, investigating which physical characteristics support groups of users in solving a task on a tangible tabletop. Our work provides a set of characteristics that need to be investigated in further empirical studies in order to understand how they impact social and cognitive aspects of the solving activity.

11.3   Case Study Design and Setup

For the case study, we set up a tangible tabletop system, based on the optical tracking framework "reactivision". The worktop was sized 95 × 120 cm, with an interactive area of 75 × 100 cm. On the table, we projected an image of the solar system,

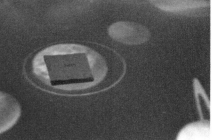

Fig. 11.1 Mapping the cards with the images of the planets

showing the sun and each of the nine planets. We further created nine cards, each with one name of the planets. A camera and projector had been placed underneath the table to track the positions of the physical objects and project feedback onto the semi-translucent tabletop surface. The implemented task was to match the correct name of a planet to the correct image of a planet.

When a user places a card onto a planet, she/he gets an immediate feedback in form of a red (false answer) or green (correct answer) circle that is shown around the planet. During the solving of the task, the system counts the number of attempts (i.e., wrong pairing of a card and a planet's image was counted as one attempt), and the time needed to solve the task. As soon as all the planets are correctly assigned, the system shows a scoring window which displays the results (Fig. 11.1).

The study was conducted with 24 participants divided into eight groups of three. The participants were randomly selected from the research department, with no deep background in astronomy. A briefing questionnaire revealed that the available knowledge was acquired at schools and through personal interests.

At the beginning of each test, the participants were explained the concept of a TUI and how it detects physical objects. We described the goal of their task and which kind of feedback they can expect from the system. They could place themselves around the table as they preferred.

The study was video recorded and at the end we distributed a questionnaire. The video recording was made from one angle, showing the movements on the table and the bodily interactions made close to the table. The questionnaire consisted of three questions asking the background knowledge on astronomy and the System Usability Scale (SUS) with 10 questions. Further, we took notes on the performance of the group and how the users placed themselves around the table.

While the results from the quantitative evaluation have been described elsewhere [13], we focus here on a qualitative analysis of the different ways of interacting with the physical objects and space as support for solving a task.

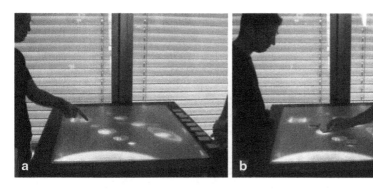

Fig. 11.2 P1 looks at a planet, and points to it: "This is the earth" (**a**). P3 grasps the card of the earth and places it on the according planet (**b**)

11.4 Video Analysis and Findings

The first step of the video analysis was to extract a set of key scenes showing the most significant moments of interaction involving the physical space and objects. Those key scenes are described with a few snapshots and a transcript of what happened.

The key scenes have then been analysed using the CLM framework [4]. This framework supports the analysis of mechanisms for collaborative learning by suggesting four categories of behaviour. Groups are discussing collaboratively through "Making and accepting suggestions", i.e., introducing and accepting knowledge and ideas, and "Negotiating", i.e., sharing statements and suggestions for joint consideration. Further, the collaboration is coordinated through mechanisms of "Joint attention and awareness", allowing to monitor ongoing activity, and "Narrations", where participants say aloud what they are doing.

As a collaborative problem solving activity can also be considered as a type of learning activity, we can assume that the CLM framework will provide us an adequate scope for focusing onto the following research questions:

- What types of behaviour can be found in the collaborative problem solving task?
- How did participants make use of the physical space to express this behaviour?

11.4.1 Collaborative Discussion: Making and Accepting Suggestions

To solve the task in a group, the participants made suggestions about potential names of different planets by speaking aloud, pointing, and making movements with the physical objects. A typical pattern was to express a suggestion through pointing to a planet and verbally suggesting the corresponding name. The acceptance of such a suggestion was then expressed in the form of an action: a second participant grasped the corresponding card and placed it on the planet's image (Fig. 11.2).

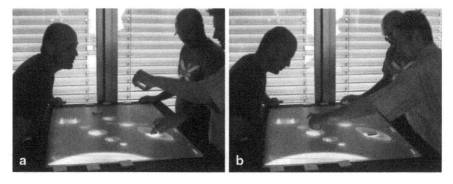

Fig. 11.3 P6 grasps the earth card and holds it high to raise the attention of P4 (**a**). He slowly lowers his arm to place the card onto earth. P4 follows his movement with his eyes and head and does not object (**b**)

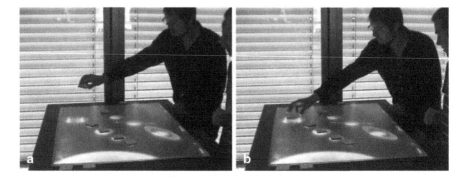

Fig. 11.4 P13 holds the Jupiter card over a planet (**a**): "Can I put Jupiter?" P14: "That seems reasonable to me" P13 places the card on the planet by letting it fall down from a small distance (**b**)

Another approach for making suggestions was to perform a slow movement with wide gestures, resulting in the placement of a card onto a planet. For example, in Fig. 11.3, one participant grasped a card and slowly moved it towards a planet to express a suggestion. During this action he makes sure that he has the attention of a second participant. The fact that the other user did not object, is interpreted as agreement to his suggestion.

In another example, a participant combined talk with a physical manipulation to express a suggestion (Fig. 11.4). He holds the card at a small distance over a planet and raises the attention onto that planet. This physical manipulation allows him to more specifically illustrate a suggestion he is making to the other participants.

11.4.2 Collaborative Discussion: Negotiating

When participants were unsure about assignments, they started to negotiate. In our analysis we identified patterns of sharing knowledge, asking questions, and disagreement, using the physical objects and space in different ways.

Fig. 11.5 P24 knows a mnemonic for remembering the order of the planets. P24 and P23 then grasp the cards one after the other and place them in this order on the bottom edge of the table

While a typical approach was to share knowledge about planets by speaking, making gestures, and pointing, we could also observe situations where the statement was underlined with physical actions. For example, Fig. 11.5 shows a situation where a group decided to first place all the nine cards on an edge of the table in order to sort them according to their distance to the sun.

In negotiation phases, we further observed different ways of asking questions. For example, a participant combined talk, with pointing and gestures:

P10, pointing to a planet: "Jupiter is not the...", *making an iconic gesture,* "...biggest planet?"

In a similar way, disagreement has been expressed through talk and pointing. For example:

P12 points with her finger onto the yellow planet: "So... here?"
P10 moves the card towards the planet and holds it slightly over it: "Here? We tried... no?"

11.4.3 Coordinating Collaboration: Joint Attention and Awareness

The working situation around a tabletop in a physical space provided an excellent environment for monitoring current activities and reflecting upon them. The participants are working on one shared space and each manipulation can be followed by everyone. We could identify a few working mechanisms that even reinforced the general awareness of what is going on.

In a number of situations, participants worked in turns, and there was always just one participant making an assignment at a time (Fig. 11.6). This allowed the other two users to follow his action and to note the corresponding feedback of the system (e.g., red or green circle). Such a situation could usually be observed when participants had already placed the planets they knew, and started to work on the remaining ones using a try and error strategy.

Fig. 11.6 P5 places a card on a planet (**a**). He sees the response turning red and removes the card very quickly (**b**). P4 follows this action while holding another card in his hand. As soon as P5 is done, P4 places his card (**c**)

Fig. 11.7 P16, P17, and P18 each hold a card in their hand. P16: "This little one, isn't it Uranus?" P18: "Ah, you may be right, yes. Go on!" P16 places it, the circle turns red: "No…"

In another situation (Fig. 11.7), we observed how participants grasped a few cards, to hold them in their hands while discussing the suggestions. Holding the objects in the hands allowed them to jointly focus on these three names and concentrate the discussions around them.

11.4.4 Coordinating Collaboration: Narrations

Although narrations in the classical sense of the word have not been observed, we identified an alternative way of telling stories, i.e., by the use of gestures and physical objects. Such practices have been observed during phases of individual working. In Fig. 11.8, we see an example of narrations based on gestures. A participant individually places the Pluto card on a planet and gets feedback that it is correct. To tell the other ones that he just successfully placed the card, he raises his arm and expresses a winning gesture.

A second mechanism related to narrations in the physical space could be observed in a few groups. When placing cards on the table, those participants made such a strong movement that the placement created a noise which could not go

Fig. 11.8 P4 looks at the image and then on the cards close to him. He spots Pluto, grasps the card and quickly places it on the planet (**a**). He sees the circle turning green, is happy and shows it by raising his arm (**b**)

unnoticed by the other participants. We can interpret that this audible aspect of physical manipulations is a way of telling the group about own actions and making it easier to follow interventions.

11.5   Discussion

To better understand what characteristics of the physical objects and space support the observed mechanisms, we analysed the respective interactions in more detail. We characterized each of the interactions based on the questions:

- Where does the interaction take place?
- What is physically manipulated during the interaction?
- Who is actively or passively intervening in the interaction?

Table 11.1 summarizes these major characteristics of the physical interactions.
    From this analysis, we can extract a few insights concerning the physical characteristics of collaborative thinking spaces, which we discuss in the following.

11.5.1   Physical Interaction Objects

In most of the mechanisms the physical cards showing the names of the planets are being used. Being small, they were hold in the hand, and moved to different locations on or next to the table.
    Participants often used the cards to interact with the system and effectively assign names to planets. In addition, we could identify a number of situations where the cards have been used for 'offline' interactions. It was a common practice to hold a card close to a planet in order to demonstrate a potential assignment. Further,

Table 11.1 Mechanisms of collaboration supported though different characteristics of the physical interaction

Physical mechanism	Physical interaction		
	Where	What	Who
Making suggestions through talk and pointing	Responsive area	Hands	Group
Agreeing by placing the card according to a suggestion	Responsive area	Hands and cards	Group
Making suggestions through slow and visible movements	Responsive area	Hands and cards	Group
Sharing knowledge through actions	Non-responsive spaces	Hands and cards	Group
Asking questions through talk, and pointing	Responsive area	Hands	Group
Asking questions through talk, and action	Non-responsive spaces	Hands and cards	Group
Working in turns	Responsive area	Hands and cards	Group
Holding cards in the hand	Non-responsive spaces	Hands and cards	Group
Narrations with gestures and body posture	Responsive area	Hands, body posture	Group
Placing cards with some noise	Non-responsive spaces	Hands and cards	Group

participants are holding several objects in their hands, to concentrate the discussion on the naming of this subset of planets. Other situations showed that the physicality of interaction objects allowed expressing an additional meaning during a manipulation. When participants placed the cards with some noise on the table, they were able to increase the awareness of the other participants. Besides assigning the name to the planet, they added additional information to their physical manipulation, which allowed for a better coordination of collaboration.

The physicality of the interaction objects allowed for a high range of flexibility in their potential manipulations. The participants had the possibility to vary the type and location of the manipulation in order to express different kinds of meanings. This freedom of action was a useful resource for mechanisms related to planning, discussion, and coordination. Such actions, that do not contribute towards the overall goal of the task, but facilitate mental computation of information, are called epistemic actions [7]. Kirsh and Maglio consider them as a valuable resource in improving human cognition and performance.

11.5.2 Shareability of the Space

The selected mechanisms all involve several participants, which communicate to each other either through talk and gestures, or through physical actions. Such a communication thus involves the faces, bodies, and hands of participants, the responsive area where the planets are displayed, and the cards. This can be illustrated, for example, through the situation described in Fig. 11.1, where one participant

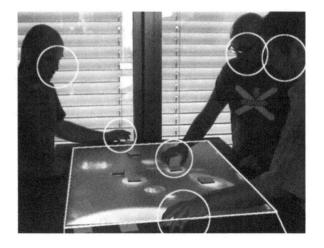

Fig. 11.9 The tabletop provides a shared space where gazes, body postures, gestures, physical actions, interaction area and storage places meet

points onto a planet and a second places the cards according to this suggestion. Such a mechanism involves the line of sights of the two participants, the pointing gesture, the card, the physical movement, and the image of the solar system.

These different elements thus need to be visible for each participant; the interaction area and physical objects further need to be reachable by them. This brings us to the conclusion that an important characteristic of this physical space is sharable on several layers. Each participant can easily follow and access what is happening (a) on the responsive area, (b) in the space between participants, and (c) on the storing place of the objects. Those areas are merged in the space above the tabletop and create a shared space for a variety of actions combining talk, gestures, body postures, and physical objects (Fig. 11.9).

This characteristic of the physical space relates to what Hornecker [6] calls a "bodily shared space", i.e., a space where users and objects are co-present and where the user experiences his body to be in the same place as the interaction objects.

11.5.3 Non-responsive Spaces

When analysing the actual places where the participants are interacting with each other, we notice that a number of mechanisms do not occur on the interaction surface itself. The participants rather specifically looked for places which are not responsive in order to discuss suggestions without interacting with the application.

For example in Fig. 11.5, the participants place the cards on the edge of the table to discuss the sequence of the planets according to their distance to the sun. Another example is described in Fig. 11.4 where a participant explicitly makes use of the space above the surface, in order to demonstrate a suggestion without entering it into the system.

These non-responsive spaces are thus a convenient way for participants to discuss aspects of suggestions. Since no movements are tracked on these areas, participants cannot enter a wrong solution, and feel comfortable with exchanging their ideas. They are thus an essential characteristic for supporting epistemic actions. Participants use them to make suggestions, demonstrate next steps, or set a common focus; activities which do not directly contribute towards the overall goal of the task, but support the participants in thinking about the problem.

A similar observation was made by Fernaeus and Tholander [3], reflecting about an "extra layer of interaction" that is enabled through actions that are "not recorded into the system". The physical space therefore allows a whole range of activities, such as planning and testing of ideas, or selecting and locating the programming cards.

11.6 Conclusions

Through analysing groups of three persons using a tangible tabletop, we have identified mechanisms of collaborative problem solving and related characteristics of the physical space and objects. We found three aspects that supported users in thinking collaboratively: the physical interaction objects, the shareability of the space, and the non-responsive spaces.

Our observations synergize with findings from related work on TUIs and the physical space. They provide another example of how the physicality of TUIs was used for a collaborative learning activity and thus contribute towards a better understanding of the design space of tangible user interfaces.

The assessment item used in this evaluation was assessing knowledge. We implemented a matching task, which is one of the classical tasks used by GUI-based assessment platforms, such as TAO [14]. This task provides only a simple example of a collaborative problem solving context, as the amount of potential solutions is very limited. Further, the system provides only limited digital feedback, and our study was done with a small number of people. Nevertheless, the analysed context was a problem solving situation in a physical interactive environment and allowed us to identify a range of very significant aspects of the physical space and objects that have been used in this situation.

These insights will allow us to set up a range of further experiments. For example, in the near future, we will study the impact of different characteristics of tangible interactions on the level of procedural knowledge. Focusing on procedural knowledge will allow us to assess problem solving skills, for example, in the context of simulations. In empirical studies, we will analyse the differences in the solving strategies and related performances of groups, when varying (a) physical characteristics of the TUI and (b) the nature of the task. This will allow us first to define a framework for designing TUIs to support collaborative problem solving tasks and second, such an understanding of solving strategies in the physical space allows us to identify new ways of measuring the different aspects of a collaborative problem solving activity and to improve techniques of technology-based assessment. A first step would be to classify the types of activities in the non-responsive spaces and to develop a taxonomy of events that we want to measure. New technologies need to be integrated into the table to measure those events. Educational data mining approaches will detect patterns in the logged events streams gathered from the non-responsive as well as responsive spaces. Those patterns can be mapped to solving strategies and cognitive behaviours during problem solving.

Acknowledgments Many thanks go to our student Warda Atlaoui, who was strongly involved in the development of the tangible tabletop. Further, we would like to thank all the colleagues who voluntarily participated in our study.

References

1. Al-Smadi, M., Gütl, C.: Past, Present and Future of e-Assessment: Towards a Flexible e-Assessment System. Special Track on Computer-based Knowledge & Skill Assessment and Feedback in Learning Settings (CAF 2008), ICL 2008, pp. 1–9, Villach, Austria (2008)
2. Fernaeus, Y., Tholander, J.: Looking at the Computer but Doing it on Land: Children's Interactions in a Tangible Programming Space. People and Computers XIX—The Bigger Picture, pp. 3–18. Springer, London (2006)
3. Fernaeus, Y., Tholander, J.: Finding design qualities in a tangible programming space. In: Proceedings of the SIGCHI Conference on Human Factors in Computing Systems—CHI 2006, p. 447, ACM Press, New York, NY, USA (2006)
4. Fleck, R., Rogers, Y., Yuill, N., Marshall, P., Carr, A., Rick, J., Bonnett, V.: Actions speak loudly with words: unpacking collaboration around the table. In: Proceedings of the ACM International Conference on Interactive Tabletops and Surfaces, pp. 189–196, ACM Press (2009)
5. Horn, M.S., Solovey, E.T., Crouser, R.J., Jacob, R.J.K.: Comparing the use of tangible and graphical programming languages for informal science education. In: Proceedings of the 27th international Conference on Human Factors in Computing Systems, pp. 975–984, ACM Press (2009)
6. Hornecker, E.: Understanding the benefits of graspable interfaces for cooperative use. In: Proceedings of 5th International Conference on the Design of Cooperative Systems, pp. 71–87 (2002)
7. Kirsh, D., Maglio, P.: On distinguishing epistemic from pragmatic action. Cogn. Sci. **18**(4), 513–549 (1994)
8. Klemmer, S.R., Hartmann, B., Takayama, L.: How bodies matter: five themes for interaction design. In: Proceedings of the 6th Conference on Designing Interactive Systems, pp. 140–149, ACM Press (2006)
9. Marshall, P.: Do tangible interfaces enhance learning? In: Proceedings of the 1st International Conference on Tangible and Embedded Interaction, p 163, ACM Press, New York, USA (2007)
10. Oppl, S., Steiner, C.M., Albert, D.: Supporting Self-regulated Learning with Tabletop Concept Mapping. In: Mühlhäuser, M., Sesink, W., Kaminski A., Steimle J. (eds.) Interdisciplinary approaches to technology-enhanced learning. Waxmann Verlag (2010)
11. Pontual Falcão, T., Price, S.: Interfering and resolving: How tabletop interaction facilitates co-construction of argumentative knowledge. Int. J. Comput. Support. Collab. Learn. **6**(4), 23–29 (2011)
12. Price, S., Falcão, T.P., Sheridan, J.G., Roussos, G.: The effect of representation location on interaction in a tangible learning environment. In: Proceedings of the 3rd International Conference on Tangible and Embedded Interaction, pp. 85–92, ACM Press (2009)

13. Ras, E., Maquil, V.: Preliminary Results of a Usability Study in the Domain of Technology-based Assessment Using a Tangible Tabletop. In: Workshop Proceedings of IHM, pp. 3–7 (2011)
14. Ras, E., Swietlik, J., Plichart, P., Latour, T.: TAO–A versatile and open platform for technology-based assessment. Paper presented at the sustaining TEL: from innovation to learning and practice, proceedings of 5th European Conference on Technology Enhanced Learning (EC-TEL 2010), vol. LNCS 6383. Springer, Barcelona (2010)
15. Resnick, M., Martin, F., Berg, R., Borovoy, R.: Digital manipulatives: new toys to think with. In: Proceedings of the SIGCHI Conference on Computer Human Interaction, pp. 281–287 (1998)
16. Rogers, Y., Scaife, M., Gabrielli, S., Smith, H., Harris, E.: A conceptual framework for mixed reality environments: designing novel learning activities for young children. Presence Tele-operators Virtual Environ. **11**(6), 677–686 (2002)
17. Shaer, O., Hornecker, E.: Tangible user interfaces: past, present, and future directions. Found. Trends® Hum. Comput. Interact. **3**(1–2), 1–137 (2009)
18. Sharlin, E., Itoh, Y., Watson, B., Kitamura, Y.: Cognitive cubes: a tangible user interface for cognitive assessment. In: Proceedings of the SIGCHI Conference on Human Factors in Computing Systems, vol. 4, pp. 347–354 (2002)
19. Stanton, D., Pridmore, T., Bayon, V., Neale, H., Ghali, A., Benford, S., Cobb, S., Ingram, R., O'Malley, C., Wilson, J.: Classroom collaboration in the design of tangible interfaces for storytelling. In: Proceedings of the SIGCHI Conference on Human Factors in Computing Systems—CHI 2001, pp. 482–489 (2001)
20. Terrenghi, L., Kranz, M., Holleis, P., Schmidt, A.: A cube to learn: a tangible user interface for the design of a learning appliance. Pers. Ubiquitous Comput. **10**(2–3), 153–158 (2005)
21. Zhang, J.: The nature of external representations in problem solving. Cogn. Sci. **21**(2), 1–25 (1997)
22. Zuckerman, O., Arida, S.: Extending tangible interfaces for education: digital montessori-inspired manipulatives. In: Proceedings of the SIGCHI Conference on Human Factors in Computing Systems (2005)

Chapter 12
End-users' Integration of Applications and Devices: A Cooperation Based Approach

Marco P. Locatelli and Carla Simone

Abstract The current organizational and technological evolution suggests to conceive tailorability and EUD also in terms of integration of off the shelf applications and devices that support collaboration. To this aim this chapter proposes an approach that leverages the ability of actors to coordinate their activities and then grounds integration on the notion of cooperation. The resulting technological environment is presented and illustrated through a case derived from an ongoing project. Some considerations derived from a short experimentation conclude the chapter.

12.1 Introduction

Environments supporting tailorability and End Used Development (EUD) are called nowadays to offer their functionalities in a different scenario with respect to earlier approaches and solutions [12]. From a technological point of view, we are witnessing an explosion of open source software applications: they are not always reaching the desired level of robustness and quality of documentation but surely they constitute a reference asset that is going to increase its quality and re-usability. In any case, today almost all available applications guarantee their openness through API (Application Programming Interface).

More interestingly, from the organizational point of view, companies need to be flexible enough to timely react to external (and sometimes internal) changes. This means that an organization survives if it balances in an effective way two complementary activities: the management of the corporate processes and information that support its mission and guarantee its overall robustness; and the management of the day-by-day activities that guarantee the fulfillment of those general goals by a distributed problem solving and coordination that involves groups of people acting at the frontiers of the organization itself and then needing a more flexible way to organize their joint work. Thus, we are witnessing an increasing number of situa-

M. P. Locatelli (✉) · C. Simone
University of Milano-Bicocca, viale Sarca 336, Milan, Italy
e-mail: locatelli@disco.unimib.it

C. Simone
e-mail: simone@disco.unimib.it

J. Dugdale et al. (eds.), *From Research to Practice in the Design of Cooperative Systems: Results and Open Challenges*, DOI 10.1007/978-1-4471-4093-1_12,
© Springer-Verlag London 2012

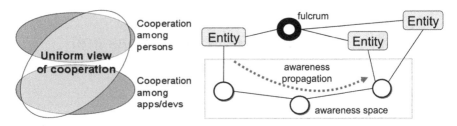

Fig. 12.1 CASMAS provides a uniform view of cooperation (*left*). The CASMAS model: entities can represent either persons or applications/devices (*right*)

tions where users need to negotiate their behavior with other users, as members of more or less consolidated communities [19]. In all these different situations, communities can take various forms and have a varying life span [2]: however, all of them have to establish some basic behavioral rules and conventions to survive and be effective toward their members and their hosting organization. To this aim, the technologies the organization makes them available (typically, corporate information systems) have to be flanked by (compositions of) technologies that, altogether, better respond to their local needs: technologies that are conceived to support local activities without a strong focus on persistency, efficiency, uniform adoption, and are instead more focused on requirements as heterogeneity, malleability, immediate appropriation, user control and the like. This view motivates a shift of interest from tailorability of single (collaborative) applications, e.g. [11], (possibly adopted across the organization) towards the tailorability of *local compositions of existing applications*, as a complement to the former kind of tailorability [20].

The point we want to make is that, irrespective of any details of how it is conceived and implemented, integration is usually proposed in terms of *mutual control* among applications, as for example in Web Services Architectures (SOA) [9] and by the so called mashups [21]. This approach takes the point of view of the professional programmers who reason in terms of system functionality and are skilled enough to deal with all the technical details implied by this kind of composition. On the contrary, end-users are driven by their needs to coordinate their individual and collaborative activities according to the aims, rules and conventions of the community they belong to. So, why not to take the *cooperation* point of view in defining a framework that supports end-users in composing the applications they deem as useful for their local needs and why not to leverage on the long tradition of collaborative work studies? Empirical studies, especially in the CSCW framework, have uncovered that the mechanisms supporting cooperation can be described as the composition of artifacts and protocols in combination with the awareness of what is going on in the context (e.g., [18]). Since actors are familiar with the above mechanisms it should be natural for them to apply the same principles not only to coordinate their mutual behavior but also to define how useful applications might interact to support it since both kinds of interactions can be defined at the same time, by means of the same conceptual tools [16] (see Fig. 12.1 (left)). This approach is in the line of component based tailorability [20] but in addition it offers an explicit way to compose/integrate pieces of software by means of a clear and hopefully friendly metaphor. In this approach, we aim to bring to the technology the "controlled flexibility" typical of human cooperation instead of constraining human beings to conceive their own behaviors in terms of the capability of the technology.

This chapter presents how we exploited the CASMAS framework[1], which supports this view of integration and illustrates its application in a case derived from an ongoing project in our University. Some considerations derived from this short experimentation conclude the chapter.

12.2   The Metaphor and the Language Underlying the Framework

Suppose that a set of applications and devices have to be integrated to support a set of actors cooperating through them. According to the Community-Aware-MAS (CASMAS) framework they all are represented as *entities* and become members of a *community*: as such, they coordinate their behaviors through a Common Information Space (CIS) [3], called *fulcrum*[2], that contains the coordinative information, possibly articulated in coordinative artifacts [13]. Moreover, the fulcrum contains the *behaviors* that are dynamically assigned to each entity to make it an active member of the community: the use of behaviors is similar as in the Actor Model [1]. Like this model, communication is asynchronous but it is not message based. Instead, when an entity *posts a request* in the fulcrum, other entities will *react to this request* according to the behaviors currently assigned to them. In addition, entities promote mutual awareness by being located in an *awareness space* where awareness information is propagated from a source entity along the space structure (topology) [4, 17]. An awareness space can represent the physical space, but also be a logical space: for example, it can represent a set of roles and their relationships as edges connecting them. Figure 12.1 (right) sketches a community, its fulcrum and awareness space. An entity can be member of more than one community and can be located on more than one awareness space: in this case it allows the exchange of information among the communities the entity belongs to.

The CASMAS framework has associated a language to specify entities, their behaviors and the awareness management. This language takes the declarative form of facts and rules (when-then constructs), which offers the possibility to express behaviors in a highly modular way, without the need to define complex and exhaustive control structures [14, 15]. The rules constituting an entity's behavior express *what* the entity is expected to do *when* some conditions are satisfied [15]. These conditions are matched against the facts contained in the community's fulcrum and in the entity's local memory, and against the awareness information from the community's

---

[1] A previous formulation was presented in [7].

[2] This term is used to emphasize the pivotal role of this space in cooperation.

spaces where the entity is located; the action(s) the entity should do updates either the community fulcrum/awareness spaces or the memory of the entity itself.

The integration of a software application/device is realized by inserting a fact in the memory of the entity representing it and by defining the behavior of this entity. The fact contains pairs attribute-value that specify the information the application/device makes available for sake of coordination with, and awareness promotion for, the other entities of the same community; the entity's behavior expresses conditions (among others) on the concrete application/device attributes (when) and invokes some of the functions the application/device exposes to the community (what): actually, the entity is a sort of wrapper that mediates between the concrete application/device and the integration environment (community). For example, if a DMS (Document Management System) is defined so as to provide the number of downloads in one of its attributes and exposes a function to build a report of some occurred events, users may define rules such as:

```
# a semi-formal rule to express the behavior of a DMS
when
   today's downloads are more than 1000
then
   share the report of the today downloads
     with the community
```

Actually, the CASMAS framework uses the Drools[3] rule editor and its capability to express rules in semi-formal terms. This possibility realizes a sort of self documentation and facilitates rules formulation and understanding. This is particularly important since end-users (in the true spirit of EUD) share with other end-users single rules up to whole behaviors: thus documentation plays an important role in reuse or adaptation of exiting rules/behaviors.

When a user wants to define or modify a coordination/awareness pattern, she is facilitated by the high modularity of the overall approach. In fact, behaviors are clearly assigned to entities and then any definition/modification of a rule constituting a behavior affects very delimited portion of the system: the behavior itself and those of the entities involved by the rule at hand. This makes it easier to cross-check the consistency of the definition/modification since it is univocally specified which entity is in charge of making true each condition and of providing each function constituting a rule [16].

12.3   The Framework Put to Work

The basic constructs of the language can be uniformly used to express entities' behaviors at any level of abstraction (see Fig. 12.2) where each level can use the primitives defined at the level(s) below. The language (constituting the first level)

---

[3] http://www.jboss.org/drools.

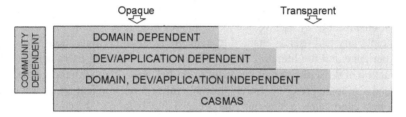

Fig. 12.2 Abstraction levels

provides the following basic constructs (only the ones managing coordination and awareness are presented): *assert, retract, modify* a fact in a fulcrum, *move* an entity in a space, *makeAware* about an information, *AwareOf* to test if an entity perceives some kinds of awareness promoting information. The next level makes available *domain/application/device independent* primitives, like *postRequest* and *copyFact*, and predicates like *Request* and *Response*: they express coarser and recurrent pieces of behaviors that are likely to facilitate integration in terms of coordination of generic components. The level immediately above contains the interfaces (services) provided by *domain independent applications/devices*: for example, the basic I/O primitives of a interactive table or the basic functionalities of a DMS (as described in the previous section). Then the *domain dependent behaviors* are defined at the highest level, possibly with different degree of visibility of the levels below, according to the needs of the community. In fact, this visibility depends on the kinds of technical skill characterizing different classes of users, on the complexity of the integration to be realized, on the organizational norms, and so on. The basic point is that any user applies the same declarative pattern at each level either to define/modify/compose the primitives/predicates available at that level, or to enrich them by using the primitives/predicates of the levels below [16]. A best practice is to organize each level so that it is clear what it makes available and the knowledge required to operate at this level: the knowledge only, since the language is always the same.

A framework supporting tailorability and EUD has to clarify how the different kinds of users are expected to use it. According to the EUD literature, there are at least three kinds of users: *developers, power-users*, and *end-users* [12]. In CASMAS developers are expected to set up and maintain the overall framework: in particular, they are in charge of the two bottom levels of Fig. 12.2. Hence, they define the basic primitives/predicates that are domain independent in that they express the elemental interactions with the fulcra and the awareness spaces, their applications and devices. In the previous section we mentioned the basic ones but nothing prevents a specific instantiation of the framework to add new primitives/predicates if needed. Developers are also in charge of constructing the wrappers for the functionalities offered by the applications/devices to be coordinated: they can be used in the right part of the rules at the next higher level of abstraction. These two activities require technical skills that the other kinds of users are not expected to possess. The highest level is the realm of end-users and power users. Power-users are end-users with technical skills suitable to manage the dynamic configuration of the coordinated applications, mainly by adding new behaviors or high level primitives/predicates. In principle any end-user is enabled to manage dynamic configurations: however our experience and the literature (e.g., [8]) show that often end-users delegate the construction of difficult interactions to more skilled users. In other words, end-users may need a "human proxy" between them and the tailored application: power users are the best candidates to play this role because they belong to the community, understand the needs of their "costumers" and know about the rules and conventions holding within the community itself. They are then able to express them in terms of behaviors, i.e., sets of rules, that can be made available to the other community members. End-users are expected to tailor existing behaviors by adapting the set of rules they contain. More experienced end-users can build completely new behaviors by writing new set of rules, possibly with the help of some power-users. In this paradigmatic allocation of responsibilities end-users are not expected to act as "systems integrators" or "software architects": instead, they are called to think in terms of which kind of coordinated behavior they are able to offer and want to get from the community in response to their common needs. This behavior has to be negotiated among the actors (as it happens irrespectively of the available technology) and then properly implemented by using the features made available by the framework.

12.4 Case Study

In the context of the GAS (Grandi Attrezzature Scientifiche)—Intelligent Building project of our University we set up a room with some facilities for group work: an interactive desk, some interactive whiteboards, a localization technology, small and medium size interactive screens, and artifacts "augmented" by means of localization tags to make them traceable in the room (for example, books with a localization tag attached). The above interactive devices allow actors to use software applications to support group work and (new) content production by accessing their own contents or the contents provided by other people.

The case study we present in this chapter involved a class of 14 students divided in three groups (two groups of five persons and one group of four persons). The students were familiar with computer usage and owned a background in psychology (one person per group own advanced skills in computer usage; two of them have been involved in doing power-user tailorability, see Sect. 12.4.2.4). The supervisor asked groups to prepare a report on a common topic in psychology. The groups met twice a week for about 2 months to collaboratively prepare the report with the support of the supervisor. From time to time the supervisor made some contents available to the class to orient the work of the three groups. To support this supervised collaboration the room was configured as follows: the desk is reserved to the supervisor and runs an application to manage personal contents and possibly make them publicly available to the class; each group owns a whiteboard providing a work space where to manage group, personal, or publicly available contents. During three meetings students and supervisor were told about the CASMAS framework

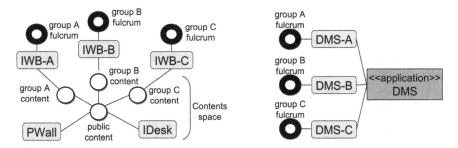

Fig. 12.3 Basic configuration (*left*). Multiple entities associated to one shared application (*right*)

and language as well as about the features made available by the basic configuration. Then they started to autonomously use this framework: when tailoring was needed students tried to solve the problem by their own and came to us only to validate their solution or to ask for our help. Students were familiar with the DMS that managed the content/documents they needed: it was configured so that single actors and groups can have their own repositories. The rest of this section describes how the basic configuration (referred to as "system") was constructed and then tailored by the students to respond the needs arisen during its usage.

12.4.1   Configuring the System

According to the approach presented in Sect. 12.2, we (as developers) implemented the initial system configuration that includes the following fulcra and awareness spaces:

- `group X fulcrum`: a community fulcrum for each group (see Fig. 12.3 (left));
- `class fulcrum`: a community fulcrum for all the actors involved, i.e. students and the supervisor;
- `contents space`: a space to promote awareness of available contents (see Fig. 12.3 (left));
- `room space`: a space representing the physical localization inside the room of all the involved actors to manage awareness promotion about their presence.

The `contents space` contains a `group-X` content node for each group: these nodes are linked to the `public content` node to support the propagation of awareness information about the availability of group and public content, respectively. Actually this is a simplification of the actual `contents space`: it is sufficient to discuss the usage of the framework presented in this chapter.

In addition, the configuration contains the entities that stand proxy for the three groups, the supervisor and the following "technological actors": one entity for the interactive desk (`IDesk`); one entity for each interactive whiteboard (`IWB-X`); one entity for the public wall (`PWall`); one entity for each group to manage its interactions with the DMS (`DMS-X`).

Figure 12.3 (left) considers only the portion of the whole configuration that will be used in the rest of this chapter and shows how the above entities are connected to the fulcra and to the `contents space`. Moreover, groups members are linked to the fulcrum related to their group, and the supervisor is linked to the fulcrum related to the class (these links and the latter fulcrum are omitted in the figure).

In a cooperative setting, some applications (typically, a DMS as in our case) are shared among several users and groups as a resource provided by the organization they belong to. However, users and groups might want to define different local interactions with this resource, according to their needs. In CASMAS this is realized by associating more than one entity to a single application instance and to connect each of them to the appropriate fulcrum (see Fig. 12.3 (right)).

Each entity of the basic configuration has associated a "standard" behavior. In the following we illustrate a small portion of system behavior concerning a case of awareness promotion that involves `IDesk` and `PWall`. Patterns related to other forms of cooperation will be shown later on. When a new content is moved from the personal to the public area of the interactive desk (typically, by the supervisor), the `IDesk` uses the `contents space` to make the other entities aware of this event (*makeAware* primitive, see Sect. 12.2). The related awareness information is propagated in the space from the `public content` location because the `IDesk` is situated there, and reaches all the `group X content` locations. `PWall` becomes aware of the new available content because it is situated at the `public content` node and owns (by design) the following rule (rule RD1_PWALL) that realizes the following reaction: `PWall` shows the new content to make it publicly available.

Rules are hereafter presented using the semi-formal notation of Drools.

```
rule "RD1_PWALL-show publicly available content"
when
  aware of content available on space CONTENTSSPACE
then
  show content
end
```

where `aware of` is a construct defined at the CASMAS language level. The `show` action is defined at the application dependent level. Notice that the `IWB-Xs` do not react to the presence of any new available content because the developers did not define a similar rule in their behavior, even though this kind of awareness promoting information reaches all the locations where they are located.

12.4.2 Tailoring the System

During the case study we observed different situations in which power users or end users felt the need to modify the basic system configuration giving rise to different kinds of tailorability.

12.4.2.1   End-user Tailorability

Two of the three groups improved the support provided by the system. Members of group 'A' recognized it was useful for them to have the public contents available for future use. Members of group 'B' identified a different requirement: they would have the public contents visualized also on their local IWB in addition to the public wall. In this way the group could elaborate their report having these contents ready at hand during their collaboration. Then Group 'A' defined two rules that illustrate a typical cooperation pattern between two applications through the fulcrum. By the first one (rule R2_IWB) the IWB-A posts a store request to group A fulcrum when it is aware of the new available content.

```
rule "R2_IWB-privately store public content"
when
   aware of new content available in space CONTENTSSPACE
then
   post a "store" request of this content to the group
end
```

post is a construct at the domain/device/application independent level, as already mentioned in Sect. 12.2.

By the second rule (rule R2_DMS) the DMS responds to the "store request" by storing the content through the functions of the DMS application. The content is stored in the current activity area of the repository.

```
rule "R2_DMS-privately store public content"
when
   there is a "store" request from the group
   group is carrying on an activity
then
   store content contextually to the current activity
end
```

request is a fact at the domain/device/application independent level, as well as post; current activity is a fact defined at the domain dependent level that models the current activity and its attributes (e.g., its name) that the group is carrying on. In the basic configuration used in the case study the current activity fact was asserted as a static information useful to allocate to a specific area the contents generated during the case. In a more general situation, this naturally dynamic information could be obtained from a WFMS application for which current activity is defined as one of its attributes (see Sect. 12.2).

Group 'B' needed to define only one rule to let the IWB-B show the content when it becomes aware of a new available content (rule R3_IWB).

```
rule "R3_IWB-show public content"
when
   aware of content available on space CONTENTSSPACE
```

```
then
  show content
end
```

After group 'B' used the system for a while, its members realized that every time a public content was available on their IWB they naturally focused on that content; in order to make its fruition easier they also minimized the current content to have more space for the new content. Hence, the group decided to change the above rule (rule R3_IWB) to minimize the current content area before the public content was shown, by adding the "as main content" clause to the action part of the rule

```
  ...
show content as main content
  ...
```

Group 'B' found group 'A' "storing behavior" very useful. Accordingly, group 'B' updated the behavior of their IWB-B with the functionality implemented by group 'A'. In this way they did not only view the public content but also had the content stored in the DMS.

12.4.2.2 Domain Language as Support of Tailorability

As mentioned in Sect. 12.2, the semi-formal language supported by Drools to define a Domain Specific Language (as Drools calls it) can be used both to offer a more user friendly version of the CASMAS language and to construct a semi-automatic documentation of system behavior [16]. Users appreciated this possibility because this made easier and more natural for them to conceive the rules, and also because the semi-formal language allows one to hide some technical details (as we will discuss in Sect. 12.5). We present here as an example the formal version of rule R3_IWB defined for the IWB-B by group 'B':

```
rule "R-F-1"
when
  AwareOf(space=="$CONTENTSSPACE$",
    type=="content available", contentURL:awarenessData)
then
  application.minimizeContent();
  application.showContent(contentURL);
end
```

This formal rule is automatically derived from rule R3_IWB by means of the following mappings where the semi-formal version is associated (by '=') with its formal counterpart and the texts in curly brackets define the rule parameters to be instantiated: in this case, the type of awareness information and the awareness space where the information is perceived.

```
[when]aware of {awareness type} on space {space name}=
AwareOf(space=="{space name}",
  type=="{awareness type}", contentURL:awarenessData)
[then] show content as main content =
  application.minimizeContent();
  application.showContent(contentURL);
```

Notice that the semi-formal formulation does not contain any reference to the information content: in fact, the rule does not define any specific condition on it. However, the content appears as an attribute in the formal specification. Although this kind of parametrization might be considered simple and not so powerful, it allows one to adapt it to compose other rules managing other types of awareness information, e.g. about an updated content. The Drools factory supports users in building the mappings through a graphical user interface (that generates the above textual mapping structure) although in a not completely satisfactory way: we will come back to this points in the conclusions.

Finally, the action show content as main content ([then] mapping) expresses the users' needs *in one sentence*: in fact, "as main content" implies that all the other contents have to be minimized. The abstraction of a sequence of actions into a single sentence is very powerful also to avoid accidental omissions, in particular when some actions have to be done only to maintain system consistency. Rule R2_DMS is an example as the response to a request implies the request deletion. This rule is translated into the following formal rule

```
rule "R-F-2"
when
  request:Request(assertedIn=="$GROUP$",
    service=="store", contentURL:params)
  CurrentActivity(assertedIn=="$GROUP$",
    activityName:name)
then
  application.store(contentURL, activityName);
  retract(request);
end
```

by means of the following mapping:

```
[then] store content contextually to the
current activity=application.store(contentURL,
  activityName); retract(request);
```

In our experience, to start using the semi-formal language end-users need the assistance of a power user: then, they start using the mappings to build new semi-formal rules. Only after a longer experience they define the needed mappings by their own, typically by adapting the ones they had used before.

12.4.2.3 Tailoring Information Provided by Applications

During the case study the students came to us to understand how to extend the set of attributes that the developers defined to convey information from the DMS to the coordination space (i.e, groups fulcra) since they didn't find a solution by themselves. During the discussion to give an answer to this request they appreciated the fact that this was possible in a way that they could understand. In fact, it would only require the invocation of some pertinent application method(s) as shown by the following example (RAPP-1) that we used to illustrate the solution.

```
rule "RAPP-1"
when
   there is a "number of docs" request from the group
then
   post number of docs to the group
end
```

where the post of "number of docs" information should be defined in the mapping as:

```
int numberOfDocs=application.getDocsCount(dir);
assert(new DirDocsCount(assertedIn="$GROUP$",
   directory=dir, count=numberOfDocs));
```

The students told us that this kind of tailoring would require the help of the developers: however, they felt they could formulate the related request with an idea of what it would require to be implemented. Power users instead were confident that, if the application methods were sufficiently well documented, they would be able to handle the simplest cases by their own.

12.4.2.4 Power-user Tailorability

The awareness promotion about new content produced by other groups was a feature required by the participants since they like to stay informed. However, end-users were not able to define this behavior by themselves, mainly because it is not simple for them to implement a message starting from the URL of the content to be shown. Hence, a couple of recognized power-users committed themselves to cooperatively build the new behavior for their colleagues. The two power users negotiated the following assignments, according to their skills. One of them defined a new rule to be added to the IWB-X behavior, which shows the desired message when this device is aware of a new content (thus, using a previously unexploited information). The second power user defined the function that creates the new message by extracting information from the URL of the awareness information content. Although this power user was not a professional developer, she was able to look for some tutorials on the Web[4] to implement the needed function, called createMessage, by adapting standard patterns they make available.

---

[4] e.g. http://www.exampledepot.com/egs/java.net/ParseURL.html.

```
rule "R1_IWB-show awareness about groups' content"
when
   AwareOf(space=="$CONTENTSSPACE$",
      type=="group content created",
      contentURL:awarenessData)
then
   # show content awareness
   String awMessage=createMessage(contentURL);
   application.showAwarenessMessage(awMessage);
end

function String createMessage(String contentURL) {
   URL url=new URL(contentURL);
   String documentName=url.getFile();
   String message = documentName + "is available";
   return message;
}
```

`createMessage` is a function that she defined at the domain dependent level, since it defines for the specific community how the actors are informed about a new content produced by other groups. To adopt this new behavior each group uploaded it in its own fulcrum so that the IWB of each group acquires this behavior and behaves accordingly to the community's agreement. The above kind of division of labor was observed in several circumstances: it is favored by the if-then structure of the language, which defines a natural "interface" between the tasks of the two power users.

12.5   Lesson Learnt and Future Developments

The experience we got from the case study has been encouraging and fruitful: the community metaphor and the cooperation based approach was naturally appropriated by the participants since they were able to recognize coordinative practices in their every day learning activities and take them as starting point to tailor the given system configuration. Sometimes users had some difficulties in separating the functional aspects of an application (what it can do) from its coordination and awareness behavior (when and how it should do something). This kind of difficulty emerged when users collaborated with developers to include a new application functionality (as reported in Sect. 12.4.2.3) or a totally new application (not reported in this chapter) into the system: often users suggested functionalities that include coordination or awareness aspects. However, this problem almost disappeared when users wanted to tailor how the application contributes to the overall system: in this case they had to recognize which basic functionality was offered by the application, and which new coordinative behavior had to be defined. The case study confirmed that any adoption of tailorability and EUD environments requires an assisted learning process: however, we perceived an increasing appropriation of the approach because the kind of support users requested was toward the solution of more complex problems of integration and tailoring [10]. At the same time the case study raised a set of basic requirements oriented to improve the usability of the approach. The first issue is about the development of a graphical interface to represent the current configuration of the system in terms of the integrated applications/devices and the proxies of their collaborating users. This graphical interface would facilitate system development and tailorability, and support rules organization. Actually, the levels of abstraction described in Sect. 12.3 and the modularity based on the notion of community of entities are a sound basis towards rules organization at each level. A second issue concerns rules definition. Here it is not a matter of syntax comprehension: users correctly understood existing rules; nor of compliance with the (semi-)formal language: Drools offers a rich syntax driven editor. When users came to us for getting support, we observed that they did not own a strategy to transform their intuition of what each entity should do into well-formed rules [5] and in so doing they encountered recurrent problems: typically, users do not list all the conditions that characterize the situation in which an action has to be executed; or they forget to retract facts that no longer represent valid situations; or they are confused about where to memorize information (i.e., facts) either in their private memory or in the shared fulcra, and by default choose the second alternative; or finally, they apply the traditional pattern of interaction based on request/response also when the post/react pattern would be more appropriate since the capabilities of the current collaborative context are not fully known. We are currently collecting the problems that the past and ongoing experiences of usage are putting in evidence [14]: the aim is to enrich the graphical interface with suitable guidelines that would warn users of erroneous or at least dangerous rules formulations. A last and even more challenging issue concerns the test of rules consistency in presence of the tailoring of a given configuration [6]. Again, the rules organization mentioned above offers an initial strategy based on modularity: however, more has to be done to support the check of consistency. A possible solution could be based on the visualization of rules dependencies, like cells dependencies in a spreadsheet: here however the solution has to take into account the different levels of abstraction in which rules are organized. In improving the CASMAS framework along the above lines we will continue to adopt the iterative method based on users feedbacks, thanks to the technological setting made available by the GAS-Intelligent Building project.

Acknowledgments This work has been supported by the GAS-Intelligent Building project and with the financial support of F.A.R. 2010.

References

1. Agha, G.: Actors: A Model of Concurrent Computation in Distributed Systems. MIT Press, Cambridge (1986)
2. Andriessen, J.: Archetypes of knowledge communities. In: van de Besselaar, P.V., De Michelis, G., Preece, J., Simone, C. (eds.) Second Communities & Technologies Conference (C&T 2005), pp. 191–214, Springer, Netherlands (2005)

3. Bannon, L., Bodker, S.: Constructing common information spaces. In: ECSCW 1997: Proceedings of the 5th Conference on European Conference on Computer-supported Cooperative Work, pp. 81–96, Kluwer Academic, Norwell, MA, USA (1997)
4. Benford, S., Fahlén, L.: A spatial model of interaction in large virtual environments. In: ECSCW 1993: Proceedings of the 3rd Conference on European Conference on Computer-supported Cooperative Work, pp. 109–124, Kluwer Academic, Norwell, MA, USA (1993)
5. Berti, S., Paternò, F., Santoro, C.: Natural development of ubiquitous interfaces. Commun. ACM. **47**(9), 63–64 (2004). doi:10.1145/1015864.1015891
6. Burnett, M., Cook, C., Rothermel, G.: End-user software engineering. Commun. ACM. **47**(9), 53–58 (2004). doi:10.1145/1015864.1015889
7. Cabitza, F., Locatelli, M.P., Simone, C.: Cooperation and ubiquitous computing: an architecture towards their integration. In: Proceeding of the 2006 Conference on Cooperative Systems Design, pp. 86–101, IOS Press (2006)
8. Dixon, D.R.: The behavioral side of information technology. Int. J. Med. Inform. **56**, 117–123 (1999). doi:10.1016/S1386-5056(99)00037-4
9. Erl, T.: Service-oriented Architecture: Concepts, Technology, and Design. Prentice Hall PTR, Upper Saddle River (2005)
10. Fischer, G., Giaccardi, E., Ye, Y., Sutcliffe, A.G., Mehandjiev, N.: Meta-design: a manifesto for end-user development. Commun. ACM. **47**(9), 33–37 (2004). doi:10.1145/1015864.1015884
11. Fogli, D.: Chap. End-User Development for E-Government Website Content Creation, pp. 126–145, Springer, Berlin (2009). doi:10.1007/978-3-642-00427-8_8
12. Lieberman, H., Paternò, F., Wulf, V. (eds.): End User Development. No. 9 in Human-Computer Interaction Series. Springer, Netherlands (2006)
13. Locatelli, M.P., Loregian, M.: Active coordination artifacts in collaborative ubiquitous-computing environments. In: Schiele, B., Dey, A.K., Gellersen, H., de Ruyter, B.E.R., Tscheligi, M., Wichert, R., Aarts, E.H.L., Buchmann, A.P. (eds.) Ambient Intelligence, European Conference, AmI 2007, Darmstadt, Germany, 7–10 Nov 2007. In: Proceedings, Lecture Notes in Computer Science, vol. 4794, pp. 177–194, Springer (2007). doi:10.1007/978-3-540-76652-0_11
14. Locatelli, M.P., Simone, C.: Integration of services based on the community metaphor: some guidelines from an experience of use. In: The 2nd International Workshop on End User Development for Services (EUD4Services). Torre Canne (Brindisi), Italy (2011)
15. Myers, B.A., Pane, J.F., Ko, A.: Natural programming languages and environments. Commun. ACM. **47**(9), 47–52 (2004). doi:10.1145/1015864.1015888
16. Repenning, A., Ioannidou, A.: What makes end-user development tick? 13 design guidelines. In: Lieberman, H., Paternò, F., Wulf, V. (eds.) End User Development, Human-Computer Interaction Series, vol. 9, pp. 51–85. Springer, Netherlands (2006). doi:10.1007/1-4020-5386-X_4
17. Rodden, T.: Populating the application: a model of awareness for cooperative applications. In: CSCW 1996: Proceedings of the 1996 ACM Conference on Computer Supported Cooperative Work, pp. 87–96. ACM Press, New York, NY, USA (1996). doi:10.1145/240080.240200
18. Schmidt, K., Simone, C.: Coordination mechanisms: towards a conceptual foundation of cscw systems design. Comput. Support. Coop. Work. **5**, 155–200 (1996). doi:10.1007/BF00133655
19. Wenger, E.: Communities of practice; learning as a social system. Syst. Think. **9**(5), 2–3 (1998)
20. Wulf, V., Pipek, V., Won, M.: Component-based tailorability: Enabling highly flexible software applications. Int. J. Hum. Comput. Stud. **66**(1), 1–22 (2008). doi:10.1016/j.ijhcs.2007.08.007
21. Yu, J., Benatallah, B., Casati, F., Daniel, F.: Understanding mashup development. IEEE Internet Comput. **12**, 44–52 (2008). doi:10.1109/MIC.2008.114

Chapter 13
Social Aspects of Place Experience in Mobile Work/Life Practices

Luigina Ciolfi, Breda Gray, and Anthony D'Andrea

Abstract This chapter examines the importance of "where" mobile work/life prac-tices occur. By discussing excerpts of data collected through in-depth interviews with mobile professionals, we focus on the importance of place for mobility, and highlight the social character of place and the intrinsically social motivations of workers when making decisions regarding where to move. In order to show how the experience of mobility is grounded within place as a socially significant construct, we concentrate on three analytical themes: place as an essential component of social/collaborative work, place as expressive of organizational needs and characteristics, and place as facilitating a blending of work/life strategies and relationships.

13.1 Introduction

Work practices are increasingly mobile, both from the point of view of spatial mobility and in terms of mobility between roles, situations and relationships. Yet there has been little research so far on the implications about *where* work is done: mobile workers accomplish their work at a variety of locations, and such loca-tions are tightly connected with practices and interactions, both in terms of in-frastructural support [18] and of possibilities for collaboration [22]. This chapter examines the social character of place in the practices of a community of highly mobile workers. It investigates motivations for mobility, both social and coop-erative: where do workers work and what affects their decisions to move in this regard? Our findings suggest that place matters in decisions about where work is done because, among other factors, it is invested by social connotations and

L. Ciolfi (✉)
Interaction Design Centre, Department of CSIS, University of Limerick, Limerick, Ireland
e-mail: luigina.ciolfi@ul.ie

B. Gray
Department of Sociology, University of Limerick, Limerick, Ireland
e-mail: breda.gray@ul.ie

A. D'Andrea
ISSP & Department of Sociology, University of Limerick, Limerick, Ireland
e-mail: a-dandrea@uchicago.edu

J. Dugdale et al. (eds.), *From Research to Practice in the Design of Cooperative Systems:*   183
Results and Open Challenges, DOI 10.1007/978-1-4471-4093-1_13,
© Springer-Verlag London 2012

meanings—something that the design of technologies supporting mobile interaction should be more sensitive to.

Mobility is a broad concept characterizing much recent socio-scientific research and technology-related research. The *new mobilities* approach involves examining 'how social relations necessitate the intermittent and intersecting movements of people, objects, information and images across distance' ([25], p. 54). It is concerned with movement but also with the economic, social and cultural organization of distance ([25], p. 54). Underpinning this approach is the view that human mobility cannot be understood outside of the movement of objects and technologies: here ensembles of technologies with people, knowledge and other agents mediate and shape everyday life. People are engaged in making work and non-work worlds in and through the ways in which they 'move, mobilize people, objects, information and ideas' ([4], p. 112). We are particularly interested in how this deep understanding of mobility is linked to the role of technology in supporting collaborative practices on the move, and on how mobility in both work and life is mediated by technology.

However, most research on the role of technology in supporting practices on the move is still overly technology-centred, focusing primarily on the design and/ or evaluation of services, protocols and applications. Studies of mobile technology use seldom extend to the broader circumstances of mobility, and almost never to *where* mobile work and life practices occur. As well as this, the *everytime-everywhere* assumption underpinning mobile technology design and development [14, 27]—whereby it is assumed that the needs of mobile actors are not location or time dependent—has led to an abstracted understanding that lifts mobility out of specific contexts. Although this approach makes an important contribution in relation to infrastructure and access (for example, in terms of providing robust connectivity and services), it makes little or no contribution to understanding human interactions on the move [8]. As Sørensen points out: 'It is tempting to assume (…) that work can be conducted at any time and anywhere through combinations of global networking and mobile information technology. However, this conclusion makes inappropriate assumptions of both the power of technology and the inherent characteristics of work' ([23], p. 4). Human interactions on the move—with technology and with other people—are much more complex, and are affected by practical circumstances related to places, organizations and social relationships: therefore, we feel that it is necessary to look at the specific physical contexts that mobile workers inhabit in their everyday practices, and to examine their strategies for movement in relation to them.

Whereas early HCI research on mobility and work focused mainly on individuals, within CSCW there have been attempts at looking at cooperative work on the move [1, 5]. The studies of mobile practices conducted so far are mainly focused on collaborative aspects of the task-at-hand: for example, how mobile software and applications support group work [10, 13] and how collaboration is accomplished while on the move (see for example [19]). In our study, we explore broader social and collaborative connotations of mobility as a strategy pervading work and life. We position our work within a stream of research in collaborative computing looking at mobility in context, an area of study still under development [21, 26]. In this chapter we reflect on data gathered as part of a project studying new patterns of mobile work and life in the context of the 'knowledge economy': grounded on a model of work that assumes flexibility, connectedness and spatial and practice-related mobility [9]. Views vary with regard to which kinds of work are most emblematic of the knowledge economy. However the main characteristics of so-called knowledge work tend to include: work with codified concepts/knowledge [24]; variety or varied work; interdependence with tasks done elsewhere; individual autonomy with workers being expected to make independent judgements in uncertain contexts [2] and a tendency for work to be undertaken across different locations and on the move [7].

Our focus is on the lived experience of these workers and how mobility characterizes their work and life practices. In particular, we look at the central role of place as socially constructed in these practices. In the following section, we discuss further how our work connects to related research on place and mobility and how we set out to conduct our investigation.

13.2   Situating Mobility in the Social World

In our project, we make the assumption that new forms of work increasingly have mobility inscribed in them and the need to manage *fluidity* and *boundaries*, with technology playing an essential part in both [23]. Our argument is that such mobility needs to be studied in context, and that such context reveals patterns of social and collaborative practices that are closely tied to mobile strategies and linked constructions of place. Mobility is a wide-ranging notion and previous research has identified various forms of spatial mobility, differentiating levels at which movements can take place [17] and various types of mobile activities [15]. We acknowledge the importance of these finer distinctions: although our analysis takes place at a broader level, that incorporates these different forms of mobility by documenting mobile practices as shaped by context. As such, our main goal is therefore to look at mobility in context.

Notions of place can help us uncover some of the social connotations of mobility. Attention to place acknowledges the debate on distance [20] and recognizes that communication, interaction and collaboration happen in different ways through co-presence. By centering place it is also possible to examine how face-to-face interaction blends with interactions established by digital means [16], and identify the awareness mechanisms in distributed group work [11]. Thus, considering place *explicitly* as a lens to understand practice within a certain physical context allows us to connect aspects of human activities and experiences to the qualities of the environment [12]. We focus on the making of places, the boundaries and trajectories between them, and we consider these places not just as locations but as scenes of our experience in the world. Technology becomes a factor in the embodied context of practice and we pay particular attention to how it mediates activities. We are not singling out locations, but address place as the multi-layered experience within the physical world that is simultaneously shaped by personal, social, physical and cultural factors [6]. As such, place is defined by social interaction, it is invested with social relationships as well as physical qualities.

Others have highlighted the importance of considering place when studying mobile practices. Brown and O'Hara [3] argue that work changes place, just as place changes work and work-time planning: places are constantly reconfigured and appropriated by people to support their activities, and being in a particular place affects work activities in terms of physical resources and other factors. Work places are made and work is made in place. In their study of nomadic study groups, Rossitto and Eklundh [22] examine how en-placed experience leads to complex patterns of collaboration and reconfiguration of the physical environment, and argue that social and collaboration needs lead to choosing a particular place of work.

Similarly, in our study, we argue that the conditions under which people choose their work place are deeply socially motivated. As such, places are socially experienced and technology becomes entwined in an individual's strategies of action. These are social and collaborative strategies: they might not be always related to a collaborative *task*, but they are related to collaborative *work* and to social relationships, both professional and personal. As work and life become more mobile, workers are faced with the question of where they are done. Decisions about where work and life take place involve considerations about interaction with others and about the differentiated mobilities in relation to everyday movement and long-distance travel. Moreover, turning to the question of how boundaries between work and life, between work and personal social relationships might be blurred by mobile work, it is clear that technology plays a central mediating role.

In the following sections we present evidence for our argument by discussing qualitative data gathered through a series of in-depth interviews with high-tech professionals, all living relatively mobile lifestyles. All the participants in the study are working in the high-tech sector in senior roles (managers, directors, CEOs, etc.) and their companies are all located in the "National Technology Park" (NTP), a regional science and technology hub housing around 80 organizations with strong emphasis on research and development. Although our participants hold slightly different roles within their organization, they present the common traits of living highly mobile lifestyles, working in positions of responsibility and doing business in the high-tech sector, also involving substantial use of digital technologies. We conducted in depth semi-structured interviews with 11 men and 7 women. The qualitative methodology we employed involved asking people about their everyday experiences of work and life, their interaction with technological artefacts as manipulated in practice and the affordances for practices they offer. The interview was loosely structured into three parts: biographical questions about the participants' background, profession, family and lifestyle; work questions about daily activities and their integration with technologies, forms of employment, connectivity and networking practices; institutional questions regarding their company's choices over location, perceptions of quality of services and interaction with support agencies. In order to show how the experience of mobile work and life is grounded within place as a socially significant construct we concentrate on three themes:

- Place as an essential component of social/collaborative work;
- Place as expressive of organizational needs and characteristics;
- Place as facilitating a blending of work/life strategies and relationships.

In the following sections, we will concentrate on each theme, presenting and discussing relevant data excerpts.

13.3   Place as Essential Component of Social and Collaborative Work

Each place of work carries implications of a social and collaborative nature. Workers choose to be somewhere in order to establish or maintain relationships and to do collaborative work. Not only do some places provide structural support, but they *mean* something with regard to these factors: being somewhere means being with others, working with them, a strategy of collaboration or simply co-presence.

Jonathan[1], the CEO of a software development company, talks about his weekly work routine at numerous places:

> I'm in here most days, because I just want to—we were taking on some, one or two new people, and I just want to get the whole, you know, importance going. But tomorrow, as an example, I'm in the city tomorrow in meetings with suppliers and S--, to see…can S-- maybe put us in the way of getting more opportunities, you know. Last week, I was in the city on Wednesday, with C---. We got an award from C--- for—it was five companies, […] and ourselves, and there was two more, we got an award at a dinner last Wednesday. What else? On a day-to-day basis, it's just really being here, being available, you know, this type of thing. (Jonathan)

Being "here", meaning at the office, is important for Jonathan in order to establish relationships with the new people. Travelling to the city is also necessary to make new partnerships, receive the important award, work with suppliers, and strengthen their institutional collaboration with C---. In general, being "here" is valued as much because it strengthens internal relationships. It's not just about travelling, choosing to work at headquarters is an important social strategy too.

Jack, technical director of a software firm, is also conscious of his team at the company headquarters. When asked about why he does not like to do work from his home, although he travels a lot internationally and finds this tiresome, he answers:

> Well I suppose because the team is here. We do actually have to meet sometime, even though I haven't spoken to them much today and I've been away since Tuesday. And also what we have here is we have our own Intranet, to our own sort of network internally, and that I can't access from home. We could, but it would be too expensive and security wise it would be a nightmare. But the main thing is just to meet the team. (Jack)

---

[1] All names have been changed to preserve anonymity.

There is certainly an infrastructural issue connected to headquarters (the secure intranet) that makes it relevant for Jack to be there, but a technical solution could be found to reduce the need for presence at headquarters. However, if for Jack the 'main thing is just to meet the team', then presence at headquarters will continue to be necessary. As the discussion progresses, Jack agrees that he could work from home at least some of the time and deal with queries over the phone, but chooses not to:

> Well the main thing, the reason I came in this morning is I had a teleconference with some folks in Greece and Italy at 10, so. I could have done that at home, but. I don't know, I just come into the office, it's handier. And all my files and stuff is here, the paper. The main thing is to meet, is to meet the team, because like it isn't just me managing the projects. It's about the guys doing the Web site, or software, or hardware, whatever. So it isn't just me. (Jack)

Although the presence of other resources is one factor in his decision to work at the office for the morning, the main motivation is a collaborative one. The specific technological infrastructure of the office and presence of 'the team' means that projects can be managed more effectively and efficiently in that specific place.

Kate, chief engineer for a telecoms company, echoes this sentiment:

> So I can do all of that from home, but I still feel the need to come in and be a bit more… You have to meet people, there's a social aspect to it that you need to, you know, I wouldn't talk to all the engineers every day on a technical level, you know what I mean, but you would try to make sure that you met them in the canteen [*inaudible*] have a cup of coffee or, you know, even you're passing in the corridor, you, you know, you ask them how the kid is or how the wife is or how their soccer match went. (Kate)

Kate's work extends beyond her engineering skills to creating good worker relations that enable smoother collaboration when she needs to talk to her engineering colleagues on a technical level.

Jack also talked about work with collaborators requiring long-distance mobility. His company is involved in EU projects, and, as the technical director, Jack oversees a number of these.

> This week we had our meeting in Skovia on…Well we had a series of meetings on Thursday and Friday. So I had to prepare for those because I'm the project manager. Eighteen partners and another five or six that came along, and we had on Thursday morning, we had a business partners meeting, which was totally business—pricing, markets, all that sort of stuff. And then at 12 o'clock, we had the official launch by the municipality of Skovia where we had the TV cameras along and journalists and all that sort of stuff. (Jack)

In his role as project manager, Jack needed to prepare for the trip and the meetings in Skovia. He also participated in a number of collaborative activities, some more focused and others regarding the visibility of the project, such as dealing with the journalists. Jack is well aware of the implications of working both at headquarters and in faraway locations: in the interview he goes on to describe his preparation for long-distance trips in order to work at his best with his international collaborators, as well as organizing things so that he can keep a connection with headquarters (for example by booking a hotel with good internet access so to be contactable by his home team). Therefore, even if his mobility means that he will not be in the presence of both groups of collaborators while he is in Skovia, his practice is conscious of having to maintain a collaborative link with them.

The choice of work place is not only between home, the office and some away location. Mobility also involves work being done *while* on the move. For example, Saul, software marketing manager, made the decision to travel to the city by train when he was involved in a project there, because working on the train helps him to focus on the work to be done collaboratively when he arrives in the city.

> I'd go from here early in the morning, but I had the train ride up and the train ride down. And what that meant was that if I was going up to meet you, I'm coming to meet you, you're busy doing all your stuff at your desk because you're at your desk and you're doing, you know, twenty minutes of this and ten minutes of that, and you know, a quarter of an hour of that, and a phone call, and so on. And I had three hours on the train to do absolutely nothing except think about [you], and to focus on the meeting. So I was extremely effective in that time (…) I have nothing else to do except prepare for you. (Saul)

When the work activities of such high-skilled workers are readily mobile, they are constantly making decisions about where and when particular aspects of their work are done. The above quotes emphasize the ways in which particular tasks and collaborations are only possible in particular places. These places are understood and inhabited primarily with regard to relations with particular others, so that certain tasks can be completed, or the way is eased for other kinds of work to be achieved. This is exemplified by the very nuanced collaborative strategies that the participants deploy with respect to doing work at particular places. The places themselves come into existence as such via the social and collaborative motivations of the workers.

13.4   Place as Expressive of Organizational Needs and Characteristics

Places are not only socially significant to individuals, but also to entire organizations. The relative significance of particular places, whether the company premises or a home office, will depend also on the organizational culture: the place of work is related to the social relationships within the organization. Where the organization is and where its people are matters. Jonathan is a managing director but also founder and owner of his company: one of the first decisions he made was the actual placement of the company itself.

> I just felt I would like to come in here because it was having the address of the Technology Park nowadays, is because we're providing more services rather than just boxes and hardware that it would give us a bit of an umpf, we'll say, in that sense. Number two, it suited. I live in K----, you know, and it suited a number of people as well, this particular area. C-----, if you go to R----, as an example, it's just very, very closed in and the companies are on top of each other. (Jonathan)

Being in the NTP expresses the values of the organization: it is a meaningful address for customers to recognize the company's degree innovation and quality of service.

Moreover, there were practical concerns regarding where the workers live, and how placing the company in the NTP would suit the members of the organization.

The organizational structure of the company is also motivated by the relationship with clients in other cities.

> What we have, we call it a sales office in C---, which in reality is now a number with a service office. So if you ring C---, it's answered here. In the city, the software company has a small office [there] which we use, but it—there's nobody permanently based there. So for all intents and purposes (…) we have a sales office in the City, a sales office in C---, but here is really where everything happens. (Jonathan)

The company is associated with other places: one of the remote offices has only a nominal presence, the other remote office doesn't have permanent staff but company employees go there when clients in the city need them. The organization is therefore physically structured around three places to aid the relationships with clients.

The organizational aspect of choosing a place of work for the company is not something that involves only the institution, but also the particular workers. For example, Charles, chief technology officer for an online services company, has made significant decisions about his personal work places: he does his day-to-day work from home and goes to the office for particular events, such as important meetings, although he lives not far from headquarters.

> I find that the advantages outweigh any disadvantages, our client base is everywhere. This means we can provide support for them, not practically 24 hours, but I can respond to support an issue at 11 pm, having the ability to do that. Whereas some people in their office, it is a situation that means that the door is closed at 5 pm and stuff like that, and that's necessary in some instances. But my type of work, I like embedding our work in what we do, so it is fairly seamless and we don't mind doing it like that. (Charles)

The indeterminacy of place with regard to where clients are located, and the embedding of work in his home life arise for Charles from an organizational culture of fluidity and multi-locatedness: he feels that being at home allows him to work beyond the boundaries of an office and provide clients with better support while being present for his family.

Place also contributes to building organizational culture *internally* and not only with respect to customers and other external stakeholders. Dan, managing director of a software consultancy firm, expresses this view with regard to having people work in the office although they could easily work remotely.

> One is to do with purely looking at results, and we don't purely look at results. We look at the actual individual as well and them fitting into the actual organization and creating a culture in the organization (…). If you're at home, you might feel that—well you have to prove yourself at home and you might be on Google, you might be searching different technical forums on the Internet trying to find the answer to your solution doing more reading. Whereas in your office, you can just say to one of the other guys in the office, "can I bounce something off you? Can I use you as a sounding board?" And those sorts of things, it's about team building. (Dan)

The office is seen as a site of more efficient work via instant collaborative problem solving, and this in turn strengthens organizational culture. Dan says so explicitly when he suggests that working from home could isolate workers from colleagues, rather than support the team.

Another participant in our study, Angela—managing director of a small software firm -, when talking about her long distance mobility, mentions both aspects of the organizational significance of being somewhere that were expressed by Jonathan and Dan. Angela travels a lot internationally because she wants her customers to see that the company cares for the personal contact. She explains how she sees her role as someone representing the organization to customers and partners, especially when establishing a relationship with a new client.

> People know where you're coming from, they know the bigger picture, and they know where you're going in general. So I find that the, actually spending time *[with clients]*, particularly at the start up project phase is worthwhile. And then we would use the teleconferencing and emailing and that afterwards, and Skype, you know. (Angela)

She also explains how she is happy to travel because all the other workers are back at the office and instantly contactable for updates and problem solving—she is mobile so that others can be productive at headquarters in responding to customer issues raised some distance away in her meetings with clients. In Angela's example, the choice of where work happens is motivated by both how the organization relates to clients and how it works and strengthens its capacity internally.

13.5   Place as Facilitating a Blending of Work/Life Strategies and Relationships

Throughout our study, we have collected examples of how the participants' mobility is a constant blend between work and life places and of how the choice of place of work is connected to social relationships within both work and private life. Because high-skilled work relies more on specific skills and abilities rather than static infrastructure, much of this work can be done in many places. We saw examples of how different people make different decisions on where to work, although generally motivated by social factors, hence creating a potential fluidity with regard to boundaries between work and life.

Charles has an office at the home he shares with his wife and two children.

> I go to my home office, and use things like email and Skype (…) we also use social media tools like Twitter and LinkedIn to keep in touch with people. And in the office we also use tools like Yammer, collaboration tools like that to share documents and stuff like that. That would be generally the set up. Then I get my children and have lunch. So that's basically how we work. (Charles)

In this description of how his company works, getting the children and having lunch are part of the same flow outlining how the company (which he refers to as "we") operates. Work and family tasks blur at Charles' home and this flexibility between work and life is also heavily mediated by technology. Although family and work tasks may be negotiated in a fluid way, some boundaries are defined: Charles chooses to leave one of the work technologies out of his home space. Charles' bedroom is kept work-free and Blackberry-free.

> Well, I'd certainly keep the Blackberry out of the bedroom for sure. In that case, you do have to have and set up rules when you don't let that interfere with your personal relationships. (Charles)

As we saw in the previous section, Charles' decision to work from home has to do with his view on how the organization can best support clients. On the other hand, Sara, the owner of a web development agency, also works from home, however she explains her preference almost entirely in personal terms:

> But my preference is to work at home. (…) It's a preference. I could do it from here and I could do it from anywhere in the world as long as there was an ashtray and some broadband, but I—it's just a personality thing really. I think I'm just a home body and I, you know, I like my husband being around. And you know, we have lunch together. I think you get into a groove and your best stuff happens where it happens. (Sara)

The ambiance of home is conducive to work productivity and once connected by efficient broadband Sara's optimum work context and her *home body* personality preference can be achieved. She also mentions how the presence of her husband (who also works at home), a deep personal relationship, is one of the reasons for her choice.

Saul's company is based in the NTP, but he lives in C---, about 100 km away, because of family reasons: his first wife is based there with their two kids and his second wife, also with kids of her own, has a job there. Saul's work practices are highly mobile not only because of the nature of his job, but also because of his personal situation.

> If I'm travelling, I take my work with me if I can at all. So I might, say work a Tuesday in the National Technology Park (…) have meetings there, stay Tuesday night, work Wednesday in the hotel or in the office, and work, come on down to C--- maybe late on Wednesday or on Thursday morning, you know? (Saul)

His decision to use his home as workplace for some days, and to work at headquarters on other days is connected to his personal life strategies. This also means creating a temporary work place in the hotel he stays at on the days when he is at headquarters.

The motivation to move a significantly long distance away from home and office could also be personal and similarly requires work strategies to be adapted around that place. For example, Angela spent an entire summer in Spain so that her son could learn Spanish.

> I was (…) just outside Malaga. So our day was pretty much the same as it would have been here, as in the school had very good wireless connections. So when he *[Angela's son]* was in class from 8 to 12, I would have done my day's work but done it in half a day. And then in the afternoon, he would have been off with activities with his friends, and then my nine-year-old daughter, my mother-in-law and extended family came out for different periods, so we kind of had our holiday then in the afternoon. (Angela)

In the interview she goes on to explain how there were issues in communicating effectively with the rest of the team back at headquarters, particularly when trying to collaboratively solve a problem. Nonetheless she was pleased with her decision as it was made for important family reasons and she arranged her work strategy to fit around that. Angela also talks about her average day when she is at the NTP, and how she also moves her work between office and home.

> I find what I have to do at home is…I have to say that there's one particular room that's work only. So it's kind of like an office. And when I close that door, it has to be a bit like closing the door here, because the danger is (…) sometimes you will just, you know, you might be doing, you know, something family, and you say, OK, I'll just go in for ten minutes and I'll check email. Now ten minutes becomes an hour and an hour can become, you know, you can get dragged into it. (Angela)

Here we see that Angela has spatially confined her work to one room while she is at home, and her strategy of balancing between work and life relies on the physical configuration of the place in order to keep a definite separation. Angela chooses to do work at home, but closing the door to her home office means dedicating herself to family: although her work is in a room nearby she can keep work activities separate from her personal life at certain times.

Nancy, head of marketing for a green technology company, often increases her spatial mobility by extending business trips with days working at her boyfriend's house in the city in order to spend more time with him.

> Yeah, to see my boyfriend, yeah. I tend to go up more, partially because, well sometimes I'm up in the city anyway for business, or for work, sorry. We're sponsored by Enterprise Initiative and so often we have meetings with them. So if I'm up in the city anyway for a meeting on a Thursday or a Friday, I would stay over. (Nancy)

However, staying overnight in the city makes planning more difficult. Nancy goes on to explain how her decision to work from her boyfriend's house leads to extra planning in order to make sure that everything she needs to do her work is with her.

> I had a meeting in the city on a Thursday, and I asked could I work from *[boyfriend's]* home on the Friday, which was no problem (…). And I just had to kind of go through my desk and make sure that I had all my stuff, and then take the laptop and, you know, that (…) It would kind of scupper things if I went, oh damn, the thing that I need is down in the Technology Park, you know. (Nancy)

For some of our participants, work and life are fluidly negotiated while for others work is done at home to facilitate family demands: it can be characterized by further planning and be managed by defining boundaries. In some cases these different approaches are defined in terms of personal preferences and in others they are required because of the specific needs of children or partners. However, all these examples demonstrate the ways in which the places described by participants are invested by complex blends of work and life relationships. These blends are experienced as an opportunity for some, and a constraint for others: overall, they highlight how mobility is very often not only work-related mobility; that places matter for professional and personal relationships and, subsequently; that the range of interactions that mobile workers perform on the move are linked to both personal and professional considerations.

13.6   Discussion and Conclusions

In the previous sections we have shown examples of how focusing on *where* mobile
professionals conduct their practices can reveal important aspects of mobile work
and life. The data highlights how, in order to understand mobility more richly, it
can be useful to extend accounts of tasks and practices by looking at the context
of activity. The notion of place helped in this analysis as it allowed us to consider
explicitly the physical context of interaction as a blend of structural characteristics
and human experience. We argued that place is socially constructed and is therefore
an important consideration in portraying how people do mobility with respect to
collaborators and other stakeholders. The data show that places of work are essentially connected to social and collaborative relationships and that their meaning
also emerges from such relationships. Jack, Jonathan and Kate all explain how their
decision to do work at their company's headquarters although they could work as
easily from another location is linked to their understanding of how important being
in that place with co-workers is to establish a good partnership with them. Their
motivation is about working on collaborative tasks, but also on establishing and
maintaining a positive personal relationship with their co-workers.

Moving to other locations is also socially motivated: Jonathan talks about the
many stakeholders that he physically travels to ensure face-to-face contact is maintained and conveying the importance of being there with them. Jack, an experienced
manager of international projects, has developed a keen sense of the importance of
his presence at particular places for the success of the project.

Moreover, the trajectory between one place of work and another and the ways
in which mobility is physically accomplished also carry social meanings: Saul explains how his choice of travelling by train rather than by car is about having time to
concentrate on the person he will meet once he arrives in the city, and on the work
to be done together. This is part of a larger strategy for managing places of work in
relation to collaborators and other stakeholders, and directly links with our second
point: that places are expressive of organizational needs and values. Where the company is placed in the first instance certainly has a meaning for potential customers:
we see in our data that the NTP is chosen not simply for its business infrastructure
but also because it makes it possible to associate an organization with values of
innovation and professionalism. Besides this institutional concern, individuals see
their place of work as representative of the mission of their organization: Charles
identifies working at home as representing his availability to customers beyond the
office (intended as a confined unit of space and of time). On the other hand, Angela
physically travels to customer sites to show the dedication of her company to its
customers. The chosen places of work may be different in these two examples, however they both show how organizational concerns drive the decision to be somewhere in particular. In another example, Dan talks about how being somewhere
with co-workers is a way to build an organizational culture internally: this example
shows how organizational concerns related to place are not only directed to clients
and external partners, but also to the team of co-workers within the same company.

The final set of examples relates to what Büscher and Urry [4] refer to as the making of work and non-work worlds through mobility: places of work carry with them life concerns, sometimes in more pronounced ways than others. The choice of being in a particular place may be entirely dependent on life demands, and in that case the environment is adapted to fit work requirements. In other situations, places are a blend of work and life and certain strategies need to be put in place to maintain balance between them and to successfully achieve both professional and personal goals.

Overall, we have shown how *where* people do mobility matters and that the *where* is almost always connected to social relationships. We see this as a contribution towards redefining mobility as a spectrum notion: mobility cannot be seen as a reified concept but as a set of possibilities. It reconfigures itself in manifold ways through practice, and reconfigurations of spatial, temporal and informational mobility emerge through different practices. Technology is an essential part of the practice and discourse of knowledge workers: it is not just about functionality, but about the *style* of work and life that technology mediates. The study presented in this chapter contributes to current research on understanding and designing mobile collaborative systems by pointing out how social concerns surrounding mobile work go beyond the cooperative execution of tasks and performance of collaborative activities and by highlighting how understanding the interrelationships between place and mobility is essential to grasp the social and collaborative motivations of movement. It also highlights the increasing significance of place in decisions about where mobile work is to be done as this work is increasingly made mobile by the affordances of technologies and associated newly imagined combinations of work and life.

Acknowledgments We acknowledge the support of Irish Higher Education Authority PRTLI and the EU Regional Development Fund through the Irish Social Science Platform. Thanks to the Institute for Studies of Knowledge in Society at the University of Limerick.

References

1. Bellotti, V., Bly, S.: Walking away from the desktop computer: distributed collaboration and mobility in a product design team. In: Proceedings of CSCW 96, pp. 209–218, ACM Press (1996)
2. Benson, J., Brown, M.: Knowledge workers: what keeps them committed, what turns them away. Work Employ. Soc. 21(1), 121–141 (2007)
3. Brown, B., O'Hara, K.: Place as a practical concern of mobile workers. Environ. Plan. A. 35(9), 1565–1587 (2003)
4. Büscher, M., Urry, J.: Mobile methods and the empirical. Eur. J. Soc. Theory. 12(1), 99–116 (2009)
5. Churchill, E.F., Wakeford, N.: Framing mobile collaboration and mobile technologies. In: Brown, B., Green, N., Harper, R. (eds.) Wireless World: Social and Interactional Implications of Wireless Technology. Springer, London (2001)

6. Ciolfi, L., Bannon, L.J.: Space, place and the design of technologically enhanced physical environments. In: Turner, P., Davenport, E. (eds.) Space, Spatiality and Technology, pp. 217–232. Springer, London (2005)
7. Cohen, R.L.: Rethinking 'mobile work': boundaries of space, time and social relation in the working lives of mobile hairstylists. Work Employ. Soc. 24(1), 65–84 (2010)
8. Cousins, K.C., Robey, D.: Human agency in a wireless world: patterns of technology use in nomadic computing environments. Inf. Organ. 15(2), 151–180 (2005)
9. Davis, G.B.: Anytime/anyplace computing and the future of knowledge work. Commun. ACM. 45(12), 67–73 (2002)
10. Divitini, M., Farshchlan, B.A., Samset, H.: UbiCollab: collaboration support for mobile users. In: Proceedings of SAC'04, pp. 1191–1195, ACM Press, New York (2004)
11. Gutwin, C., Greenberg, S.: Workspace awareness for groupware. In: Proceedings of CHI 1996, pp. 208–209, ACM Press, New York (1996)
12. Harrison, S., Dourish, P.: Re-Place-ing space: the roles of place and space in collaborative systems. In: Proceedings of CSCW'96, pp. 67–76, ACM Press, New York (1996)
13. Izadi, S., Coutinho, P., Rodden, T., Smith, G.: The FUSE platform: supporting ubiquitous collaboration within diverse mobile environments. Autom. Softw. Eng. 9(2), 167–186 (2002)
14. Kleinrock, L.: Nomadicity: anytime, anywhere in a disconnected world. Mob. Netw. Appl. 1(4), 351–357 (1996)
15. Kristoffersen, S., Ljungberg, F.: Making place to make IT work: empirical explorations of HCI for mobile CSCW. In: Proceedings of GROUP'99, pp. 276–285, ACM Press, New York (1999)
16. Licoppe, C.: 'Connected' presence: the emergence of a new repertoire for managing social relationships in a changing communication technoscape. Environ. Plan. D Soc. Space. 22, 135–156 (2004)
17. Luff, P., Heath, C.: Mobility in collaboration. In: Proceedings of CSCW '98, pp. 305–314, ACM Press, New York (1998)
18. Mark, G., Su, N.M.: Making infrastructure visible for nomadic work. J. Pervasive Mob. Comput. 6(3), 312–323 (2010)
19. Morrison, A., Mulloni, A., Lemmelä, S., Oulasvirta, A., Jacucci, G., Peltonen, P., Schmalstieg, D., Regenbrecht, H.: Mobile augmented reality: collaborative use of mobile augmented reality with paper maps. Comput. Graph. 35(4), 789–799 (2011)
20. Olson, G., Olson, J.: Distance matters. J Hum. Comput. Interact. 15(2), 139–178 (2000)
21. Perry, M., O'Hara, K., Sellen, A., Brown, B., Harper, R.: Dealing with mobility: understanding access anytime, anywhere. ACM Trans. Comput. Hum. Interact. (TOCHI). 8(4), 323–347 (2001)
22. Rossitto, C., Eklundh, K.S.: Managing work at several places: a case of project work in a nomadic group of students. Proceedings of ECCE 2011. doi:10.1145/1362550.1362562 (2007). Accessed 30 Nov 2011
23. Sørensen, C.: Enterprise Mobility. Tiny Technology with Global Impact on Work. Palgrave Macmillan, London (2011)
24. Thompson, P., Warhurst, C., Callaghan, G.: Ignorant theory and knowledgeable workers: interrogating the connections between knowledge skills and services. J. Manag. Stud. 38(7), 923–942 (2001)
25. Urry, J.: Mobilities. Polity, London (2007)
26. Weilenmann, A.: Negotiating use: making sense of mobile technology. Pers. Ubiquitous Comput. 5(2), 137–145 (2001)
27. Wiberg, M., Ljungberg, F.: Exploring the vision of anytime, anywhere in the context of mobile work. In: Malhotra, Y. (ed.) Knowledge Management and Virtual Organizations, pp. 157–169. Idea Group, Hershey (1999)

Chapter 14
Maintaining the Instant Connection—Social Media Practices of Smartphone Users

Sanna Malinen and Jarno Ojala

Abstract In the last few years, using social media via mobile phone applications has become increasingly common. However, there are only few studies exploring people's mobile application usage behavior. In order to understand users' mobile social media practices in the context of everyday life, 30 owners of high-end smartphones were interviewed for this study. The context of their mobile SNS use cases was studied through diaries kept by 15 of the participants. The results show that mobile social networking is typically about briefly checking the latest updates and news, most often while in transit and when immersive use of the internet is not possible. Also, there are more browsing activities on the mobile phone than content creation, which is better done with PC. In the use of social media, immediate access to the most interesting content, such as photos, status updates and news, is highly valued; in this respect, the mobile phone adds value to the use of social media by enabling access to it in a great variety of situations and locations. As a practical result, we present design implications for mobile SNS applications and point out that there is currently a lack of features for effective selection, storing and filtering of content produced through the various social media sites.

14.1 Introduction

With the greater prevalence of smartphones containing internet access and social media applications, the mobile internet, i.e. accessing internet via a mobile device, has emerged as a common way to browse social media alongside the stationary web. Today, social media is increasingly consumed and content is created using mobile devices, and there is a plethora of mobile applications and services designed specifically to enable mobile phone users to update, browse and create content. Mobile phones have changed people's communication practices, as they allow us to remain

S. Malinen (✉) · J. Ojala
Tampere University of Technology (TUT), Human-centered Technology,
P.O.Box 589, 33101 Tampere, Finland
e-mail: sanna.malinen@tut.fi

J. Ojala
e-mail: jarno.ojala@tut.fi

J. Dugdale et al. (eds.), *From Research to Practice in the Design of Cooperative Systems:* 197
Results and Open Challenges, DOI 10.1007/978-1-4471-4093-1_14,
© Springer-Verlag London 2012

connected to others irrespective of location. For the most part, research carried out in the area so far has explored phone calls and SMS as forms of mobile communication, with the more recent phenomenon of mobile social networking remaining a relatively unexplored research topic.

This study presents the results of a user study with 30 qualitative interviews, and aims to understand the participants' mobile social media consumption practices. The participants were owners of high-end smartphones and consumed various social media sites and SNSs through their mobile phones regularly. The aim of the study was to understand the role that mobility plays in social media consumption, and to explore how the physical and social contexts of the use affect the selection of the device and the content that is consumed. Furthermore, in this chapter we describe the situations in which social media is typically consumed in order to identify the patterns of mobile social media use. By exploring the social media practices of the participants, we aim to find out whether the mobile device is bringing any additional value to the use of social media compared to the PC and to identify any typical patterns for sharing and browsing social media content through mobile phone applications.

This study focuses on owners of high-end smartphones who have the opportunity download a variety of existing mobile applications for their phones. We assume that because the latest mobile applications for the most common SNS are relatively simple to use, easy to open and usually enable instant access to the site, they are facilitating the overall use of social media.

14.2 Related Work

In recent years, social network sites (SNS), such as Facebook, Twitter and MySpace, have integrated into people's daily communication practices. Boyd and Ellison [1] define SNSs as web-based services that allow individuals to construct a public or semi-public profile within a bounded system, articulate a list of other users with whom they share a connection, and view and traverse their list of connections and those made by others within the system. A feature common to all forms of social media is that they enable users to communicate, create, share and view digital content of interest, and to reciprocally give and receive support and information.

So far, research on social media has not widely discussed the characteristics of its use via mobile devices, making it interesting to discover whether there is some extra value that mobility can add to it. There are many characteristics associated with the mobile device that separate it from the stationary internet. A mobile phone is usually personal, whereas a PC is often shared with others; for this reason, the mobile phone is generally considered a more intimate medium [3, 9]. A mobile internet connection is fast and easy to use, as it is almost always available and enables quick access almost anywhere and anytime. Consequently checking behavior, i.e. brief usage sessions repeated over time, comprises a large part of smartphone use [11].

In a survey reported by Kaikkonen [8], the mobile internet users mostly read email and followed some social media sites, such as blogs and discussion forums. However, active contribution to social websites was less common when using mobile devices compared to desktop computers. According to the participants, this was due to mobile web sessions being shorter and more prone to interruptions, which meant that the desktop computer was perceived as more appropriate in situations that required peace and privacy [8]. Cui and Roto [4] introduce a habit of using the mobile internet during micro breaks that can take place anywhere. The activities engaged in during these micro breaks mainly consisted of checking updates. The duration of the micro breaks can be very brief, and the attention span of the user may be as short as 4 s. In their large scale study of the usage of mobile applications, Böhmer et al. [2] found that application usage is at its highest in the afternoon and evening, peaking around 6 pm, with the average usage time being less than a minute, and that social applications are most likely to be used in late evening from 9 pm to 1 am.

Recently, many social media services and applications have been developed for use via mobile devices; social media services such as Foursquare in particular are bridging the gap between online and offline, as they support users' association with physical locations [10]. With GPS-enabled phones, people are able to employ location-based social media services, making the boundaries between online and offline even more blurred.

Based on previous research [7, 14], it seems that some forms of social media are better suited for mobile use than others. Particularly microblogging, a form of blogging enabling brief updates usually limited to 140 characters, is commonly done via mobile phone: for example, the majority of Twitter users engage with the site using multiple devices [14]. The fascination with microblogging lies in momentary and brief postings on experiences that would not be shared via other, familiar channels and achieving a presence, a sense of being "out there" with friends, by checking each other's updates [5]. We assume that a mobile device is particularly suitable for creating brief postings at a specific moment in time and encourages sharing them instantly and spontaneously.

Until recently, the use of the mobile internet has been somewhat limited by technical issues and had thus been considered as narrower in terms of the user experience. Previous research [8, 9, 13] has pointed out that users of the mobile internet have experienced difficulties in understanding the structure and layout of websites viewed through the mobile phone; also, the first internet services for mobile phones were based on tailored content and therefore offered only limited content compared with full internet [8, 9]. Hinman et al. [6] compared mobile internet use with PC use and found that users wanted to do the same things with the mobile device as they were used to doing with a desktop computer, but felt it was not possible, as internet browsing on the PC is immersive and invites exploration and discovery, whereas when browsing the web via a mobile device the attention is divided and it is difficult to get totally immersed.

However, previous research on mobile internet use [4] has found that even though the mobile is used most often in stationary situations with no internet access, it was surprisingly also opted for in locations providing internet access due to being perceived as a more convenient means to use the internet in certain situations, such as when watching television at home. Böhmer et al. [2] noticed that the choice of browser over application was to some extent dependent on location or activity to be performed on the internet: for example, checking flight status at the airport was more likely to be done using a browser than an application, probably due to the inadequacies of native applications.

As the popularity and variety of social media sites has increased rapidly during the last couple of years, we assume that social media consumption currently plays a major role in mobile web browsing. Due to previous limitations in mobile browsers, mobile versions were produced of the social media web solutions, with the identical full web sites becoming available only after sufficient development of mobile devices [8, 9]. As the selection of mobile applications available to consumers has grown rapidly during the past few years, it seems that social media is now being used increasingly via mobile applications tailored for specific websites, and less with a mobile browser.

14.3 Data Collection

14.3.1 Participants

The research data consists of 30 qualitative user interviews that were collected in Finland in two phases; the first phase in September–October 2010 and the latter in January–February 2011. The participants were recruited through mailing lists and discussion forums intended for various student and hobby groups, one of which was aimed at the fans of Apple products. A total of 51 persons enrolled for the study and filled in an online screening questionnaire containing questions about their background on topics such as age, occupation, current mobile phone model, and how often they used social media through a PC and a mobile device.

Based on the screening, a total of 30 participants were selected on the basis of their current mobile phone model and the amount of social media usage through the mobile. Out of the participants, 10 were female and 20 male, with ages ranging from 17 to 56 (average age 29). The majority of them (16) were students, and the rest worked full-time: seven in field of ICT and seven in non-ICT occupations. Their mobile devices were: iPhone (11), Nokia N900 (5), HTC (4), Nokia Xprss-Music (2), Nokia E71 (2), Google Nexus One (1), some other Nokia smartphone (5), Sony Ericsson Xperia (1) and Samsung Galaxy S (1). In addition, two participants mentioned using iPad and two iPod Touch to browse social media. Six of the participants reported using more than one device for mobile web browsing. The most often used social media sites by participants are presented in the Table 14.1.

The group of participants consists of high-end mobile phone owners, who presumably had fixed rate access to mobile internet. As the participants were selected partly based on their ownership of the most recent and most advanced smartphone

Table 14.1 Most popular social media sites among participants (N = 30)

Social media site	Mentions
Facebook	29
YouTube	25
Online discussion forums	22
Twitter	10
MySpace	7
Flickr	4
LinkedIn	4

models, the group of participants can be defined as early adopters of technology. Previous literature [12] on the social shaping of technology suggests that early adopters tend to be social leaders, as their understanding and use of technology may influence others.

In the screening survey, the persons who had enrolled for the study were asked how often they used social media sites through a mobile device. As participants to the study were selected based on their activity, they were more familiar with social media sites than the average population. Out of the group of the participants (30), 13 (43 %) reported browsing social media with a mobile phone more than five times a day, with 10 participants (33 %) citing a frequency of one to four times a day. The rest (7) used a mobile device to browse social media weekly.

14.3.2 Method

We used a semi-structured interview method for investigating the informants' social media browsing and content sharing practices. The main themes of the interviews were: motivations for using social media services, description of the context of use, content creation and sharing, and routines and patterns of mobile social media use.

The duration of face-to-face interviews varied from 1 to 2 h. In the interviews, the informants were asked to show on their mobile phone the social media applications most commonly used by them. The interviews were recorded in audio and transcribed in order to conduct a qualitative content analysis. All the interviewees were rewarded for their participation with a EUR 20 gift voucher.

In order to gain more detailed information on the context and situations of mobile use, 15 of the participants were asked to keep diaries of all their mobile social media usage during 2 days of their choice. In the diaries, they were advised to write down each time they used social media and to describe in detail the situation and duration of use, what they did and if any problems occurred and, especially, if the context of use affected on the use of social media in some way. In total, we obtained descriptions of 125 use situations. The diaries were written down on a form provided by the research group and submitted via e-mail before the face-to-face interview. The diaries were then thoroughly discussed in the interviews.

Fig. 14.1 Duration of social media use sessions (total = 122)

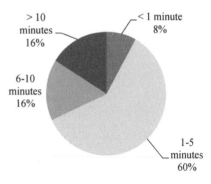

> 10 minutes 16%

< 1 minute 8%

6-10 minutes 16%

1-5 minutes 60%

Table 14.2 Social media content browsed (total = 97) and created with mobile phone (total = 26)

Social media content browsed (total = 97)	
Reading status updates, newsfeed, latest comments on Facebook	41
Reading private messages	16
Reading discussion forum messages	13
Reading e-mail messages	11
Browsing a friend's profile on SNS	6
Listening to music/viewing a video on SNS	5
Browsing pictures uploaded to SNS	3
Reading Twitter feed	2
Social media content created (total = 26)	
Commenting on something	9
Composing private messages	6
Writing status updates	6
Liking something	3
Voting/rating	2

14.4 Results

14.4.1 Social Media Use Cases

The diaries were analyzed in order to understand the context of mobile social media use and to identify the daily routines and recurring practices of the users as well as the more exceptional and extraordinary situations of use. The participants were asked to estimate the duration of each of their social media sessions carried out via mobile, which provided us with the durations of a total of 122 use cases (see Fig. 14.1). The results show that the participants' social media use consisted of brief recurrent sessions, as the majority of sessions lasted only from 1 to 5 min (60 %). The longest session mentioned in the diaries lasted approximately 70 min, the shortest being only few seconds in duration.

As shown in Table 14.2, the number of occasions of browsing content (97) was more than three times greater than the number of sessions involving content cre-

Table 14.3 The situations of use mentioned in diaries

Situations	Mentions
At home:	*44*
In bed (morning and night)	16
Watching TV on a sofa	6
During a break (coffee, tea, food)	5
Other	17
Outside the home:	*44*
At work, school or lecture	13
When walking to school, work, etc.	11
In a shop, city centre	10
When visiting someone	5
Other	5
On transportation:	*37*
Bus	19
Train	13
Car	5

ation (23), which indicates that mobile social media use is primarily about reading and browsing content, and less about content creation and sharing.

In the interviews, the participants were asked why they did not create and share content with their mobile device, which elicited several mentions of problems regarding the usability of devices. The most commonly cited reason for not creating content on the mobile phone was difficulty in text input: typing with a small virtual touch-screen keyboard was slow and errors were easily made. Particularly when traveling in a shaky bus or car, the conditions were too unstable for typing longer texts. Many of the discussion forums popular among the participants currently lack suitable mobile applications. Therefore, writing messages on forums was considered too time-consuming. Difficulty in sharing links with a mobile phone was also mentioned as one reason for not posting on SNSs. Especially users with phones other than the iPhone stated that difficulties in photo uploading caused them to prefer uploading them from PC.

14.4.2   Daily Routines of Mobile Social Media Use

With the diaries, we wanted to understand the daily social media routines of the participants and how the mobile phone is integrated into them. The situations of reported social media use via mobile are listed in Table 14.3.

At home   Contrary to the assumption that the mobile device is most often opted for in situations where stationary internet is not available, a common context for mobile social media use seems to be at home. Based on both the diaries and the interviews, the most common use case for browsing social media with the mobile phone was at home while in bed. The mobile phone is usually positioned by the bed and enables quick and easy access to the internet before going to sleep at night. The participants also wanted to see the latest news and updates as first thing before getting up in the morning and opening the PC. The mobile was also considered a discreet device, as you can browse it in the dark without disturbing others, in contrast to having to turn on the light to read a book, for example.

> The first thing in the morning is to check Facebook with my mobile from bed. (male 27 years)

> Before going to sleep I read the different forums and Facebook with the mobile. That way I don't have to turn on the computer. (Female 38 years)

At home, the mobile phone is always at hand, and the participants reported that in situations where they wanted to have a quick look in social media during a commercial break on TV, or in the middle of other activities, they preferred to browse it with their mobile rather than bother going on the stationary computer, which is often located in another room. There were also mentions of situations where the PC is being used by another person or there is some other software, such as a game, running on it.

> I don't want to walk to the computer when I'm lying comfortably on the couch. (female, 25 years)

> I don't want to close the game on the PC when I am taking a break. (male, 26 years)

At work and in school Social media is used in the workplace and at school during the day. Those who have stationary internet and work with a PC used the PC as their primary social media device. However, there were many exceptions, as the use of SNSs is not in allowed in all companies. The diaries and interviews contained numerous mentions of social media use during lunch or coffee breaks, or checking with phone whenever possible, e.g. during boring meetings or lectures, between lectures, or when there are no customers nearby. As a device, the mobile was also considered discreet and unnoticeable, as it allows the user to browse personal content with more privacy.

> During a lecture, if you are sitting in the front row, you tend to go for the mobile so that your Facebook is not visible to everyone behind you. (female, 24 years)

In public places and on the move As expected, the mobile internet is commonly used in situations where stationary internet is not available. Most common use cases mentioned were transitions from home to workplace or school, when traveling by bus, train, or car. The mobile phone was preferred to a book because it is easy to carry, open and put away in case the browsing session turns out to be a short one. Typically, the participants were engaging in short social media sessions whenever possible, even when walking and stopping at the traffic lights for a few seconds.

> When you are caught in a red light and you have to wait, you can take a quick look in Facebook. (female, 24 years)

The mobile device was often taken out and found useful in public locations around town, often as a result of an ad hoc need in a particular context; for example when shopping in a grocery store and looking for recipes in a discussion forum or a blog. Another common use case mentioned was spending time in the city during lunch or coffee breaks.

Special and exceptional occasions In addition to their daily routines and commonly occurring situations, the participants were asked about special and exceptional occasions regarding their mobile social media use. They reported about various special events such as traveling and visiting new places and meeting new people. Such situations prompted the users to be more active in their use of social media, particularly in terms of creating content and sharing it with others. Especially traveling in interesting places and experiencing new things were mentioned as occasions that were exceptional and therefore worth sharing with others:

> If I am attending a concert or a play, I can write about it immediately and recommend it to others. (male, 56 years)

Other exceptional use cases mentioned were situations in which the users needed to quickly check something while on the move, such as the address of the place they were going to, a phone number or details of an event they were about to attend.

Also social situations in which social media was used collectively with others, for example by sharing content with friends by showing them the mobile display, were mentioned as exceptional. Usually content was shared as links via SNS or e-mail, but there were a couple of mentions of social situations in which a funny video, picture or song was shared by showing the screen to others.

14.4.3   The Value of Mobility in the Use of Social Media

> Because social media services are based on continuous presence, I'll check them every day. Checking them only once a week, you would miss lots of things. (male, 31 years)

In the interviews, the temporal aspects of social media usage were clearly highlighted; photos, events, news, and other content shared on social media should be read at the earliest opportunity, and are considered to be the most interesting immediately after they are posted. The mobile use cases mentioned most frequently in the diaries were short checks of the latest updates on the Facebook feed. Briefly checking their newsfeed several times a day enabled the users to catch information on the most recent events as soon as it was posted. All interviewees emphasized that reading the updates as soon as possible was important for them and if there was a long break from social media, especially Facebook, they felt that they might have missed something important going on in their network of friends. They also describe situations where, having been online at the right moment, they had been invited to a spontaneous get-together.

> My friend once invited everyone sledging, and then a bunch of us went sledging just like that. I check it regularly to find out if something special is going on. (female, 24 years)

Some participants described their frustration at having missed something important because they either had not checked social media regularly, or had otherwise failed to notice an important update.

> I did not have a clue that there had been a baby born in the family, because I didn't see it on Facebook. I felt like I had totally missed out on the happy news and I was only told about it 3 months later. (female, 31 years)

The results show that for the participants, social media had become an important part of their daily routines and practices. Social media was read first thing in the morning and before going to sleep at night. Social media was also used whenever the respondents had extra time or were bored, and the mobile device allowed them to pick up the latest news and updates in a greater variety of contexts and situations compared to the stationary web.

Social media was used when there was a lack of company, as well as in the presence of other people. However, there seemed to be a social norm against checking social media when accompanied by others. In such a context, the mobile phone was considered more inconspicuous than the PC and thus less rude. Other people's presence was also considered to be distracting, which also contributed to the suitability of the mobile phone for browsing the internet when accompanied by others, as browsing with a phone is a less immersive experience.

> I'll try not to use it if I have company, but if I'm bored or not participating in the discussion, I can take a quick look in Facebook or check the news. (male, 31 years)

Based on the interviews and diaries, it can be concluded that the value of mobile social media use lies in its' immediacy and independence of place and time: the mobile allows instant access to the essential content. Reaching for the mobile phone in your pocket and opening an application is easy and quick, and the device can also be switched off and put aside instantly if attention is to be focused on other things. Another advantage of the mobile phone is its private nature and the fact that it does not disturb others, or draw too much attention, but enables the creation of a private space and is therefore suitable for browsing personal content and communicating privately.

To our surprise, the mobile phone is used mostly for reading and not so much for content creation, even though it allows people to share their experiences and feelings instantly. Especially social media status updates were perceived as content that should be written and shared the moment they are experienced:

> Sometimes I have a thought in my mind that might be a good status update and I need to share it immediately. It would seem somehow false to post it 3 h later. (female, 30 years)

14.4.4 Roles and Functions of Mobile and PC

Even though the participants of this study represented the most active group of mobile social media users, the majority of them still reported using PC as their main social media device. With the interviews, we wanted to understand their social media use as a whole, and to see the general view of how social media use is divided between mobile and stationary device; are there some tasks or services that are perceived as more suitable for PC, or is the selection of the tool mostly down to context?

The results show that mobile social media use is about quickly checking the latest updates and finding out if something interesting has occurred. If something specific comes up, the interesting content is often viewed later in more detail on the computer screen. In particular, users prefer to revisit content such as videos and photographs of good quality and long texts and articles on the PC when there is more time available and the content can be viewed from a large screen. The participants also reported that the current mobile SNS applications were lacking some important features, which made them want to return to some of the content using a PC:

> With the mobile, you are not able to see the quality of photos and mark them as favorites on Flickr. (male, 26 years)

> A mobile app is great for an overview, but it's like seeing thumbnails on the PC. You can't really see the details in the pictures on the mobile phone (male, 29 years)

Even with the latest technology, the mobile web still seems to involve certain limitations regarding browsing and content sharing. The participants mentioned some usability problems that limited or reduced their use of the mobile internet, and thus led them to prefer using certain functions via PC only. Particularly text input of long text items, viewing photographs and videos, listening to music, reading long stories and articles and adding photographs and videos were considered as tasks better suited for PC.

In addition to technical and usability issues, also some context-related factors impacted the selection of browsing tool. In situations where the time available for reading or writing was particularly short, the users opted for the mobile device since it requires a lower level of engagement than the PC.

14.4.5 Design Implications for Mobile SNS Applications

All participants preferred to use the most popular sites, such as Facebook, Twitter and YouTube, with native applications designed specifically for each site. The mobile browser was mostly used for browsing other websites than social media, such as reading the news. The applications were considered better than a browser because the connection was instant and did not require login every time and the essential features were clearly laid out. Especially Facebook applications were appreciated because they offered only the most relevant content without games, applications or advertisements, which the majority of respondents perceived as disruptive. Also, many of the Facebook applications displayed the content of the newsfeed in a preview form, meaning that the users could easily take a quick glance at it and use the mobile browser for a closer look at items that appear interesting enough.

In the interviews, the participants were asked what kind of social media content they find the most interesting. According to the responses, the following four content categories were valued the most:

- Content that is related to me and where someone is paying attention to me specifically, e.g. personal messages.
- Content that people have produced themselves, e.g. personal photographs.
- Content that is new and fresh.
- The latest news distributed and commented on by friends.

Mobile applications should allow for a quick overview to the latest content and enable users to easily relocate the most important content items later on. Most SNS content, such as status updates, comments, likes and links from external sources, is browsed quickly and glanced at only once. The content that is considered the most personal and interesting in the long run is often returned to later on and read more carefully when the user has more time.

The participants reported that their current mobile applications for Facebook were suitable especially for browsing content to be quickly glanced over, such as newsfeeds, whereas content that required closer viewing, particularly photographs, was difficult to find. The users had to come up with their own ways of bookmarking interesting content by clicking on the like button or adding comments on Facebook in order to find their way back more easily.

Sharing content that was linked from external sources, such as news, videos and interesting articles, was common particularly on Facebook and Twitter plugins, and reading the content brought to SNS and recommended by friends was often considered more relevant than reading the content on the original site:

> I never read news on online news sites. I want to get recommendations and links from my friends on Facebook: that way, they have already filtered the content for me, and selected the most interesting pieces of information. (male, 27 years)

However, the amount of the data linked from other social media sites, such as Sportstracker, YouTube, Spotify or LastFM, was sometimes experienced as excessive, resulting in users wanting more control over what they share with others and avoiding automatic sharing through social media plugins such as Facebook connect, in order to avoid spamming. Particularly on Facebook, the amount of information received through the newsfeed was perceived as too great, and as a result almost all of the participants reported having filtered content by blocking unwanted applications, games and people. Types of content most often filtered out included uninteresting people or persons who post too much, useless applications and games, commercial content from Facebook pages liked by the users, and location-based content that is currently non-relevant:

> If you're abroad, it's annoying when your hometown sends daily updates and messages about events there. (female, 25 years)

All participants mentioned having hidden people not so interesting or close to them from their newsfeed at least temporarily. Yet, completely blocking out certain SNS friends was not common, because even people not considered to be very close or personally important to the users were thought to sometimes write interesting updates. In order to maintain an element of surprise, the users did not want to filter out too much of the content and continued to also retain some more peripheral people in their networks.

The most preferable way to filter social media content was to arrange it according to people. On Facebook, this can be done by grouping people into the different categories according to importance, relationship type or real-life group they belong to using the Groups feature. However, the most used features for filtering were lacking from the mobile applications, and the adjustments had to be made with the PC browser. When asked how they would feel about automatic filtering of content, the participants did not consider it reliable enough: they were suspicious of whether the system would really be able to detect what is relevant for them personally and felt it might cause them to miss some interesting content. Also, the participants emphasized that urgency, personal relevance and the need to react or respond varies greatly depending on the type of content. The status updates of friends were considered interesting but usually non-urgent, and could thus also be read later. Private messages were mentioned as important and requiring immediate attention, whereas postings and pictures related to the user were perceived as the most interesting though non-urgent content category.

The participants expressed a need to receive immediate notifications of the most important and urgent content. Most of the social media applications used push-notifications for the latest SNS activities. However, more customizing was needed for separating the most important content, such as personal messages, from the news stream. Voice feedback was perceived as useful only for the most important news, as the notifications were deemed annoying if they appeared on the screen too many times of times per day.

The participants who used many social media services regularly expressed a wish to manage all their social media content, including discussion forums and blogs, using the same application. Currently, they were able to combine the accounts for the most popular sites such as Twitter and Facebook, but since the personal relevance of social media feed varies between the different services, they did not wish to read all content merged into the same newsfeed: for example, updates from Twitter, LinkedIn or YouTube contacts did not have the same personal value as those posted by Facebook friends.

The relevance of personal e-mail was estimated at the same level with SNS feed, and the idea of combining the two in the same application was positively received, even though many participants said that messaging through Facebook, chat or IRC had replaced e-mailing between friends. However, there was no interest among the participants for combining their work e-mail account with social media updates: in their free time, they try to remain up-to-date with their SNS feed on an instant basis, but did not want to receive their work e-mail in real time, finding it could wait until the next work day.

14.5   Conclusion

Our results show that the importance of using social media via a mobile device lies in being able to check the latest news and staying in perpetual contact with others. The immediate contact with people in one's social networks enables instant reaction and participation. The mobile phone allows checking the latest news and social media updates briefly in situations when more immersed and extensive browsing is not possible, such as in transit, at work or at school. Still, mobile applications were also used at home when stationary internet was available, as simply reaching for the phone was considered convenient and easy when there was no need to perform lengthy or immersive tasks.

The results show that most often social media was browsed when people were bored or just wanted to keep up with latest updates by their friends. Even though the mobile phone can be used instantly in a moment of need and allows synchronous communication and sharing content in real-time, it still lacks many of the features and elements of the full web, and the browsing experience remains narrower than with PC. The mobile is not perceived as engaging as the stationary web in terms of time spent on each session. This assumption is supported by our findings, as the diaries contained only a couple of mentions of browsing sessions lasting longer than 30 min. Due to the instant connection, the mobile phone is used for social media browsing more frequently than the stationary web, which is often kept open in the background and opted for in tasks better accomplished via the PC.

On the basis of the results, we can say that ownership of a high-end smartphone with specifically tailored social media applications seems to encourage and motivate people to use social media in various contexts and thus increase the overall use. Even though all the participants mentioned the PC as their main social media tool, they felt that mobility adds value to the use of social network sites since it allows instant and more frequent use of SNS.

Regarding the design of SNS applications, the participants felt that reading the latest news on their feed is currently easy but that there is a lack of features for storing and bookmarking the most important content items for later use. As a result, this was done most commonly via PC. The number of social media updates was also often perceived as too great, and uninteresting content should be filtered out more effectively. The most commonly used filters were not available on mobile applications, which led to filtering adjustments being made with a PC browser. In addition, the participants' opinions of the type of content that should be filtered out varied to some extent. Also, they did not find automatic filtering reliable enough and wanted to be able to decide for themselves what kind of updates and news they wanted to receive, in order to maintain an element of surprise.

The social media site usage by the participants of our sampling follow the popularity of social media sites among Finns in general, with Facebook as clearly the most popular social media site and Twitter being used by less than half of the participants. Thus, the affordances of Facebook and reasons for using it seem to impact our results to some extent.

Acknowledgments The authors wish to thank Nokia Research Center for enabling this study. This research was part of the project "PROFCOM—Product-Internationalization with Firm-Hosted Online Communities", mainly funded by Tekes, the Finnish Funding Agency for Technology and Innovation (decision number 2283/31/07).

References

1. Boyd, D.M., Ellison, N.B.: Social network sites: definition, history, and scholarship. J. Comput. Mediat. Commun. 13(1), article 11 (2007)
2. Böhmer, M., Hecht, B., Schöning, J., Krüger, A., Bauer, G.: Falling asleep with angry birds, facebook and kindle—a large scale study on mobile application usage. In the 13th International Conference on Human Computer Interaction with Mobile Devices and Services (MobileHCI 2011), pp. 47–56, ACM Press, New York, NY, USA (2011)
3. Chae, M., Kim, J.: What's so different about the mobile internet? Commun. ACM. 46(12), 240–247 (2003)
4. Cui, Y., Roto, V.: How people used the web on mobile devices. In the 17th International Conference on World Wide Web (WWW '08), pp. 905–914, Beijing, China (2008)
5. Grace, J.H., Zhao, D, Boyd, D.: Microblogging: What and How Can We Learn From It? In: CHI 2010 extended abstracts on Human factors in computing systems (CHI EA 2010), pp. 4517–4520, Atlanta, Georgia, USA, (2010)
6. Hinman, R., Spasojevic, M., Isomursu, P.: They call it "surfing" for a reason: Identifying mobile Internet needs through PC deprivation. In: CHI 2008 extended abstracts on Human factors in computing systems (CHI EA 2008), pp. 2195–2208. Florence, Italy (2008)
7. Java, A., Song, X., Finin, T., Tseng, B.: Why we twitter: understanding microblogging usage and communities. In: 9th WebKDD and 1st SNA-KDD 2007 workshop on Web mining and social network analysis, pp. 56–65, ACM Press, New York, NY, USA (2007)
8. Kaikkonen, A.: Full or tailored mobile web- where and how do people browse on their mobiles? In: International Conference on Mobile Technology, Applications, and Systems (Mobility '08), Article 28, ACM Press, New York (2008)
9. Kaikkonen, A.: Mobile internet: past, present, and the future. Int. J. Mob. Hum. Comput. Interact. 1(3), 29–45 (2009)
10. McCarthy, J.: Bridging the gaps between HCI and social media. ACM Interact. 18(2), 15–18 (2011)
11. Oulasvirta, A., Rattenbury, T., Ma, L., Raita, E.: Habits make smartphone use more pervasive. Pers. Ubiquitous Comput. 16(1), 105–114 (2012)
12. Rogers, E.M.: Diffusion of Innovations, 5th edn. Free Press, New York (1995)
13. Roto, V., Kaikkonen, A.: Perception of narrow web pages on a mobile phone. In HFT 2003 (2003)
14. Zhao, D., Rosson, M.B.: How and why people twitter: the role that micro-blogging plays in informal communication at work. In: ACM International Conference on Supporting Group Work (GROUP '09), ACM Press, pp. 56–65. New York, NY, USA (2009)

Chapter 15
Supporting Collaborative Work in Socio-Physical Environments: A Normative Approach

Catherine Garbay, Fabien Badeig, and Jean Caelen

Abstract We propose a normative approach to collaborative support system design in distributed tangible environments. Based on activity theory, our goal is to mediate rather than drive human activity and to integrate components from the physical, numerical and social environments. We propose an original architecture coupling a physical space (tools supporting human activity), a processing space (agent performing activity, be it human or artificial), an informational space (traces reflecting activity), and a normative space (filters regulating activity). We further consider collaboration as a conversational process grounded in the objects of the working space. To this end, tangible objects of various kinds are designed to support multi-threaded activity. Heterogeneous trace properties may then be fused to situate activity and ground the filtering process. Interface agents are designed to provide appropriate visual feedback and support mutual awareness. Beyond the mere sharing of individual or group activity, we approach awareness as involving mutual knowledge of the activity constraints. We show through simple examples from the RISK game the potential richness of the proposed approach.

15.1 Introduction

We propose in this chapter a normative approach to design collaborative support system in distributed tangible environments, in the framework of the TangiSense infrastructure [13]. In accordance with activity theory, the guiding principles of our design are (1) to mediate rather than drive human activity, (2) to articulate within a single framework tools from the physical environment and rules from the social realm. Collaboration in our design does not amount to sharing the most visible part

C. Garbay (✉) · F. Badeig · J. Caelen
LIG, Université de Grenoble, UFR IM2AG—BP 53, 38041 Grenoble Cedex 9, France
e-mail: Catherine.Garbay@imag.fr

F. Badeig
e-mail: Fabien.Badeig@imag.fr

J. Caelen
e-mail: Jean.Caelen@imag.fr

J. Dugdale et al. (eds.), *From Research to Practice in the Design of Cooperative Systems:*   213
Results and Open Challenges, DOI 10.1007/978-1-4471-4093-1_15,
© Springer-Verlag London 2012

of activity, but further involve the mutual understanding of laws and rules that forge its background in more or less explicit ways. In addition, we propose that sharing be addressed in the framework of privacy constraints that may be placed at the individual or group level. Another guiding principle is to recognize the dynamic nature of both environments: the components of activity such as tools, goals and rules are constantly changed, constructed and transformed in relation to the outcome of the activity system.

To this end, we propose an original architecture coupling four spaces: a physical space (tools supporting human activity, be it tangible objects or virtual displays), a processing space (agent performing activity, be it human or artificial), an informational space (traces reflecting activity), and a normative space (filters regulating activity). In this framework, the trace embeds the mutual relationships between tools, agents, and constraints from their social environment; agents are responsible for the activity dynamics while filters implementing the norms are responsible for its regulation. Traces are meant to register activity as well as its compliance to the systems of norms at hand, to reflect the constraints tying the collaborative effort. They may in turn be communicated or transformed, thus mediating future activities. To support rich conversational exchange from distant places, within the constraint of tangible environments, we propose to embody communication within tangible objects and virtual displays representing various threads of activity. Collaboration may then be seen as a conversational process grounded in the objects of the working space. The fusion of trace properties then allows situating activity and grounding the filtering process. Interface agents are designed to provide appropriate visual feedback and support mutual awareness. The degree of awareness is further modulated by privacy constraints regulating the extent to which the activity is to be tracked and made visible. We show through simple examples from the RISK game the potential richness of the proposed approach.

15.2   Application Framework

The TangiSense table [13] may be seen as a magnetic retina which is able to detect and locate tangible objects equipped with RFID tags (Fig. 15.1). This retina is made of 25 blocks containing 64 antennas and readers of 1 inch^2 each. Each block of antennas further contains two microprocessors, one dedicated to the management of the RFID readers and another one to the handling of Ethernet communications. The density of antennas allows a spatial and temporal resolution compatible with the real-time detection of moving objects by users. The blocks are driven by the Infrastructure Layer running on the PC host. The role of this layer is to deal with the infrastructure communication, to filter potentially unstable tags IDs and positions, or as well to aggregate information in case a tag is crossing between two blocks. When RFID tags are pasted underneath tangible objects, it is possible (1) to detect their presence on the surface of the table, (2) to proceed to their identification, since RFID tags are unique and (3) to store relevant information directly in

Fig. 15.1 a The *TangiSense* table as equipped for the RISK game with tangible objects and virtual led displaying the ground map as well as tangible objects moves; **b** distributed view: objects handling is transmitted in real time, whatever the distance between the two tables

the object tag's memory (for example their last position, or their last owner). Each RFID antenna is further equipped with four multicolor light emitting diodes (leds). The primary role of these diodes is to provide feedback, that is to *react* to tangible objects positioning and moves, assessing for the user their effective detection by the table. Their secondary role is to provide additional information to the user, from the mere assessment of action correctness, to the display of color pattern enriching the feedback to the user by indicating places where events occur.

The Risk game is a strategic board game for two to six players. The standard version is played on a board depicting a political map of the Earth, divided into 42 territories, which are grouped into six continents. Upon start, each player is allocated an army (cannons, soldiers, cavalrymen) and a set of territories that his army occupies. He is further assigned a mission card specifying his target, be it to conquer some territories or to defeat a given army. An attack takes place according to a well-defined process: the attacking player first of all designates two territories, the first one, from his own territories, supporting the attacking armies, and the second one, from the board, being attacked. The attacking player defines the number of attacking armies in moving army pieces. The attacking and attacked players then throw dices to determine who is losing or winning this round. The attacking player may conduct as many attacks as wanted: the assault continues until he decides to retire, or until one of the two is eliminated. The attacking player may finally operate some army moves, before it is the turn of the other player. A player is eliminated in case all his territories have been lost. The game is finished as soon as one player has reached its mission goal. Figure 15.1 displays example views of the RISK game, as played on the TangiSense table. The potential interest of this application, as regards our proposed modeling, is to offer a static environment of limited complexity, with players operating at the same organizational level, under strict coordination rules. In this context, the goal of the proposed design is to offer a coordination framework ensuring smooth interplay, considering that the players have no communication means except the table and its tangible and virtual equipments. We will illustrate our modeling approach in Sect. 15.6, in the framework of three main functionalities: initial setting up of the players, management of player privacy and management of inter-player coordination.

15.3   State of the Art

To design collaborative support systems, a major issue is to preserve the spontaneity and fluidity of human activity while ensuring the consistency and proper coordination of action [17]. We consider these issues in the framework of activity theory and normative multi-agent system design, with the goal to integrate in a unified view the physical, numerical and social realms of human activity. Activity theory articulates within a single dynamics the individual and social components of human activity (the subject, the object and the tool, on the one hand, the group, its organization and rules, on the other hand). According to this theory, the object is seen and manipulated not *as such* but within the limitations set by the instrument [7]. The tool restricts the interaction to be from the perspective of that particular tool or instrument only [12]. It mediates the structure and objectives of activity; it is in turn transformed and built along this activity and therefore keeps track of user experience [3]. As quoted by [15], "the structuring of activity is not something that precedes it but can only grow directly out of the immediacy of the situation". The involvement in action create circumstances that could not anticipated in advance, and the object and motive reveal themselves only in the process of doing. As a consequence, the limitations set by the instrument may not be modeled a priori, rather they reveal in the course of action. A tool can be physical, mental, or semiotic, it can be a heuristic that one follows to transform an object, or it can be a speech act that transforms a situation [5]. Communication may therefore be thought of as *grounded* in the objects of the working space, which may be designed as coordination objects and raise action. Kraut et al. [11] for example analyzes the role of visual information as a conversational resource in performing collaborative tasks, to maintain mutual awareness, ground conversation and facilitate mutual understanding. According to [19], tangible objects might be used as full resources to support epistemic action, be it oriented toward the physical or numerical world (reference to situate action, sensorial or perceptual resource to sustain involvement into action,...). Coordination is considered as driven implicitly by [20], thanks to an increased consideration of human coordination capacities, and to the search for a balance between the handling of affordant objects and the application of implicit communication norms. Activity theory further recognizes the dynamic nature of context, i.e. the fact that the activity tools, goals and rules are constantly changed, constructed, and transformed in relation to the outcome of this activity [5, 10]. Context is defined as the coupling of two main components, one internal (mental context, private objectives) and the other external (physical and social environment in which activity develops) [6]. According to [14], an integrated computer-supported collaboration environment should provide, configure and handle for each actor the set of tools he needs, accounting for his rights and duties for this activity.

Mutual awareness both of the state of task objects and of one another's activities [11] is a core issue to sustain collaboration; it is defined as sharing mutually manifest information or events [18], and implying belief in mutual attention [6]. Physical co-presence provides multiple resources for awareness and conversational grounding (e.g., sights, smells, touch) which have to be complemented in the case of distant communication. Traces of activity have been proposed by several researchers as a way to represent, share and visualize human experience in its interaction with numerical platforms. Interaction traces have further been explored to enhance synchronous collaboration, and sharing traces at a group level has been advocated to support group awareness [4]. The notion of *social translucence* has been proposed by [8] to represent the degree to which distant actors share the constraints potentially limiting their activity, in terms of visibility, awareness and accountability. A new tool called *social proxy* is proposed in this respect: these graphical representations display socially salient aspects of some situation (distant talks, bidding, queuing...) with a variable degree of visibility.

Normative agents have been proposed by the COIN (Coordination, Organization, Institutions and Norms in Agent Systems) community to face the conceptual antagonism between the autonomy of a system and its control. Coordination in this approach is seen as a social paradigm: agent behavior is not only guided by their mere individual objectives but also regulated by norms specifying which actions are considered as *legal* or not by the group. The norms may operate at several levels in the system, they specify in a declarative way actions considered as legal or accepted. They may be adopted or not by the agents, which may result in penalties, and adapted to cope with the evolution of context [1, 2]. The system dynamics therefore depends not only on the agent dynamics but also on the dynamic of the norms. The approach has been recently extended to specify the interaction modes of agents belonging to the same organization [2]. The goal of such specification is to provide tools allowing to reason on these interaction modes and to check their appropriateness. Another major issue is to maintain consistency, especially in contexts where human actors do not know each other, are communicating from distant places, and may display opposite or conflicting goals. An application to the control of multi-player computer games has been studied in [9]. The purpose is to constrain players and their avatars to adopt a team-like behavior and to respect rules, while allowing some autonomy to keep the game appealing. One further requirement concerns the evolution of the game, since rules change according to rounds of the game. The proposed design articulates two layers using a normative organizational model: the multi-agent interactive game in which avatars evolve as autonomous agents, and an institutional multi-agent middle-ware called SYNAI (SYstem of Normative Agents for Institution) dedicated to the management of the organization and to the arbitration. The role of this arbitration system consists in rewarding or punishing agents when they respect or not their agreements. Finally mention is made in [16] of a distributed and situated approach to normative design. The proposed normative infrastructure is composed of normative objects and normative places, and further allows the spatial contextualization of norms.

15.4   Proposed View

Human activity is multi-threaded: collaboration may be seen as a conversational act, where the signs of dialog are multiple (moving, designing, acknowledging, referring, turn taking, giving speech). These signs of dialog are missing in the course of distant collaboration. To benefit from the tangibility offered by the infrastructure at hand, we propose to design dedicated tangible objects, called tangigets, to support distant communication and use them to produce signs and traces of conversational activity. We will for example distinguish between a *designation tangiget* (a tool to delineate zones on the table surface or points out an object, thus indicating its relevance to distant actors), an *annotation tangiget* (a tool to express acceptance or rebuttal of a given utterance), and a *coordination tangiget* (a tool to indicate the starting or ending of activities). A *privacy tangiget* has been added to account for modifications in the privacy rules.

Collaborative activity does not reduce to exchanging views, or sharing the production of results. More deeply, it amounts to sharing common goals and intentions, and to understand the physical or social constraints surrounding activity. Privacy rules may in addition rule out the degree of sharing. These constraints are often kept implicit and thus remain invisible; they vary from one individual to the other (preferences, own objectives), from one organization to the other (rules for turn taking or for conducting operations), and may as well depend on the current goal or physical environment. Some of these rules may hold for the whole collaborative session or evolve according to the processing stage or as well depending on individual decisions.

To cope with these various issues, we ground our design on an extended notion of trace, where traces reflect both human activity and its relationship to the norms under consideration, through a set of property values and types. The norms are represented explicitly via filters deposited in the system environment, which may evolve along the various stages of collaboration or more opportunistically in case of some tangible object moves (privacy tangiget for example). Filters are triggered in a situated way, via the fusion of trace properties expressing a pattern and context of activity. They further enrich these trace properties by reflecting their compliance to the norms.

They finally participate to the system regulation by launching agents, whose role is to keep track of tangible objects moves and process the trace accordingly, to generate feedback to the users and to maintain the system of norms at hand by removing or depositing filters. Interface agents are designed to provide appropriate visual feedback. Feedback is operated in a dual way, to reflect activity (virtual display reflecting tangible object moves on distant tables), and to reflect norm compliance (virtual display underneath a tangible object reflecting the legitimacy of its move to the actor responsible for this move). Such feedback is regulated by privacy rules.

In this framework, norms do not act as a prerequisite to action or as a way to prevent action. Rather, they allow grounding the physical infrastructure of the collaborative environment into the realm of a social organization. These norms are not static, but may evolve, to account for dedicated contexts or demands. They further reveal in the course of action in the form of new trace properties, a set of signs revealing potentially complex relationships and facets, which will afterwards be interpreted, possibly in different contexts by different actors.

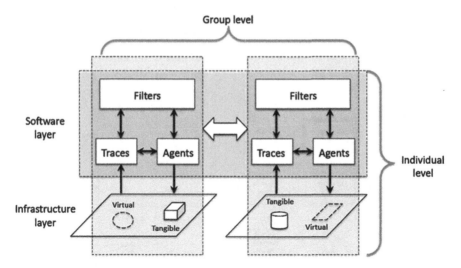

Fig. 15.2 Collaboration as the joint management of traces (representing activity), norms (regulating activity) and agents (performing activity).

15.5   Proposed Architecture

We finally model collaboration as a situated process coupling four spaces: the physical space (human activity tools, be it tangible objects or virtual displays), the informational space (activity traces), the processing space (activity performers, be it human or artificial agents) and the normative space (activity regulation rules). Four kinds of elements are therefore distinguished in the proposed architecture (Fig. 15.2): (1) tools, i.e. tangible objects and their virtual representatives, that appear in the physical environment; (2) traces, i.e. numerical objects, which keep track of human and artificial agent activity and register the privacy of this information as well as its compliance to the system of norms at hand; (3) actors, i.e. human and artificial agents, whose role is (a) to handle tools, thus generating and updating traces of activity, and (b) to handle the normative space, i.e. to deposit filters in the system; (4) filters, condition-action rules, which regulate the system activity by (a) modifying the privacy of trace properties, (b) checking the compliance of activity with respect to the system of norms at hand and (c) launching agents to react to trace modifications.

In this framework, human and artificial agents are responsible for the activity dynamics while filters implementing the norms are responsible for the regulation of this dynamics. Traces evolve jointly under the regulatory action of filters and the processing action of human and artificial agents, which are operated in an asynchronous and concurrent way. To the dynamics of traces corresponds a dynamics of norms, deposited along the collaboration process. Filters are deposited by agents and may be set as active or inactive. Active filters are repeatedly checked for application to the information space (traces), under control of a dedicated engine (not

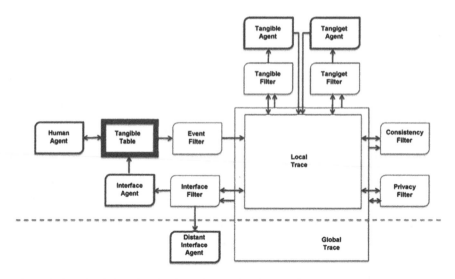

Fig. 15.3 Functional view showing the various types of agents, filters and traces.

shown in the figure). They launch agents as soon as some pattern of interest is detected over the information traces.

When activated, the system operates according to the following information flow (also shown in Fig. 15.3): (1) Early detection of a tangible or tangiget object move by event filters operating at the infrastructure level: creation or update of the corresponding local trace; (2) Triggering of the consistency and privacy filters: update of the corresponding local traces; (3) Triggering of the tangible, tangiget and interface filters: computation of some local trace property, feedback to local and distant human actors.

We distinguish between four types of agents: (1) Tangible agents: their role is to perform the computation required by the application and enrich the trace properties (decision resulting from dice roll results for example); (2) Tangiget agents: depending on the tangiget that has been handled, their role is to launch the requested coordination policy, that it is to modify the policy at hand by depositing the corresponding set of filters; (3) Interface agents: their role is to provide visual feedback, by means of led display, informing either about a distant tangible object move, about the result of consistency analysis (consistency of tangible object move, result of consistency filter) or about a request (request for a tangible object move, result of a coordination filter); (4) Global agents further operate on some global trace properties, under the regulation of dedicated global filters, to maintain the directory of actors and for the sake of global processing consistency (they are not displayed in Fig. 15.3, for the sake of simplicity).

The advantage of distant collaboration is to benefit from a free and private space of action that may not be accessed from the outside. Another key element is the possibility to continue active working in phases where one has to wait for results from distant tables, by drafting in a concrete way various potential intermediate solutions and keeping them private. Some privacy rules may therefore hold for the whole collaborative session or evolve according to the collaboration stage or to individual decisions. We therefore propose (1) that private/public spaces be delimited from start by means of dedicated privacy filters (in the RISK game for example, the player mission card must be kept private) and (2) to dynamically open and (re)open these spaces as soon as it is decided or necessary for the course of action (in the RISK game for example, a player may want to simulate some attacks and keep them private before entering the full play). This kind of closing/opening action may for example be ruled by means of a dedicated tangiget.

Traces in our present design are attached to tangible and tangiget objects, to describe their properties and current state. They are further attached to the virtual representatives of these objects. Any trace is considered as a set of (property, value) pairs. We propose that properties be typed, to register their privacy and compliance to the norms. As a consequence, a trace is expressed as follows:

$$Trace = \{(p, v)\} \text{ where } p = \langle name : consistency : privacy \rangle$$
$$\text{with } consistency \in \{valid, invalid\} \text{ and } privacy \in \{private, public\}$$

Valid (resp. invalid) expresses the fact that the given property is compliant (resp. not compliant) with respect to the norms at hand. Private (resp. public) means that the property is not accessible (resp. accessible) to distant agents. Newly created traces are considered as private, with a non-assigned (null) consistency. As soon as some trace property is public, it becomes accessible to distant filters.

Any trace is defined as possessing the following minimal properties (identifying name, type of tangible object, tangible table where originated, spatial position on this table, time of move). The type of a trace may be either tangible, tangiget or abstract (to refer to global properties of the whole system of tables).

We distinguish between five kinds of filters (Fig. 15.3): (1) Event filters: filters that regulate the creation of traces from stream of events generated by objects move on the table surface; these filters are part of the infrastructure layer and not considered into more details in the following; (2) Interface filters: filters that launch interface agents as soon as some trace is created or modified (under the constraint that privacy rules hold); (3) Tangible (resp. tangiget) filters: filters that launch tangible (resp. tangiget) agents; (4) Consistency filters: filters that check the compliance of human activity with respect to some norms, and thus enrich the trace via the field consistency of trace properties; (5) Privacy filters: filters that modify the trace local visibility and accessibility to distant actors, and thus enrich the trace via the field privacy of trace properties.

15.6 An Application to the RISK Game

The goal of this section is to illustrate the potential of the proposed design and provide some concrete hints regarding representation and processing issues. We ground this analysis on an application to the RISK game that has been presented in

Table 15.1 Description of the player trace

Property name	Property consistency	Property privacy	Value
Type	Null	Private	(Player card, tangible)
OnTable	Null	Private	idTable1
Name	Null	Private	Dupont
Id	Valid	Private	2
Position	Null	Private	(0.3, 0.5)

Table 15.2 Description of the $F_{consistency}$ filter elements

$F_{consistency}$	Property name	Property field	Parameter	Operator	Value	
Conditions	Type		?Trace1	=	(Game, abstract)	(1)
	PlayerNumber		?Trace1	<	6	(2)
	Type		?Trace2	=	(Player card, tangible)	(3)
	Type	Consistency	?Trace2	=	Null	(4)
	Id		?Trace2	=	?id	(5)
	Type		?Trace3	=	(Coordination, tangiget)	(6)
	Status		?Trace3	=	Initialization	(7)
	Handled		?Trace3	=	?id	(8)
Actions	$\forall i; p_i.consistency(?trace2) \leftarrow Valid$					(9)

Sect. 15.2. We focus on three activity/regulation stages (player identification, privacy, attack coordination protocol) exemplifying different aspects of our modeling.

Player Identification The player identification process starts as soon as a player handles his player identification card and puts in place his coordination tangiget. Handling this tangible object results in the creation of a trace, which is described in Table 15.1.

Such creation triggers a validation filter $F_{consistency}$ whose role is to check whether this player is legitimate or not and modify the player trace accordingly. $F_{consistency}$ is described in Table 15.2.

As may be seen, the condition part of this filter involves the composition of heterogeneous trace elements: global trace of the game, to check the number of players already entered in the game (must be under six), status of the player's coordination tangiget (must be "Initialization"), presence of a new player identification card.

An agent attached to the follow-up of this new player is then created, thanks to a new filter, $F_{newplayer}$, described in Table 15.3. The role of this filter is to launch the player agent and the coordination agent, whose role is to ensure any further processing for this new player.

Privacy As regards privacy, the default policy is that any player (or player action) be known and visible to other players. However, this policy holds under the condition that the corresponding information or action are valid, according to the norms at hand. This basic policy may further be changed by handling a dedicated tangiget, to declare some action as private (not discussed further in this section).

Table 15.3 Description of the $F_{new player}$ filter elements

$F_{new player}$	Property name	Property field	Parameter	Operator	Value	
Conditions	Type		*?Trace1*	=	(Player card, tangible)	(1)
	Position	Consistency	*?Trace1*	=	Valid	(2)
	Position		*?Trace1*	=	?pos	(3)
	OnTable	Consistency	*?Trace1*	=	Valid	(4)
	OnTable		*?Trace1*	=	?t	(5)
	Id		*?Trace1*	=	?id	(6)
	Type		*?Trace2*	=	(Coordination, tangiget)	(7)
	Status		*?Trace2*	=	Initialization	(8)
	Handled		*?Trace2*	=	??id	(9)
Actions	*Launch(agent$_{coordination}$, ?t, succeed)*					(10)
	Launch(agent$_{player}$, ?t, ?Trace1)					(11)

Table 15.4 Description of the $F_{privacy}$ filter elements

$F_{privacy}$	Property name	Property field	Parameter	Operator	Value	
Conditions	Type		*?Trace1*	=	(Player card, tangible)	(1)
	Type	Consistency	*?Trace1*	=	Valid	(2)
	Type	Privacy	*?Trace1*	=	Private	(3)
	Id		*?Trace1*	=	?id	(4)
	Type		*?Trace2*	=	(Coordination, tangiget)	(5)
	Status		*?Trace2*	=	Initialization	(6)
	Handled		*?Trace2*	=	?id	(7)
Actions	$\forall i; p_i.privacy(?Trace1) \leftarrow Public$					(8)

We have shown in Table 15.1, the example trace of a newly created player, with some properties kept private. We give in Table 15.4, the description of a filter, called $F_{privacy}$, whose role is to transform these trace properties, under the condition that the current stage of the player's coordination tangiget is "Initialization".

As soon as the player trace is valid and public, a new filter may be triggered, whose role is to launch the Interface agent in order to provide feedback of this new event to distant tables. This filter, called $F_{interface}$, relies on a complex condition part, checking that the player trace properties are simultaneously valid and public, that the state of the coordination trace is "Initialization", and finally that distant player traces are valid and public.

Coordination The purpose of this section is to illustrate inter-player coordination, based on a simple example from the RISK game: launching of an attack by a given player. According to our framework, inter-player coordination is ensured (1) by the players themselves handling dedicated tangigets, (2) by the normative system expressing policies of action and (3) by the visual feedback provided to each player. Two different tangigets are considered in the following: a coordination tangiget (a dice with sides representing various stages of the game) and a designation tangiget (to point out the attacking and attacked territories).

As exemplified in Fig. 15.4, such coordination finally involves interleaved tan-gigets, filters and agents handling. Filter description may easily be derived from the descriptions in Tables 15.2, 15.3 and 15.4. The whole process may be decomposed as follows:

- Tangiget handling: handling the coordination and designation tangigets modify the corresponding traces, which triggers the tangiget filter F_{attack}; this filter which launches tangiget agent 1 on the attacking player local environment to-gether with tangiget agent 2 on the attacked player distant environment (F_{attack}, acting at a global level in the game, is actually provided the rights for creating a relationship between both players and launching these agents);
- Policy management: it is then the role of both tangiget agents to deposit the pol-icy they plan to follow, in the form respectively of the Interface filter $F_{interface}$;
- Communication management: the role of $F_{interface}$ is to launch interface agent 2, so that information about the attack under preparation be provided to the dis-tant player (lightning of leds underneath the distant player identification card, coordination tangiget and attacked territory); $F_{interface}$ condition part involves information about both distant players identification, coordination and designa-tion traces;
- Tangiget handling: upon receipt of this feedback, player 2 reacts by handling his own coordination tangiget, thus acknowledging receipt of this action;
- Communication management: the role of $F_{interface}$ is now to launch interface agent 1, to transmit player 2's acknowledgement of receipt (lightning of leds un-derneath player 1 coordination and designation tangigets); $F_{interface}$ condition part involves information about both distant players identification, coordination and designation traces;
- Player 1 may now proceed forward by handling his fighting army.

15.7 Overview of the Correlations Between Agents and Filters

To show the system dynamics, we finally summarize in Table 15.5 the various types of filters and agents involved in this short scenario, together with their roles, trig-gering events, results and dependencies.

15.8 Conclusion

We have presented a design to support collaboration under tangible environments. Our core contribution is to provide a seamless integration between elements from the physical, numerical and social world, in a design grounded into normative multi-agent system theory. Human collaboration in our design is mediated via tangible ob-

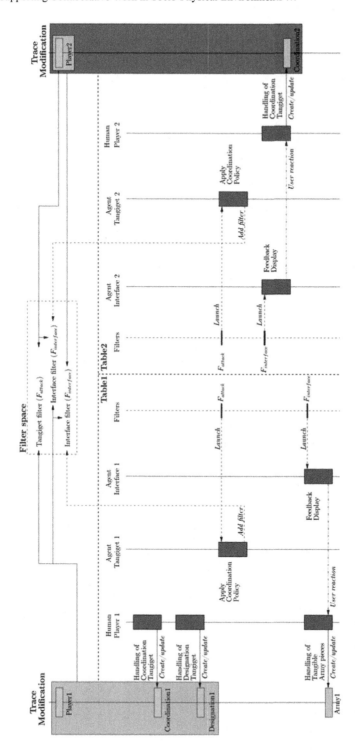

Fig. 15.4 Interleaving of tangiget, filter and agent activity to ensure activity coordination in a specific phase of the RISK game

Table 15.5 Correlations between agents and filters in the short RISK game scenarios

Interaction scene	Player identification	Attack	Consistency	Privacy	Interface
Role	New player joining the current game	Regulate interplayer coordination during attack state	Verify human activity consistency	Update the accessibility of traces	Operate visual feedback on distant table
Filter	$F_{new\ player}$	F_{attack}	$F_{consistency}$	$F_{privacy}$	$F_{inter\ face}$
Trigger components	Tangible object: player Tangiget: coordination	Tangible object: player Tangiget: coordination, designation	Property: consistency	Property: privacy	Tangible object tangiget Property: consistency, privacy
Action-trace	Ø	Modify traces	Modify traces	Modify traces	Ø
Action-agent	Launch: $Agent_{Player}$ $Agent_{Coordination}$	Launch: $Agent_{Attack}$ $Agent_{Coordination}$ $Agent_{Designation}$	Ø	Ø	Launch: $Agent_{Inter\ face}$
Dependencies	Consistency	Player identification	Ø	Ø	Consistency Privacy
Consequences at the agent level	Subscribe to local and global policies in terms of consistency, privacy and interface	Add appropriate privacy, consistency, interface filters for this specific phase	Ø	Ø	Ø

jects and registered via multi-dimensional numerical traces. These traces are made to evolve under the application of normative rules, to keep track not only of a given activity, but furthermore of the normative context surrounding this activity. Visual feedback is further provided, to reflect activity, in a way that is situated with respect to the norms at hand. Context awareness is therefore approached as involving both activity and norm awareness.

In accordance with the principles of activity theory, norms do not act as a prerequisite, or as a way to apply a priori constraints on action. Rather, they are meant to situate action, by evaluating properties that may then be considered by other agents, in proper contexts. Human collaboration in this context is mediated rather than assisted by complex computerized systems; it is regulated rather than constrained. Collaboration is finally defined as a process by which individual and collective norms are appropriated and co-evolve. Further specification and implementation, in front of a real application, is of course mandatory to more thoroughly investigate the potential, difficulties and limitations of this approach.

Acknowledgments Work supported by Agence Nationale de la Recherche (ANR) under grant IMAGIT—project ANR 2010 CORD 01701.

References

1. Boella, G., van der Torre, L.V.N., Verhagen, H.: Introduction to normative multiagent systems. Comput. Math. Org. Theory. **12**, 71–79 (2006)
2. Boissier, O., Balbo, F., Badeig, F.: Controlling multi-party interaction within normative multi-agent organisations. In: Coordination, Organization, Institutions and Norms in Agent Systems VI (LNAI 6541). Springer, Heidelberg (2011)
3. Bourguin, G., Derycke, A., Tarby, J.: Beyond the interface: co-evolution inside interactive systems a proposal founded on activity theory. In: IHM-HCI 2001 Conference, People and Computer XV—Interactions Without Frontiers, pp. 297–310. Springer, Berlin (2001)
4. Clauzel, D., Sehaba, K., Prié, Y.: Enhancing synchronous collaboration by using interactive visualisation of modelled traces. Simul. Model. Pract. Theory. **19**, 84–97 (2011)
5. Cole, M.: Cultural Psychology: A Once and Future Discipline. Harvard University Press, Cambridge (1996)
6. Dumazeau, C., Karsenty, L.: Communications distantes en situation de travail: favoriser l'établissement d'un contexte mutuellement partagé. Le travail humain **71**, 225–252 (2008)
7. Engestrom, Y.: Developmental work research: reconstructing expertise through expansive learning. In: Nurminen M., Weir G., (eds.) Human Jobs and Computer Interfaces, pp. 265–290. Cambridge University Press, New York (1991)
8. Erickson, T., Kellogg, W.: Social translucence: using minimalist visualizations of social activity to support collective interaction. In: Höök, K., Benyon, D., Munroe A. (eds.) Designing Information Spaces: The Social Navigation Approach, pp. 17–41. Springer, London (2003)
9. Gâteau, B., Boissier, O., Khadraoui, D., Dubois, E.: Controlling an interactive game with a multi-agent based normative organizational model. In: Coordination, Organization, Institutions and Norms in Agent Systems Workshop (COIN) at the 17th European Conference on Artificial Intelligence (ECAI), Italy (2006)
10. Greenberg, S.: Context as a dynamic construct. Hum. Comput. Interact. **16**, 257–268 (2001)

11. Kraut, R.E., Fussell, R., Siegel, J.: Visual information as a conversational resource in collaborative physical tasks. Hum. Comput. Interact. **18**, 13–49 (2003)

12. Kuutti, K.: Activity theory as a potential framework for human-computer interaction research. In: Nardi B. (eds.) Context and Consciousness: Activity Theory and Human Computer Interaction, pp. 17–44. MIT Press, Cambridge (1995)

13. Lepreux, S., Kubicki, S., Kolski, C., Caelen, J.: Distributed interactive surfaces using tangible and virtual objects. In: Workshop DUI 2011 Distributed User Interfaces, at CHI 2011, pp. 65–68, Canada (2011)

14. Lewandowski, A.: Vers de meilleurs supports aux activités coopératives en accord avec la co-évolution: application au développement logiciel coopératif. Ph.D. thesis, Université du Littoral Côte d'Opale (2006)

15. Nardi, B.: Activity theory and human-computer interaction. In: Nardi B. (eds.) Context and Consciousness: Activity Theory and Human-computer Interaction, pp. 69–103. MIT Press, Cambridge (1996)

16. Okuyama, F., Bordini, R., da Rocha Costa, A.: A distributed normative infrastructure for situated multi-agent organisations. In: 6th International Workshop on Declarative Agent Languages and Technologies (DALT) to held as part of AAMAS-2008 (2008)

17. Pape, J.A., Graham, T.C.: Coordination policies for tabletop gaming. In: Proceedings of the graphics interface poster, pp. 24–25 (2010)

18. Salembier, P., Zouinar, M.: Intelligibilité mutuelle et contexte partagé, Inspirations conceptuelles et réductions technologiques. Activités. **1**, 64–85 (2004)

19. Shaer, O., Hornecker, E.: Tangible user interfaces: past, present and future directions. Hum. Comput. Interact. **3**, 1–138 (2010)

20. Sire, S., Chatty, S.: Vers des interfaces à collaboration directe pour le travail de groupe. In: Proceedings of the GRESICO communication, société et internet, pp. 259–275 (1998)

Chapter 16
Exploring Collaboration in Group-to-Group Videoconferencing

Petr Slovák, Peter Novák, Pavel Troubil, Vít Rusňák, Petr Holub, and Erik C. Hofer

Abstract Prior work on videoconferencing shows that various design changes can have profound impacts on group dynamics. In order to further explore the available design space, we report on a qualitative study that compares behaviour of groups in two group-to-group videoconferencing environments and face-to-face communication during a complex social dilemma game. There are pronounced differences in participant behaviour between the two videoconferencing designs, indicating higher cooperative behaviour in one of the videoconferencing conditions. Based on qualitative analysis of the gameplay, we hypothesise that the decisive factor is a discrepancy in the type of group identity that develops during the game. Our results suggest that the differences in behaviour are due to differences in design of the two videoconferencing environments. In particular, the incorporation of personal displays and individualised videostreams likely contributed to these outcomes.

16.1 Introduction

Videoconferencing is coming into focus of researchers and industry again, both in the context of workplace (e.g., [12, 16]), as well as everyday life (e.g., [1, 7], and success of Skype as a family video chat). A number of recent studies shows how often even subtle changes in the design of videoconferencing systems strongly affect interaction of users [9–12, 16, 18].

A common scenario for distributed interaction in the workplace is *group-to-group* communication, where several people are collocated at a number of distributed sites. While this has not been so extensively researched by the videoconferencing community, previous studies have found that specific problems arise when computer-mediated communication (CMC) channels such as email, chat, audio or

P. Slovák (✉) · P. Novák · P. Troubil · V. Rusňák · P. Holub
Masaryk University, Botanická 68a, Brno, Czech Republic
e-mail: slovak@ics.muni.cz

E. C. Hofer
School of Information, University of Michigan, 1075 Beal Avenue, Ann Arbor, USA

J. Dugdale et al. (eds.), *From Research to Practice in the Design of Cooperative Systems: Results and Open Challenges*, DOI 10.1007/978-1-4471-4093-1_16,
© Springer-Verlag London 2012

commodity videoconferencing are used in this setting. For example, groups might exhibit strong in-/out-group effects on each site [4], leading to *collocation blindness* [5] or *presence disparity* [15]. Efforts to support group-to-group communication through specialised video conferencing environments appeared [9, 12, 18], reporting significant improvements over the commodity videoconferencing design (i.e., units consisting of a large shared screen and camera per group such as Cisco TelePresence series and similar). These specialised environments are based on various design factors, such as individual viewing positions allowing for eye-contact [9], "blending" of physical spaces by careful choice of furniture and camera angles [12], or effects of seating arrangements [18]. Moreover, all design concepts above build on technically complex solutions and include components that are not directly accessible to many users.

To inform further development of group-to-group videoconferencing environments, it is important to understand these design factors much better, as well as analyse how they play out in various settings. To explore this design space, we have previously developed a group-to-group videoconferencing prototype called GColl [14]. As some form of gaze awareness has been implicated as an important factor in most of prior videoconferencing work (e.g., [10, 18]), we aimed to design for a compromise between supporting gaze-awareness, individual viewing positions and ease of deployment. In comparison to commodity videoconferencing, GColl design includes a screen for each user (e.g., a personal laptop), a videostream from each user (instead of one shared videostream from each site) and a restricted gaze awareness functionality.

In this study, we were interested in exploring if and how the behaviour of groups of participants using GColl differs in comparison with face-to-face interaction (FTF) and commodity videoconferencing design. Our choice of face-to-face and commodity videoconferencing as the two comparison environments allowed us to draw out any gross differences in participants' behaviour over these dissimilar conditions, as well as highlight design choices that provide benefits over the commodity videoconferencing. We adapted a complex social dilemma game as the basis for interaction, with no restrictions on interaction among participants. Lessons learned from such open ended observation help us inform future work and suggest factors that merit further analysis.

In particular, qualitative analysis of the game play revealed pronounced differences in participant behaviour among the two videoconferencing designs and face-to-face, indicating higher collaboration and cooperative behaviour in GColl videoconferencing condition and face-to-face. Based on gameplay analysis, we propose that the decisive factor is a discrepancy in the type of *group identity* that develops during the game. GColl design seems to have facilitated creation of shared group identity similarly to the FTF condition, diminishing the in-/out-group effects observed in groups using commodity videoconferencing, and thus leading to better cooperation among the group members. Contrary to expectations, the observed differences were not due to the gaze awareness affordances available in GColl. In the Discussion section, we suggest how the remaining differences in design between GColl and commodity videoconferencing (i.e., personal screens and videostreams) could have contributed to the observed results.

The differences in observed behavior between the two video mediated communication outcomes highlight the significant impacts that design choices have on the use and performance of communication systems. Our analysis suggests that the combination of two specific design factors is most likely responsible for these outcome differences, due to facilitating a shift in the group dynamics. One of the contributions of this study is this illustration of the ways such design choices impact the observed use of two comparable video communication systems. Overall, our results do not dispute the importance of gaze awareness for remote collaboration, but point to other aspects that may be also important, such as design dependent changes in group identity.

In the rest of this chapter, we first outline the related work. We continue with description of the study design and the analysis of the gameplay videorecordings. The discussion then ties our observations to the proposed changes in group identity.

16.2 Related Work

In addition to work already mentioned in the Introduction, a number of previous papers focused on various aspects of the interface and how they affect interaction of users. For example, [11] shows that including the whole upper body rather than a head image increases subsequent helping behaviour towards a stranger. Several videoconferencing systems supporting multi-person (but not group-to-group) interaction explored effects of facilitating gaze awareness and other non-verbal information (e.g., Hydra [13]). Venolia et al. [16] show how providing a dedicated physical proxy used for videoconferencing in collocated teams with a single remote collaborator improves the felt presence in meetings.

Designed specifically for group-to-group interaction, Multiview system [9] was shown to support trust more successfully than commodity videoconferencing, yielding results that were statistically indistinguishable to those achieved by face-to-face communication [10]. This difference is attributed to gaze awareness Multiview provides and commodity videoconferencing does not. Seating positions together with support for directional gaze awareness and non-verbal signals improved task outcome and discussion structure in [18]. Similarly, contemporary top-end videoconferencing installations, often dubbed as telepresence, (e.g., [12]) report supporting collaboration better than commodity videoconferencing.

16.3 Method

As discussed above, the study aims to explore differences in behaviour of groups using three communication environments: an environment analogous to current commodity solutions (denoted as *standard videoconferencing*—SVE), a prototype design called *GColl* [14], and *face-to-face*. We first give a detailed description of the chosen task. We then go on to provide further details about the used videoconferencing environments and the study procedure.

16.3.1 Task Description

Our choice of social dilemma game is motivated by prior work showing that these types of tasks are (1) sensitive to changes in communication environments (e.g., [3]), and (2) tap into concepts as collaboration and trust that are important for remote teamwork [6]. Similarly to previous research using social dilemma games in CMC (e.g., the Daytrader Game [3, 10]), we used a more complex social dilemma than the well known game-theoretic tasks such as the "Prisoner's Dilemma". To simulate a broader range of real-world interactions, we were interested in a task that retains most properties of common social dilemma games, but allows for long term planning and imitates prolonged group interaction by adding a relationship between the history of actions and the current game state (in contrast with repeated trials of the same situation used in many more formal social dilemma tasks).

To this end, we have adapted a game called The Goldminers, used for example in social skills courses. The Goldminers game is an instantiation of a social dilemma, which forces each player as a group member into the decision between the two basic strategies each turn: she can either cooperate with the other group members, which may not be optimal for her personal score, or defect to possibly gain a higher score than the others. In addition, Goldminers allow for two possible end-game scenarios (cooperative vs. individualistic). These scenarios are based on the end-game score achieved by the group members and impact distribution of rewards after the game.

Goldminers differ from game-theoretic social dilemmas in several ways: first, no restriction on communication is given; second, there are three possible actions to be taken and their effect differs depending on the context; and finally, payback for individual actions changes (in a predictable and known way) during the course of the game depending on the history of previous moves. These differences make the game problematic to analyze by quantitative methods—for example, possible outcomes of one rounds are dependent on the rounds and actions played previously. However, it makes the game more interesting for the participants[1], as well as demanding higher cooperation among the players should they try to achieve the cooperative scenario, as a quite complex strategy needs to be created early in the game if the group is to succeed. Moreover, the motivation for these changes comes from real-world activities, where team communication is key and history of actions done affects the current situation. As our study aims for qualitative understanding of behaviour differences among the environments, difficulties with quantitative analysis are not an issue.

The rules of the game are as follows: Participants represent goldminers and try to mine gold from a river. The river has an attribute called *gold density*, which is set to US\$ 30,000 at the beginning of the game. Every round, each participant simultaneously chooses one of three possible actions: (1) **legal mining**, which gives the participant lower personal profit (current value of *gold density* minus 25 % tax) and causes no harm to the others; (2) **controlling** the river costs the participant a small

---

[1] For example, more than half of our groups played a second round of the game "just for fun".

amount of gold (US$ 15,000 divided evenly among all participants controlling that round) while incurring a great loss to all illegal miners; (3) **illegal mining** makes the participant either lose or gain US$ 50,000 depending on whether a control action had been played that turn. In both cases, *gold density* attribute is decreased by a US$ 1,000 for each illegal miner. Once every three rounds the river partially "cleans itself", increasing the attribute by a US$ 1,000, up to its original value of US$ 30,000. Once all participants choose their action, the round is evaluated and the numbers of particular actions taken (but not who actually took them) are displayed. The game ends after 15 rounds, or if the *gold density* attribute is ever lower than US$ 1,000. Participants were aware of the exact game ending conditions.

Two ending scenarios were possible: (1) a *cooperative scenario* is achieved if at least five out of six participants have more game money than a given threshold (US$ 330,000) when the game ends—participants were awarded with a chocolate bar each for this outcome; (2) *individualistic scenario* was acquired in all other cases—group members were given chocolate bars according to the game money gained (first two participants got two bars, the next two got just one bar, and the last two did not receive any chocolate bars). Thus, incentives for cooperative as well as uncooperative play were present. Note that the overall number of chocolate bars for the whole group remained constant in both scenarios and the only difference was in how they were distributed. The cooperative scenario threshold was chosen so that the group had to cooperate extensively to reach it. Several forms of cooperation are possible in the Goldminers game: the most common one is if everyone in the group agrees to play a particular action. Highest score for each player is achieved if all participants play only legal mining moves for the first 10 rounds, and continue with illegal mining till the 15th round.

A simple Goldminers application was developed in Java.

16.3.2 Videoconferencing Environments

The study compares three communication environments for interaction of groups: the *standard videoconferencing environment*, the *GColl* environment, and *face-to-face*. The standard videoconferencing environment uses a single screen and camera for each group, resulting in setup analogous to the one shown at Fig. 16.1. Diagram of the setup for FTF condition is at Fig. 16.2.

There are several differences between GColl [14] and the "standard" commodity videoconferencing system: (1) in GColl, each user uses her own display; (2) there are two cameras aimed at each user (called *focus* and *side* cameras), plus one *group* camera per each site. Additionally, each user can, independently of others, "focus" on any other participant on her display, which was designed to enhance gaze awareness functionality. However, participants in this study did not find the "focus" function useful and have not used it during the game. The explanation was that the game required mainly addressing all others at once, so there was no need to "focus" on a particular player. Due to space restriction, we refer the reader to [14]

Fig. 16.1 SVE site
configuration

Fig. 16.2 FTF site
configuration

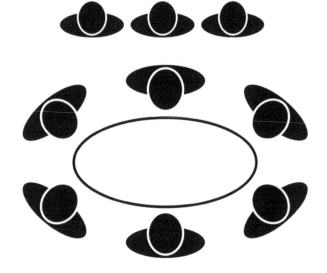

for details on the intended gaze awareness functionality and other details regarding
GColl. Diagrams depicting screen and GColl site layout are at Figs. 16.3 and 16.4.

16.3.3 Subjects and Study Procedure

Overall, 126 participants (i.e., 21 groups of 6) took part in this study. Similarly to
prior work on social dilemma games (e.g., [5]), we made sure that participants did
not know each other prior to the experiment. All participants were students of various national universities and fields of study, and received a small, non-monetary
reward for their participation in the study. We asked about previous use of other
videoconferencing software: no participant indicated any experience more than "using Skype once in a while".

Each group of six participants communicated over a particular communication
channel (i.e., seven groups per channel), using the Goldminers social dilemma game

Fig. 16.3 GColl display
layout

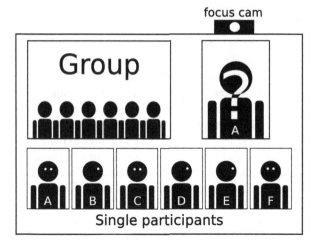

Fig. 16.4 GColl site
configuration

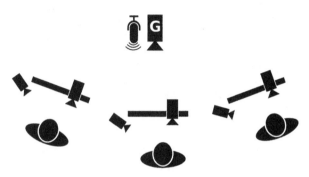

as the basis for their interaction. We videotaped their communication and logged the progress of the game. In computer-mediated settings, the participants were divided into two three-person groups communicating over the videoconferencing environment. Each group has participated in one session only.

Technical setup was as follows: All users were provided with a laptop with widescreen display or a PC with a 17" LCD, running the Goldminers applications. GColl users were captured by two Logitech QuickCam Pro 9000 USB webcams at each workstation. At both sites, the group view was captured by an Elmo PTC-15S camera. The game application did not obstruct any GColl windows. In the "standard" videoconferencing setting, the group camera and the sound were captured exactly in the same way as in GColl, and an NEC MT1060 projector was used to display the remote group. The screen was located in front of the seating arrangement, approximately 2 m from the participants, placed at a height corresponding to a normal sitting position. The image of the remote participants was slightly smaller than life-size. The same audio setup was user in both videoconferencing conditions: by a ClearOne AccuMic PC microphone at one site and SHURE EasyFlex EZB/C microphone at the other.

Participants in each group played one 15-round session of a social dilemma game called Goldminers and attended a debriefing. Each session took 60–90 minutes, depending mainly on the length of gameplay (5–25 min, mean 14 min). An explanation of the game rules was given by the facilitator with a time for questions, and the participants tried out the game application. Care was taken not to inform the participants about the aims and indicators of the study. Participants consented the game could be logged and videotaped. In computer mediated conditions, the facilitator first explained features of the environment on a running instance. Participants were divided into two subgroups of three, and one of these subgroups moved into another game room. After we made sure that the videoconferencing environment and the game application worked correctly, the participants were left alone to play the game. In the face-to-face condition, the group played together around a large oval table in one of the rooms. A technical team was prepared to help in case any issues arose. When the game ended, we led the participants back to the first room. Additionally, participants from the last six groups attended a short focus session. Afterwards, we handed out the rewards: an USB flash disk or a chocolate bar to each player, and six additional chocolates split among players depending on the game outcome. The session ended with a voluntary debriefing.

16.3.4 Methodology

Two of the authors and one of their colleagues conducted thematic analysis of the video-recordings, alternating periods of independent interpretation of the data with joint discussion and merging of the proposed concepts. We iteratively annotated the videostreams (using Advene tool [2]) in dependence on the emerging concepts, transcribing relevant parts in detail. The resulting coding scheme addressed the types of discussion for each round—see next section for more details. The analysis was carried out by two of the authors. Additionally, 9 of the 21 videostreams (approx. 42 % of the data) were independently coded by an additional researcher. Interrater agreement was 100 %, showing that the concepts were clearly identifiable in the data. Due to technical problems, video from one FTF group was not available—overall, video-recordings of six groups using FTF, seven using SVE and seven communicating over GColl were analyzed in this section.

16.4 Results

Thematic analysis of the video-recordings showed profound differences in behaviour of groups using different communication environments during the task, pointing our attention to the topics presented below: We first outline analysis of the discussion structure, strategies used, and the value groups attached to cooperative play. Second, we present indices of in-/out-group behaviours that appeared in most SVE groups, but very few GColl or face-to-face groups. The Discussion section

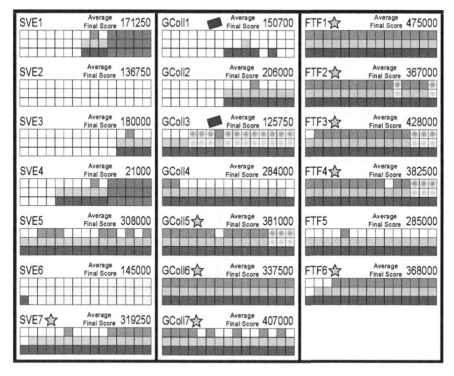

Fig. 16.5 Round-by-round overview for SVE, GColl and face-to-face groups

then suggests an interpretation of the observed differences in behaviours in terms of changes in the type of group identity created.

16.4.1 Strategies and Discussion Structure

We analyzed the gameplay discussion for each group. Initial analysis pointed to differences among the three environments in both the amount of game-oriented discussion as well as the type of proposed strategies, with GColl groups showing behaviour much closer to FTF than SVE groups. In particular, we focused on occasions where a discussion of a joint strategy for the following round(s) took place, if it was accepted and adhered to by the participants, and what kind of strategy was discussed (e.g., long-term vs. just for the current round)[2].

Figure 16.5 gives an overview of how each group behaved during the game: each 3×15 grid corresponds to a particular group, with rows representing types

---

[2] Initially, we have also looked at the amount of technical coordination connected to the game application used, social talk such as jokes or other remarks that were not directly connected to the game, and other similar concepts; however, none of these features differed substantially among the environments.

of discussion present, and columns particular turns. Squares in the lowest rows (red) are filled if any kind of game oriented discussion was present in that turn; the middle row (yellow) is marked if the group came to an agreement on how to play for that round; the squares in the top row (green) are filled if the group adhered to the agreement exactly. Half-filled squares represent rounds where the group explicitly agreed on playing arbitrary actions; gray parts of the two SVE games show turns that were not played as the game ended prematurely due to heavy illegal mining. A star attached to a group name symbolizes that the group reached the cooperative scenario. Similarly, a brown "chocolate bar" symbol next to a group name marks two GColl groups that reached a cooperative outcome in a special way, as discussed later in this section.

We now present a brief description of main differences between FTF, GColl and SVE in terms of used strategies. *Face-to-face groups* are characterized by abundance of strategy oriented discussion, which always started before the first turn and was often long-term (for five out of six groups). Except for one group, FTF-5, participants followed the accepted strategy in the majority of rounds. This group is actually the only FTF group not reaching the cooperative scenario ending. *GColl groups* were generally similar to face-to-face in terms of the tendency to discuss the gameplay from the first round and agree on long or short-term strategies (five out of seven groups), even though the discussion starts later into the game in two cases. Although the ability to keep agreements is lower when compared to FTF (but still higher than SVE), most of the groups continued trying until the end.

Two GColl groups that did not create long-term strategies (i.e., GColl-3 and GColl-1), repeatedly discussed a meta-strategy: the participants noted that as the number of chocolate bars handed out in both possible end-game scenarios is equal, it does not matter whether they manage to "formally succeed" (i.e., end the game cooperatively) as they can always redistribute the chocolate bars themselves to simulate cooperative scenario payout. One of the groups (GColl-3) really did so right after the game; while it is probable that the GColl-1 group did so as well, we cannot be certain as in this case the rewards were handed out off the recording. This shows that these GColl groups strongly preferred the cooperative scenario, even if they were not able to reach it by coordinated game-play[3].

SVE groups took a different approach: very short-term plans (i.e., for the current round only) are most common, with more sophisticated strategies appearing only late into the game, if ever. In an example of this very narrow-sighted planning, members of groups SVE-1 and SVE-4 agree on several short term plans from the 8th and 5th round, with both groups ending the game in the 10th round due to heavy illegal mining that dries up the river. Members of these groups are very surprised at first, but understand the situation soon with exclamations as "...*I knew we forgot about something!*". Additionally, there are two SVE groups that never reach any agreement during the whole game.

---

[3] Only one SVE group (SVE-6) had a similar idea suggested by a participant during gameplay, but was dismissed immediately. Actually, it was understood as a very good joke by the others: "<laughing> you mean that I'll get the two chocolates for being the winner, and get even more from you? Yeah, I'd definitely take that."

Table 16.1 Percentages of rounds where a common strategy was accepted; the second row shows how many of these agreements were then actually kept

	FTF (%)	GColl (%)	SVE (%)
Strategy accepted	98	79	44
Strategy then kept	79	61	39

There were differences among the three environments also in the number of rounds where an agreement was accepted/kept. Table 16.1 provides percentages of rounds where (1) any joint strategy was agreed upon by the group; (2) and how often were such agreements kept. Again, SVE and FTF groups are strikingly different from each other, with GColl groups somewhere between the two extremes.

16.4.2   Tendency to Collaborate

Groups using different communication environments also differed in how they valued reaching cooperative goal. In particular, FTF groups strongly preferred the cooperative scenario, similarly to many groups in GColl condition. Most SVE groups preferred individualistic gameplay.

In all *face-to-face groups*, the discussion immediately focused on way in which the cooperative scenario could be reached with more-or-less whole group joining in to suggest various strategies. This means that all face-to-face groups implicitly chose the cooperative goal as the preferred scenario, although this was not suggested by the game rules in any way. Three *GColl groups* exhibited the same implicit preference for cooperative play as the face-to-face groups (and these were actually the three GColl groups to reach the cooperative scenario). Another two GColl groups agreed to redistribute the rewards after the game themselves, as they were not able to coordinate well enough to reach the cooperative scenario in the game but wanted to at least simulate cooperative outcome. The remaining two GColl groups also preferred collaborative play, but had problems with some of the participants defecting. *SVE groups* exhibited a much different pattern: except for one group, SVE-5, remaining groups either did not talk about cooperative play at all (three groups), or had to discuss it explicitly with several participants arguing and persuading the others to aim for the cooperative win (three groups). Out of these three groups, only one has eventually accepted the arguments and tried to play cooperatively.

16.4.3   Group Dynamics

Many participants interacted differently with collocated vs. remote colleagues. This was mainly common in the majority of SVE groups (substantial effects in five out of seven groups). Almost no such signs appeared in GColl groups, with the exception of GColl-3; and even this particular group showed very mild effects when compared to most of the SVE groups.

For example, in the following exchange, the SVE-3 group is waiting for someone to click on their "Ready" button to continue the game (A/B represent the sites, numbers distinguish players at a site):

A1:   (*to the screen*) Uhh, this takes a bit long, right?
B1:   Yeah, everything is still shadowy.
A1:   (*turning to a collocated player, quietly*) What did she say?
A2:   (*quietly, turned to A1*) Don't know, I didn't understand either. (*turning to the screen, speaking loudly*) Hey, what did you say?

Two effects common for many SVE groups are visible in the transcript. The first is the tendency to consult just the collocated rather than all players in the case of a problem. Additionally, many players tended to speak slightly louder than normal when addressing the remote participants, but very softly when interacting with collocated ones. As these effects did not appear in GColl environment, where the very same audio setup was used, this is likely to be connected to the influence of the SVE environment, and not just technical difficulties. The second are moments when members in both sub-groups talked in parallel, each about a different topic, and each effectively ignoring completely what goes on at the remote site. Often, one of the groups started discussing a topic first, and the second site focused on something else after a while. As such, these effects cannot be attributed only to turn-taking problems commonly associated with video-mediated communication.

Majority of the SVE groups also exhibited strong *in-group/out-group effects* at each site; for example, the following conversation occurred very shortly into the SVE-6 game:

(*site B talking quietly on how they could strategize without allowing the other site to see/hear it*)
B1:   […] but if we show it on the screen, they can't see that, can they?
A1:   (talking to collocated colleagues) So, we are split into 'us' and 'them' (gesturing towards the screen), right?
       < *everyone laughs* >
B1:   Like, we should play against each other?
       (A1 and B2 speaking over each other)
B2:   Yep, lets choose the safe way.
A1:   Well, I guess it's the technology's fault….

Similar examples of the collocated sub-groups understanding themselves as "us" and the others as an out-group, though not always so pronounced, appeared also in most of the other SVE groups. This was pointed out by the participants themselves during focus group sessions (done with SVE-5, SVE-6 and SVE-7); interestingly, even the two most successful SVE groups, SVE-5 and SVE-7, report the same problem. For example:

(*SVE-5 focus group*)
P1:   I felt like we were separated [by the environment] into two teams…
P2:   < *agrees* >

Table 16.2 Average percentage of individual/group-related pronouns	FTF (%)	GColl (%)	SVE (%)
Individual (e.g., "I")	28	37	50
Group-related (e.g., "we")	72	63	50

P1: I mean, even if it wasn't part of the game, we played as two teams …

P3: (*interrupts*) yeah, we always thought that the problem is on their side, that it must be someone from them [who kept defecting].

Seeing such strong differences in group dynamics between SVE and GColl/FTF groups, we analysed usage of individual and group related pronouns such as "I" or "we". Prior literature shows how usage of these pronouns can reflect whether or not individuals consider themselves as part of a group [17], implicating cooperative (first-person plural pronouns such as we, us, and our) vs. competitive play (first- and second-person singular pronouns e.g., I, me, my, you, your). Returning to the video-recordings, we counted the ratio of these two types of pronouns individually for every group. Averages for each communication channel are shown in Table 16.2. While not conclusive, these percentages further illustrate the observed differences in group dynamics.

16.4.4 Summary of Gameplay Analysis

In a typical *face-to-face* session, the Goldminers game was played cooperatively with a lot of discussion on what is the best strategy and effective cooperation. While there might be some rounds where one or more participants do not follow the group strategy, these are not common. Face-to-face group typically reach the cooperative end-game condition. On the contrary, strategy related discussions are diminished in most *SVE groups*, with the majority of groups playing without a common plan of action for most of the time. Cooperative play, if present at all, needs to be usually explicitly discussed and argued for by the participants. Even if accepted by the group, many participants often do not comply (either by "staying on the safe side" due to a low group trust, or by actively abusing the trust of others). *GColl groups* prefer cooperative play much more often than in SVE and the level of strategy oriented discussions is very similar to that of face-to-face. However, some groups exhibited problems with defecting members or the inability to reach effective cooperative strategies (e.g., they start the discussion too late, or do actions without considering the long term effects).

Overall, the used communication environment had strong effects on participants' behaviour: GColl and FTF groups behaved similarly and shared the cooperative goal approach, but GColl groups were sometimes not able to coordinate well enough to reach it. SVE groups present radically different patterns of behaviour, with emphasis on individual play.

16.5   Discussion

We have compared three communication environments (face-to-face, GColl and standard videoconferencing (SVE)), analysing interaction during a social dilemma game. The game was played by groups of six strangers, each using a particular environment. Qualitative analysis of gameplay shows that interaction in groups using GColl was, in comparison to SVE, much closer to face-to-face discussions in terms of the tendency to cooperate, the amount of strategy oriented discussion, and the ability to reach a cooperative outcome scenario.

So what is it that makes the GColl environment more like face-to-face than another video-mediated communication system? Contrary to our expectations, participants did not make use of the gaze awareness functionality offered by GColl so enhanced gaze awareness cannot explain observed differences in behaviour.

One explanation, supported by our analysis of communication differences between local and remote participants, suggests that *group identity* developed differently in the SVE conditions than in the GColl and face-to-face conditions. Participants in the SVE condition used behavior that indicated they perceived the other participants as belonging to one of two groups—either a local group or a remote group. Moreover, their use of significantly more personal pronouns indicates a more individualistic approach to the game. In both the face-to-face and GColl conditions, we do not see evidence that the participants made a similar grouping.

As all other aspects were held constant, differences between GColl and SVE interfaces likely played a key role in shaping the perception of group identity. In SVE, only the remote participants are shown in a single video window which is shared by everyone at the site. A GColl user sees any other participant (1) in the same place (on her personal display); (2) in an individual videostream. This means that, for any GColl player, all others are represented in the same virtual space. When analyzing the videorecordings, we found that most GColl users actually preferred to use the common virtual space (i.e., face their display) even when reacting to a remark by a collocated player. On the contrary, SVE users were forced to choose between looking at the remote, or collocated players at all times. We believe that this difference in how video streams were presented contributed to the GColl users' tendency to consider all players as a single group and to create a shared group identity (which is what happened naturally in all FTF groups), while the SVE players perceived two groups (local and remote).

Further supporting this explanation, the observed changes in behaviour are consistent with prior work on the effects of group identity on social dilemma games. In one study, shared group identity helped transform participant's understanding of a Prisoner's Dilemma task (where a "successful defection" is the most effective outcome) into an Assurance game that favors cooperation; and playing against a member of an antagonistic group (e.g., an out-group) diminished the tendency to collaborate [8]. Similarly, Bos et al. [6] show how groups with strong group identity bonds (e.g., fraternity members) played more cooperatively in the Daytrader social dilemma task. Shared identity in FTF and GColl groups might be therefore the key factor in their preference for cooperative interaction; whereas the perception of two distinct groups in the SVE condition may have contributed to participants taking a more adversarial approach to game play.

16.5.1   Future Work

Qualitative analysis shows substantial differences among the behaviour of groups in FTF, GColl and SVE, suggesting that differences in group identity were one of the key aspects. While effects of group identity on collaboration in face-to-face are already known, our observations suggest that differences in videoconferencing interface design can shape and/or change it. This opens interesting directions for further work, but also suggests that group identity might have played an important role in other settings. For example, the less effective seating conditions in [18], where collocated participants were seated side-by-side, might have induced stronger in-group behaviour, similarly to the SVE condition in this chapter.

We identified a combination of two design aspects present in GColl that were likely to affect the observed differences in behaviour. We argue how this combination of personal displays showing individualized videostreams from each participant (instead of a shared videostream depicting members from remote site), could have facilitated development of shared group identity. Further studies are needed to disentangle this combination and understand in detail how individual factors contribute to the observed effects. Additionally, it is not yet clear if and how these effects transfer into settings where the users know each other well, such as long term work-teams or family interactions.

16.6   Conclusion

This chapter reported on how group cooperation and collaboration patterns differed when groups of six discussed a task face-to-face, over a novel desktop videoconferencing design called GColl, or a commodity videoconferencing. Results show that groups interacting over GColl exhibit substantially lower in-/out-group effects when compared to commodity videoconferencing, and preferred collaborative over individual interaction similarly to face-to-face groups. The gaze awareness properties of GColl were not responsible for the observed changes in behavior. We argue instead, that the decisive effect is most likely based on the combination of having one display for, and a videostream of, each participant. We also suggest that the observed effects stem from differences in how group identity developed in groups using particular communication environment, and how the design differences contributed to this effect.

Acknowledgments We thank the participants in our study. We are also especially grateful to our technical team, in particular Milan Kabát and Lukáš Ručka, who made sure that the videoconferencing systems ran smoothly during the tests.

References

1. Ames, M.G., Go, J., Kaye, J.J., Spasojevic, M.: Making love in the network closet: the benefits and work of family videochat. In: CSCW 2010, p. 145. ACM Press (2010)
2. Aubert, O., Prié, Y.: Creating and sharing hypervideos with advene. In: HYPERTEXT 2005, p. 298. ACM Press, Sept 2005 (2005)
3. Bos, N., Olson, J., Gergle, D., Olson, G., Wright, Z.: Effects of four computer-mediated communications channels on trust development. In: CHI 2002, pp. 135–140. ACM Press, New York, NY, USA (2002)
4. Bos, N., Shami, N.S., Olson, J.S., Cheshin, A., Nan, N.: In-group/out-group effects in distributed teams. In: CSCW 2004, p. 429. ACM Press, New York, NY, USA (2004)
5. Bos, N., Olson, J., Nan, N., Shami, N.S., Hoch, S., Johnston, E.: Collocation blindness in partially distributed groups: is there a downside to being collocated? In: CHI 2006, pp. 1313–1321. ACM Press, New York, NY, USA (2006)
6. Bos, N.D., Buyuktur, A., Olson, J.S., Olson, G.M., Voida, A.: Shared identity helps partially distributed teams, but distance still matters. In: GROUP 2010, p. 89. ACM Press, New York, NY, USA (2010)
7. Judge, T.K., Neustaedter, C., Kurtz, A.F.: The family window: the design and evaluation of a domestic media space. In: CHI 2010, p. 2361. ACM Press (2010)
8. Kollock, P.: Transforming social dilemmas: group Identity and Cooperation. In: Danielson, P. (ed.) Modeling Rational and Moral Agents, pp. 186–210. Oxford University Press, Oxford (1998)
9. Nguyen, D., Canny, J.: MultiView: spatially faithful group video conferencing. In: CHI 2005, pp. 799–808, ACM Press, New York, NY, USA (2005)
10. Nguyen, D.T., Canny, J.: Multiview: improving trust in group video conferencing through spatial faithfulness. In: CHI 2007, pp. 1465–1474, ACM Press, New York, NY, USA (2007)
11. Nguyen, D.T., Canny, J.: More than face-to-face: empathy effects of video framing. In: CHI 2009, pp. 423–432, ACM Press, New York, NY, USA (2009)
12. O'Hara, K., Sellen, A., Harper, R.: Embodiment in brain-computer interaction. In: CHI 2011, p. 353, ACM Press, May 2011 (2011)
13. Sellen, A., Buxton, B., Arnott, J.: Using spatial cues to improve videoconferencing. In: CHI 1992, pp. 651–652, ACM Press, New York, NY, USA (1992)
14. Slovák, P., Troubil, P., Holub, P.: GColl: a flexible videoconferencing environment for group-to-group interaction. In: INTERACT 2009, Volume 5727 of Lecture Notes in Computer Science, pp. 165–168. Springer, Berlin (2009)
15. Tang, A., Boyle, M., Greenberg, S.: Display and presence disparity in mixed presence groupware. In: AUIC 2004, vol. 28, pp. 73–82, Australian Computer Society, Inc. (2004)
16. Venolia, G., Tang, J., Cervantes, R., Bly, S., Robertson, G., Lee, B., Inkpen, K.: Embodied social proxy: mediating interpersonal connection in hub-and-satellite teams. In: CHI 2010, p. 1049, ACM Press, New York, NY, USA (2010)
17. Wiener, M., Mehrabian, A.: Language Within Language: Immediacy, a Channel in Verbal Communication. Irvington Pub., New York (1968)
18. Yamashita, N., Hirata, K., Aoyagi, S., Kuzuoka, H., Harada, Y.: Impact of seating positions on group video communication. In: CSCW 2008, p. 177 (2008)

Chapter 17
Use of Graphical Modality in a Collaborative Design Distant Setting

Stéphane Safin, Roland Juchmes, and Pierre Leclercq

Abstract In this chapter, we are interested in studying the use of the graphical modality (digital sketch and document annotations) as a tool for collective design and remote communication. This study takes place in the framework of a 3 months long collaborative architectural design studio, gathering students from Belgium and France to remotely work together in three small groups. The study focuses on the role of the graphical modality inside synchronous remote meetings supported by the Distributed Collaborative Design Studio (DCDS). The DCDS enables multimodal real-time remote exchanges, and aims at remotely re-creating the conditions of co-present meetings. This environment associates a videoconference tool (supporting verbal and non-verbal communication) and an original real-time shared digital hand-drawn sketches system (supporting graphical communication). We identify the types of digital annotations made on the imported document (thanks to the electronic pen), as well as their role in the cognitive design processes and in the collaborative and communication processes. We also identify the different practices of digital sketching, in regard to each group and its collaborative strategies. We discuss the utility of the graphical modality as an efficient support for collaborative synchronous activities and show that the DCDS environment supports different strategies of collaborative design (co-design and distributed design). We conclude on recommendations for improving the system and for designing sketch-based collaborative environments.

17.1 Introduction

In a wide range of activity sectors, collaboration has been intensified, notably in the design domains. Collective work is increasingly organized simultaneously (rather than sequentially as it used to be in the past [1]). Moreover, design teams are often

S. Safin (✉) · R. Juchmes · P. Leclercq
LUCID-ULg—Lab for User Cognition and Innovative Design, University of Liège,
1 chemin des chevreuils B52, 4000 Liège, Belgium
e-mail: stephane.safin@ulg.ac.be

R. Juchmes
e-mail: r.juchmes@ulg.ac.be

P. Leclercq
e-mail: pierre.leclercq@ulg.ac.be

J. Dugdale et al. (eds.), *From Research to Practice in the Design of Cooperative Systems:*   245
Results and Open Challenges, DOI 10.1007/978-1-4471-4093-1_17,
© Springer-Verlag London 2012

geographically distributed, and the need for distant real-time interaction is consequently emerging.

While the best way of ensuring effective co-ordination and collaboration remains face-to-face meetings, convening all participants at the same time in the same place can often be problematic: travel costs, ecological impacts and immobilization of human resources have to been considered. Moreover, complex activities such as design are characterized by the use of numerous documents, which are annotated or modified. In architecture, these documents are an integral part of the design process, translating existing perceptions and representations, then simulating and testing possible interventions: these documents include sketches, drafts, plans, specifications, etc. They are jointly produced by multi-disciplinary teams and are modified in real time (through annotation) to support the collective decision-making process. There is therefore a need to support rich distant interactions, helped by new means of communication made available, among which one can distinguish two categories:

• Asynchronous systems, which allows file sharing, such as emails, file servers or electronic document management systems. Although they may be very efficient, they are not sufficient: individually used, they force collaborators to construct information incrementally, by successively accumulating content ('versioning'), rather than incorporating it. Making decisions through successive interventions does not encourage connections to be made between different points of view nor the incorporation of all opinions into the final decision;
• Synchronous real-time communication tools such as telephone, video-conferencing or web chatting. Being more and more efficient, they however only convey partial interaction: voice and (to a certain extend) gestures. They are not designed to convey representations of content but only comments on them, i.e. they do not allow an evolving graphic representation to be shared.

In this context, some devices and environments are emerging, enabling rich distant interactions, and are increasingly used in professional but also in educational settings. In this study, we are interested in understanding the use of the graphical modality (digital sketches and annotations) as a tool for collective design and remote communication, through the observation of a remote collaborative architectural design studio using a multimodal real-time collaborative environment, the Distributed Collaborative Design Studio (DCDS). This environment has the particularity to convey in real-time several modalities of exchange: verbal and visual (via video-conferencing), but also graphical (with digital annotation and document sharing).

17.2 Collaborative Design

Collaborative design requires three types of activities: task-oriented activities, process-oriented activities and interaction management activities [7].

Task-oriented activities are directly related to the content of the design. Usually, one can distinguish problem framing, solutions generation and solutions evaluations. Those activities occur in individual design, but also in collective design, through argumentation processes [5]. Communication is therefore an essential point for solving the design problem: a common understanding of the problem allows to structure it (e.g. suggesting goals), the ideas must be generated by the different actors and communicated to the group (e.g. propositions of design) and, to be efficient, the ideas must be collectively evaluated through communication processes (e.g. criticisms). Stempfle and Badke-Schaub [15] showed that those content-oriented activities account for about 2/3 of the interactions between group members.

Process-oriented activities are necessary to coordinate group actions. These activities are linked to the management of viewpoints, the synchronization and coordination tasks, the conflict management, and the building of a common knowledge [16]. Two modes of coordination can usually take place in collaborative design [6].

- Distributed design where the actors perform distinct but interrelated tasks, each one mobilizing its own resources and its own temporality to carry out specific objectives serving the joint project. The actions are simultaneous, but not joint. The key issue is the coordination of different partners' activities and their temporal articulation.
- Co-design where all the designers respond to the problem in an integrated way, share common goals, generate solutions and evaluate those together. The challenge of this type of collaborative design is the cognitive synchronization, i.e. the creation, through actions of communication, of a shared common context that enables the entire group to coordinate more efficient action.

In collaborative activities, primarily in distributed design activities taking place remotely and in the management of interdependencies between tasks and designers, actors need to have a collective consciousness of the situation, of the changes made on the design object, of the tasks, and of the partners' skills and activities. This mutual consciousness is called situation awareness [3]. While in face-to-face situations actors share a common context, remote interaction can be disrupted by many constraints: reduction of the richness of communication channels (e.g. reduced field of view) and difficulty in sharing information and objects (e.g. troubles communicating spatial reference). To achieve this mutual awareness, it is necessary to share a part of the context.

The different views on the object must be coordinated and integrated to build a common vision. This mechanism, called grounding, involves the construction of a common reference space consisting in all the knowledge that group members have in common and that they are aware to have in common. This space is called a shared common ground [4] or joint problem space [10]. This common ground is not just understanding which actor undertakes any action and how the task is globally conducted, but rather building a strong inter-understanding of each other and solve the problem together. The grounding affects both the problem (a framework for the generation and evaluation) but also the procedures, representations and the knowledge that partners have of each other. The construction of a common ground is a prerequisite for negotiating solutions.

Interaction management activities. These include all activities related to the process of communication. To communicate, one needs to develop a message, but also to check that this message has been understood. It is also necessary to provide

Fig. 17.1 Virtual Desktop

clues and positive evidence to the partner(s) to show that the message has been under-stood: acquiescence, confirmations, start of next speaking turn, and so on [4]. These activities are simple in the case of face-to-face communication using everyday lan-guage, but are much more complicated in the case of remote communication, of asyn-chronous exchanges, and in case of high degree sophisticated or abstract messages.

The communication has therefore a "cost". The different costs of communication are associated with the constraints of environments for sharing and supporting col-laboration. The media of communication can be characterized by several properties that can facilitate exchanges and the construction of a shared common referent: possibility to see and hear each other, simultaneity of actions, sequentiality of the messages, reviewability, etc. [4].

17.3 DCDS

In order to support remote synchronous collaboration, the LUCID-ULg lab has de-veloped the Digital Collaborative Design Studio (DCDS). The idea is to support real time exchanges with a complete approach, by associating a shared document space and a graphical modality interaction to the classical verbal and visual chan-nels. The aim is to reinforce awareness of each other's actions and to facilitate grounding and argumentation, by sharing the same contents.

This prototype is composed of two parts.

A hardware part, the Virtual Design Desktop (Fig. 17.1), consisting of an elec-tronic A0 drawing table with a suspended ceiling equipped with a projection system

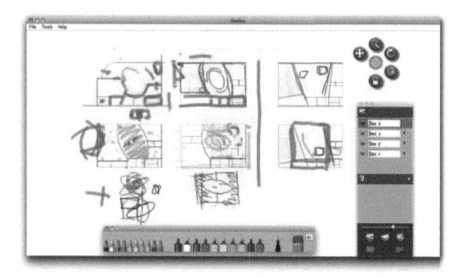

Fig. 17.2 SketSha Interface

offering a large working surface (approximately 150×70 cm). An electronic pen allows the drawing of virtual sketches on this surface. Manipulation widgets are specifically designed to interact only with the stylus in this environment.

A software called SketSha (for "sketch sharing"—Fig. 17.2) constitutes a shared drawing environment allowing several users to be connected to the same virtual drawing space. Various functionalities, such as a panel of colored pens (and an eraser) and a navigation tool (to zoom, translate, rotate), are available through intuitive graphical widgets. Some layout facilities also have been included in the prototype, such as the possibility of drawing and managing different sheets of virtual paper, of deleting or duplicating them, and of managing their transparency. The software also enables users to import Computer Assisted Design (CAD) plans and bitmap images. This software captures the strokes that compose the sketch, shares them between the different distant locations (through a standard internet connection) and transmits the complete information in real time onto the active boards through video-data projectors.

A 24-inch screen completes the system, with an integrated camera which enables the participants to talk to each other, and to see each other face, arms and hands during the real-time conference. Pointing, annotating and drawing are made possible due by the electronic pen. Social exchanges are transmitted through the external modules of video-conferencing in order to support the vocal, the visual and the gestural aspects of the collaboration (Fig. 17.3).

In respect to the user-centered framework underlying the development of the DCDS, the system has already been tested in different short and long collaborative work settings with students and professionals [see 2, 8, 9, 12, 13].

Fig. 17.3 Meeting on the
DCDS

Fig. 17.3 Meeting on the
DCDS

17.4 Issues and Setting

This study aims at understanding the role of multimodality and interactive annotations in the collaborative process of designing. In particular, we address two types of issue in this chapter.

First, we wish to know the impact of the document sharing on collaborative process. The system, by allowing the real-time sharing of documents and interactive annotations, may support the awareness, the grounding and facilitate negotiation of solutions. We therefore expect its use to be associated with a strong quality of collaboration and to support "coupled" versions of collaboration (i.e. co-design, [6]). The second issue is related to the way the graphical modality is used to support the collaborative design process. We wish to understand how the designers use the graphical modality to support their design process (generating solutions, reframing the problem and evaluating solutions) and their remote collaborative process (awareness, grounding, interaction management). This study is a first attempt to identify and describe the role of interactive distant annotations in collaborative design.

To answer these questions, we observed a collaborative architectural design workshop, co-organized by the Nancy School of Architecture (France) and the Faculty of Applied Sciences of the University of Liège (Belgium). Three groups of five students (mix with French and Belgian students) worked during one term (3 months) on an architecture program. Each group had to design collaboratively and remotely a building (a cultural center), starting from a program completely defined.

For this purpose, the groups had several tools at their disposal: asynchronous collaborative tools (mails, file exchange servers,…); usual synchronous collaborative tools (chat, videoconferencing…); and a 1-h meeting each week on the DCDS. They were allowed to upload their documents in the system, to annotate them during their discussion, and to save the edited documents.

This study focuses on the weekly synchronous meetings with the DCDS. We videotaped each session and recorded all the documents, digital drawings and digital annotations. The video data represents eight 1-h meetings for each of the three groups, for a total of 24 h of video. More than 700 documents were analyzed to identify types of annotation.

17.5   Method

Our method is a comparative descriptive approach. We compared three groups in the same specific setting, in order to identify similarities and differences on collaborative activity, that can inform us on the benefits provided by the system and its limits. The large corpus enables us to make a first identification of the different roles, types and functions of annotations.

17.5.1   Assessment of the Collaboration

In order to understand and describe the collaborative process, we made video analysis supported by a grid to assess the quality of collaboration. This grid, inspired by Spada's works in the CSCL domain (see [14]), enables to quickly assess the collaborative process according to six dimensions, based on the observation of behavioral indicators (see Table 17.1).

These dimensions cover the task-related, group management and communication processes and enable to calculate both a score on each dimension and a global score on the collaboration quality. This grid has proven to have a strong inter-coder reliability (see [2] for details).

17.5.2   Graphical Activity Analysis

We made video analysis of a sample of video extracts in each group. These videos have been analyzed together by an ergonomist and an architect. This sample has been made in order to have a representation of all kinds of drawings and annotation, in each group and in different moments in the design process.

We tried to identify the uses of the graphical modality, i.e. digital drawings and annotations, in the collaborative design process. Our observation focuses on the roles and functions of annotation in the communicative process, the graphical characteristics of the drawings and the difference between the groups, according to their modes of collaboration. Complementary to these we also analyzed all the documents used during the DCDS sessions.

17.6   Comparison of the Groups' Collaborative and Graphic Activity

Clearly, the three groups do not collaborate in the same way.

The **group 1** sets up a "distributed design" process: the members work individually asynchronously, take some decisions, and the propositions are presented to the

Table 17.1 Dimensions and indicators of our method

Dimensions	Definition	Indicators
1. Fluidity of collaboration	It assesses the management of verbal communication (verbal turns), of actions (tool use) and of attention orientation	Fluidity of verbal turns Fluidity of tools use (stylet, menu) Coherency of attention orientation
2. Sustaining mutual understanding	It assesses the grounding processes concerning the design artefact (problem, solutions), the designers' actions and the state of the AR disposal (e.g. activated functions)	Mutual understanding of the state of design problem/solutions Mutual understanding of the actions in progress and next actions Mutual understanding of the state of the system (active functions, open documents)
3. Information exchanges for problem solving	It assesses design ideas pooling, refinement of design ideas and coherency of ideas	Generation of design ideas (problem, solutions, past cases, constraints) Refinement of design ideas Coherency and follow up of ideas
4. Argumentation and reaching consensus	It assesses whether or not there is argumentation and decision taken on common consensus	Criticisms and argumentation Checking solutions adequacy with design constraints Common decision taking
5. Task and time management	It assesses the planning (e.g. task allocation) and time management	Work planning Task division Distribution and management of tasks interdependencies Time management
6. Cooperative orientation	It assesses the balance of contribution of the actors in design, planning, and in verbal and graphical actions	Symmetry of verbal contributions Symmetry of use of graphical tools Symmetry in task management Symmetry in design choices

group during the synchronous sessions. Specific issues are resolved collectively in those synchronous meetings and the work is divided. Each member leaves the session with specific tasks to be done for the next weekly synchronous meetings. Between two DCDS sessions, students exchange documents and questions by email. Intermediary scores on the collaboration quality scale characterize the group during their synchronous meetings. Comparatively to the other groups, they have a weak score for the "argumentation and consensus" dimension: solutions are chosen amongst the individuals' propositions, but are not clearly negotiated. But the group globally manages well the design process: the teachers judge the results of the design as excellent.

In general, the **group 1** uses graphical modality for presentation: the documents are brought into the workspace by the different designers, each in turn explains the contents of the documents, using the annotation as a medium of presentation. Designers highlight essential parts of the design, add pieces of information to explain the document or draw pointing annotation to identify the elements of design to which they refer. They mainly use annotation, which does not convey new infor-

Fig. 17.4 Highlighting
annotations

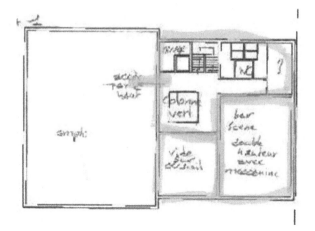

mation to the document, like pointing and especially highlighting (Fig. 17.4). Sets of questions and answers regularly take place between students and teachers (or between students themselves) and the graphical modality is used to identify the elements of design on which the discussion focuses. Most of the time in this group, the documents are only annotated by their authors and the teachers. Nevertheless, the frequent highlighting of documents elements seems more than just communicating about the drawing. We have shown, in individual architectural design, the importance of highlighting for the decision making process [11].

The primarily purpose of annotations is communication, for building a shared vision of the project and for taking decisions. The generation of solutions therefore takes place outside the meeting sessions, and synchronous DCDS sessions are used to evaluate those solutions and to reframe the problem.

Group 2 establishes a "co-design" process: key structural decisions are taken during DCDS sessions, a lot of collective propositions are done during those meetings. Between two sessions, students work locally in small groups to implement the decisions and propositions (by drawing plans and model). The formal exchange for explanation and presentation of the documents takes place by email before the synchronous sessions, to free up time during the DCDS sessions for collective decision-making. The group has excellent scores on the quality of collaboration scale all along the process. Especially, it surpasses the other groups in the "information exchanges", "argumentation and consensus" and "cooperative orientation" dimensions. They are truly engaged in a collaborative design, where all members participate to all decisions. The teachers judge their design outcome as excellent.

This group is characterized by a very different mode of operation. Very quickly, the members choose a unique concept for the project and the meetings on the DCDS are used to solve important issues, to suggest ideas and take strategic decisions. The students spend much less time to present documents to each other, in benefit of the generation of solutions and collective decision-making. Here, the graphical activity is directed towards the design. Students use annotation to bring new information to previous representations: about 2/3 of the annotations conveys original piece of

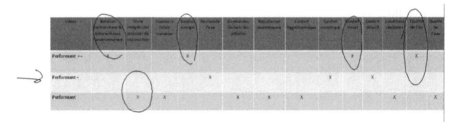

Fig. 17.5 Pointing annotations on a document

information to complete or modify the imported documents. In particular, this group uses a lot of complex drawings over the plans and images, which are mainly used to generate ideas. The various documents are annotated by all group members, which indicates a real sharing of representations. We may note that this group draws also more digital sketches than the others (on virtual white sheet).

This characterizes the common generation of solutions and a common decision process. The focus here is on the generation and criticism of novel ideas. The precise resolution of the generated ideas (i.e. increasing accuracy, reducing ambiguity, choosing one solution among the several possible solutions) is done asynchronously.

Group 3 is characterized by the establishment of a "distributed design" process and by the emergence of conflicts early in the workshop. Each student in this group makes his own propositions alone and the DCDS sessions are used to present each own work, to try to convince the others of one own ideas and to require teachers help and comments if necessary. Students present themselves each other's work, but there is little interaction within the group. Most of the discussions are held between the student presenting his own work and the teachers. These discussions are sometimes punctuated by questions and answers from other participants. The group obtains weak score on collaboration scale. In particular, they are globally weaker than the other groups in three dimensions: fluidity of collaboration, mutual understanding and information exchanges for problem solving. This functioning generates (or is generated by) a climate of conflict within the group. It is accompanied by an inability to agree on a unique concept or a common vision of the project. Thus, ambiguities and disagreements about the project persist until the end of the workshop. The synchronous collaboration sessions and the large number of emails exchanged between sessions fail to resolve the conflict. After 8 weeks, the conflict being too important, this mode of cooperation is interrupted by the teachers, who decide to impose a formal structure for sharing responsibilities and for distributing the tasks. Thanks to this external help, the group manages to finish the workshop decently. Their design outcome is nevertheless judged as weak.

In terms of graphic activity, this group mainly uses pointing annotation (see Fig. 17.5). Once again, this observation reflects the collaborative activity of the group. They take few or no decision together and use DCDS synchronous meetings to try to convince each other that their own solution is better. For this purpose, it seems that pointing is the most efficient way of using the graphical modality. Annotations are almost exclusively done by the authors of the documents, in order to convince their partners.

Here, the aim of the synchronous sessions is neither to generate all solutions, nor to collectively evaluate the propositions, but rather to convince the partners. The graphical modality is essentially used to support the presentation of documents, which explains the prevalence of pointing annotations. Errors are poorly detected and poorly recovered: in-depth analysis of the proposals rarely occurs.

These descriptions highlight three clearly different modes of collaboration and three different annotation practices. The possibility to use shared representations and to annotate them interactively does not seem to produce strong collaboration. Rather, the groups' collaborative practices seem to determine the graphical behaviors.

17.7 Graphical Activity Analysis

We identified several functions of annotation as well as differences in the uses by groups and individuals. According to our observations, digital annotations serve different roles during the collective activities.

Draw attention to one element of the design. This function aims at supporting communication by spatially contextualizing the discourse on the documents. It is the deictic role of annotations. This role is carried on by pointing annotations but also by some highlighting annotations. These annotations are similar to pointing gestures and can spatially locate a question or comment. This feature of the annotation is temporary: once made, the trace is no longer necessary.

A second function, close to the previous one but however distinct, consists in **putting in correspondence elements present in several documents**. Thus, the annotations do not only support the speech, but also help to make connections between multiple representations, on a graphical mode. In the illustration below (Fig. 17.6), the designer, explaining to its partners the principles underlying its construction, explicitly shows on five drawings where is the "heart of the project." This function is supported by highlighting or pointing annotations. No new information is specifically added to the document, but this mapping can convey a specific message, namely the identification of several drawings of a common concept.

Designers also use annotations to **contextualize the document** on which they are drawn. They may typically indicate North or elements of surrounding context (road, buildings neighborhood, etc.). This contextualization is important in the course of communication, but does not create new information to be conserved. These annotations are explicitly intended to reduce ambiguity and synchronize the different viewpoints.

Another function is **to complete the document** with information not present explicitly, relative to the "functioning", the use or the atmosphere in the building. These are elements that traditional architectural representation does not contain, such as circulation information, ambiance, luminosity, etc. Indeed, plans adopt a strictly geometric perspective on the architectural object. This added information

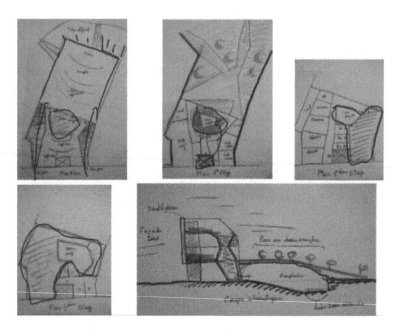

Fig. 17.6 Identification of the "heart of the project" (in *blue*) with digital annotations on previous documents (scanned pen-and-paper sketches)

explains how to interpret the plan. The digital annotation, accompanied by speech, can compensate the weaknesses of other representations (models, plans, images, etc.). Some complementary digital sketches can also be made next to the document, such as perspective drawing, detailed design or synthetic cross-section.

Graphical annotations are also used to **"synthesize" the document**. In this case, the designers highlight specific parts of the plans or models to emphasize the main elements of the building. The design is synthesized into "functional areas" which make up the premises of the building. This function is performed with highlight annotations and no new information is brought to the document. This synthesis reduces the complexity of the design and some of the uncertainty, but it does not add precision to the design, the underlying document being often more accurate than the annotation.

Sketches and annotations are obviously also used to **come up with ideas**. These generations of solutions, acts of conception, are supported by drawings and elements such as annotations as well as digital sketches. The group members and teachers can directly visually and graphically assess these new ideas.

Annotations sometimes meet several of these functions, and it is not easy to establish a strict correspondence between the form of annotation and its function. Note that all these functions have been identified in all groups.

In the groups, we moreover observe that each group member usually uses a specific color to annotate the document. This may allow the group to identify the annotations' authors and to trace the argumentation process. But this behavior is not systematic. Participants change pen color when they have to make several sketches or annotations, not when they just have to make a quick note.

Our observations show that graphical modality is a flexible tool for collaborative design, which can serve three main purposes.

Support the communication. This is primarily to support the speech and the argumentation, by highlighting the spatial elements to which the designer refers to when he explains the documents. It is also a way to convey gestures, weakly supported in our remote environment. The graphical modality and digital sketching provides a "cheap" and quick way to perform temporary pointing gestures.

Support the design (idea generation, questions and answers). The graphical modality enables to express ideas, to complete plans and models, to ask and answer questions, to share reflections by expressing them geometrically, etc. One can thus observe sequences of questions and answers with pointing, verbal criticism with drawn counter-proposals, etc. The graphical modality therefore supports the argumentative episodes, typically observed in co-presence activities.

Support the construction of a common ground. By adding information not explicitly present on the documents, by adding elements of context and by graphically comparing several documents, the group ensures that everyone understand the architectural object being designed in the same way, and share a common vision of the project.

A striking element emerging from our observation is the differentiation between two attitudes regarding the annotation practices. In particular, these attitudes concern the link between annotations and underlying documents.

- The first approach is to perform many annotations in a very spontaneous way, directly on the drawings (no matter who is the author) without erasing them. It seems that for some individuals the annotation is by nature ephemeral, and therefore it can be used flexibly and intensely. This is using the environment as a **temporary workspace**, allowing all compositions, simulations and graphic gestures. Here, it seems that the process is more important than the result.
- In the second approach, the annotations appear to have an informative and durable role. This is using the environment as a **document editor**. The authorship of the document is an important matter: users annotate much less the documents created by the others, use the eraser and make drawings more accurate. From this perspective, users 'respect' documents and draw on them only to add relevant information. This information is used after the synchronous meeting. The focus here is on the content of the annotation, rather than on the process.

Both of these attitudes depend on three factors:

- The group collaborative process: group 2 is clearly more engaged in using the DCDS as a temporary workspace, to generate ideas without constraints. The group 1 and 3 use the DCDS rather to edit their documents quite cleanly.
- The authorship: students tend to use their own documents (i.e. the documents they produced personally between two DCDS sessions) as a temporary workspace, whereas they tend to draw much less annotations, and do it in a more cleaner way, when on others' documents.

- We also observed some personal preferences. For example, one of the two observed teachers is always annotating intensely all documents (workspace) whereas the other one is always more accurate and tends to erase his graphical comments if they are no more necessary.

17.8 Conclusion

This study aims at understanding the role of the graphical modality in remote collaborative design. We followed three groups of students during a 3-months workshop and observed their annotations practices during weekly synchronous distant collaborative sessions. These meetings are supported by the DCDS, a multimodal collaborative environment, which enables to communicate by speech, to see each other, and to draw and annotate on a shared space thanks to an electronic pen.

This first study, specifically focusing on the use of the graphical modality during distant collaboration, brings three types of results.

- The graphics behaviors are largely dependent upon the group collaborative process. Although the digital drawings and annotations enable to support very "strong" versions of collaboration (in which group members share ideas and resources and in which solutions are collectively elaborated and evaluated), the availability of the graphical modality does not seem to generate those kind of collaborative processes. Rather, our observation shows a flexible use of the digital drawings.
- There are several functions of digital annotations, which support communicative processes, design content and the construction of a common ground. Those are three essential processes in collaborative design.
- We identified two attitudes towards the interactive annotation of documents.

Our future work will be to extend these results by examining them in a more systematic way: by the mean of experimental studies allowing to change the conditions of distant sharing, and by the development of proper methods to address the role of graphical modality and its complementarities with other modalities (gestural and verbal).

To enhance our system, and in general to design sketch-based communication tools, we suggest two main recommendations according to this study.

- Support communication and design activities by specific means. The idea is to reconcile the two attitudes: "document edition" (which necessitate lasting annotations) and "workspace" (in whom a lot of annotations are temporary). To convey this last type of information, using gesture recognition or temporary traces tools may be an efficient solution.
- Support seamless integration with other tools. The vast majority of collaborative activity takes place on previously made document. The system should favor an easy import and export of the documents, to enhance possibilities and allow more flexible organization.

Acknowledgments This work is supported by a funding from the Research Council of the University of Liège, and by the ARC grant, financed by the French Community of Belgium. The authors wish to thank all the students and teachers who took part to the study.

References

1. Boujut, J.-F.: Workshop Proceedings of 9th International Conference on the Design of Cooperative Systems. Improving shared representations by linking discursive and graphical aspects of design. Int. Rep. Socio Inform. 7(1), 177–190 (2010)
2. Burkhardt, J.-M., Détienne, F., Hebert, A.-M., Perron, L., Safin, S., Leclercq, P.: An approach to assess the quality of collaboration in technology-mediated design situations. In: Proceedings of ECCE 2009: European Conference on Cognitive Ergonomics. Helsinki, September (2009)
3. Carroll, J.M., Neale, D.C., Isenhour, P.L., Rosson, M.B., McCrickard, D.S.: Notification and awareness: synchronizing task-oriented collaborative activity. Int. J. Hum. Comput. Stud. **58**, 605–632 (2003)
4. Clarck, H., Brennan, S.: Grounding in communication. In: Resnick, L., Levine, J., Teasley, S. (eds.) Perspectives on Socially Shared Cognition. American Psychological Association, Washington, DC (1991)
5. Darses, F.: Processus psychologiques de résolution collective des problèmes de conception: contribution de la psychologie ergonomique. Unpublished HDR—habilitation à Diriger des Recherches, Université Paris V—René Descartes (2004)
6. Darses, F., Falzon, P., Béguin, P.: Collective design processes. Paper presented at the COOP 96, Second International Conference on the Design of Cooperative Systems, Juan-les- Pins (1996)
7. Détienne, F., Boujut, J.-F., Hohmann, B.: Characterization of collaborative design and interaction management activities in a distant engineering design situation. Paper presented at the COOP 2004—Cooperative systems design: scenario-based design of collaborative systems (2004)
8. Elsen, C., Leclercq, P.: A sketching tool to support collaborative design. CDVE'08, 5th International Conference on Cooperative Design, Vizualisation and Engineering, Mallorca, Spain (2008)
9. Kubicki, S., Bignon, J.-C., Lotz, J., Gilles Halin, G., Elsen, C., Leclercq, P.: Digital Cooperative Studio. ICE 2008 14th International Conference on Concurrent Enterprising, Special session ICT-supported Cooperative Design in Education, Lisboa, Espagne (2008)
10. Roschelle, J., Teasley, S.: The construction of shared knowledge in collaborative problem solving. In: O'Malley, C.E. (ed.) Computer Supported Collaborative Learning, pp. 69–97. Springer, Heidelberg (1994)
11. Safin, S., Juchmes, R., Leclercq, P.: Du crayon au stylo numérique: influences des IHM à stylo et des interprétations numériques sur l'activité graphique en tâches de conception. J. Interact. Pers. Syst. **2**(1), 1:1–1:31 (2011)
12. Safin, S., Leclercq, P.: User studies of a sketch-based collaborative distant design solution in industrial context. In: Proceedings of CDVE 2009. The 6th International Conference on Cooperative Design, Visualization and Engineering, Luxembourg, September (2009)
13. Safin, S., Verschuere, A., Defays, A., Burkhardt, J.-M., Détienne, F.: Quality of collaboration in a distant collaborative architectural educational setting. Workshop W1: Analysing the quality of collaboration in task-oriented computer-mediated interactions, in COOP 2010: 9th International Conference on the Design of Cooperative Systems. Aix-en-Provence, May (2010)
14. Spada, H., Meier, A., Rummel, N., Hauser, S.: A new method to assess the quality of collaborative process in CSCL. Paper presented at the Conference on Computer support for collaborative learning: learning 2005: the next 10 years! (2005)

15. Stempfle, J., Badke-Schaub, P.: Thinking in design teams-an analysis of team communication. Des. Stud. **23**, 473–496 (2002)
16. Visser, W.: Conception individuelle et collective. Approche de l'ergonomie cognitive. INRIA—Institut national de la Recherche en Informatique et Automatique, Le Chesnay, France (2001)

Chapter 18
Struggling Against Social Isolation of the Elderly—The Design of SmartTV Applications

Malek Alaoui and Myriam Lewkowicz

Abstract This chapter charts a work in progress in the frame of the European project AAL FoSIBLE. Our hypothesis is that virtual networks and online generational communities could offset the lack of relationship, prevent isolation and increase self-esteem for older people living alone at home. Following this purpose, we are then aiming at defining services by rethinking the use of well-known existing technologies and to broaden their scope to be more affordable by older people. This chapter describes related work on the use of the Internet for social interactions among the elderly. The living Lab approach we follow and our results on understanding the actual use and needs of the elderly are presented, followed by the SmartTV platform which is iteratively developed. The analysis of the use of this platform being designed in a user-centred approach will permit us to answer our research issues.

18.1 Introduction

For the most developed world countries the chronological age of 60 and over represent the border where is defined an "elderly" or "older person". This definition is in general associated to the age at which people get retired. Europe represents the highest proportion of elderly[1]. In France they represent 22.5% of the entire population[2]. For the next 25 years they are estimated to reach 1/3 of the entire population [1].

---

[1] http://www.who.int.

[2] http://www.france24.com/fr/20100119-647-millions-fran-ais-plus-500-millions-deurop-ens.

M. Alaoui (✉) · M. Lewkowicz
Troyes University of Technology (UTT), ICD/Tech-CICO—UMR CNRS 6279, 12 Rue Marie Curie—BP2060, 10010 Troyes Cedex, France
e-mail: malek.alaoui@utt.fr

M. Lewkowicz
e-mail: myriam.lewkowicz@utt.fr

J. Dugdale et al. (eds.), *From Research to Practice in the Design of Cooperative Systems: Results and Open Challenges*, DOI 10.1007/978-1-4471-4093-1_18,
© Springer-Verlag London 2012

Ageing is a new step of life with a lot of changes that could be related with physical, cognitive and social frailty. Physical and cognitive frailties have been addressed in several research and industry initiatives focusing mainly on the development of a variety of assistive technologies for maintaining elderly with disabilities at home as long as possible. These technologies mainly offer services for health monitoring and security, and are designed to give the elderly a means of living independently while being able to rely on help in case of emergency.

From our point of view, even if these technologies are interesting and useful for the security of elderly people, they have two kinds of limitations:

First, all those technologies are often considered as intrusive and raise ethical, psychological and social issues [2, 3]. The more the disability and loss of independence faced by the elderly is great, the more is the need of private information by these new systems to be more effective. Caring for older people while taking into account their concerns about their privacy and the social isolation they suffer still represents a major research issue. Secondly, successful ageing cannot be reduced to being in good health and has to take into account well-being and self-esteem.

Rather than addressing autonomy and dependency, our aim is then to define how ICTs could alleviate isolation and loneliness, in order to cope with social frailty which is however an important health-related issue. Indeed, the diminution of social ties with former colleagues after retirement, the loss of spouses, friends, distance from children and the gradual reduction of the mobility and autonomy can contribute to isolation, depression and may have negative impacts on elderly' general health status. A recent study [4] has even showed that the lack of social relationships influences the risk of mortality of ageing people.

Our hypothesis is that virtual networks and online generational communities could offset this lack of relationship, increase self-esteem and prevent isolation for older people living alone at home and who want to stay at home like the majority of them [5]. Having access to social support from their peers online and anytime, could enable elder people to talk about their problems rather than letting worries accumulate for a long time before they find a hearing, especially for them who are reluctant or unable to participate in face-to-face discussions or to go and see a professional caregiver.

This chapter starts by describing existing work on the use of the Internet for social interactions among the elderly. We then list our research issues linked to the creation of services for the elderly by rethinking the use of well-known existing technologies and to broaden their scope to be more affordable by older people. In order to create these services, we have adopted a Living Lab approach in the frame of the European project AAL FoSIBLE[3]. After describing this approach and our results on understanding the actual use and needs of the elderly, we present the platform which is iteratively developed. The analysis of the use of this platform being designed in a user-centred approach will permit us to answer our research issues.

---

[3] Fostering Social Interactions for a Better Life of the Elderly.

18.2   Related Work

Several online services dedicated to social networking among elderly exist, most of them aiming at finding companions (Netsenior[4], Voisin-Age[5] ...).

Elderly also participate into online discussion forums. Some studies on this phenomenon have been conducted recently, for instance comparing online and offline settings. For instance, Pfeil et al. [6] highlight that older adults' perception of social support in online settings (such as online forums, chat rooms and social networking sites) is different comparing to their offline experiences; On one hand physical co-presence is very important for older adults for disclosing one's feelings to others and establishing a level of trust, which is a prerequisite for exchanging personal information in online settings. But on the other hand, the concern of being a burden—which is a reason for elderly' reluctance to talk about their problems—does not exist when disclosing information about oneself in online settings due to the anonymity and the fact that people do not have to face the other person directly when writing a message.

This finding is in line with other studies, such as the qualitative analysis of Israeli retirees by Blit-Cohen and Litwin [7] which suggests that the virtual world is a potentially important arena for the production of social capital among older adults. They have showed that elderly connections occur in both physical and virtual world, and that the participation in cyberspace allows elderly persons to develop social ties, to strengthen the flow of information and to enhance norms of reciprocity through computer mediated networks.

For Wright [8] friendship on the Internet network enables older people to bond with different kinds of groups. They thereby create and develop relationships not only with other elderly people, but with members of different backgrounds and different generations as well. The expansion of elderly persons' interpersonal environment by means of virtual communities enables them to feel more integrated into society. Elderly' social worlds do not necessarily reflect participatory decline and social isolation. They could be engaged in strengthening or enlarging their networks, both the physical ones and the virtual ones. Internet interaction is then one of many types of social interaction, such as meetings in local communities or clubs. Wright [8] has also showed that the amount of time older adults spend in an online support community has a positive impact on their network size and the satisfaction with the received support. Respectively, older adults who spend less time communicating with online community members rated their satisfaction with support from their offline network higher.

Lepa and Tatnall [9] have analyzed the formation and operation of virtual networks of older people using the GreyPath community portal. The major component of the portal is the Village, an innovative virtual community. Communities of interest such as book or art lovers are established when accessing the chat facilities

---

[4] http://www.netsenior.fr.

[5] http://www.voisin-age.fr.

and message boards. The findings are that GreyPath is a technology that has the potential to strengthen the bonds between older people living in a region that may be geographically far-flung, to make it into a virtual community.

Older adults could be concerned about misbehaviour and misunderstandings in virtual communities based on the fact that online interaction is generally text-based. Kanayama [10] studied an online community for Japanese older adults with a focus on self-disclosure and the exchange of social support. She states that text-based online communication for older adults, much like writing letters, is enhancing rather than limiting their ability to interact on a personal and emotional level. She also mentions that older adults perceive the asynchronous nature of online communities and the possibility to edit messages before sending them as beneficial.

These studies about the use of the Internet by elderly people, the complementarity between online and offline interactions, the features which are the most interesting for this populations are very fruitful, but few of them include implication for design, questioning the medium and ergonomical concerns; many questions still remain to be answered about how to design systems for social interactions among elderly.

18.3   Research Issues

Our researches are devoted into creating services for elderly by rethinking the use of well-known existing technologies and to broaden their scope to be more affordable by older people.

The questions are: (1) could we consider the development of innovative services based on an interactive Smart TV platform as a solution for elderly' social isolation issues? (2) Acknowledging that the development of online applications for supportive ties among older people by interaction on the Internet is technically possible, will the feelings of mutual trust and of belonging be sufficient to build virtual community between elderly who are used to face-to-face interactions? (3) Will they be more willing to stick to virtual groups if they have less reluctance about using TV than computers? (4) Older people tend to have particular problems with the interaction of new technology because devices are not designed to accommodate their special needs [11]. How could we adapt existing interfaces and interaction modes to fit their needs and enhance communication and social support?

18.4   A Living Lab Approach

A living lab is a real life experiential environment which allows all stakeholders to concurrently consider both the performance of a service and its adoption by users at the earlier stage of research and development [12].

Various models of User Centred Design, such as Cooperative Design [13], Participatory Design [14], Contextual Design [15] and Experience Design [16] are intended to consider user requirements right from the beginning. These are considered as development processes and not innovation systems. The basic ideas might be similar, but they do not cater for the systematic foundation of an innovation system [17]. However, Living Labs as new paradigm are operating as a User Centred Open Innovation Ecosystem [18], to promote a more proactive role of users from User Centred Design and User Experience towards user co-creation. Living Lab is defined as an experimentation environments in which technology is given shape in real life contexts and in which (end) users are considered 'co-producers' [19] or co-creators involved in all of the product or service development lifecycle [20]. Living Lab is more than experimental facility as its philosophy is to turn users, from being traditionally considered as a problem, into value creation [21]. Living Lab represents a user-centric research methodology for sensing, prototyping, validating and refining complex solutions in multiple and evolving real life contexts. The key aspect of differentiation regarding Living Labs is the involvement of the users as stated in [22], "the real challenge may lie in involving users in a sociological sense, that is to say, by taking into account the micro-context of their everyday lives". The development of Living Labs is supported by the belief that the full potential of ICT today is not in the continued innovation of new technical products with superior technical performance, but rather the understanding of the user situation and innovation of solutions to match those in a changing society [17].

Living Labs move research out of laboratories into real-life contexts to stimulate innovation. A Living Lab instruments and stimulates users to drive and take active part in research, development and innovation, in their normal real-life environment. The approach is intended to [18, 21], (1) Engage all stakeholders, especially user communities, at the earlier stage of research and innovation for discovering emerging scenarios, usages and behaviours; (2) Explore, experiment, and evaluate (including socio-ergonomic, socio-cognitive and socio-economic aspects) new ideas and innovative concepts as well as related artefacts in real life situation; (3) Observe the potentiality of a viral adoption of new artefacts through a confrontation with user's value models. (4) Result in more accurate and reliable products and services. As an example of a living lab used for developing solutions dedicated to elderly "Caring TV" is the Finnish Well Life Center. It was established by the city of Espoo and Laurea University of Applied Sciences [23] Caring TV is a television functioning as a user interface designed to improve the quality of life of elderly. The TV is controlled by a touch-screen. Through the TV one can broadcast programs meant for elderly, for example physiotherapeutic advice, rehabilitation programs and cooking tips. In addition Caring TV enables elderly people to communicate with health care professionals, who in real-time through a view phone give advice in areas concerning healthcare and well-being[6].

Current technological advancements promise very exciting opportunities that seek to address different areas in the lives of the elderly. Overall, there are many

---

[6] http://www.caringtv.fi/.

successful systems. However these are mostly health systems, ambient technologies, or monitoring tools. Through the living lab approach and the fact of integrating end-users on the development process, we are not just attempting to provide solutions by addressing issues related to aging (general health situation, security, ergonomic...) but to provide social support and a higher quality of life for the elderly based on their expected needs.

As the integration of users and stakeholders is crucial in setting up and running a Living Lab, for the FoSIBLE project stakeholders from both the public and the private sectors are currently involved. We are adopting the living lab approach to explore new ideas and concepts on creating innovative applications based on existing technologies to foster elderly quality of life, experiment prototypes and evaluate breakthrough scenario that could be turned into successful innovations. The experimentation and evaluation of the resulting scenarios and smart TV applications are driven by users within a real life context.

In order to be able to design services which will be usable and useful for elderly staying at home, we need to clearly understand how do they live, what are their actual interactions and communication modes and to explore in what areas of their social life digital technology could bring a meaningful contribution.

10 end-users were recruited in France by the intermediary of elderly associations for recruiting end-users. We organized a meeting with the help of our partnership Les arcades (a gerontology prevention centre financed by the Malakoff Médéric group which is one of the biggest players in complementary medical insurance in France). Two brochures were made for this occasion and given to the participants. One gives a general overview of the project and the other includes a set of usage scenarios of social television, so that participants can get an idea on some potential opportunities for using the system that we intend to design. The selection was made upon their age and familial situation. The volunteers are eight women and two men aged between 65 and 90 years and showing no apparent health problems that prevent them from leaving or being in contact with their friends and family. However, one woman suffers from arthritis affecting her hands and feet, which forced her to stop working 10 years before retiring.

Semi-structured interviews were used to understand participants' daily practices, how do they live and what are their actual needs in relation to the use of TV as a medium of communication and collective activities. We conducted the interviews in the participants' homes, which was an opportunity to observe the environment in which participants live. Each interview lasted between 1 and 2 h.

18.4.1 Daily Activities and Expected Needs

The social network of participants interviewed in the project is limited to their families and to some friends. Most of them use the telephone to communicate and do not feel isolated as long as they can travel to visit them or to participate in group activities organized by Les Arcades: roundtable discussions organized by the psycholo-

gist of the centre, philosophy-coffee, theatre, yoga, annual travel, embroidery…
Unfortunately, recently all of these activities are no more organized by Les Arcades
but by an independent association. This change affects the people we interviewed
and as a result, they do not participate so often.

The participants receive regular visits from members of their families (mostly
children) to help them for shopping, to do some work in the house (mowing the
lawn, cleaning the gate…), or to accompany them on journeys. They had no contact
with their neighbours, however some of them said that they know that they can
count on them in case of problems or if she needs help.

At home, the days of our participants are mostly organized the same way. They
share their time between cleaning the house, reading, playing crosswords, arrow
words, coded words, sudoku… and especially watching TV programs by selecting
them from a program guide or a magazine. However, the time they spend affront
television varies from one participant to another. Some of them watch television at
specific times (noon for news, series…), while others say they keep it on to have a
kind of presence in the background even they are not watching it.

The phone is still their main communication medium. They mainly call their
children, grandchildren and friends, especially when they cannot see them. All the
participants evoke the lack of communication with their grandchildren, and the fact
that they miss sharing moments of their lives or seeing them growing.

Some of them expressed problems using remote controls: when they have a separate remote for the TV and for the TNT decoder (for digital TV which became mandatory since September 2010), some features suddenly become redundant (such as
volume control for example which can be provided by the two remote controls). The
participant suffering from arthritis also has difficulties pressing buttons that are too
small and with the confusion to select channel numbers with more than one digit
(for example channel 32 which is the one for the local TV where she lives). Most of
the participants usually use the remote only to turn the TV on and off, to control the
volume and to change the channel. They do not use advanced features.

Participants have expressed many wishes. Their first needs were communica-
tion-oriented: they would appreciate more communication with family member and
friends, especially for those who have friends at the retirement house (which main
occupation is to watch TV).

In terms of sharing, our participants also proposed virtual guided tours on TV
for cities and museums, attending courses (computers, cooking, gardening, for-
eign languages …), sports sessions, playing remotely games (crosswords, sudoku,
bridge…), online book club exchange, online round table, sharing a TV program,
having a photo album on TV and being able to annotate the photos to remember the
context in which they were taken.

Participants also expressed the need for more accessible and less complicated interfaces than computers. About control interface, participants who do not have disabilities think using a keyboard would be possible but not very practical. They prefer a digital tablet, even if they find that the voice control is also a simpler interface
than the keyboard. The digital control interface could be used for collective games
as crosswords, puzzles or sudoku, and to exchange drawings with small children.…

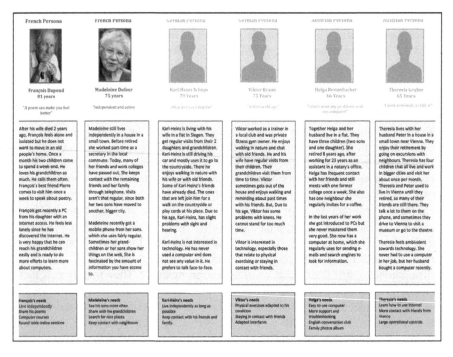

Fig. 18.1 FoSIBLE Personas

18.4.2 Personas, Storyboards and Scenarios

Elderly people have limited experience with information technology, which implies that the perception of their needs in this term raises special design issues; likewise designing for them cannot be made just through common methods such as the application of guidelines.

Based on the data collected during the interviews, a set of personas have been created [24]. Although personas are fictional, they describe attributes of our real users. Each persona has a name and a picture. They are carefully described in terms of needs, goals and tasks. Two primary personas were created for each participating country of the project (France, Germany and Austria). Such detailed personas are a key to avoid tendency for the developer to usurp or distort the real end-user. To enhance the presence of users in the development process instead of talking about "the users", technical partners develop for these personas as real persons. The persona must be a concrete individual in every one's mind. These personas are the link between designers, developers and end-users. Figure 18.1 represents the FoSIBLE personas panel.

Scenarios and storyboards are used for describing how the personas can use the defined services. They allow rapid communication on the potential uses and needs and especially about the technical feasibility. We have also presented scenarios to end-users to enrich and refine them iteratively during the development process. The analysis of the first scenarios by the developers revealed that not all the features can be implemented. The decision was made to consolidate and specify all scenarios to fit the potential of the selected Smart TV platform (HBBTV) and control interfaces (gesture recognition and tablet). Here is an example of a consolidated scenario:

> François is staying on his armchair watching a literary program "le bateau livre" on "France 5" channel. He likes to be abreast of literary news. The show discussion was about Jonathan Franzen's new novel "Freedom". He activates his buddy list and sees that Madeleine is online, watching "Arte" channel. Using his tablet, he activates the chat box and sends her a message by typing on the virtual keyboard to invite her to switch to "France 5" channel. On Madeleine's TV the chat box appears on the corner of the screen highlighting the message of François. Then they start to exchange messages about the TV show. Madeleine says, "This is a great show I did not hear about it before". François is very happy that he can find someone who shares his passion for books.
>
> François has an idea: "it will be nice to recommend this book to my book club community". He activates the FoSIBLE widget. To have access, he does not need to identify himself as he chose to connect automatically by saving his login and password. Once connected, François uses left and right gestures to navigate and find the "Clubs" service. Existing clubs appear and with the tablet he chooses the "Book Club". François can see on his main page persons who joined the club recently, the most recommended books and the last active discussion(s) on the forum. On his tablet, he clicks on "Recommend a book" icon. A recommendation form is represented. He fills in the form using the virtual keyboard on the tablet -with the book title and author name. From the "Share Book Recommendations" space, François can see what his friends are reading now, and he can keep track of what he would like to read by marking some recommendations as "book to read". As François wants his best friend Pierre to be notified of this recommendation, he sends him a dedicated message "A really good book! Come this weekend and we can discuss around a cup of tea". Pierre receives the message instantly on his "Stay in Touch" space with a notification displayed on his tablet.
>
> To help the members of the "Book Club" to stay in touch and being aware of the activity of the community, a monthly letter is sent to them by the system on their "stay in touch" inbox. This monthly letter is a kind of newsletter that contains book reviews from the club members and the most recommended readings.

Mockups have been defined to illustrate scenarios and help in collecting feedback and comments concerning the services and interface development. They are used as a way to test end-users abilities to interact with specific devices and technologies and imagine alternative design features. It is also a way to focus on problem areas of the project and verify the feasibility of design choices.

We have defined four services that users can select when looking at their TV set: WatchTV, Play, Stay in Touch, Participate in clubs:

- If the user selects Watch TV, s/he will be able to watch any program (like in a traditional TV), but also to see her/his buddy list, to interact with her/his buddies, to recommend programs and to look at recommended programs.
- If the user selects Play, s/he will be able to play games, to invite others to a game, to compare scores.
- If the user selects Stay in Touch, s/he will have the access to all the materials that her/his relatives want to share with her/him (photos, videos, drawings), s/he will be able to send/receive message, etc.
- If the user selects Participate in clubs, then s/he will see existing clubs (yoga, philo cafe, cooking, poetry, reading…), and s/he will be able to create a new one.

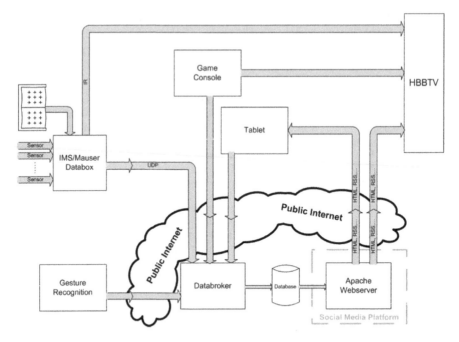

Fig. 18.2 Overall FoSIBLE Platform

18.5   The FoSIBLE Platform

Different existing TV platforms and user interfaces have been analysed to choose the more adapted configuration. According to the goals of the FoSIBLE project and the competitive analysis that was done to compare existing social TV systems, the standard HBBTV (Hybrid Broadcast Broadband TV) was chosen. This choice was motivated by the fact that HBBTV is an open platform that provides an alternative to proprietary technologies on the European market.

The central element of the FoSIBLE platform (Fig. 18.2) is the Smart TV system using the standard Hybrid Broadcast Broadband Television (HBBTV). Smart TV[7] is a set of web-based services running on an application engine installed in digital TV connected to the Internet. A Smart TV application is a special type of widget that is implemented on a browser and runs on the TV screen. Viewing an application is very much like viewing web pages using a web browser on an ordinary PC. Screen resolution, hardware specifications and remote controller make differences between applications and web pages. An application is a web page consisting of HTML, CSS and JavaScript. The HTML page shows the structure of the application, the CSS file does the style, and the JavaScript file controls the behaviour of the application. The smart TV service makes possible to extend the functions of the TV, so that users can obtain useful information and interesting contents on their TV screen. Ap-

---

[7] http://www.samsungdforum.com.

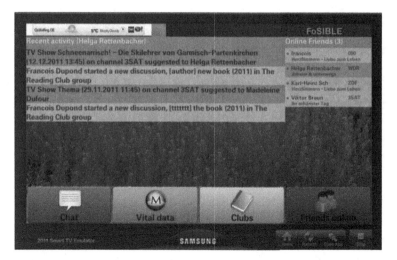

Fig. 18.3 "Online Friends" Widget

plications implementing social features and functionalities requested by our users are developed on a social media platform (JoomSocial). In addition to traditional manufacturer-specific remote controls, gesture recognition and tablet PC are implemented and completed by sensor information to detect the presence of the user. The gesture recognition modules are used to generate commands to control the menu of widgets (see scenario). Users will be able to use a tablet PC as an additional input terminal, which they can use to navigate on the TV, but also to enter text (e.g. during chats or when writing a short article). The tablet can additionally be used to display messages, when the TV is switched off or to be able to read messages in another room (e.g. read a recipe sent by a friend in the kitchen). Central orchestration of the system is guaranteed by the use of a web-based data-broker. It provides an easy integration of new data sets from various devices or software e.g. vital data, gestures...

The FoSIBLE platform is accessed by the end users by widgets. The background is slightly transparent so the image of the TV can still be visible.

The blue button of the remote control makes appear the "online friends" widget which lists all the friends who are watching TV at that time, with the channel information and their recent activities on the platform (Fig. 18.3).

Chat can be opened and closed via the red button on the remote control. It allows sending short messages to the online friends for instance to initiate a discussion when watching a TV program. The messages are typed on the tablet (Fig. 18.4).

The yellow button lists existing clubs (Fig. 18.5). Either with the gestures or by using the tablet, the user can select the club s/he wants to participate in.

After looking at all the topics in a club (Figs. 18.6 and 18.7), s/he can comment or create a new topic by using the tablet.

The last widget called "Vital Date" is based on sensors data (blood pressure, blood sugar measurement, and weight measurement...) and depicts an "Activity Index"—this is another part of the FoSIBLE project which we do not focus on.

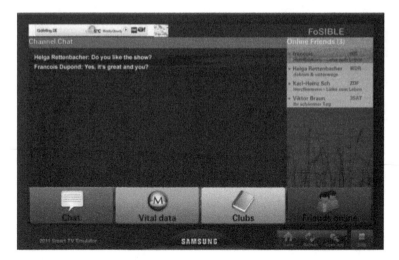

Fig. 18.4 "Chat" Widget

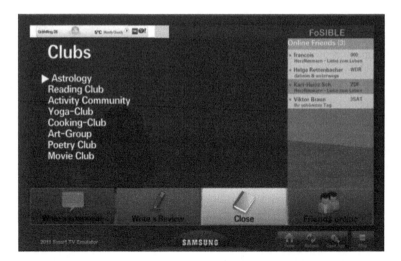

Fig. 18.5 "Clubs" Widget

Focus groups will be organized in 1 month to allow users to develop their own ideas on the applications they will evaluate and control interfaces. The focus group will include 10 end-users; with the support of a group leader, the participants will be able to speak freely about the system during a session lasting about 2 h. The objective will be to collect data on how users perceive the system, and therefore to obtain their feedbacks, initial reactions to the design and to examine their preferences. After implementing focus groups results into the platform, participants will be equipped at home with the FoSIBLE system, and we will follow their use during 1 year.

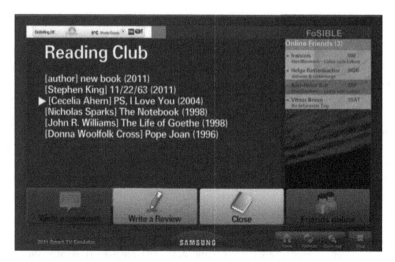

Fig. 18.6 Browsing reviews in the Reading Club

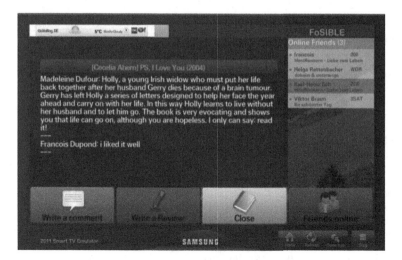

Fig. 18.7 Reading a review and a comment in the Reading Club

18.6   Conclusion

Monitoring is a solution for older people to be able to live in their environment as long as possible, especially for those suffering from disabilities related to age or diseases. However, we believe that we need to take into consideration the quality of their life by improving their well-being and self-esteem. Based on the fact that social isolation due to loss of relatives and week social network could contribute to depression and may have negative impacts on their general health status, we would like to allow them to interact with their peers. To address this challenge, we have adopted a Living Lab approach consolidated by the use of personas, scenarios and mockups to define TV services. We have iteratively designed SmartTV applications to support socially oriented activities for older people. They are actually being developed and the household rollout will start in 3 months and will last 1 year. The use of these applications by the elderly will help us to asses if virtual networks and online generational communities could offset elderly' lack of relationship and social isolation by creating new ties among peers.

By inviting the future users to participate actively in the creation of the future services, in the early stages of design, bringing their ideas from their experience, practice, desires and frustrations, we expect significant impact of the qualitative work on the development, acceptance, appropriation, and usage of our technology in fostering the social life of elderly.

Acknowledgments This work was partly funded by the European Community and the National Research Agency (ANR) through the AAL 169 program (FoSIBLE Project No. ANR-09-AALI-002-04).

References

1. Robert-Bobée, I.: Projections de population pour la France métropolitaine à l'horizon 2050, La population continue de croître et le vieillissement se poursuit. Insee Première n° 1089 (2006)
2. Sixsmith, A.: An evaluation of an intelligent home monitoring system. J. Telemed. Telecare. **6**(2), 63–72 (2000)
3. Whitten, P., Collins, B., Mair, F.: Nurse and patient reactions to a developmental home telecare system. J. Telemed. Telecare. **4**(3), 152–160 (1998)
4. Holt-Lunstad, J., Smith, T.B., Bradley, J.: Social relationships and mortality risk: a meta-analytic review. PLoS Med. **7**(7), 1–20 (2010)
5. Riche, Y., Mackay, W.: PeerCare: supporting awareness of rhythms and routines for better aging in place. Comput. Support. Coop. Work. **19**(1), 73–104 (2010)
6. Pfeil, U., Zaphiris, P., Wilson, S.: Older adults' perceptions and experiences of online social support. Interact. Comput. **21**(3), 159–172 (2009)
7. Blit-Cohen, E., Litwin, H.: Elder participation in cyberspace: a qualitative analysis of Israeli retirees. J. Aging Stud. **18**(4), 385–398 (2004)
8. Wright, K.: Computer-mediated social support, older adults, and coping. J. Commun. **50**(3), 100–118 (2000)
9. Lepa, J., Tatnall, A.: Using actor-network theory to understanding virtual dommunity networks of older people using the internet. J. Bus. Syst., Gov. Ethics. **1**(4), 1–14 (2006)
10. Kanayama, T.: Ethnographic research on the experience of Japanese elderly people online. N. Media Soc. **5**(2), 267–288 (2003)
11. Jetter, H.-C., Gerken, J., Reiterer, H.: Natural User Interfaces: Why we need better model-worlds, Not better gestures. Paper presented at the CHI 2010 Workshop—Natural User Interfaces: The Prospect and Challenge of Touch and Gestural Computing, Atlanta, USA (2010)
12. Schaffers, H., Sallstrom, A., Pallot, M., Hernandez-Munoz, J.M., Santoro, R., Trousse, B.: "Integrating Living Labs with Future Internet experimental platforms for co-creating services within Smart Cities," Concurrent Enterprising (ICE), 2011 17th International Conference on Concurrent Enterprising, pp. 1–11, 20–22 June (2011)

13. Erlbaum, J., Kyng, M.: Design at work: Cooperative design of computer systems. Lawrence Erlbaum Associates, Hillsdale (1991)
14. Schuler, D., Namioka, A.E.: Participatory Design, Lawrence Erlbaum 1993 and chapter 11 in Helander's Handbook of HCI. Elsevier, Mahwah (1997)
15. Beyer, H., Holtzblatt, K.: Contextual Design: Defining Customer-centered Systems. Morgan Kaufmann, San Francisco (1998)
16. Aarts, E.H.L., Marzano, S.: The New Everyday: Views on Ambient Intelligence, p. 46. 010 Publishers, Rotterdam (2003)
17. Eriksson, M., Niitamo, V.-P., Kulkki, S., Hribernik, K.A.: Living labs as a multi-contextual R&D methodology. In: Proceedings of the 12th International Conference on Concurrent Enterprising, 26–28 June 2005, Milan, Italy (2006)
18. Pallot, M.: Engaging Users into Research and Innovation: The Living Lab Approach as a User Centred Open Innovation Ecosystem. Webergence Blog. http://www.cwe-projects.eu/pub/bscw.cgi/1760838?id=715404_1760838 (2009)
19. Ballon, P., Pierson, J., Delaere, S.: Test and experimentation platforms for broadband and innovation: examining European practice. In: Proceedings of the 16th European Regional Conference by the International Telecommunications Society (ITS), 4–6 Sept 2005, Porto, Portugal (2005)
20. Schumacher, J., Feurstein, K.: Living labs—the user as co-creator. In: Proceedings of the 13th International Conference on Concurrent Enterprising, 4–6 June 2007, Sophia-Antipolis, France (2007)
21. ECOSPACE Newsletter No 5.: http://www.ami-communities.eu/wiki/ECOSPACE_Newsletter_No_5
22. ISTAG Working Group on Experience and Application Research: "Involving Users in the Development of Ambient Intelligence" (2005)
23. Mäkäräinen-Suni, I.: Best practices, innovation and development: experiences from five living lab innovation environments. In: Proceedings of the 14th International Conference on Concurrent Enterprising, 23–25 June 2008, pp. 129–136, Lisbon, Portugal (2008)
24. Cooper, A.: The Inmates Are Running the Asylum: Why High Tech Products Drive Us Crazy and How to Restore the Sanity. Sams—Pearson Education, Upper Saddle River (2004)

Chapter 19
Examining Multiactivity Using Multi-camera Recordings: The Use of Text Chat in a Call Center

Karine Lan Hing Ting

Abstract Call center work cannot be reducible to talking on the phone. Parallel to their talk, call center agents manage computer/screen activity and collaboration with co-workers present on the floor. The situated work activity that is achieved is an artful management of several forms of interaction occurring simultaneously. Among these parallel activities is the use of text chat. This keyboard writing of short messages is a quick and easy way to share information and coordinate action. More importantly, being a 'silent' communicative medium and modality, it allows coordination with colleagues to occur at the same time as the phone call. Focusing on text chat allows a questioning of the place and use of computer technologies in call center work. However, in order to fully understand how this artifact supports collaborative work, it is important to examine the multiactivity the agent is engaged in. The analyses of the whole situation of work presented in this chapter are based on multi-camera video extracts, giving access to the phone conversation, the screen activity and content, verbal communication and gestures with co-workers around.

Index of abbreviations and transcript symbols

CCA   Call center agent
Sup   Supervisor
Pro   Prospective Customer
(( ))   Description of non-verbal actions
* #   Delimitates agent's actions description
......   Continuing gesture or action
↑   Rising inflection
?   Moderate rising inflection
,   Continuing intonation
.   Stopping fall in tone
:   Extension of sound or syllable
(3.0)   Pauses or silences in seconds
=   Latching or rapid successive actions
-   Interruption
•hhh   Audible out breath

K. Lan Hing Ting (✉)
LASMIC, Université de Nice-Sophia Antipolis, Nice, France
e-mail: karine.lan@gmail.com

J. Dugdale et al. (eds.), *From Research to Practice in the Design of Cooperative Systems:*   277
Results and Open Challenges, DOI 10.1007/978-1-4471-4093-1_19,
© Springer-Verlag London 2012

19.1   Introduction: Beyond the Talk in Call Center Work

Call centers are representative of new service activities that have expanded in recent years, made possible by advanced information technologies. A call center is a
centralized office, where a dedicated workforce specializes in the telephone service
provision function, managing incoming and outgoing calls by telephone. It is a
workplace where communication is not just part of the job description, in essence
it *is* the job description [1]. Talk is central in call center interactions: Service is delivered over the phone through language and social interaction within the calls [2].
    Analyses on call center interactions have most often adopted a dyadic perspec-
tive: telephone calls have usually been viewed as two-party interactions in which
participants have access only to each others' speech. In this "speech-only interface",
can work be described only in terms of a verbal conversation between two interloc-
utors—a customer and a call center agent? Even though talking on the phone is considered as the main activity, there are two activities, both of them language-based,
involved in workers' routine. The first is talking to customers on the telephone, the
other is inputting and retrieving data by computer [1], as the agent faces his/her
computer screen. Linguists and sociologists of work, many in France, have been interested in the industrial rationalization of talk in these "communication factories".
This highly standardized job, which leaves very few autonomy to the agent, is based
on a taylorized model of work design, which can be systematized by new call center
technologies: Automated Call Distribution regiments the pace and rhythm of work,
scripts prescribe what to say and how, performance is constantly being monitored
and measured. Computer technologies in call centers have, therefore, mostly been
examined in terms of codifications and surveillance of an individual work activity. Other aspects—how the technology supports the call management and communication for collaboration and teamwork—have been the object of interaction
researches.
    Examining both the phone conversation and the whole situation of technology-
equipped work, several studies on call centers [2–4] have shown that call center
agents' activity cannot be reducible to its most visible aspect. Video recordings
make possible the observation of the complexity of work activities in this technologically-equipped workplace. More than "talk at work" or "talk as work", call
center work is characterized by *multiactivity* [4]. As we will see in the analyses of
this chapter, several other activities, alongside the main foregrounded frontline talk,
are involved in call center work.

19.2   Documenting Technologically-supported Multiactivity

The research literature on the notion of multiactivity is relatively recent and is
mostly interested in highly specific workplaces. The issue of the management of
concurrent courses of action began to be raised with the arrival of the multiplicity

of communication tools and technical objects in the workplace. Henceforth, the terms "equipped organizational environments" and "equipped co-presence" [5]. Multiactivity has been described as the simultaneous or parallel occurrence of the conversation with other activities. It is "not just *two* successive independent actions, but *one* multiactivity constituted by two or more parallel streams of action". It implies that these parallel courses of action be attended at the same time by the participants, in ways that can be more or less autonomous, more or less dependent, within relations that can change through time [6]. The simultaneous flows of action can be distributed in a dynamic way between a 'main' and a 'secondary' activity, and can be sensitive to the sequential relevancies of the foregrounded talk [4], that is the phone conversation. If the two parallel streams of action are compatible, they can be carried out simultaneously. At other times, they are mutually exclusive and consequently suspend one another. Designing their streams of action as being parallel or embedded requires from the participants that they coordinate their multiactivity, achieving a hierarchization work in shifting from one activity to the other. This necessity to coordinate a complex array of simultaneous tasks and activities in a 'multimedia' work environment [7] is just one of the characteristics that call centers share with other "centers of coordination" [8], which have been the object of workplace studies.

Workplace studies constitute a growing body of sociological studies concerned with work, technology and interaction in organizational environments. They address the social and interactional organization of workplace activities, and the way in which tools and technologies, ranging from paper documents through to complex multimedia systems, feature in everyday work and collaboration [7]. The interest of adopting a workplace studies approach, that is a naturalist video-based studies of organizational interaction, for analyzing call center work, is the workplace studies' interest for situated action. Video recordings can capture how personnel draw on resources—whether interactional, spatial or technological—to coordinate their action and achieve their work activity in collaboration with others.

Examining how call centre agents manage multiple work activities running simultaneously, this chapter focuses on the use of text chat. The interest of examining this keyboard writing of short messages is twofold. First, text chat is afforded by call center technology and takes place on the computer screen. Analysis reveals an artful use of this function for coordination between co-workers, far from aspects of surveillance and codification of work practices, which studies have mostly described so far. Second, the use of text chat occurs simultaneously to the call management activity. Through this mediated modality of communication, which has the advantage of being 'silent', agents are able to read incoming messages or type and send messages, while they are talking on the phone. We will see how text chat is used for collaboration in place of talk, examining its situated context of use: we will consider the participants' co-location on the same floor, and how text chat is used in relation to the agents' management of their main activity, which is talking on the phone. Analysis will demonstrate how in prioritizing the talk on the phone, over another course of action within the multiactivity, agents orient to the pre-eminence of the call management as the main foregrounded activity. Therefore, this chapter is interested in multiactivity, less in terms of doing several individual actions at the same time, than in terms of an interactional phenomenon: How multiactivity situations are organized, managed, and accomplished in social interaction

The analyses presented in this chapter are based on video analysis and fine transcripts of the agents' actions, which draw on interactional, multimodal and material resources. The video extracts have been collected through a multi-camera device, giving a synchronized access to the phone conversation, the screen activity and content, body torque and gestures of the agent as he/she orients to co-workers around, as well as a general view of the spatial work environment. These multi-camera recordings make available for observation and analysis the whole range of activities that occur simultaneously to the phone talk. Before examining the extracts, it would be interesting to have an understanding of the characteristics and the use of writing of short messages in professional settings.

19.3   Digital Writing for Information Sharing and Coordination

The growing use of Instant Messaging (IM) by business executives has given rise to studies questioning the efficiency of this form of communicative mode at the office. Research on IM demonstrates that it promotes the exchange of information and collaboration in the workplace by its speed and easiness of communication. It ensures coordination between distributed groups, overcoming limitations of time and space [9]. This quasi-synchronous digital writing, where the sequentiality of turns is ideally maintained like in conversation, allows refined forms of coordination [10], as well as minimal interruption. Through the "media substitution effect" [11], where IM replaces other forms of communication, the exchanges are shorter, characterized by quick clarification questions and collaboration of moderate intensity. Because of its elasticity, and as workers achieve an "articulation work" between their multiple solicitations, these "equipped interactions" are not intrusive [5]. Therefore, IM reveals to be an efficient tool.

Like the use of IM at the office, text chat in the call center where the data have been collected allows information sharing and coordination in minimum time and intrusiveness. However, as opposed to IM, allowed by dedicated software and an internet connection, the text chat function is integrated in the Customer Relationship Management (CRM) software. IM allows communication with a list of buddies not restricted to co-workers, whereas text chat in the call center allows only a hierarchical communication between logged in agents and their co-present supervisors or floor leader (agents cannot communicate in between themselves). The integration of this communication function alongside other call management functions raises interesting design/use questions. Is the necessity for collaboration and information sharing on the floor as important as the call management?

Fig. 19.1 Text chat window

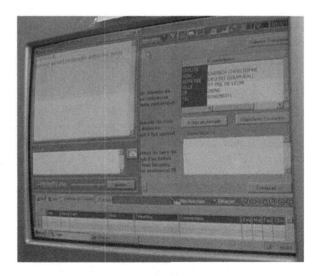

In order to address this question, it is necessary to see how incoming messages pop-up on an agent's computer screen. The pop-up window appears on the top left part of the screen. In proportion to the screen's size, and the size of the text it contains, the size of the text chat window is quite big—about a third of the computer screen (Fig. 19.1).

More importantly, when popping-up, it covers other buttons that are potentially necessary for managing the end of the current call. This requires that the call center agent processes the message, before closing the window (1) in order to be able to access the call qualification buttons (2) and next call dialing (3) (Fig. 19.2).

19.4   Analyzing the Context of Use of Text Chat

Whether the call management implies inputting data and making actions on the computer (actions 2 and 3 in figure below) or talking on the phone, text chat allows an additional interaction to this main work activity. This quasi-synchronous processing of pop-up message, occurring simultaneously to the call, rests on a different participation framework and a different communication mode (writing as opposed to talking). Therefore the collaborative communication or information-sharing remains invisible on the *frontline*, as the customer has only access to the "main" publicly-displayed activity, which is the phone talk. However, our focus is on the other activities that occur simultaneously to this main talk, and how they are socially organized. Analyzing multiactivity means analyzing, not only the shifting from one activity to the other, but the situated interdependence between these activities. This means that text chat is examined within its social context of use, considering the complex array of social, technical and interactional resources, which inform the mundane and accountable use of this specific communication artefact.

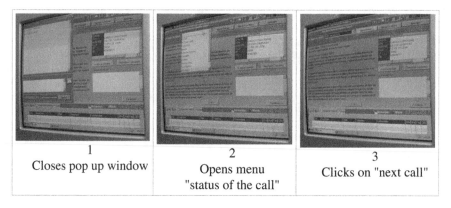

1	2	3
Closes pop up window	Opens menu "status of the call"	Clicks on "next call"

Fig. 19.2 Actions on the screen

The two extracts below occur at a few minutes interval. The call center agent has to attend a religious ceremony and needs her supervisor's authorization to leave work earlier. The literal translation of the message is "Later I leave at 5 p.m". Even if these exchanges constitute a form of talk at work, the topic of the request is not linked to the call management activity at hand, and is not directly linked to the production task either. Her supervisor is seated next to her, at the same cluster. They can mutually see and hear each other. The way the agent orients to sending a message by text chat, or verbally addressing the supervisor, shows that floor interactions between call center workers cannot be considered as ordinary face-to-face interactions, precisely because of the modes of communication the agents draw on to achieve multiactivity.

In the extracts below, the talk (in French, appears in bold) has been transcribed and translated (line underneath). The agent's actions on the screen are restituted, described in between double brackets and notified by "→". The numbering of lines and the connection symbols aim at preserving the temporality of the actions. The transcript begins when the agent starts typing the message, while talking to the prospective customer.

Extract 1

```
21.CCA    simplemen:t pour vou↑s annoncer que
          simply to tell you that
22.       >vo*tre nu*méro d télé#phone fixe#,<
          your phone number
   →      *((types « GH »))
   →      #((erases « GH »))
23.       hhh a été sé*lectionné:↑ par l'agence
          has been selected by the agency
   →                  *..((types « TALEUR »))....
```

```
24.        de XXX* ce matin, et de ce fait, nous
           of XXX this morning and therefore we
           ..... *
25.        vous o*ffrons un téléphone porta:ble.*
           offer you a mobile phone
    →              *...((types « JPAR A »))...... *
26.        *j'e:spère que cela vous fait plaisir?*
           I hope that this pleases you
    →           *......((types « 17HR »))..............*
27.        monsieur?
           sir
28. Pro    ((Prospect's turn not restituted)
29. CCA    *((selects the text))
30.  →     ((right click « cut »))
```

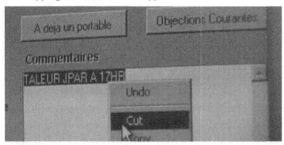

```
31.  →     ((opens recipients' list, selects supervisor))
```

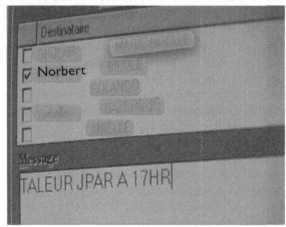

```
32.  →     ((« paste » in message zone))
33. CCA    oui:,
34.  →     ((clicks to send message))
```

35. →   ((back to « comments » zone, starts
          inputting customer's data))

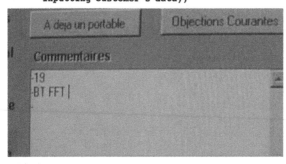

In this first extract, we see how her writing the message occurs simultaneously to her conversation on the phone with the prospective customer. She starts typing the message as she gives the reason for the call, after the opening sequence. The symbols in the transcript are meant to restore the fine temporality between her talk and her keyboard actions visible on the screen. But even if we do not get into detail in this very fine coordination, it is possible to see that these two independent activities are managed simultaneously. She starts typing at line 22, in the "comments" zone on her screen. The comments zone is situated on the right part of the screen and is where agents are expected to type in the personal information of the customer. The agent then selects the text (line 29) she has just written, cuts (line 30) and pastes the text in the chat window (lines 32) after having selected the addressee (line 31) and sends the message. She has typed the message while presenting the reason for the call to the customer (till line 27), and makes the other actions while the latter is responding. The transcript of the customer's turn has not been transcribed here so that the analysis can focus on the agent's text chat actions.

By examining the parallel actions achieved by the agent in the set of data, we can observe a difference in the coordination of the simultaneous actions of talking and typing. It is one thing to type in customer information on the computer while talking to the customer, as both actions are tied to the call management activity. It is another thing to write a message, like the one the call center agent types, from lines 22–34. Managing the text chat appears here as a completely separate and independent activity from the call management, and there is no apparent "coordination" work between the two courses of action. The talk and the text chat do not only rely on two different modes of communication, they also have two different addressees and participation frameworks, different topics, different statuses in terms of talk as work, which seem hardly linked to each other.

Extract 2 occurs 11 minutes after Extract 1. The message in Extract 1 did not produce any answer on the supervisor's part. The agent starts typing a message before talking to her supervisor.

Extract 2

```
10. CCA      vous↑ annoncer? que vo:tre numéro d
             to tell you that your
11.          téléphone fi::↑xe (0.5) a été
             phone number has been
12.          sélectionné:: ce matin par l'agence
             selected this morning by the agency
13.          de XXX (.) et de ce fait? vous êtes
             of XXX and therefore you are
14.          l'heu↑reuse gagnan:te d'un magnifique
             the lucky winner of a great
15.          téléphone portable. (.) j'es*pè-•hhh
             mobile phone. I hope- ((interrupts))
     →                                *((types
16.          « Je »))
17. CCA      co:mment?
             pardon?
18. CCA →    ((types « pourai partir tale »)) =
```

```
19. CCA      = ((lifts her mike)) =
20.          = norber:t? (0.5) nor#bert, (.)
21. Sup                            #((turns his
             head))........................#
```

```
22. CCA        *cinq* heures la prière taleur.#
               five o'clock the religious ceremony later
               *((turns back to the screen))*
23. Sup        ((turns back his head and nods slowly
               5 times))
24. CCA        ((qualifies the call, clicks to dial
25.            next call))
```

The agent starts writing line 15, when sequentially in the conversation, she has finished giving the reason for the call and initiates the question. The question "I hope that this pleases you?", that she repeats at each and every call, projects the customer's answer. However, the customer is not interested and hangs up. The message that appears on the screen is "je pourai partir tale", that can be translated as "may I go later", a question that she does not finish typing. She does not need to. The call having abruptly ended, the agent is no more engaged in the telephone conversation. She is therefore available for other types of verbal interaction.

She interrupts her writing line 18, quickly lifts her mike which makes visible her disengaging from the phoning activity, and summons her supervisor by calling him by name (line 20). As the supervisor turns his head and looks at her (before being summoned, he was looking at his screen, line 18), she produces her request verbally. She then quickly orients back to her screen and completes the call management actions on her screen, lines 24 and 25. These rapid successive actions make clearly visible for analysis that call management cannot be reduced to talking: even though the phone conversation has ended at line 17, the call needs to be qualified[1] before another call can be made. Analyzing the "call" based on video recordings allows a revisiting of the boundaries of a telephone call, and to examine the place of computer technology in managing it from a global perspective.

Most importantly concerning multiactivity, this extract allows an analysis of the artful management and the fine coordination between multiple layers of activity, and the different modes of interaction that are mobilized to support their achievement. The use of text chat appears as being situated and contextual. Since the supervisor is next to her, she can see that he is not interactionally engaged, and being given that her phone conversation has ended, she is available and can engage in a face-to-face interaction. The agent addresses her supervisor, and produces her request verbally. This confirms the use of quasi-synchronous digital writing, whether text chat or Instant Messaging, as characterized by the "media substitution effect" [11], where writing of short messages replaces other forms of communication. We see in the extract above that text chat or talk are used interchangeably, in a situated and contextual way, depending on the contingencies. Analyzing the work activity implies to take into consideration not only the talk as work, but also the praxeological, spatial and material environment of the call centre agent.

---

[1] These data are used to generate statistics about performance rate.

In these two extracts, we have examined two "outgoing" text chat messages, where the agent being observed writes and sends messages to a specific addressee who is seated next to her. Though we have been able to examine the agent's multiple streams of activity, her use of text chat did not allow a questioning of, what we may call, the intrusiveness of text chat, and of the potential problems of having to manage several courses of action at the same time.

Extract 3a

```
70.    Pro    a↑11ô
              hello
71.    CCA    (3.0)
72.    Pro    a:↑11ô:
              hello
73.    CCA    (( ))
74.           oui: bonjou:r, mada↑me savo::che↑
              yes good morning, mrs savoche
```

What is of interest in this short transcript is the interactional disruption at the beginning of the call. Contrary to the first two examples above where the agent's multiactivity remained transparent in the phone conversation, there is a disruption that occurs here, which is oriented to by the prospective customer. The customer answers the phone with a first "hello" (line 70). Line 72, she produces a second "hello" with a rising intonation. In between the two, there is a silence, which lasts 3 seconds. The call center agent starts talking at line 74. This disruption may be considered as a minor one, probably perceived as a simple communication problem by the customer, who has only access to the audio resources in the conversation. The transcript in Extract 3a adopts this phone conversation perspective.

However through a multimodal analysis of the whole situation of work, it is possible to see that what is actually accomplished—both on the screen in the spatial work environment of the floor—in parallel of this interactional disruption, is actually rich and complex. Below is the multimodal transcript of the video recording of the same extract.

Extract 3b

```
67.    →    ((call dialing screen))
            ((Message pops up))
```

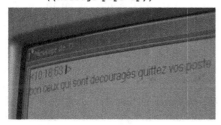

```
68.    CCA    (3.0) ((looks at the screen))
```

```
69.    →      ((customer record page appears))
70.    Pro    a↑llô
              hello
71.    CCA    (3.0)     ((turns her head,
              maintains gaze towards floor leader))
```

```
72.    Pro    a:↑llô: =
              hello
73.    CCA    = ((orients back to her screen)) =
74.           = ((lowers her mike))
              oui: bonjou:r, mada↑me savo::che↑
              yes good morning, mrs savoche
```

The message has been sent by the floor leader in a go to all the workers present on the floor. The message examined here is the third message in a collection of eight, that the floor leader sends successively in a few minutes' time. The message, which pops up at line 67, is "well, those who are discouraged, leave your position". The analysis will focus on the orientation of the call center agent to this message in particular.

When the customer hangs up, line 69 (the customer record page appears when communication is put through), and produces the first "hello", line 70, the agent is reading the message (lines 68–71). Line 71, she turns her head towards the floor leader, the sender of the message. What is heard as a "silence" in the conversation corresponds to her action of gazing at the floor leader, which lasts 3 s. The agent orients back to her screen after the customer has produced a second "hello". Contrary to the first, which was an answer, this second "hello" constitutes a summons, which strongly projects an answer from the caller. It is produced line 74, and the prospective customer can hear "yes good morning mrs savoche". Apart from the fact that this first turn accomplishes three conversational actions—(i) the answer to the summons ("yes"), (ii) a greeting ("good morning") and (iii) a confirmation of the identity of the called ("mrs savoche[2]" with a rising intonation)—what is of interest is the set of non-conversational actions accomplished as part of "the answer".

Lines 73–74, three actions quickly follow each other. Line 73, she orients back to her screen and quickly reads the customer's name on the record page, which she enunciates ("mrs savoche"). Line 74, the agent lowers her mike, activating it. So far, the agent could hear the customer but the customer could not hear the agent. This characteristic is specific to call center interactions and the type of mediated communication that is made possible in this technologically-equipped workplace. By her practical action of lowering her mike, she makes visible for analysis that she is engaging in the phone conversation. She produces her first turn almost at the same time.

By the agent's orientation of gazing at the floor leader, and by the supervisor's same orientation, it appears that it is less the moment at which the message pops up, than its content, which is oriented to. Whereas the two previous messages did not produce any disruption in her ongoing phone conversation, this particular message appears as being problematic since it prevents her from managing the beginning of the call. By analyzing the multiactivity, this extract allows a quick insight into the contextual use of this digital mode of managerial communication, and allows a first questioning of the intrusiveness issue, which needs to be developed elsewhere.

19.5   Conclusion

By examining the use of text chat as a specific form of talk as work, and looking at the screen activity as part of the call management, this chapter has shown how multiactivity is achieved in this call center. Focusing on aspects of multimodal interaction—whether mediated communication or gestures and bodily conduct—analysis has shown that in this "open space" workplace, characterized by co-presence, text chat cannot be analyzed as an independent and isolated form of communication. The additional interaction it permits, when examined in a situated and contextual way, reveals that the efficiency of this communicative tool is highly contextual. Whether this interactional equipment is to be considered as useful for collaboration or disruptively intrusive depends on the situated use that is made. The approach of this chapter has been to understand as precisely as possible this actual use: the type of collaboration that it makes possible and what is meant by "collaborating through text chat". Analyzing text chat as part of multiactivity has allowed an understanding of the medium, as well as of the ordinary communication practices it affords. Through the type of analysis presented in this chapter, it is possible to grasp how work practices in this setting is currently organized with respect to text chat, with

---

[2] The participants' or customers' names are fake, to ensure their anonymity.

a view to considering opportunities and implications for other mediated-communication technologies.

It is interesting to observe the artful management of this mode of communication together with other courses of action in call centers, these "communication factories". What is known as a call center will evolve into what has started to be known as a contact center. Today, customers contact companies by calling, emailing, chatting online, visiting websites, faxing, and even by instant messaging. The fine knowledge of how call center personnel manage different streams of activity and participation frameworks, and make use of digital writing as mediated forms of communication may be helpful to accompany the "next step". It is recognized that systems will become increasingly concerned with supporting collaborative and organizational, rather than individual, conduct. Call/contact centers are no exception. A fine understanding of collaborative work, distributed teams, use of technology can be useful to designing technology-mediated services, or new forms of distant collaboration like homeshoring.

References

1. Cameron, D.: Good to Talk? Living and Working in a Communication Culture. Sage, London (2000)
2. Whalen, J., Zimmerman, D.H.: Working a call: multiparty management and interactional infrastructure in calls for help. In: Baker, C., Emmison, M., Firth, A. (eds.) Calling for Help: Language and Social Interaction in Telephone Helplines, pp. 309–345. John Benjamins, Amsterdam (2005)
3. Licoppe, C., Relieu, M.: Entre système et conversation. Une approche située de la compétence des téléopérateurs dans les services d'assistance technique. In: Kessous, E., Metzger, J.-L. (eds.) Le travail avec les technologies de l'information, pp. 177–199. Hermès, Paris (2005)
4. Mondada, L.: Using video for a sequential and multimodal analysis of social interaction: videotaping institutional telephone calls. Forum Qual. Soc. Res. 9(3), 88 paragraphs (2008)
5. Licoppe, C.: Pragmatique de la notification. Tracés. 16, 77–98 (2009)
6. Mondada, L.: The organization of concurrent courses of action in surgical demonstrations'. In: Streeck, J., Goodwin, C., LeBaron, C. (eds.) Embodied Interaction: Language and Body in the Material World. Cambridge University Press, Cambridge (2011)
7. Heath, C., Knoblauch, H., Luff, P.: Technology and social interaction: the emergence of 'workplace studies', Br. J. Sociol. 51, 299–320 (2011)
8. Suchman, L.: Centers of communication: a case and some themes. In: Resnick, L.B., Säljö, R., Pontecorvo, C., Burge, B. (eds.) Discourse, Tools and Reasoning: Essays in Situated Cognition, pp. 41–62. Spinger, Berlin (1997)
9. Quan-Haase, A., Cothrel, J., Wellman, B. Instant messaging for collaboration: a case study of a high-tech firm. J. Comput. Mediat. Commun. 10(4), article 13 (2005)
10. Denis, J., Licoppe, C.: L'équipement de la coprésence dans les collectifs de travail: la messagerie instantanée en entreprise. In: Bidet, A., et Pillon, T. (eds.) Sociologie du travail et activité, pp. 47–65. Octares, Toulouse (2006)
11. Garrett, R.K., Danzinger, J.N.: IM=Interruption Management? Instant messaging and disruption in the workplace. J. Comput. Mediat. Commun. 13(1), article 2 (2007)

Chapter 20
Agentville: Supporting Situational Awareness and Motivation in Call Centres

Tommaso Colombino, Stefania Castellani, Antonietta Grasso, and Jutta Willamowski

Abstract Call centres are high pressure work environments where agents work strictly according to shifts and time schedules. Typically, agents are grouped into teams with supervisors from whom they receive only periodic performance feedback. It is a challenge to maintain high motivation and performance amongst the agents in this environment. Agents may lack awareness of their individual status with respect to their objectives, and the performance of their team and the call center as a whole. In this chapter we describe the design of a system that we are building to provide the agents with real-time information on their work environment's status and on potential improvements in performance, while hopefully also improving their work experience. The solution is based on the introduction in the call centre of some game mechanics whose selection and instantiation has been informed by case studies conducted by the authors.

20.1 Introduction

Call centres are an example of high pressure office workplaces where agents work very strictly according to shifts and time schedules, in cubicles situated in large open spaces, while receiving calls assigned to them one after the other immediately as they become available as long as the calls stack up in the call centre queue. Typically, agents are grouped into teams of 10–15 workers to which supervisors are assigned from whom they receive periodic (weekly and monthly) feedback on their performance. Supervisors report to Operations Managers, who in turn

T. Colombino (✉) · S. Castellani · A. Grasso · J. Willamowski
Xerox Research Centre Europe, 6, chemin de Maupertuis, 38240 Meylan, France
e-mail: Tommaso.Colombino@xrce.xerox.com

S. Castellani
e-mail: Stefania.Castellani@xrce.xerox.com

A. Grasso
e-mail: Antonietta.Grasso@xrce.xerox.com

J. Willamowski
e-mail: Jutta.Willamowski@xrce.xerox.com

J. Dugdale et al. (eds.), *From Research to Practice in the Design of Cooperative Systems: Results and Open Challenges,* DOI 10.1007/978-1-4471-4093-1_20,
© Springer-Verlag London 2012

are responsible for groups of 10–15 supervisors. In call centres doing inbound activity (receiving phone calls from customers) agent performance is measured according to metrics, here on referred to as Key Performance Indicators (KPIs) which are derived from the call centre telephone switch and from assessments performed by quality analysts who listen to recorded phone calls and "score" the agents' performance on a set of pre-defined categories (e.g. "average", "very good", etc.). An example of a KPI derived from the telephone switch is Average Handle Time (AHT), which represents the average time an agent spends on a phone call with a customer. The call centre as a whole is expected to keep their aggregate average KPI values within a certain threshold (or upper and lower threshold values)—agents are therefore in turn expected to manage their phone calls so that their average values fall within those thresholds. This organizational hierarchy is designed to ensure control and supervision of a "floor" that may total 800–900 agents in some of the larger call centres. It also creates a reporting structure where agents are held to account for their own individual performance alone and where activity-based compensation mechanisms for agents reflect their individual performance but not that of the call centre's operations as a whole. The challenges that characterize this environment can be translated into two broad and interrelated requirements:

- Providing agents with the right level of "situational awareness", i.e. an understanding of their ongoing performance within the broader context of the operations of the call centre as a whole;
- Providing the right motivation and performance related incentives to employees.

In the absence of the appropriate levels of situational awareness and motivation for the agents, it becomes difficult for call centres (represented operationally either by supervisors or operations managers) to justify the need for agents to push their performance beyond their minimum requirements, even when and where there is room for improvement at the individual agent level that would in turn improve the aggregate performance of the call centre as a whole.

In some call centres, Information Management Systems available to agents may provide access to switch data. However, to reflect the performance trends of specific agents or teams the data needs to be aggregated into "reports", the creation of which is time consuming and dedicated to specific organizational processes, such as reporting on the call centre's overall performance or in the course of "coaching sessions" with individual agents. The net result is that agents receive feedback on their individual and team performance only periodically, and not in the course of their routine work of taking phone calls—which is precisely when it is most needed for agents to effectively monitor their own performance. Therefore, call centre services providers are interested in finding solutions to the problem of providing agents with continual, dynamic information about individual, team and call centre performance.

Our observational studies suggest that supervisors and operations managers in call centres are skilled at providing agents with valuable feedback on their performance metrics in their weekly one-to-one coaching sessions. While supervisors would like to have more one-on-one time with their agents, there is obviously a limit to how much time a supervisor can spend with any one of his or her agents in the course of a week, and to the time the call centre can afford to pull agents out of production time (i.e. taking phone calls) to receive coaching. Moreover performance targets and objectives need to be perceived as fair and attainable, and provide a reasonable balance between individual performance objectives and organizational requirements, in order to motivate performance.

In this chapter we illustrate the design of a system, called Agentville, which we are building for addressing the situation awareness and motivation issues in call centres. What our system offers is a feasible way of closing the agent-supervisor feedback loop by providing agents with near real-time access to their current performance metrics and trends (without having to log in to a separate system while they are taking calls)—this empowers the agents to self-monitor more effectively between the weekly milestones that are already in place. Our system also provides clear and shared objectives with direct access to relevant metrics: through our systems the agents and supervisors are able to compare their performance to that of their team and the call centre as a whole and better understand the relationship between their performance and the organizational goals of the centre. Supervisors will be able to easily identify agents and teams which have the best margins of improvement on strategically relevant metrics at any point in time and challenge or encourage them to improve. The challenges could also be configured by the supervisors to be automatically triggered by the system when specific situations are detected.

We first describe more in details the analysis of performance and work experience issues in call centres that has inspired the design of our system. Then we describe the interaction supported by Agentville and discuss related and future work.

20.2 Performance and Work Experience in Call Centres

The goal of this section is to provide more context for the focus on performance management strategies in our work with call centres. Part of the focus comes from a specific concern with the high level of attrition experienced by the call centres we collaborated with. To some extent, high levels of attrition are endemic to the business model. Call centres ramp up or down their workforce depending on projected call volume, new product releases, and other factors usually tied to the client organization's needs. In turn, agents who are treated as expendable to the short term business requirements of the organization will not necessarily show a lot of loyalty to their job. But even taking these factors into account, agent turnover remains excessively high and carries a cost in terms of training and loss of experience within the workforce. Part of our remit in collaborating with the call centres was therefore to gain some insight into the aspects of the job that agents find stressful, above and beyond the pressure that the job itself brings (inflexible pacing, pressure to deal with unhappy customers, and more). One of the issues we identified was in the occasional misalignment of organizational goals and objectives, performance management strategies, and the agents' own self interest.

20.2.1 Working to the Numbers

The business model of an outsourced call centre is to deliver a business service or process to the outsourcing company at an appropriate level of quality, but at a lower cost than if the company was to manage that service or process itself. The expected level of quality is defined by what is commonly referred to as a Service Level Agreement (SLA). This contractual document sets performance targets for the outsourced service provider, along with bonuses and penalties for exceeding or failing to meet the relevant thresholds. The key performance metrics in the SLA are typically the same ones used to assess the performance of the agents (albeit at different levels of aggregation). The performance of the call centre as a whole therefore relates, quite directly, to the aggregate performance of its individual agents.

We do not intend to go into the operations management strategies of a call centre operation in detail here—suffice it to say that they have all the expected workforce, quality management and assessment processes—all designed to optimize that difficult relationship between quality and quantity. What we do want to describe in more detail is what we observed happening in practice, and in particular the ways in which agents are forced to balance the often contradictory relations between performance metrics (both quantitative and qualitative), compensation mechanisms, and organizational policies.

A very simple example of the interconnectedness of performance metrics is the relationship between AHT and Calls per Hour (CPH). This is a very straightforward relation: The higher your AHT the lower your average number of Calls Per Hour is going to be, but if we add Customer Satisfaction Survey responses to this equation, the balancing act becomes less straightforward. These surveys are administered at random to customers after a phone call with a call centre agent. Agents do not know which of their calls will be attached to a survey score, but they do know that a negative evaluation will directly affect their compensation (as agent pay rates are calculated using a combination of quantitative and qualitative performance measures). They also know that a way of minimizing the chances of a negative score is to spend as much time as needed with each customer in order to resolve their issue—which in the long run may negatively affect their AHT and CPH values.

In one particular call centre we encountered a situation where the company policy was that agents should only offer limited phone support to customers who have not paid for the company's optional support package. The agents, however, were aware that offering only limited support to non-eligible customers might result in a negative customer satisfaction survey. So the problem for the agent then becomes one of balancing "risk" between two potentially contradictory factors which will affect their performance assessment and pay rate: enforce the client organization's policy and risk incurring in negative surveys, or ignore (or not fully enforce) the policy and risk negatively impacting the SLA (which states that the call centre should only offer limited support to non-eligible customers). Providing full support to ineligible customers may also affect the agents' individual performance assessment, but in this case the impact of a negative survey score, from an agent's point of view, was far more damaging.

Realistically, call centre operators understand that agents, when faced with these kinds of contradictions, will tend to put their own interests ahead of those of the organization as a whole (in so far as these are visible to them). Even when not faced with contradictory relations between different performance metrics, many agents learn how to "work to the numbers"—i.e. leverage their understanding of the performance assessment and compensation mechanisms in order to, for example, hit the highest compensation rates without necessarily providing the best value to their organization. There is no criticism of the agents' behavior implied here—to the extent that they are treated as expendable resources they cannot be expected to sacrifice their own self-interest for the greater good of the organization.

20.2.2 Motivation Through Gamification

If an organization such as call centre wants to "optimize" the value of the work of its agents it must therefore ensure that it is providing agents with (a) coherent and attainable objectives, and (b) the right level of awareness of where they are with respect to those objectives. Insofar as the needs of the call centre as a whole are not always going to be a perfect match with the self-interest of the agents, the call centre also needs to provide the appropriate incentives. Some of these are meant to be managed through Activity Based Compensation (ABC) mechanisms. The problem with ABC is that it encourages agents to "work to the numbers". The call centres' response, then, is to regularly tweak the ABC mechanisms to attempt to "drive" the agents towards better performance in specific areas. This can lead to confusion on the part of the agents, and it can, as described above, occasionally introduce contradictions between organizational policies and the agents' own interest.

To provide an additional incentive system that does not rely on the manipulation of compensation mechanisms or on the potentially punitive character of traditional performance management and tracking strategies, many call centres have turned to the use of simple "games" such as challenges and competitions. These are usually performance related (i.e. tied to specific KPIs) and may pit individual agents, teams, or entire call centres against each other for rewards that range from the nominal (a few extra minutes break time) to the substantial (flat screen TVs and laptops). The question of the effectiveness of the use of challenges and competitions in call centres is outside of the scope of this chapter. Trends in performance are routinely tracked within call centres, but challenges and competitions are just two out of any number of factors that could be affecting agent performance at any given moment in time. What encourages their use, more than hard evidence of their impact on performance, is the perception on the part of call centre managers that they give agents a much needed morale boost. Based on observations made during our field studies, there are nevertheless some observations that we would like to make about the current implementation of challenges and competitions in call centres.

In the first instance, they are often tied to specific organizational requirements (for example, drive a specific performance metric, or the sale of a particular product or service). The consequence of this is that the challenges and competitions can be biased towards a specific skill set, and therefore specific agents, and then not be motivating for all the agents.

The challenges and competitions are also implemented in a fairly "low-tech" manner. This means that ongoing games are tracked using pen and paper, and represented using whiteboards or paper wall displays. This does not mean that the call centres do not put any effort into the running of the competitions. The problem is that this type of representation is not very dynamic and not visible to all the agents on the floor (depending on where they are seated). Like other types of performance management and motivation strategies in the call centre, this type of implementation has a fairly slow feedback cycle. The agents' engagement is therefore mostly dependent on the nature of the reward rather than in taking part in the game itself. This is fine insofar as the call centres are prepared to provide substantial rewards for occasional challenges and competitions, but not very sustainable if they wanted to use them more pervasively

20.3   Agentville

On the basis of the observations made during recent field studies conducted in call centres but also during previous studies [2, 6] we have identified two major problems in call centre work environments: first agents are missing clear and up to date information enabling them to take appropriate decisions on their work; second call centres have difficulties in providing the right motivation and performance related incentives to their agents. We have designed and are building a system, called Agentville, that aims at addressing these problems. Agentville provides the agents of a call centre with a visualization of important elements of information on the work environment and it integrates some game mechanics. More precisely, it offers:

- a visualization of the salient elements of information on the unfolding work status, at call centre, team, and agent levels, in an integrated and real-time fashion;
- visual indications of current trends and potential performance issues, and
- indications and means on how to potentially address these issues;
- a direct integration of selected individual and collective game mechanics with the performance feedback features of the system.

The vision of the future work in a call centre supported by a 3D virtual world multiplayer game environment, including avatars, etc. is discussed in [11]. Although the idea of integrating the game mechanisms in a fully developed virtual environment with a coherent narrative in a workplace like a call centre looks like an interesting challenge, what we advocate here is the feasibility and the benefit of adopting a more modular and incremental approach, that is, to introduce only the following *game mechanics* [3, 4, 7]: *Progression, Virtual Currency, Levels, Badges, Leaderboards*, and *Challenges*. The game mechanics that we propose have been selected and instantiated according to our understanding of the requirements for improving both performance and motivation of call centres operators and our direct observation of work dynamics in call centres.

This section illustrates the design of the system describing its two main components: (1) a server side through which data on call centre activities are collected and processed and (2) a client side rendering the resulting information to agents, enabling them to assess the situation at a glance, and providing them with some means to react accordingly.

20.3.1 Server Side

The server side of the Agentville system is devoted to the collection and aggregation of relevant information, e.g. KPIs data, and the support to gaming elements, used to provide on the client side integrated information on current work status and trends and indications on how individual and collective performance and quality of work experience could be improved.

20.3.1.1 Key Performance Indicator Data

The KPI data that are used by the system and dynamically collected by wrapping various call centre data sources and systems include:

- Call centre SLA, i.e. the call centre KPIs, e.g. the minimum and maximum acceptable length for a call. The call centre KPIs are related to the individual call centre agent's KPIs. For instance the constraints on the acceptable call length are translated into minimum and maximum values for agent's AHT.
- Agent specific data

    - Agent status information (e.g. handling a call, presence at desk)
    - Call specific data: Start and duration of the current call, hold time, transfer, etc.; Average Handle Time (AHT); Calls Per Hour (CPH).
    - Scheduling data: agent scheduling data including planned shifts and breaks.

- Call specific data

    - Call timings: meta-data about a call obtained on the fly analyzing the call audio content: talk time, dead air time, etc.
    - CSAT scores: satisfaction scores assigned to calls on the base of surveys.
    - Quality scores: obtained and aggregated from quality assessments carried out on e.g. a weekly basis by quality assurance officers who listen to agent calls and mark them on a number of categories related to policy adherence, technical capabilities, soft skills, etc. This score is often also a KPI in the SLA.
    - Topic: a set of keywords from a predefined list that are assigned to the call when CSAT score are assigned, describing the call content.

20.3.1.2 Selected Game Mechanics for Call Centres

Agents are evaluated and paid essentially based on the KPI values they obtain. Therefore the KPIs also play a central role in the following game elements that we consider and integrate in our system.

Virtual Currency: The system awards agents for their work in terms of a virtual currency (credits). Credits are attributed for and associated to the different categories of actions or achievements relevant within a call centre and depending on the configuration of the call centre, typically wrt its SLA:

- Handling an individual call in a timely fashion: the amount of credits awarded depends on the correct timing (satisfying call related KPIs, e.g. AHT, dead air time, etc.). The timing thresholds and relevance of the individual KPIs will be specific to each call centre and depend on the SLA agreed with the customer. After each call the system can verify automatically from the switch board data if these constraints are met and award corresponding credits to the agent.
- Satisfying a not-individual call time-related KPI, e.g. adherence to the schedule. These conditions can be verified automatically from the switch board data and corresponding credits awarded in regular time intervals corresponding to the overall value achieved by the agent, e.g. overall adherence per shift computed at the end of each shift.
- Satisfying quality requirements, e.g. obtaining a good quality assessment/CSAT score; each time a quality assessment or CSAT becomes available within the system corresponding credits are automatically awarded.
- Showing topic expertise: strong topic expertise can be identified during the quality assessments. In that case corresponding credits are awarded.
- Helping other agents: If the system detects that one agent helps out another agent credits can be awarded to the helping agent. This is possible for instance when an agent with strong topic expertise tutors another agent with initially weaker expertise on that topic; if over time the second agent shows significantly increased expertise this provides evidence that the first agent did a good tutoring job.

All these credits are continuously accumulated on the individual agent's account and visible to the agent (see Client side section). The agent can spend them, according to agreements within the call centre, at any time for various things like virtual goods, earning 'time-outs' (just for some seconds, so agents can catch their breath) etc.

Badges: Badges materialize the agent's level of performance for a given category over a long time period. They are attributed to the agents in regular time frames (corresponding to meaningful evaluation periods, such as the agent's regular review periods with their supervisor). In each category the agent obtains a badge if he earned a minimum amount of credits in this category. Different levels may exist for each category badge (e.g. gold, silver, bronze) corresponding to the amount of credits earned over the corresponding time period (i.e. corresponding to the achieved level of performance). Different badges indicate e.g. that an agent has handled a corresponding amount of calls in a timely fashion, that he satisfied the not-individual call time-related KPIs up to a certain level, how well he satisfied quality requirements or that the agent has shown expertise in certain topics or that he provided relevant help to his colleagues.

Levels: Agents are situated at different levels according to the badges they own. An agent starts on the lowest level—without any badge. Once he obtains a bronze badge in all categories, indicating that he has reached a certain level of performance in all required categories he will level up to the next level etc. Similarly he might move down to a lower level if later on he only obtains lower level badges in some categories over consecutive time periods.

Leader boards: Leader boards can be presented for each level to the corresponding agents indicating how the agent is placed with respect to his colleagues.

Progression: The system provides information about the current situation for the agent's KPIs, the trends, and estimations of the KPI for the near future. It also detects when an agent is close to change level, i.e. level up or down. It can then alert the agent indicating what he can do to achieve an improvement for the level or to prevent to loose a level, e.g. suggesting trying to limit the next calls handle time if the recent AHT was a bit too high. As badges are distributed in regular time intervals corresponding to the reviewing periods of the agents such alerts will mainly happen when the reviewing date is close and the estimation becomes more and more accurate. However, particularly big deviations from prior performance values or rare data such as quality assessments which are carried out only a limited number of times might generate earlier alerts.

Challenges: In our system challenges that can be issued are bets for the agents on improvements of a given KPI or on their overall performance. Two options are considered: either bets are controlled by supervisors or they are automatically issued by the system. In the first case a supervisor can use the system to suggest to the agent to bet on improvements of not satisfactory KPIs or when the agent is close to change level, i.e. level up or down. The agent can accept the bet or ignore it. In the second case the system suggests to the agents to bet on improving particular KPIs. For example for the CPH the system detects that the parameter for an agent is below threshold and provides an estimation of how this can be improved on the basis of the scheduling of the work and the time interval in which the parameter is evaluated, e.g. 1 week or 1 month, and allows the agent to bet a minimal and a maximal amount of points according to a given scale. If the agent ignores or delay (resp. reject) the bet the system can periodically re-submit the suggestion to the agent (resp. discard it). Satisfying an accepted bet will in turn result in an increased amount of credits granted whereas missing it will remove a corresponding amount of credits.

Similar to what we defined above for the individual agent's, the same game mechanics can also be introduced for agent teams. Therefore the corresponding values are averaged over all team members. This represents the overall team level and allows situating the team performance with respect to the other teams. It identifies and visualizes global strengths/weaknesses in the team and allows the supervisor to address them with appropriate actions, e.g. training, or exceptional awards to increase performance on particular critical performance measures. Again the system can detect positive and negative trends and alert the supervisor accordingly.

From the team agent's varying topic expertise information the system can furthermore identify and highlight other interesting situations, e.g. the presence within the team of agents with strong and other with weak expertise with respect to a particular topic. In this case it can be useful to organize pairs of buddies in such a way that the stronger agent tutors and forms the weaker one. This can be organized by the supervisor or proposed by the system directly to the concerned agents. The pair of agents can then bet on an improvement of the weak agent within a given time frame; if after that the expertise level of the initially weaker agent rises significantly the system can recognize this and award corresponding credits to the tutoring agent. (The weaker agent will be rewarded directly because he improved his topic expertise.) Another situation that can be identified is a general lack within the team of a particular expertise. In this case the supervisor might want to organize corresponding trainings.

The system also integrates information about the general call centre situation. From past observations it can determine the maximal queue length that can still be appropriately processed by the call centre at a given time (i.e. with a given number of scheduled agents). Monitoring the actual situation in terms of queue length and present agents allows foreseeing critical situations and tackling them in time. Alerts can be given when such critical situations may arise; the system can then e.g. propose that the agents can bet on faster handling of calls enabling to keep the whole centre within an acceptable situation. Another possibility is to propose rescheduling of agent presence (breaks) rewarded with additional credits for agents that accept rescheduling.

20.3.2 Client Side

The client side of Agentville provides the agents with a synthetic graphic representation of information on their own performance and credits, as well as the opportunities for improvement. Given the typical characteristics and constraints of a call centre, we believe that in order to be effective the interface must be easily accessible and always visible to keep the users permanently aware of the actual and evolving situation. It must also be simple and intuitive such that the user can understand at a glance without any particular effort and without distracting her from her "real" work. Finally, it must be of small size, especially for the agents because the large majority of the screen estate is already occupied by the various tools needed to perform their work. For example, the typical desktop of an agent in a call centre is crowded with tools providing access to knowledge bases and Customer Relationship Management environments used to record call data and to access content that may be relevant to answer the customer's questions or to perform a required task.

Fig. 20.1 Multiple KPI
visualization

We therefore propose that the client interface for the actors of Agentville mainly consists of a desktop widget of small size that sits permanently on their desktop providing all required information at a glance.

20.3.2.1   Agent Visualization

We propose a visualization mechanism that includes for each agent a visualization of a customizable selection of KPIs, typically varying in number between 1 and 10, which provides at a glance information about (a) whether the average value for the displayed KPIs for that agent fall within or without the required threshold at a specific point in time or in real time; (b) the trending of the average values for the displayed KPIs for the agent's ongoing work day across regular time intervals or in real time and (c) for all selected KPIs the badges representing their current skill level (bronze, silver or gold). Figure 20.1 shows an example of the widget. In the centre the widget displays customizable information (in Fig. 20.1 the current AHT value together with the total number of credits earned over the ongoing reviewing period).

Using the navigation tabs at the bottom of the widget, the agent can access additional visualizations, such as an overview of their current level, credits and badges gained (Fig. 20.2). Invitations to bet on improvements of the KPI performance are displayed e.g. if the agent is close to achieving a new level for a particular KPI.

Another kind of information provided to the agent is a detailed, comparative visualization of an individual, selectable KPI for an agent versus the team or the overall centre average values with customizable time intervals (day, week or month). This provides at a glance information about whether the average values for the displayed KPI for that agent, the team, and call centre as a whole, fall within or without the required threshold at all points in time for the selected time interval and provides information about the corresponding performance levels. An example is shown in Fig. 20.3.

Fig. 20.2 Example of an
agent's current level, credits
and badges

Fig. 20.3 Detailed KPI view
with thresholds and trends

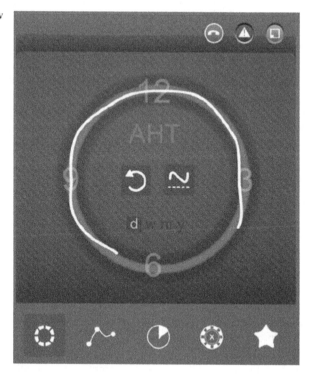

Fig. 20.4 The remaining
time on the agent's shift can
be used to visualize a projection of the current performance trend through to the
end of the shift

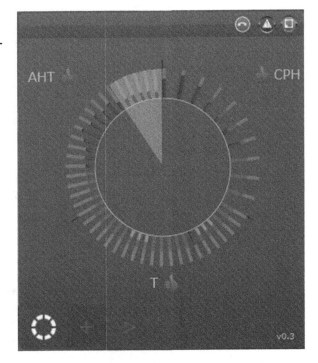

The system also shows *Prospective Information* as follows:

- given the current trend for any given KPI, the widget shows the projected performance for the rest of the shift, week, or month;
- given the distance of the current average performance value for any KPI from
  the current threshold value(s) for that KPI the widget shows: (a) for agents who
  are underperforming, the necessary effort to bring, the average value within the
  expected threshold(s) over the rest of the shift, week or month (see Fig. 20.4);
  and (b) for agents who are not underperforming, the necessary effort to maintain
  the current average values over the rest of the shift, week or month.

20.3.2.2   Supervisor Visualization

Team supervisors have their own version of the client which displays the same
information present in the agent client, but gives supervisors the ability to select
and visualize the performance of any of the agents on their team, or the average
performance of the whole team. Figure 20.5 shows an example of the visualization
of the performance of an individual team member:

Fig. 20.5 Supervisor
visualization

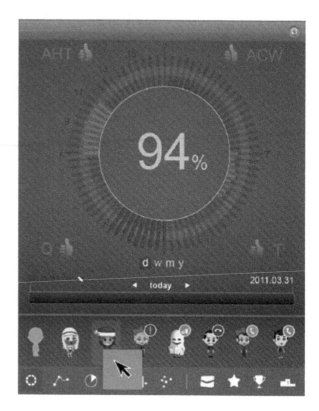

20.4   Related Work

Gamification of work environments is a recent trend which broadly speaking refers
to adding elements of competition, direct reward, team supported learning and play
around the execution of real work activities. The most mature and known category
is also referred to as "serious games". These environments are typically simulation
environments that provide training and support in a game space where users can
learn by experimenting, interacting with other colleagues represented as avatars
and winning rewards. Only recently however this approach has been proposed also
in support of routine on-going work [10, 11] and not only in support of specific
learning activities. This last attempt is challenging as the gamification should be
attractive enough to engage the actors in the system dynamics but at the same time
not too distracting from the actual execution and focus on the work tasks. Reeves
and Read [11] list the key elements of gamification of a work environment where
it provides self representation, meritocracy mechanisms, transparency of the activities, and teamwork added value. Also, recently there are examples of social games
designed for the workplace like for example Taskville [10], a distributed social media workplace game that gamifies the process of routine task management, intro-

ducing light competitive play within and between teams. The game "incorporates a city-building metaphor where the completion of tasks leads to the growth of cities in the game world".

Reeves and Read [11] also provide a scenario of how a call centre environment may be gamified. Their scenario includes the ideas of a supervisor checking her team's progress ("after the last shift, how do they rank on number of call resolutions, who in the group has leveled up and who needs encouragement?"). Also, "All the once familiar call centre metrics are now cast as points, ranks, and virtual currency within a large and engaging multiplayer game complete with a compelling narrative, interesting 3D environment". And "Data about the team are available for all to see (just right-click a character to discover its experience level, wealth in gold pieces, availability for new assignments, or recent compliments from other team members.)". This scenario is quite similar to our general problem statement and solution approach and includes a number of the aspects of what we propose for the gamification part but it considers a full-fledged multiplayer game instead of selected game elements as in our approach.

The http://www.callcentregames.com web site provides a number of games that are meant to motivate agent performance. While the motivations are quite the same of our system, a key difference is that they provide games that are implemented outside the working system, therefore lacking the continuous monitoring of performances and the higher degree of engagement due to the integration with the work environment.

Some commercial companies are working on offerings for the "gamification" of call centre work, which seem to be more oriented to exploit narratives in the game to motivate the users [9] and to use games [8] ("*Your avatar would participate in the game along with other agents. The concept of the game would be simple. Complete a mission—the agent's task—and earn gems or badges.*"). [1] suggests an approach that also exploits games, but in that case they address call centres doing outbound activity (phoning customers or perspective ones) instead of inbound ones like in our case.

Rypple (http://rypple.com) proposes "a social performance platform built for teams to share goals, recognize great work, and help each other improve." This tool essentially supports the definition of goals and people involved and the collection of relevant feedback on the individual's work. Employees, their managers, and colleagues can access all or part of the collected feedback in real time, and use it to assess and evaluate performance. It does not include any linkage of real data on performance to quantified feedback (our credits mechanism). It is also a generic tool so not specifically designed for call centres.

Also related to our work are systems where virtual points can be gained and spent in online communities in a work environment. For example the Personal Assessment Tool [5], relates "green points" to the activity of printing. Green points are consumed when printing and when saved in the system they can be used to perform actions, e.g. a donation for an environmental cause.

20.5 Conclusion

The call center work environment is rich in challenges. The outsourcing business model requires efficiency in the operational management of the workforce. This can create differences in perspective between different layers of the operation, notably in that the agents may fail to see the relation between their work and the interests of the call center as whole. Through Agentville we are trying to bridge that difference in perspectives—notably by (a) providing agents with a higher degree of situational awareness with respect to the core performance metrics that drive their compensation and productivity of the whole operation; (b) integrating some game mechanisms directly into the call centre's performance management strategies and information systems.

We are aware that this system faces some challenges. In particular, we understand that more access to information and better situational awareness will not on their own address contradictions between performance metrics and other factors like compensation mechanisms and organizational policies. But insofar as agents are required to balance factors which are correlated in non-obvious ways, better situational awareness can only ease the task. We also understand that game mechanics like the ones we propose here have yet to demonstrate their effectiveness in providing motivation outside of learning and training environments and over what is already implemented in the call centers we observed.

We designed our system based on our understanding of the call centers' requirements and our ethnographic observations of agents at work. The current prototype of Agentville is ready to be deployed on a trial basis in a real-life production environment—we will gather data about its use in the coming months and hope to report on our findings in future publications.

References

1. ARCARIS.: http://thenextweb.com/la/2011/08/26/how-chilean-born-arcaris-is-bringing-gamification-to-call-centres/ (2011)
2. Castellani, S., Grasso, A., O'Neill, J., Roulland, F.: Designing technology as an embedded resource for troubleshooting. Comput. Support. Coop. Work. **18**(2), 199 (2009)
3. GamificationEncyclopedia.: The Gamification Encyclopedia. http://gamification.org/wiki/Encyclopedia (2011). Accessed 17 Aug 2011
4. GamificationOrg.: http://gamification.org/wiki/Gamification (2011)
5. Grasso, M.A., Willamowski, J., Ciriza, V., Hoppenot, Y.: The personal assessment tool: a system providing environmental feedback to users of shared printers for providing environmental feedback. In: Proceedings of the Ninth International Conference of Machine Learning and Applications (ICMLA), 12–14 Dec 2010, Washington, DC, US (2010)
6. Martin, D., O'Neill, J., Randall, D., Rouncefield, M.: How can I help you? Call centres, classification work and coordination. J. Comput. Support. Coop. Work. **16**(2), 231–264. Springer, Dordrecht (2007)
7. MEG.: Media Evolution, Gamification (2011)

8. Modelmetrics.: "Gaming the Call Centre"—April 19, 2011, http://www.modelmetrics.com/joel-dubinskys-blog/gaming-the-call-centre/ (2011)
9. MOTIVITI.: http://www.motiviti.com/blog/serious-games-gamification/, http://www.motiviti.com/blog/playrocket-sneak-preview/ (2011)
10. Nikkila, S., Linn, S., Sundaram, H., Kelliher, A.: "Playing in Taskville: Designing a Social Game for the Workplace". CHI 2011 Workshop on Gamification: Using Game Design Elements in Non-game Contexts (2011)
11. Reeves, B., Read, J.L. Total Engagement: Using Games and Virtual Worlds to Change the Way People Work and Business Compete. Harvard Business Press, Boston (2009)